# The Mating Game

Third Edition

*For my girls—Emma, Piper, and Phoebe.*

# The Mating Game

A Primer on Love, Sex, and Marriage

Third Edition

Pamela C. Regan

*California State University, Los Angeles*

Los Angeles | London | New Delhi
Singapore | Washington DC

Los Angeles | London | New Delhi
Singapore | Washington DC

FOR INFORMATION:

SAGE Publications, Inc.
2455 Teller Road
Thousand Oaks, California 91320
E-mail: order@sagepub.com

SAGE Publications Ltd.
1 Oliver's Yard
55 City Road
London EC1Y 1SP
United Kingdom

SAGE Publications India Pvt. Ltd.
B 1/I 1 Mohan Cooperative Industrial Area
Mathura Road, New Delhi 110 044
India

SAGE Publications Asia-Pacific Pte. Ltd.
3 Church Street
#10-04 Samsung Hub
Singapore 049483

Acquisitions Editor: Lara Parra
Editorial Assistant: Morgan Shannon
Production Editor: Laura Barrett
Copy Editor: Diane Wainwright
Typesetter: Hurix Systems Pvt Ltd.
Proofreader: Lawrence W. Baker
Cover Designer: Gail Buschman
Marketing Manager: Katherine Hepburn

Copyright © 2017 by SAGE Publications, Inc.

Printed in the United States of America

ISBN 978-1-4833-7921-0

This book is printed on acid-free paper.

16 17 18 19 20 10 9 8 7 6 5 4 3 2 1

# Brief Contents

# Detailed Contents

# Preface

"Is She 'The One'?" (*Men's Health*)

"How to Know If a Guy Likes You" (*Glamour*)

"New Tricks for the Bedroom" (*Maxim*)

"10 Little Ways to Say 'I Love You'" (*Woman's Day*)

"Is She Flirting or Just Being Nice? Here's How You Know for Real"
(*AskMen*)

"What Everyone Else Is Really Doing in Bed" (*Cosmopolitan*)

"Love vs. Lust: How You'll Know the Difference" (*Woman's Own*)

"Why Do Men and Women Cheat?" (*Woman's Day*)

"10 Red Flags to Watch Out for in a Significant Other" (*Maxim*)

"How to Get Over an Ex" (*CosmoGIRL!*)

"8 Ways to Ask for What You Want in Your Relationship" (*Women's Health*)

"Help Your BFF Through a Breakup" (*Seventeen*)

"5 Problems That Can Sink Your Relationship" (*Men's Health*)

These quotations, taken from the headlines of several contemporary men's and women's magazines, underscore the deep interest (and even fascination) with which many of us approach topics of love, sex, and romance. And our interest is certainly justified. The intimate connections that we establish with other people, whether for a few moments or for a lifetime, affect our emotional and physical well-being and even the survival of our species. Without love and sex—without mating and pair-bonding and reproduction—we would feel empty, isolated, and lonely; our societies would wither; and humankind would literally perish.

My goal in writing this book is to bring together in one text past and present theory, supposition, and knowledge about human mating relationships. The first section of the text focuses on mate selection and marriage. We begin with an examination of theoretical frameworks for understanding human mating, and we consider research on men's and women's mate preferences. We then explore the early stages of romantic relationship formation with a particular focus on attraction and affiliation (in both face-to-face and online encounters), flirting, and courtship. Theories of relationship development are discussed, along with research on mate choice and marriage, conflict and dissolution, and therapeutic interventions for distressed relationships. The next two sections of the text focus on two important aspects of mating relationships—love and sexuality. First, we consider the topic of love, beginning with an exploration of theoretical discourse (and empirical investigation) into the nature of love. Special attention is given to the two love types that have received the most scrutiny from social and behavioral scientists: passionate and companionate love. The section ends with a consideration of problematic aspects of love relationships, including unrequited love, obsession and relational stalking, relational aggression or intimate partner violence, and loss of passion. The third section of the text explores relational sexuality. We examine men's and women's beliefs and attitudes about the role of sex in dating and marital relationships, and we consider sexuality—frequency, preferences, and practices—in beginning and established relationships. Problematic aspects of relational sexuality are considered, including sexual disinterest, sexual assault, sexual infidelity, and sexual jealousy. The final section summarizes what is currently known about individual differences in relationship orientation. We consider how maleness and femaleness, global personality traits, and interpersonal belief systems may influence a person's romantic opportunities, behaviors, and outcomes.

## ❖ WHAT'S NEW IN THIS EDITION?

This third edition differs from the second in a number of ways:

The chapters in each section of the textbook have been updated (with more than 400 new references and numerous real-life examples) to reflect and illustrate the most recent theoretical and empirical advancements and have been expanded to cover additional areas not included in earlier editions. Specifically, in Part I (Mating Relationships), Chapter 1 (Mate Preferences) includes an updated discussion of methods used to examine mate preference, presents new work on historical changes in men's and women's partner preferences and the ways in which individuals are willing to compromise or alter their mate selection standards, and considers additional research that speaks to the issue of whether or not investigations of people's ideal preferences reveal anything truly meaningful about the mating decisions they make in real life. Chapter 2 (Attraction, Affiliation, and Courtship) has been renamed and expanded and now includes brand-new sections on the factors that influence romantic attraction and affiliation in initial encounters (such as similarity, familiarity, physical attractiveness, responsiveness, accessibility, and so on), additional research on flirting or the communication of romantic interest, and a section devoted entirely to E-courtship—that is, attraction, affiliation, and flirting in cyberspace (e.g., web-based environments, chat rooms, online dating sites). The material in Chapter 3 (Relationship Development) has been reorganized in order to incorporate new empirical evidence on the process of relationship development. Chapter 4 (Marriage and Mate Selection) has been significantly updated to reflect recent changes in the legal status of same-sex marriage in the United States (and worldwide), as well as new research on polygamy or plural marriage, cohabitation, and the recently-identified phenomenon of "stayovers" among partners in long-term romantic unions. Additional material in Chapter 5 (Conflict and Dissolution) includes an expanded discussion of the role played by attributions in conflict, an entirely new section on how conflicts end, and new research on relationship dissolution, bereavement, and loss. The first section in Chapter 6 (Intervention) on identifying distressed relationships now includes research on dysfunctional attributional styles, and the remainder of the chapter presents new details on the techniques and clinical effectiveness of each of the major forms of couple therapy.

Like Part I, Part II (Love) has been thoroughly updated. Chapter 7 (General Theories of Love) includes new information on the reliability of scales used to assess different types of love, as well as new empirical research on individual and group differences in love. The material presented in Chapter 8 (Passionate and Companionate Love) on the characteristics of the two most important types of adult romantic love—passionate and companionate love—has also been updated to reflect current findings from the social and behavioral sciences. For example, there are new sections exploring specific components of passionate love (including partner idealization and cognitive preoccupation, exclusivity, and sexual attraction) and new material on the features of companionate love as well as the biochemical underpinnings of both of these love varieties. Chapter 9 (Love Gone

Bad: Problematic Aspects of Love) has been reorganized and significantly expanded. For example, to address the burgeoning empirical work on relational stalking, there are now separate sections detailing the prevalence of obsessive pursuit and stalking, factors (individual, interpersonal, and sociocultural) that are implicated in the occurrence of relational stalking, the consequences of stalking for victims as well as the prevalence and relative effectiveness of various coping methods, and the growing problem of cyberstalking. This chapter also now includes an entirely new section on relational aggression or intimate partner violence, with particular emphasis given to situational couple violence and domestic abuse.

Although the general organization of Part III (Sex) is unchanged, the material has been extensively revised. For example, Chapter 10 (Sexual Attitudes) includes discussion of recent national and global surveys that allow for an examination of individual and cultural differences (and similarities) in sexual attitudes and an entirely new exploration of the topic of consensual non-monogamy (swinging, open relationships, and polyamorous relationships). Chapter 11 (Sex in Beginning Relationships) includes new information on the factors that make up "sex appeal" in men and women, the relative importance placed on chastity or premarital virginity in various cultures around the world, and the relational consequences of a couple's decision to have sex early (as opposed to later) in the developmental trajectory of their relationship. All of the material in Chapter 12 (Sex in Established Relationships) focusing on sexual frequency, sexual preferences and practices, sexual satisfaction, sexual communication, and the link between sexuality and relationship satisfaction has been updated with particular emphasis on the results of recent national and international surveys, as well as research on the experiences of men and women in same-sex relationships. Chapter 13 (Sex Gone Bad: Problematic Aspects of Relational Sex) has undergone the most significant change; the section on sexual dissatisfaction has been replaced with an in-depth discussion of sexual disinterest or diminished sexual desire (a particularly painful form of interpersonal rejection). Similarly, entirely new material on the prevalence, types, origins, and consequences of nonconsensual sex between partners in intimate relationships is now provided, as is an updated discussion of infidelity and sexual jealousy in the United States and other countries.

The three chapters comprising Part IV (Individual Differences) also have been updated, with new material presented on the major individual difference variables that are associated with interpersonal behavior and relationship outcomes, including maleness and femaleness (biological sex and psychological gender and gender role orientation) in Chapter 14; global personality attributes (the supertraits of extraversion or positive affectivity and neuroticism or negative affectivity), self-monitoring, and sociosexual orientation in Chapter 15; and interpersonal belief systems, including attachment styles, rejection sensitivity, and romanticism in Chapter 16.

This new edition remains highly "reader friendly." Each chapter includes a detailed outline that serves to guide readers through the material, and I provide a list of key concepts (with page references) to assist readers in identifying and comprehending important terms, theories, and findings. Most chapters also now include real-life examples provided (anonymously) by men and women who have experienced the interpersonal events or phenomena discussed in the chapter (e.g., passionate love, online dating, relational stalking, nonconsensual sex, etc.). Each chapter presents readers with a set of recommended readings, as well as updated discussion questions that are designed to spark debate and discussion about the chapter content. These questions may also be used as in-class or take-home activities. Most, if not all, of these essential features are missing from current texts in this area; I hope that their inclusion will promote active learning and enhance readers' educational experience.

And finally, a multiple-choice test bank is now available for instructors to use in creating quizzes and exams for their students.

Love, sexuality, and mate selection are fundamental human experiences. I believe that the comprehensive review and up-to-date information contained in this text will not only provide answers to questions about these important life events but also encourage readers' interest in the diverse and multidisciplinary field of interpersonal relationships.

# Part I

# Mating Relationships

Mating relationships have enormous personal, social, and evolutionary significance. Not only do most people spend a good
portion of their adolescence and adulthood eagerly seeking a mate, but
these relationships are highly socially valued and regulated. (In fact,
there are more norms, rituals, and even laws governing behavior in this
kind of relationship than in any other variety.) And from an evolutionary perspective, mating relationships are incredibly important because
it is through pair-bonding and reproduction that the human species
developed over time and continues to exist today.

This section of the text focuses on the fundamental features of, and
the processes involved in, long-term mating relationships. Chapter 1
presents theoretical approaches to understanding the dynamics of
human mating relationships and discusses research on mate preference
or the desires that guide men's and women's choice of a long-term partner. Chapter 2 explores attraction, affiliation, and courtship—the factors
that determine who men and women like and wish to approach romantically, and how they actually communicate romantic interest and
obtain a mate in both face-to-face and online encounters. Chapter 3
considers theories designed to explain how mating relationships
develop and are maintained over time, and Chapter 4 discusses marriage and mate selection, including types of mating systems that exist
around the world, the nature of marriage, how marital relationships
have changed over time, and alternatives to marriage. Chapter 5
focuses on conflict and relationship dissolution, and Chapter 6 presents
therapeutic interventions available for helping couples in distressed
relationships.

# 1

# Mate Preferences

This chapter is divided into two sections. The first section explores the theories that social and behavioral scientists have formulated in an attempt to make sense of human mating dynamics. The second section examines research that speaks to the utility of these theoretical frameworks; specifically, it explores what is known about the attributes, traits, and characteristics people actually prefer and seek in their dates and mates.

## ❖ THEORETICAL APPROACHES TO HUMAN MATING

In general, theoretical approaches to human mating relationships tend to fall into two broad categories. The first category emphasizes how mate preferences are influenced by social forces created by and residing within the contemporary environment. The second category focuses on evolutionary forces that arose in the ancient past and that form part of our species' heritage.

### Social Context Theories: The World That Is

*Social context* frameworks focus on proximal mechanisms—that is, forces located in the contemporary social, cultural, and historical milieu—that influence mate preferences and mate selection.

*Social exchange or equity models* of mate selection represent one such framework (e.g., Blau, 1964; Murstein, 1970, 1976; Walster, Walster, & Berscheid, 1978; for reviews, see Hatfield & Rapson, 2012, and Sprecher, 1998). According to these models, the process of mate selection resembles a marketplace in which people attempt to maximize their rewards and make social interaction as profitable as possible by exchanging their own assets—beauty, health, intelligence, a sense of humor, kindness, wealth, status, and so on—for desirable attributes in a partner. A person's own "value" as a potential partner is presumed to influence the extent to which he or she is able to attract and retain a high-value partner. Since people seek the best possible value in a potential mate, but are constrained by their own assets, this process is assumed to result in the pairing of individuals of roughly equal value. That is, "wealthy" individuals who possess a great many desirable characteristics, or who have high amounts of a few particularly valuable attributes, will be able to attract and pair with others of equally high value. "Poorer" persons, or those who have fewer assets to offer a potential mate, inevitably will form liaisons with less valuable and less "expensive" others.

Exchange theorists argue that mating mistakes are costly. For example, in his discussion of the early stages of mate selection, theorist Bernard Murstein (1970) noted that although an individual may run less risk of rejection if he or she seeks a less desirable partner (low cost), the rewards of such a conquest are correspondingly meager (low profit); at the same time, the increased likelihood of rejection (high cost) associated with seeking a partner who is substantially more desirable than oneself (high profit) renders this enterprise equally risky.

Consequently, an accurate perception of one's own qualities and what one has to contribute or offer to a relationship is believed to be extremely important. In sum, based on a consideration of the basic principles of social exchange models of mate selection, we might expect people to prefer potential partners who possess a host of socially desirable characteristics, to moderate these preferences by taking into account their own attributes, and to ultimately pair with similar others.

*Social role theory* is another social context perspective that has been used to understand and explain (heterosexual) mate selection (e.g., Eagly, 1987; Eagly & Wood, 2012; Eagly, Wood, & Johannesen-Schmidt, 2004). Social role theorists posit that people develop expectations for their own and for other people's behavior based on their beliefs about sex-appropriate behavior and attributes. Such beliefs and expectations are assumed to arise from the distribution of men and women in different social roles in natural settings. For men, these roles have historically been occupational and economic; for women, these roles have traditionally been domestic. To the extent that people prefer others to behave in accordance with existing sex role stereotypes, traditionally "male" characteristics and attributes—including having a high-paying job; accruing resources; and displaying assertiveness, ambition, strength, competitiveness, and other "masculine" traits—may be viewed as important features for men to possess (and may be valued more by [heterosexual] women than by men when considering and selecting a potential mate). Conversely, traditionally "female" characteristics and attributes—including expressing nurturance; displaying emotional warmth, intimacy, and cooperation; and being concerned with one's physical appearance—may be considered important features for women to possess and therefore may be valued more by (heterosexual) men than by women when selecting a potential partner. Based on this perspective, then, we might expect that the features that are considered desirable in a mate will shift as the social roles that men and women typically occupy change over time.

Social context theorists also have identified a variety of other social forces that shape men's and women's mating behavior, including *social and cultural scripts*, which are normative expectations that define and organize social experience and are used to guide and assess social behavior (e.g., Gagnon & Simon, 1973; Reiss, 1967, 1981, 1986; Simon & Gagnon, 1986); *social learning processes*, including the patterns of reinforcement and punishment that people receive for their romantic and sexual behavior (e.g., Hogben & Byrne, 1998; Mischel, 1966); and *sexual regimes*, which consist of culturally specific normative orientations and traditions associated with sexuality (e.g., Laumann et al., 2006; Widmer, Treas, & Newcomb, 1998). Individuals learn the prevailing sociocultural "rules" of love, sex, and mating from a host of social forces including the media (e.g., television, Internet, magazines), parents and peers, the educational system, religious and political ideologies, legal principles, and so forth. For example, modern U.S. society and other Western cultures emphasize the importance of mutual attraction and individual choice in the selection of a romantic partner and hold fairly permissive attitudes with respect to male and female sexuality. Other societies emphasize family involvement in the choice of a marriage partner and hold more restrictive views of sexuality (particularly female sexuality). Given these existing sociocultural differences, we might expect to find that preferences for particular partner attributes, along with attitudes about love, sex, and marriage, will vary as a function of culture.

All of these contemporary social mechanisms—scripts, sexual regimes, social learning processes, sex-based beliefs and expectations, and social exchange—undoubtedly contribute to men's and women's mating preferences, behavior, and outcomes.

## Evolutionary Models: The World That Was

*The mind is a set of information-processing machines that were designed by natural selection to solve adaptive problems faced by our hunter-gatherer ancestors.*

—Cosmides and Tooby (1997, p. 1)

*Evolutionary models* of human mating are derived from the theoretical principles of evolutionary psychology, encapsulated in the preceding quotation. Specifically, according to noted evolutionary theorists Leda Cosmides and John Tooby (1997; also see Tooby & Cosmides, 1992), evolutionary psychology is concerned with the design of the human mind or the neural circuits we possess that process information. Evolutionary psychologists conceive of the mind as composed of many specialized processing systems. For example, we possess neural circuitry that is specialized for use in mate selection, just as we possess neural circuitry for language acquisition and for food selection. In addition, evolutionary psychologists agree that the human mind (all of our neural circuitry) was designed by the processes of natural and sexual selection originally articulated by naturalist Charles Darwin (1859, 1871). Relatedly, the human mind is believed to be designed to solve *adaptive problems* or recurrent issues in human evolutionary history that had implications for reproduction and survival. One of the most significant of these adaptive problems involved the selection, attraction, and retention of a suitable mate. Finally, evolutionary psychology is oriented toward our species' distant past. The human mind was designed to solve adaptive problems that existed eons ago and that affected the daily lives of our earliest ancestors. With these principles in mind, evolutionary models of mating consider the ways in which contemporary mating behavior might be influenced by evolved psychological heuristics that were selected because they overcame obstacles to reproduction located in the human ancestral past and therefore maximized reproductive success.

Evolutionary models target four different types of partner attributes that could conceivably have affected reproductive success among early humans (see Buss & Kenrick, 1998; Cunningham, Druen, & Barbee, 1997; Gangestad & Simpson, 1990, 2000; Regan, 2002). The first attributes center on the partner's *emotional fitness*. Evolutionary models recognize that the human biological design favors the formation of enduring (long-term and committed) relationships. Specifically, because human offspring are characterized by a period of dependency that extends well beyond infancy, successful pair-bonding and child rearing in the ancestral past depended, for both sexes, on the ability to select a mate who could and would provide sustained social and emotional support. Those early humans who selected emotionally fit partners achieved greater reproductive success than those who did not; hence, the former's genes survived. As a result of this genetic legacy, contemporary men and women are presumed to be particularly desirous of a long-term partner who possesses prosocial personality characteristics that indicate an ability and a willingness to emotionally commit to the reproductive partner, the reproductive relationship, and any resulting offspring.

In addition to dispositional attributes related to emotional fitness, evolutionary models suggest that reproductive success would have been dependent, for both sexes, on selecting a partner who possessed *physical or genetic fitness*—namely, a sexually mature, healthy individual who was capable of reproduction; who would pass on "good" genetic material to any resulting offspring; and who was physically able to contribute to the reproductive relationship, the partner, and the offspring. Insofar as physical appearance served as an external indicant or "honest advertisement" of underlying genetic fitness, reproductive status, and health in the ancestral environment (e.g., Fisher, 1958; Gangestad, 1993), appearance attributes are believed to play an important role in the mating decisions of both sexes today.

A third class of adaptively significant feature includes those inter-personal attributes that promote the successful formation and mainte-nance of a committed pair-bond. Evolutionarily speaking, an appropriate mate is one who not only possesses emotional and physical fitness, but who additionally demonstrates *relational fitness*—the ability and motiva-tion to become exclusively attached to one particular individual, to ignore the temptations posed by other individuals, and to confine repro-ductively relevant behaviors (e.g., emotional, sexual, economic, social) to the primary relationship. A number of characteristics are indicative of relational fitness, including mutual attraction or love, exclusivity, and similarity between partners. Those early humans who chose to pursue and establish a relationship with an individual who did not reciprocate their feelings of attraction, who did not confine his or her sexual and emotional activities to the primary relationship, and/or whose charac-teristics were not compatible with their own would have experienced lower levels of reproductive success than would those men and women who selected a more appropriate partner. Thus, contemporary men and women are presumed to prefer as a mate an individual who loves them passionately (and with whom they are themselves in love); who is will-ing to form an exclusive (i.e., monogamous and faithful) partnership; and who resembles them along important demographic, personality, and attitudinal dimensions.

The final category of feature that may have served to promote reproductive success in the ancestral environment is *social fitness*. In the ancestral environment, men and women who based their repro-ductive decisions at least partly on social fitness considerations—that is, who selected as mates individuals with strong ties to the existing community; with some degree of status or position within that com-munity; and with the ability to provide tangible resources in the form of food, shelter, and physical protection—would have enjoyed a higher degree of reproductive success than would men and women who chose to ignore or undervalue social fitness. Consequently, con-temporary humans are presumed to prefer mates who possess attri-butes that reflect the ability to successfully negotiate the social hierarchy.

Although all men and women are assumed to be desirous of mates who possess emotional, physical, relational, and social fitness, some evolutionary models posit sex differences in preferences for particular partner attributes. *Parental investment-based* models (e.g., Buss & Schmitt, 1993; Kenrick, Sadalla, Groth, & Trost, 1990) hypothesize that women, who invest more direct physiological resources in their off-spring than do men (e.g., contributing body nutrients during pregnancy and lactation), will be more sensitive to resource limitations and thus will be particularly attentive to a reproductive partner's social fitness (e.g., status, ability to provide resources). Men, on the other hand, are assumed to be constrained by access to women who can produce viable offspring and thus should be relatively more sensitive than women to characteristics that reflect physical fitness, including health and reproductive capacity.

Although men and women are assumed to differ with respect to the emphasis they place on particular partner attributes, they are believed to hold similar standards and to be relatively equally selective with respect to their partners. Specifically, because human males as well as females invest heavily in offspring, mating mistakes— selecting a partner who is unable to provide resources, who is capricious and emotionally unstable, who is infertile and unhealthy—are extremely costly to both sexes in the long-term relational context. Thus, parental investment theories posit that both men and women will be highly—and equally—discriminating in their choice of a long-term partner.

## ❖ METHODS USED TO EXAMINE MATE PREFERENCES

Not only have a variety of theories been developed to explain human mating, but there also are several different methods for exploring the attributes people seek in potential (hypothetical) partners. By far the most common methods used involve self-report. For example, many of the early (and some of the more recent) investigations employed a *ranking procedure* in which participants ordered or organized features in terms of their importance or desirability (e.g., Hill, 1945; Regan & Berscheid, 1997). Other researchers have chosen to use a *rating procedure* in which participants evaluate the importance or desirability of features with Likert-type scales (e.g., Dijkstra, Barelds, Groothof, Ronner, & Nauta, 2012; Wiederman & Allgeier, 1992). Still others have used a *percentile ranking procedure* in which participants indicate how much of a particular characteristic they would like a potential partner to possess relative to other same-sex people (e.g., Kenrick, Groth, Trost, & Sadalla, 1993; Regan, 1998d). And some researchers have utilized a *budget allocation procedure* in which participants receive a set number of "mate dollars" that they can distribute among (that is, use to "purchase") various attributes in a hypothetical partner (e.g., Li, Bailey, Kenrick, & Linsenmeier, 2002; Li, Valentine, & Patel, 2011). These four self-report methods are illustrated in Table 1.1.

**Table 1.1**    Four Self-Report Methods for Investigating Mate Preferences

**Instructions**

We are interested in exploring the attributes that people seek in a long-term, romantic partner—a steady date, a spouse or domestic partner, someone with whom you might cohabit and/or raise children. Below, you will find a list of attributes or characteristics that you might want a long-term, romantic partner to possess. After you read over the entire list, please evaluate these characteristics using the four different methods described below. Take your time and think carefully about your ratings.

**Scoring**

*Column 1: Rank order*

Read over the entire list of attributes and rank order them from most to least important (1 = most important characteristic to me, 2 = second most important characteristic to me, etc.).

*Column 2: Rating scale*

Rate the importance of each attribute to you in this type of partner using the following scale:

| 1 | 2 | 3 | 4 | 5 | 6 | 7 |
|---|---|---|---|---|---|---|
| Not at all important | | | | | | Extremely important |

*Column 3: Percentile ranking*

Indicate how you would like your partner to rank on each attribute, compared to other men or women, using the following scale:

My perfect partner is above _____% of other men (women) on this attribute.

Note: Scores can range from 0 to 99. For example, a score of 50 means that your partner is above 50% and below 49% of others on this characteristic (exactly average). A score of 35 means that your partner is above 35% and below 64% of the population (below average). A score of 80 means that your partner is above 80% and below 19% of all other men/women on this attribute (above average).

*Column 4: Budget allocation*

You have a budget of 500 "mate dollars" you may use to obtain percentile points across these 10 characteristics. Each dollar corresponds to one percentile point. An allocation of $50 for a particular characteristic means that your partner will be average (at the 50th percentile) on this characteristic; an allocation of $100 means that your partner will have more of that attribute than other men (or women). Use your budget to create your ideal partner.

| Characteristic Allocation | Column 1 Rank Order | Column 2 Importance | Column 3 Percentile | Column 4 Budget |
|---|---|---|---|---|
| Intelligent | _____ | _____ | _____ | _____ |
| Kind and understanding | _____ | _____ | _____ | _____ |
| Emotionally stable | _____ | _____ | _____ | _____ |
| Honest and trustworthy | _____ | _____ | _____ | _____ |
| Physically attractive | _____ | _____ | _____ | _____ |
| Good sense of humor | _____ | _____ | _____ | _____ |
| High social status | _____ | _____ | _____ | _____ |
| Similar to you (interests, values, etc.) | _____ | _____ | _____ | _____ |
| Good housekeeper | _____ | _____ | _____ | _____ |
| Sexually experienced | _____ | _____ | _____ | _____ |

Some researchers have chosen to conduct *content analyses* of personal ads in an attempt to identify the partner attributes people seek (e.g., Davis, 1990; Deaux & Hanna, 1984; Lawson, James, Jannson, Koyama, & Hill, 2014; Smith, Konik, & Tuve, 2011). Finally, some researchers have examined the importance of particular attributes *experimentally* by manipulating the features that a target individual possesses and examining the impact of this manipulation on participants' perceptions (e.g., self-reported desire to date the target; Graziano, Jensen-Campbell, Todd, & Finch, 1997; Ha, van den Berg, Engels, & Lichtwarck-Aschoff, 2012; Townsend & Levy, 1990). As discussed below, some of these methods may provide a more accurate picture of mate preference than others.

## ❖ EMPIRICAL EVIDENCE

The mate preference literature is enormous and encompasses a myriad of research studies, all of which generally indicate that men and women overwhelmingly prefer a long-term partner who possesses intelligence, emotional stability, an honest and trustworthy disposition, an exciting overall personality, and a physically attractive appearance. In two of the first documented examinations of mate preference, both conducted during the late 1930s and early 1940s, social scientists Harold Christensen (1947) and Reuben Hill (1945) asked college students at their respective universities to rank order a list of characteristics in terms of their importance in a romantic partner. The two most important attributes, according to both samples of participants, were "dependable character" and "emotional stability and maturity." Men and women also emphasized a "pleasing disposition," "good health," "desire for home and children," and "mutual attraction or love." Less important attributes included "similar political background" (unimportant to men and women in both samples), "good cook/housekeeper" (unimportant to women), and "good financial prospect" (unimportant to men). Other researchers have since replicated these results using the same or very similar lists of features (e.g., Hudson & Henze, 1969; McGinnis, 1958; Perilloux, Fleischman, & Buss, 2011; Regan & Berscheid, 1997). Table 1.2 illustrates these findings.

In more recent years, researchers have examined people's preferences for a larger variety of characteristics. For example, social psychologist Pamela Regan and her colleagues (Regan, Levin, Sprecher, Christopher, & Cate, 2000) asked men and women to indicate their preferences for 23 individual attributes. Both sexes reported desiring a

**Table 1.2**    Top 10 Desired Characteristics in a Marriage Partner

| *What Do Men Say They Want?* | *What Do Women Say They Want?* |
| --- | --- |
| Good overall personality | Honesty and trustworthiness |
| Honesty and trustworthiness | Kindness and compassion |
| Attractive appearance | Good overall personality |
| Intelligence | Intelligence |
| Good health | Attentive to one's partner |
| Kindness and compassion | Good sense of humor |
| Good sense of humor | Self-confidence |
| Self-confidence | Good health |
| Attentive to one's partner | Attractive appearance |
| Easygoing nature | Easygoing nature |

SOURCE: Regan, P. C., & Berscheid, E. (1997). Gender differences in characteristics desired in a potential sexual and marriage partner. *Journal of Psychology and Human Sexuality (9)*1, 25–37. Copyright © 1997 by the Haworth Press Inc.

NOTE: In this study, men and women were asked to rank order (from most to least desirable in a marriage partner) a list of attributes similar to the ones used by Christensen (1947), Hill (1945), and other early mate selection researchers. This table shows the top 10 most desired characteristics, arranged in order from highest to lowest ranking. As can be seen from the results, men and women tend to desire similar attributes in a marriage partner, although there is also evidence that men rank external attributes (health, appearance) higher than do women.

long-term romantic partner who possessed a great deal of the following characteristics, in order of importance:

1. *Prosocial personality attributes.* First and foremost, participants desired a mate who possessed prosocial personality attributes related to interpersonal responsiveness. Men and women emphasized the importance of a good sense of humor and an exciting personality, and they sought someone who was expressive and open and who had a friendly and sociable disposition.

2. *Characteristics related to intellect and mental drive.* Only slightly less important were characteristics related to intellect and mental drive. Both men and women sought a partner who was intellectually gifted and driven—who possessed intelligence, who was educated, and who was ambitious.

3. *Physically appealing attributes.* Although considered less important than the first two attribute categories, participants also desired a mate who was physically appealing. Both men and women emphasized a physically attractive, athletic, sexy, and healthy appearance when evaluating a long-term romantic partner.

4. *Similarity.* In addition, similarity—on demographic characteristics, values and attitudes, and interests and hobbies—was considered relatively important by the participants.

5. *Characteristics related to social status.* The least important (but still moderately desired) partner attributes were those related to social status and resources. Specifically, participants preferred a partner who was above average with respect to earning potential, who possessed at least moderate social status, and who had access to material possessions.

In addition to exploring what people seek in potential partners, some researchers have examined the attributes that people seek to *avoid* when selecting dates or mates. For example, social scientists Michael Cunningham, Anita Barbee, and Perri Druen (1996; also see Ault & Philhower, 2001; Cunningham et al., 1997; Cunningham, Shamblen, Barbee, & Ault, 2005) argue that the process of mate selection requires individuals to evaluate their partners not only in terms of the positive qualities they offer but also in terms of whether their negative qualities can be endured. Research on these undesirable partner attributes or *social allergens* reveals that men and women are repulsed by people who consistently violate social norms and rules of conduct, including drinking to excess, cheating at games, gossiping about others, arriving late all the time, and lying. In addition, they dislike partners who are oversexed— that is, who brag about sexual conquests or skills, constantly talk about or mention previous relationship partners, or gaze longingly at other men or women. People also seek to avoid partners who have uncouth habits (e.g., demonstrate poor grooming, display poor table manners, stand too close or stare inappropriately, use a loud speaking voice). In sum, individuals seek a potential mate who not only fulfills their desires but who also manages to avoid doing the things that repulse them.

Not only do men and women desire—and seek to avoid—similar features when considering a potential mate, but they are equally discriminating. Psychologist Douglas Kenrick and his colleagues (1993) asked a sample of young adults to indicate their minimum mate selection standards or the lowest level of various characteristics that they would consider acceptable when selecting a marriage partner. Their results revealed that neither men nor women would consider marrying someone unless he or she was above average (the 50th percentile) on nearly all attributes. In fact, summed across all characteristics, men's minimally acceptable mate scored at the 56th percentile and women's minimally acceptable partner scored at the 60th percentile. Regan (1998a) reported similar results. When it comes to choosing a long-term mate, both sexes appear to be highly selective.

## Individual and Group Differences

We have seen that men and women have similar preferences with respect to their long-term romantic partners. In fact, there are only two attribute categories on which men and women demonstrate consistent differences, at least in self-report studies: physical appearance and social status. Specifically, when considering attributes in a hypothetical romantic partner, men tend to emphasize physical attractiveness more than do women, and women tend to emphasize social or economic position more than do men (for an early review, see Feingold, 1992). For example, Susan Sprecher, Quintin Sullivan, and Elaine Hatfield (1994) asked a large, national sample of men and women to indicate how willing they would be to marry someone who possessed a variety of characteristics. The results revealed that men reported being significantly less willing than women to marry someone who was "not good looking," whereas women reported being significantly less willing than men to marry a partner who was "not likely to hold a steady job" and who "would earn less than you." *Neither* sex, however, was very willing to marry an individual with these attributes. Thus, it is not the case that attractiveness is *un*important to women or that social status does *not* matter to men; rather, both sexes appear to value each of these two attributes, but to different degrees.

Interestingly, men's and women's preferences for these characteristics appear to be changing over time. Using the same measurement instrument as Christensen (1947) and Hill (1945), social scientists David Buss, Todd Shackelford, Lee Kirkpatrick, and Randy Larsen (2001) compared the preferences of men and women across a 57-year span (from 1939 to 1996). Not surprisingly, they found that the same core set of positive personality attributes were highly valued across time (i.e., dependable character, emotional stability and maturity, and pleasing disposition). In addition, however, the researchers discovered that "good looks" became more highly valued by women over time (that is, rose in rank value from 1939 to 1996), whereas "good financial prospect" became more highly valued by men over time.

Culture is another variable that appears to be associated with romantic partner preferences. Although men and women from around the world value the same set of dispositional features (e.g., emotional stability, honesty and trustworthiness, kindness, humor, openness, a dependable character, intelligence; see Lippa, 2007; Pearce, Chuikova, Ramsey, & Galyautdinova, 2010; White; Pearce, & Khramtsova, 2011), robust cultural differences exist. For example, adults from traditional, collectivist countries and regions, such as China, Malaysia, Singapore, India, and Eastern Europe, tend to value demographic similarity (e.g., same religion, caste) and "practical" characteristics that reflect competence as a potential spouse and parent (e.g., family orientation, neatness, chastity, money-mindedness) more than do adults from modern, individualist countries and regions, such as the United States, the United Kingdom, Canada, and Western Europe (Buss et al., 1990; Goodwin & Tang, 1991; Sprecher & Chandak, 1992; Toro-Morn & Sprecher, 2003). The emphasis placed on these particular constellations of features is understandable when we consider that many collectivist cultures have a history of (and still practice) arranged marriage. Selecting a partner on the basis of practical considerations and demographic similarity increases the likelihood that the partners will be compatible, that the marriage will function smoothly, and that the couple will receive approval and support from their families and other social groups. Scientist Yacoub Khallad (2005) examined mate preferences among a sample of men and women from a collectivist and highly conservative patriarchal culture in the Middle East (Jordan). Although mutual attraction and love and positive personality attributes received the highest ratings, participants also emphasized characteristics associated with the traditional social values of their culture. They desired a partner who was religious, who possessed refinement and neatness, and who wanted a home and children, and they were strongly opposed to marrying someone who had been divorced. In sum, culture appears to be a very powerful correlate of mate preference (see Goodwin, 1999).

## ❖ CONTINUING DEBATES

Of the variety of topics in the human mating literature, very few have received the kind of sustained empirical attention that the topic of mate preference has received. As a result of scores of investigations, a good deal is now known about the attributes people say they prefer in their ideal romantic partners, yet two primary issues continue to plague researchers in this area.

### Do We Always Get What We Want? The Issue of Compromise

The first issue that must be addressed when interpreting research on mate preference concerns compromise. Most researchers interested in exploring partner preferences focus on what people want—that is, on the characteristics or attributes they seek in potential, and often idealized, partners. However, one of the realities of human existence in general—and certainly of human mating—is that, to quote the Rolling Stones, "You can't always get what you want." In other words, although we might ideally want to date or marry someone with a particular set of features, we might not be able to attract someone with those attributes. Perhaps the desired partner is so attractive that he or she has many mating choices, and we are merely one among many possible options. Perhaps we simply do not meet the desired partner's ideals. Maybe we are already paired with someone else and therefore not free to select a partner. Regardless of the reason, the bottom line is that we cannot always obtain the kind of partner we ideally desire. And so we must compromise.

The ability to make compromises in the arena of sex, love, and mating is extremely important. For example, if most people were completely unwilling to deviate from their ideal standards—if they absolutely refused to consider less than perfect partners and to enter into less than ideal mating relationships—little actual mating would take place; instead, everyone would be stuck in mating limbo waiting for that "perfect someone" to come along. Because a great deal of mating does occur, it is obvious that some degree of compromise must characterize the process of mate selection. Recognizing this, a few researchers have begun to explore when and how people make those compromises.

One of the first studies that provided evidence for the fact that people can and do alter their mating standards was conducted by psychologist James Pennebaker and his colleagues (1979). This creative field study took place over a 3-hour period in a number of bars and taverns located near a college campus. Specifically, at three preselected times—9:00 p.m., 10:30 p.m., and midnight (half an hour before closing)—the researchers entered the various establishments and asked a sample of randomly selected men and women to indicate how attractive they found the other bar patrons present at each of those times. Participants evaluated both same-sex and opposite-sex patrons. The researchers' results indicated that as closing time neared, the perceived attractiveness of opposite-sex (but not same-sex) bar patrons increased significantly. In other words, the men got handsomer (according to the women) and the women got prettier (according to the men) as closing time approached. Assuming that the bar patrons actually did not alter their appearances over the course of the evening, and assuming that one goal of the participants was to select a potential mate from the existing pool, these results suggest that men's and women's mating standards are not set in stone but rather are actually quite flexible. When we think we are running out of time to select a mate, the available alternatives become more attractive.

Researchers have also found evidence that people moderate their mate preferences to take into account their own desirability or *mate value*. For example, in one study, Regan (1998d) asked a group of men and women to identify how much intelligence, attractiveness, humor, and so on they desired in a perfect romantic partner and then to estimate how much of each attribute they themselves possessed. She found a strong and positive correlation between ideal preferences and mate value. For example, women who thought that they possessed high levels of attributes related to intellect, interpersonal skill and responsiveness, and social status demanded equally high levels of these desirable attributes from their potential partner, whereas women who believed they had lower levels of those characteristics expected correspondingly lower levels from their potential partner. Similarly, men who possessed a strong family orientation (e.g., desire for children and related "hearth and home" attributes) preferred a long-term partner with the same high level of these characteristics. In addition, the greater a man estimated his own social status to be, the less willing he was to compromise on that dimension with respect to a potential romantic partner.

Similar results were obtained more recently by Carrie Bredow, Ted Huston, and Norval Glenn (2011). In their investigation, a large sample of unmarried men and women rated themselves on six attribute dimensions: warmth and communality, responsibility and impulse control, expressiveness, human capital and resources, emotional stability, and physical attractiveness and health (these ratings were summed to yield a measure of each participant's "perceived market value"). Participants also (1) indicated the extent to which their potential mates (defined as other people "who were potentially available for a romantic relationship") possessed a variety of positive internal and external characteristics adapted from other mate preference research (e.g., kind and understanding, unselfish, follows through on commitments, good looking, handles money responsibly); (2) indicated how important it was for their future spouse to possess those attributes; and (3) estimated their own chances of actually securing a suitable partner (i.e., one with those essential qualities). The results revealed that participants' perceived market value was positively associated with the other three measures; that is, the higher a man's or a woman's perceived mate value, the greater the perceived quality of his or her potential mates, the higher his or her standards for a future spouse, and the greater his or her confidence about marrying someone with those desirable attributes. Thus, people's own mate value is linked with their romantic preferences and mating expectations.

There is also evidence that people are sometimes willing to compromise in another way—specifically, by allowing their partners to score lower on attribute dimensions that they themselves possess in abundance (perhaps because they reason that if they have sufficient levels, there is less need for the partner to bring those features to the relationship). An interesting study conducted by Christine Stanik and Phoebe Ellsworth (2010) illustrates this phenomenon. Here, a large sample of college women were given a standard intelligence test and then asked to rate how much they desired the attributes "good financial prospect," "social status," and "ambition/industriousness" in a future spouse (these three items were summed to create an overall index of the partner's ability to provide). The results revealed a strong negative correlation between intelligence scores and preferences for this partner attribute. Specifically, the higher a woman's intelligence score was, the *less* she desired traits associated with the ability to provide financial resources. The authors conclude that women (and, presumably, men) with high levels of intelligence or other attributes have fewer constraints on their mating decisions and can be more flexible when considering potential partners:

> Our data suggest that for women with access to education and career opportunities, intelligence makes a difference in what they look for in a man. As college women's intelligence increases, their reported desire for traits in a long-term partner that are associated with ability to provide decreases. This may reflect women's flexibility in prioritizing traits in a partner when a man's resources need not be of the utmost importance. (p. 214)

The fact that people seem to link their expectations to their own mate value provides support for the social exchange theories discussed earlier in the chapter as well as additional evidence for the important role played by compromise in mate selection.

People also appear willing to moderate their preferences by making "trade-offs" among various sets of features. For example, Cunningham and colleagues (1997) found that both men and women selected partners who combined physical attractiveness with a pleasing personality over partners who possessed the combination of physical attractiveness and wealth or the combination of a pleasing personality and wealth. Similarly, Lauri Jensen-Campbell, William Graziano, and

Stephen West (1995) reported that women preferred as dates men who possessed high levels of both agentic (e.g., active, assertive, bold, talkative) and agreeable (e.g., considerate, cooperative, kind, sympathetic) features over men who were agentic and disagreeable, nonagentic and agreeable, or nonagentic and disagreeable. And in a more recent study, Joanna Scheib (2001) found that women asked to imagine that they were selecting a husband overwhelmingly chose a less physically attractive man with a good character (e.g., dependable, faithful, kind and understanding, mature, patient) over a more attractive man with a less desirable character.

In sum, research indicates that men and women are willing to compromise their ideal mate standards by paying attention to external factors (e.g., selection time) that affect mate choice, by taking into account their own mate value, and by selectively choosing one characteristic or combination of characteristics over others.

## Do We Always Know What We Want? The Issues of Self-Report and Hypothetical Ideals

The second issue that plagues research in this area concerns whether the self-report methodologies and hypothetical "rate your ideal partner" scenarios that most researchers use adequately capture people's real-life mate preferences. There is growing evidence, in fact, that these methodologies may contribute to a misleading view of men's and women's mating desires. For example, sex differences are greater in self-report paradigms than they are in behavioral research paradigms, and greater when participants are evaluating hypothetical as opposed to actual partners (see Eastwick & Finkel, 2008; for a review, see Feingold, 1990). Paul Eastwick and his colleagues (Eastwick, Luchies, Finkel, & Hunt, 2014) reviewed 95 articles that examined preferences for physical attractiveness and earning potential in real-life encounters (that is, studies in which participants evaluated romantic partners they were married to, dating, or had at least met face-to-face). The authors' analyses revealed that, unlike in studies where people rate hypothetical dates or spouses, there were no sex differences with respect to preferences for these two attribute dimensions in the "real world." Across all studies, the higher a real partner's physical attractiveness and earning potential, the more positively both men and women evaluated him or her. In other words, the factors that people pay attention to and value in real-life mates do not necessarily match the ones they focus on when reporting their ideal, hypothetical preferences.

A study conducted by Sprecher (1989) provides an early and compelling illustration of this phenomenon. In her investigation, men and women received information about an opposite-sex target who was presented as possessing high or low levels of three attributes: physical attractiveness, earning potential, and expressiveness. After rating the target's desirability as a dating partner, participants then were asked to indicate which of these factors they believed had influenced their evaluations. Men reported being more influenced than women by the target's physical appearance. Recall that this is the first of the two major sex differences commonly reported in the literature (i.e., men value physical attractiveness in potential romantic partners more than do women). However, the experimental data revealed that men and women were equally affected by the manipulation. That is, the physically attractive target was overwhelmingly preferred as a dating partner by both men and women. Similarly, women believed more than did men that their evaluations had been affected by the target's earning potential. This is the second major sex difference often found in the literature (i.e., women value social status and resource attributes in potential mates more than do men). As before, however, there was no actual sex difference in the impact of that variable on perceptions of the target; men and women were equally affected by the target's earning potential. These results suggest that men and women may be differentially aware of (or motivated to reveal) the factors that influence their perceptions and evaluations of potential mates—an important consideration to keep in mind when evaluating research on partner preferences.

## Summary

The preferences and choices that men and women demonstrate as they enter, maintain, and terminate mating relationships undoubtedly are influenced by both contemporary and distal mechanisms. As was predicted from both of the theoretical frameworks we reviewed, men and women generally prefer partners who possess a constellation of positive characteristics, ranging from internal or dispositional traits (e.g., emotional stability, humor, intelligence), to interpersonal attributes (e.g., friendliness, sociability), to physical features (e.g., attractiveness), to social variables (e.g., status). In addition, they seek to avoid certain particularly repellant features, and they seem willing to modify their preferences as a function of various factors, including their own mate value. In Chapter 2, we turn to a consideration of the ways in which people go about fulfilling their desires and obtaining the type of mate they seek.

## Key Concepts

Social context frameworks (p. 4)
Social exchange or equity models (p. 4)
Social role theory (p. 5)
Social and cultural scripts (p. 5)
Social learning processes (p. 5)
Sexual regimes (p. 5)
Evolutionary models (p. 6)
Adaptive problems (p. 6)

Emotional fitness (p. 7)
Physical or genetic fitness (p. 7)
Relational fitness (p. 8)
Social fitness (p. 8)
Parental investment-based models (p. 8)
Self-report methodologies (p. 9)
Social allergens (p. 13)
Mate value (p. 17)

## Discussion Questions

1. In what ways does the process of mate selection resemble a "social marketplace"? Do we always pay attention to our own and our potential partners' "bargaining power"?

2. How do social roles, sociocultural scripts, social learning processes, and sexual regimes contribute to mating behavior? Consider how these factors might explain sex differences and cultural differences in partner preferences.

3. Consider how various attributes (e.g., emotional fitness, physical vitality, resources and status) may have contributed to personal survival and reproductive success in the ancestral environment.

4. Compare and contrast the various methodologies available for examining mate preferences. Which one do you think provides the most accurate view of people's desires? Which one provides the least accurate view?

5. Consider what is known about men's and women's mate preferences. How does the empirical evidence support or contradict the social context and evolutionary theories reviewed in the first part of the chapter?

6. Collect a sample of personal ads. What do people seek in a potential partner? What do they advertise? Make a list. Are there any similarities among your sample of writers? How do the preferences contained in the ads compare with research from self-report studies of mate preference?

7. Think about your own dating experiences. Have you ever compromised when considering someone as a potential romantic partner? What characteristics do you personally feel are absolutely essential in a long-term partner (i.e., you would not be willing to compromise)? What attributes are luxuries (you desire them, but they are not absolutely essential)? In answering this question, it might be helpful to look at the list of attributes in Tables 1.1 and 1.2.

## Recommended Readings

These articles present theories that can be applied to human mate preferences and that have been used to explain sex differences in mating behavior. The first article focuses on social role theory, the second presents social learning theory, the third reviews a number of social context and evolutionary theories, and the fourth presents an overview of social exchange models.

Eagly, A. H., Wood, W., & Johannesen-Schmidt, M. (2004). Social role theory of sex differences and similarities: Implications for partner preferences of women and men. In A. H. Eagly, A. Beall, & R. J. Sternberg (Eds.), *The psychology of gender* (2nd ed., pp. 269–295). New York, NY: Guilford Press.

Hogben, M., & Byrne, D. (1998). Using social learning theory to explain individual differences in human sexuality. *The Journal of Sex Research, 35,* 58–71.

Oliver, M. B., & Hyde, J. S. (1993). Gender differences in sexuality: A meta-analysis. *Psychological Bulletin, 114,* 29–51.

Sprecher, S. (1998). Social exchange theories and sexuality. *The Journal of Sex Research, 35,* 32–43.

The authors of these articles use different methodological approaches to investigate mate preferences.

Deaux, K., & Hanna, R. (1984). Courtship in the personals column: The influence of gender and sexual orientation. *Sex Roles, 11,* 363–375.

Jensen-Campbell, L. A., Graziano, W. G., & West, S. (1995). Dominance, prosocial orientation, and female preferences: Do nice guys really finish last? *Journal of Personality and Social Psychology, 68,* 427–440.

Kenrick, D. T., Groth, G. E., Trost, M. R., & Sadalla, E. K. (1993). Integrating evolutionary and social exchange perspectives on relationships: Effects of gender, self-appraisal, and involvement level on mate selection criteria. *Journal of Personality and Social Psychology, 64,* 951–969.

Li, N. P., Bailey, J. M., Kenrick, D. T., & Linsenmeier, J. A. W. (2002). The necessities and luxuries of mate preferences: Testing the trade-offs. *Journal of Personality and Social Psychology, 82,* 947–955.

Regan, P. C., & Berscheid, E. (1997). Gender differences in characteristics desired in a potential sexual and marriage partner. *Journal of Psychology and Human Sexuality, 9,* 25–37.

Wiederman, M. W., & Allgeier, E. R. (1992). Gender differences in mate selection criteria: Sociobiological or socioeconomic explanation? *Ethology and Sociobiology, 13,* 115–124.

The first of these two important meta-analyses reveals that people's stated preferences for potential romantic partners do not always predict their actual mating choices (in other words, just because people say they value particular qualities in a mate does not necessarily mean that they will actually pursue a relationship with someone who possesses those desired qualities). The second analysis reveals that physical attractiveness is as important a social asset for men to possess as it is for women to possess. In this paper, the authors argue that theories emphasizing sex differences (e.g., parental investment-based evolutionary frameworks) may be less accurate than others in explaining the social impact of physical attractiveness.

Eastwick, P. W., Luchies, L. B., Finkel, E. J., & Hunt, L. L. (2014). The predictive validity of ideal partner preferences: A review and meta-analysis. *Psychological Bulletin, 140,* 623–665.

Langlois, J. H., Kalakanis, L., Rubenstein, A. J., Larson, A., Hallam, M., & Smoot, M. (2000). Maxims or myths of beauty? A meta-analytic and theoretical review. *Psychological Bulletin, 126,* 390–423.

# 2

# Attraction, Affiliation, and Courtship

❖  ❖  ❖

How do two people—often total strangers to each other when they first meet—establish an intimate romantic connection? What is it that initially sparks their attraction to each other and leads them to conclude that such a connection is possible? And how, once they feel attraction, do they communicate their interest to each other and enter into an actual relationship? This chapter explores these and related questions.

## ❖ WHO DO WE LIKE? PRINCIPLES OF ROMANTIC ATTRACTION

Social and behavioral scientists have identified a number of factors that are associated with *attraction* (liking or positive sentiment) and that appear to play a role in the initiation of mating relationships.

### Physically Appealing Others

Recall from Chapter 1 that men and women around the world consider an array of characteristics to be highly desirable in a potential mate, including honesty and trustworthiness, kindness and sensitivity, emotional stability and dependability, humor and intelligence, physical attractiveness, and various other positive attributes. Of all these characteristics, none appears as capable of eliciting romantic interest as *physical attractiveness*—at least in initial encounters when people meet for the first time.

The powerful impact of physical appeal on romantic attraction was first demonstrated in the late 1960s in a classic study conducted by social psychologists Elaine Hatfield (then Walster), Vera Aronson, Darcy Abrahams, and Leon Rottman (1966). In their study, incoming first-year students received information about a "Computer Dance" being offered as part of a series of university-sponsored activities for new students. Those who arrived to purchase advance tickets were asked to complete a questionnaire about their interests and characteristics, which they believed would be fed into a computer and used to pair them with another student—their date for the dance—who possessed similar attributes. (Students actually were randomly paired for the dance.) As each student went through the process of completing the questionnaire and purchasing a ticket, the four people supervising the activity (who were actually confederates working for the researchers) surreptitiously assessed his or her physical attractiveness. Later that week, the students arrived at the dance and met the partners who had been (randomly) assigned to them. Then, during intermission, they completed a questionnaire that asked, among other items, how much they liked their dates and whether or not they would like to go out with them again. The researchers had predicted a matching effect; that is, they expected that people would prefer partners at their own attractiveness level (for example, they hypothesized that moderately attractive people who happened to be assigned highly attractive dates would like their partners less than would moderately attractive people who happened to be assigned moderately attractive partners). However, this was not the case. For both men and women, and irrespective of their own level of attractiveness, the more physically appealing the date, the more he or she was liked and the more often participants wanted to go out with him or her again.

Recent research using similar "live interaction" methodologies has confirmed these early findings, revealing that when people initially encounter a potential mate, they tend to focus on features that are readily seen and easily evaluated, such as physical appearance (e.g., Asendorpf, Penke, & Back, 2011; Eastwick & Finkel, 2008; Fletcher, Kerr, Li, & Valentine, 2014; Lenton & Francesconi, 2010; Luo & Zhang, 2009). Of course, over time and with repeated interactions, partners have the opportunity to come to know and value each other on the basis of less visible, interior qualities. Indeed, scientists have found that external, physical attributes become substantially less important in determining romantic attraction once partners move beyond initial encounters (see Eastwick, Luchies, Finkel, & Hunt, 2014).

## Familiar Others

*Familiarity* is another powerful predictor of attraction. It is certainly possible to feel an instant romantic or sexual interest in a complete stranger (particularly one who is physically appealing, as we have discussed). Nonetheless, research consistently finds evidence that people show a marked preference for, and tend to be attracted to, familiar as opposed to unfamiliar others. This psychological phenomenon is known as the "mere exposure effect"—merely being exposed to another individual repeatedly over time tends to generate liking for that person (Bornstein, 1989; Zajonc, 2001). In one early laboratory experiment, for example, psychologist Robert Zajonc (1968) told participants that he was studying "visual memory" and asked them to view a series of yearbook photographs of male college students. To create different levels of familiarity, each of the photographs was presented a different number of times (ranging from one to 25 exposures) for a period of 2 seconds. At the end of the trial, participants rated how much they liked the men in the photographs. The results revealed a significant association between number of exposures and liking ratings; specifically, the more often participants had seen a particular man's face (that is, the more familiar he was), the more attracted they were to him. Zajonc's initial findings have now been replicated outside of the laboratory as well, demonstrating that in real-world settings, repeated exposure to another person does produce liking for him or her (e.g., Moreland & Beach, 1992; also see Reis, Maniaci, Caprariello, Eastwick, & Finkel, 2011).

Interestingly, in the process of exploring the familiarity-attraction connection, scientists have discovered an important caveat to the mere exposure effect. Repeated contact only generates liking when a person's initial reaction to the unfamiliar other is positive or neutral. If, on meeting someone for the first time, our initial reaction is negative (for whatever reason, we find him or her to be unpleasant), then repeatedly being exposed to or coming into contact with that same individual is unlikely to produce attraction (in fact, it is likely to produce repulsion). Thus, familiarity seems to strengthen first responses, so that a person who is initially liked comes to be liked even more, and a person who is disliked comes to be disliked even more, with increased exposure.

## Similar Others

Like familiarity, *similarity* also appears to spark romantic attraction. Both men and women prefer potential mates who resemble them on demographic, dispositional, attitudinal, and interest dimensions (Markey & Markey, 2007; Sprecher & Regan, 2002), and similarity (both actual and perceived) also produces liking in laboratory experiments as well as in real-life contexts (Klohnen & Luo, 2003; Tidwell, Eastwick, & Finkel, 2013; for reviews, see Montoya, Horton, & Kirchner, 2008; Regan, 2015a). Social psychologist Donn Byrne and his colleagues have conducted the most rigorous and extensive examination of the association between similarity and attraction (for a review of this literature, see Byrne, 1997). For example, in one elegant early experiment (Byrne, Ervin, & Lamberth, 1970), a large pool of single heterosexual undergraduates completed a lengthy attitude and personality questionnaire. Next, the researchers matched male and female participants according to their degree of attitudinal and personality similarity. Pairs with the highest or the lowest number of matching responses were then given a small amount of money and sent on a 30-minute "get acquainted" date to the student union on campus. When each pair returned from the date to the research office to receive their final instructions and con-clude their participation in the study, two measures of romantic attrac-tion were collected. The first was behavioral and consisted of the physical distance between the two participants while they stood together in front of the researcher's desk (e.g., touching one another, standing at opposite corners of the desk). The second was self-report and consisted of the participants' private ratings of each other in terms of desirability as a potential dating partner and as a marriage partner. The results revealed that similarity had a strong impact on both mea-sures of romantic attraction. Specifically, the highly similar pairs stood closer together and rated each other as more desirable as a date or spouse than did the dissimilar pairs.

One reason similarity (and familiarity, for that matter) promotes attraction is that it increases the probability that early interactions between potential romantic partners will be pleasant. Two people in the initial stages of getting acquainted are likely to have easy, positive, mutually rewarding exchanges to the extent that they endorse similar attitudes and values, share similar interests, possess similar personality traits, express similar behavioral tendencies, and are familiar with one another's attributes, preferences, and characteristic ways of respond-ing. A second reason for the similarity-attraction link lies in people's general tendency to assume that similar others will like them (and dis-similar others will dislike them). That is, most of us assume that some-one who is similar to us will respond positively to us, and that, in turn, produces attraction (e.g., Condon & Crano, 1988).

## Responsive Others

The responsiveness of two people to each other lies at the very heart of interpersonal interaction and what it means to be in a relationship; thus, it should come as no surprise that responsiveness is another factor that is strongly associated with romantic attraction (see Berscheid & Regan, 2005; Gable & Reis, 2006; Reis, Clark, & Holmes, 2004). *Responsiveness* generally is conceptualized as a property of verbal and nonverbal communication as well as a general belief that another is supportive, understanding, and caring.

Research consistently reveals that men and women report greater liking for, interest in, and attraction to individuals who are responsive than individuals who are not (e.g., Davis & Holtgraves, 1984; Davis & Perkowitz, 1979; Lemay & Clark, 2008; also see Sprecher, Treger, Wondra, Hilaire, & Wallpe, 2013). For example, psychologists Gurit Birnbaum and Harry Reis (2012) used a live interaction paradigm to explore the association between perceptions of a partner's responsiveness and a particular form of interpersonal attraction—namely, sexual interest. In their investigation, university student volunteers were randomly paired with another opposite-sex student whom they did not know for a brief interaction lasting between 5 and 7 minutes. Prior to the interaction, the members of each pair were randomly assigned to the role of "discloser" or "responder." Participants assigned to be disclosers were asked to discuss a recent personal negative event they had experienced (such as failing an examination), and those assigned to be responders were instructed to respond as they would under normal circumstances. Following the discussion, the disclosing participants completed a *responsiveness scale* that assessed perceptions of how understood, validated, and cared for they felt when interacting with the responding partner (e.g., he or she "really listened to me," he or she "was aware of what I am thinking and feeling," and so forth). They also completed a measure of *sexual attraction* that assessed their interest in engaging in various pre-sexual and sexual activities with the responding partner (e.g., "to what extent would you be interested in kissing the responding participant?"). The results revealed a strong positive correlation between perceptions of a partner's responsiveness and subsequent sexual attraction to that individual. Specifically, the more responsive (validating, understanding, and caring) that men and women perceived their interaction partners to be, the greater the sexual attraction they reported feeling for those partners. In discussing their findings, Birnbaum and Reis (2012) observed that responsiveness may play a key role in fostering initial romantic attraction between potential mates:

> During initial encounters, people evaluate the suitability and compatibility of newly met potential partners . . . these evaluations include sexual desire. In this context, sexual responses to a new acquaintance may serve as a diagnostic test of his or her mate value and suitability. . . . Because responsiveness is geared toward promoting a partner's welfare, it is likely to be particularly valued in a potential long-term relationship partner. . . . It is thus reasonable that perceived responsiveness affects the results of this sexual attraction "test" (i.e., the desirability of a potential partner), as indicated by our findings. (p. 954)

It makes definite sense to pay close attention to another person's responsiveness because it imparts important information about the likelihood of a future relationship with him or her. People who are unresponsive—who avoid eye contact, lean away or orient their bodies away from us, refuse to respond (or respond inappropriately) to our conversational salvoes, or remove themselves from our company—are signaling a clear lack of interest in establishing any kind of connection with us (romantic, sexual, or otherwise). In fact, as we will discuss in Chapter 6, lack of responsiveness between partners is often a potent sign of interpersonal distress and dysfunction. It is no wonder that responsiveness is such an appealing characteristic.

## ❖ WHO DO WE APPROACH? PRINCIPLES OF ROMANTIC AFFILIATION

Feelings of attraction are the most common reason people attempt to initiate interaction with a potential mate. But attraction does not guarantee *affiliation*—we do not always approach others to whom we are attracted. Two factors play an important role in determining affiliation: accessibility and receptivity.

### Accessible Others

One of the realities that every individual must face as he or she goes about the process of mate selection is that life rarely offers up a smorgasbord of romantic possibilities. Rather, as sociologist Alan Kerckhoff (1974) observed, people's selections are limited to their *field of availables*, defined as those individuals who are available and accessible for interaction (and, therefore, potential romantic relationships). Research reveals that *interaction accessibility* is a key determinant of romantic affiliation and relationship initiation.

Potential partners may be accessible physically, virtually (electronically), or socially. Numerous studies demonstrate the powerful impact of *physical proximity* on relationship initiation, revealing time and time again that people who live (or work, shop, attend school, participate in hobbies, etc.) close to one another are much more likely to meet, interact, and establish a relationship than those who live even just a little bit farther away (see Berscheid & Regan, 2005; Regan, 2015a; Sprecher, Felmlee, Metts, & Cupach, 2014). Most romantic relationships, in fact, are hatched out of the day-to-day interactions that occur between individuals who come in contact regularly.

In addition to providing access to potential mates, proximity may promote feelings of attraction between people. For example, close physical proximity virtually guarantees that two people will become familiar with one another, and familiarity generally produces liking (recall the mere exposure effect). Moreover, individuals who live in the same neighborhood, attend the same school or church, work in the same location, and/or belong to the same social club or community organization are likely to resemble each other on important demographic, attitudinal, interest, and dispositional dimensions—and similarity, as we have discussed, also generates liking. (There are no guarantees, however. Physical proximity merely provides the opportunity to interact—it does not ensure that those interactions will be pleasant. We are just as likely to be repulsed by people we meet as we are to be attracted to them, primarily because we have an increased likelihood of discovering things about them that we find unappealing.)

Today, people need not be in close physical contact in order to interact or initiate a mating relationship. Increasing numbers of men and women now use the Internet to search for romantic opportunities (McKenna, 2008; Sprecher, 2009), and many of them do so because of a lack of physical access to available partners (Madden & Lenhart, 2006). In the online world, *virtual proximity* replaces physical proximity in determining interaction accessibility:

> In order for two people to meet online, they have to be in the same chat room at the same time (closest approximation to "real life" proximity), post messages on the same message board forum (one that archives past postings), be part of the same listserv (where users interact both on the list and off), or have the same software as other people (i.e., AOL's Instant Messenger or ICQ messaging software). Any one of these things [increases] the possibility of two people crossing paths and communicating. (Levine, 2000, p. 566)

Interestingly, although the Internet has undoubtedly widened the field of available partners for many people, most men and women who seek romance in cyberspace tend to ultimately meet their romantic partners as a function of physical proximity. One national survey of Internet users revealed that only 3% actually met their spouse or long-term partner online; the majority (56%) had met the partner at work or school; at church; at the gym; at a nightclub, bar, or café; because they lived in the same neighborhood; or because they had a "chance encounter" in a random physical location (e.g., were on the same street at the same time) (Madden & Lenhart, 2006). We will consider the topic of *e-courtship* (online or web-based relationship initiation) in greater detail later in this chapter.

In addition to physical and virtual proximity, *social proximity*—how close potential partners are to each other in the social environment or the extent to which their social networks overlap—also influences interaction accessibility. Research reveals that increased social proximity is associated with a greater likelihood of initial contact; that is, many people meet their future romantic partners through their current social network of friends and family members (e.g., Madden & Lenhart, 2006; Parks & Eggert, 1991). For example, if Jean is part of Susan's social network (they are close friends) and Jean is also part of Hugh's social network (she is his sister), it is likely that Susan and Hugh will meet at some point due to the overlap in their respective social networks (i.e., Jean). This, in turn, will provide them with the opportunity to interact, develop feelings of attraction, and possibly embark on a romantic relationship.

Members of an individual's social network also may actively facilitate initial encounters with desirable partners (and prevent encounters with those they consider undesirable). Researchers have found that family members, third parties (a common friend or acquaintance), and even professional matchmakers (see Chapter 4) may arrange initial meetings or dates between men and women in hopes that they will "hit it off" and become romantically involved (e.g., Parks, 2007; also see Arriaga, Agnew, Capezza, & Lehmiller, 2008). For example, Catherine Clark, Phillip Shaver, and Matthew Abrahams (1999) examined men's and women's accounts of the initiation of their romantic relationships and discovered that friends and family often were highly instrumental in promoting the relationship—for instance, by discovering whether a potential partner was available and interested in dating, by encouraging the selection of a particular partner, and by introducing the partners to each other.

It is apparent that our opportunities for interacting with a potential mate are influenced not only by the nature of the physical and virtual environments we inhabit, but also by the closeness of our social connection to that person and the extent to which others in our social network approve of and directly facilitate the initial encounter.

## Receptive Others

A potential partner not only must be accessible for interaction but also must be receptive to our initiation attempts. A number of relationship theorists and researchers have discussed the important role played by *receptivity* in determining whether one person will attempt to affiliate with another (e.g., Bredow, Cate, & Huston, 2008; Davis, 1973). For example, Ted Huston and George Levinger (1978) proposed a two-factor model of affiliation:

> The person contemplating initiating an encounter must consider at least two factors: (a) the degree to which he [or she] finds the attributes of the potential partners attractive; and (b) the degree to which

he [or she] anticipates they would find his [or her] attributes attractive and hence respond favorably to the initiative. (pp. 126–127)

Essentially, this model suggests that we are most likely to approach and attempt to interact with a potential mate when we are highly attracted to that person and when we believe that he or she is attracted to us and open to the possibility of a relationship (and, thus, there is a good chance that he or she will be receptive to our overtures).

Research supports this supposition. People are, in fact, most likely to initiate romantic encounters (and potential relationships) with those they believe will respond favorably to them. For example, in one investigation (Huston, 1973), men received an array of photographs of women of varying levels of physical attractiveness (ranging from above average in attractiveness to extremely attractive). Half of the men were told that each of these women would welcome the opportunity to go out with them, whereas the other half received no information at all about the women's willingness to go out with them. Each man was then given the opportunity to select one date from among the sample of women. The results revealed that the men who had been assured of acceptance consistently chose the most physically attractive women in the array. Those who were unsure about whether the women would respond positively to them, however, chose one of the less physically attractive women (presumably because they felt that a less attractive woman would be more likely than a highly attractive one to agree to go out with them). These findings demonstrate that people will generally not attempt to interact with someone they suspect might reject their overtures—it was only when receptivity was guaranteed that men felt free to select a partner based solely on the extent of their attraction to her.

In sum, people tend to approach those who are accessible for interaction and who they believe will be responsive to their initiation attempts.

## ❖ HOW DO WE CONVEY ROMANTIC INTEREST? PRINCIPLES OF FLIRTING

Researchers have identified a repertoire of facial expressions, gestures, and other nonverbal behaviors that serve as signals designed to communicate attraction and romantic interest to a potential partner (see Moore, 2010). For example, in one study, psychologists Naomi McCormick and Andrew Jones (1989) examined the nonverbal flirting behavior of heterosexual couples. Trained confederates, working for the researchers, observed 70 pairs of unmarried men and women interact-ing in bars, taverns, and cocktail lounges. Each couple was watched for a period of 15 minutes, and their nonverbal behaviors were coded. The results revealed that men and women engaged in a number of flirting behaviors designed to communicate romantic interest. One of the most common behaviors displayed by both sexes was that of moving closer to the potential partner and gazing into his or her eyes. Other acts included smiling, laughing, and displaying other positive facial expressions along with such grooming activities as self-touching, smoothing one's hair, tightening one's abdomen, arching one's back, and stretching.

Similar results were reported by anthropologist David Givens (1978), who observed male-female pairs of college students in initial encounters ranging from having coffee together for the first time after class to conversing for the first time at a cafeteria table. Typical nonver-bal behaviors displayed by both men and women included facing the partner, gazing directly at the partner as well as in a downward direc-tion, smiling, and such "auto-manipulation" behaviors as clasping the hands, covering the mouth, and touching the cheek or neck. Givens posited that these nonverbal actions contain a mix of friendliness and submissiveness that conveys "an interest in the partner that is coupled with covert denials of aggressiveness and threat" (p. 355). Such behav-iors serve as a potent signal that romantic overtures will be well received.

Although few cross-cultural investigations of flirting behavior have been conducted, the available evidence suggests that men and women around the world use many of the same nonverbal behaviors to communicate romantic interest. In several early studies, ethologist Irenäus Eibl-Eibesfeldt (e.g., 1975, 1989) surreptitiously filmed the social interactions of people from a variety of nonindustrialized tribal cultures. He discovered that smiling was one of the most common ways in which both sexes conveyed romantic attraction to another per-son. In addition, women tended to engage in a particular sequence of nonverbal behaviors when flirting with men. Specifically, a woman would make brief eye contact with her partner, smile at him, and then display a behavior that Eibl-Eibesfeldt termed the "eyebrow flash" (a quick arching of the eyebrows to widen the eyes followed by an immediate lowering of the brows). Immediately following the eyebrow flash, a woman would typically avert her gaze by tucking her chin down and to the side, put her hands on or near her mouth, and then smile or giggle. Although subsequent researchers generally have not found much evidence for the "eyebrow flash" as a flirting behavior among U.S. populations, smiling and eye contact do appear to be uni-versal methods used by men and women to convey romantic interest.

Research also reveals that interpersonal touch is another powerful communicator of attraction. Men and women in one investigation were asked to provide a detailed description of their most recent flirtation episode (Abrahams, 1994). A second group of participants then rated these accounts in terms of how flirtatious they appeared to be. Accounts rated as highly flirtatious tended to contain references to interpersonal touch, including specific actions such as "I began to rub my fingers up her arm," "I then lightly hit her with a pillow, which led to a pillow fight that ended in us holding each other," "I lightly touched him on the shoulder," and "I moved my head closer to his [and] we put our arms around each other." Other researchers have similarly found that interpersonal touch communicates attraction, interest, liking, and intimacy (Burgoon, Buller, Hale, & deTurck, 1984).

Smiling, touch, and other nonverbal actions are not the only means by which men and women convey romantic interest to potential mates. Social scientists Jerrold Downey and Katharina Damhave (1991) set out to explore people's perceptions of what constitutes flirting. Participants in their study were asked to read a number of hypothetical scenarios involving an interaction between themselves and a stranger. These scenarios differed along three dimensions: location (school hallway or restaurant bar), amount of effort expended by the stranger (makes inadvertent eye contact vs. goes out of his or her way to approach), and type of comment made by the stranger (pays a compliment vs. asks for the time). For each scenario, participants indicated whether they believed the stranger was flirting with them or not. The results revealed significantly higher percentages of "yes" (i.e., flirting) responses when the stranger was in the restaurant bar as opposed to the school hallway (61% vs. 49%), when the stranger made an effort to go out of his or her way as opposed to making inadvertent and non-effortful eye contact (68% vs. 41%), and when the stranger paid a compliment as opposed to asking for the time (83% vs. 26%). Not surprisingly, given this pattern of results, the scenario that produced the highest percentage of "yes" responses (74%) was that involving a stranger who went out of his or her way to compliment the target while in the "flirt-friendly" setting of a restaurant bar.

In sum, researchers have identified a wide array of nonverbal and verbal actions that are used by men and women to convey romantic interest.

### Does Flirting Work?

The real question, of course, is whether or not these flirting behaviors actually "work." Do glances, smiles, touches, effortful approaches, and sincere compliments do what they are designed to do—that is, prompt romantic interest and overtures from potential mates? To answer this question, psychologist Monica Moore (1985) unobtrusively observed 40 women (ranging in estimated age from 18 to 35 years) in four different social settings: a local singles bar, a university snack bar, a university library, and a meeting at a university women's center. Women were selected for observation only if they were surrounded by at least 25 other people and if they were not accompanied by a man. During each hour-long observational period, both the type (e.g., smiling, sustained gazing, hair flipping, head tossing) and the number of flirting behaviors demonstrated by each woman were recorded.

There were a number of interesting results. First, Moore (1985) found that women's flirting behavior was context specific. That is, women in the singles bar (the most likely setting in which to meet a mate) flirted significantly more frequently than did women in the other three settings. In addition, women in the snack bar flirted more than did women in the library, who in turn flirted more than did women in the women's center (the least likely setting to meet a mate, assuming a heterosexual sample). Second, Moore found that women in the singles bar *increased* their rate of flirtatious display over the observational period; they flirted more as the hour passed. However, flirting behavior was constant (i.e., did not change over time) in the other three contexts. Third, and perhaps most important, the results revealed that women's flirting behaviors actually were quite effective at eliciting interest from potential mates. Specifically, regardless of the setting, the women who engaged in the most flirting behavior were also those who were approached most often by men.

Similar results were reported by Lee Ann Renninger, Joel Wade, and Karl Grammer (2004), who were interested in exploring the effectiveness of men's flirting behavior (also see Back et al., 2011). In this investigation, the researchers unobtrusively observed 38 men (ranging in age from 21 to 34 years) in bars located near college campuses. Men were selected for observation only if they were surrounded by at least 10 other people and were not seated in a booth or accompanied by a woman. During each 30-minute observation, the researchers recorded the men's nonverbal behavior and also determined whether or not the men successfully initiated romantic contact with a woman (defined as achieving at least one minute of continuous conversation). The results indicated that the men who successfully initiated romantic contact with women exhibited a greater number of particular kinds of nonverbal flirting behavior than men who did not establish romantic contact. Specifically, "contact successful" men directed more brief glances at their intended targets, engaged in a greater number of "space maximization" movements (positioning the body so that it takes up more space, e.g., extending one arm across an adjacent chair, stretching so that both arms extend straight up in the air), changed their location in the bar more frequently, and displayed greater amounts of nonreciprocated touching to surrounding men (e.g., playfully shoving, touching, or elbowing the ribs of other men). In discussing their findings, the researchers concluded that men who provide signals of their positive intentions (through glancing behaviors) and their status (through space maximization and nonreciprocated intrasexual touch) receive preferential attention from women. Thus, for both sexes, flirting does appear to work!

## ❖ E-COURTSHIP: ATTRACTION, AFFILIATION, AND FLIRTING IN CYBERSPACE

Online or *computer-mediated communication* (CMC) has become an increasingly common way of interacting with other people (including potential and current romantic partners), particularly in the United States and other North American countries (see InternetWorldStats. com, 2012). A variety of CMC options now exist, ranging from asynchronous, static interactions that do not involve mutual exchanges between individuals in real time (e.g., sending or replying to e-mail, posting or responding to blog, discussion group, forum, or social networking site posts) to synchronous, dynamic exchanges in which participants are online and communicating at the same time (e.g., via Skype and other voice-over-Internet [VoIP] or instant messaging [IM] forums, in chat rooms, during interactive role-playing games).

Irrespective of whether or not they occur in real time, all forms of online communication differ from offline or face-to-face interaction in several ways (e.g., Cooper & Sportolari, 1997; Haythornthwaite, Wellman, & Garton, 1998; Kiesler, Siegel, & McGuire, 1984). In particular, most types of CMC lack many of the verbal and nonverbal cues that allow people to regulate their interactions and effectively communicate their intentions and feelings, such as smiling, head nodding, eye contact, physical distance, touch, and tone and volume of voice. In addition, with the exception of video chat forums or online dating sites, CMC often provides limited information (if any) about the participants' demographic characteristics (e.g., age, race or ethnicity, gender), personal features (e.g., physical attractiveness, height, weight, dress), or social attributes (e.g., socioeconomic status).

Because CMC users typically have a reduced array of social cues on which to rely, they often must use other methods for communicating their feelings of attraction to a potential date or mate (see Levine, 2000; Whitty & Carr, 2003). For example, a man or woman who is interested in pursuing a romantic relationship with someone he or she met in a chat room might respond promptly to that person's messages and include emoticons (;-o), emojis (☺), lexical surrogates ("hmm" or "ha ha"), and acronyms (e.g., LOL—laughing out loud) in his or her own messages to establish intimacy and convey feelings of warmth, connection, and interest. If the other person responds in kind, he or she may elect to send a picture, sound file, or other personal information, or the two may decide to video chat. Eventually, of course, they may decide to meet offline. Although relatively little research has been conducted on how people actually communicate romantic attraction in online forums, a survey of 5,000 chat room users by psychologist Monica Whitty (2004) revealed that the two most common cyberflirting behaviors were nonverbal in nature: Both men and women reported primarily using emoticons and acronyms to demonstrate laughing, smiling, winking, and other physical gestures and displays. These results are in accord with the face-to-face flirting literature we reviewed earlier in the chapter. Thus, it seems that people convey their feelings of romantic attraction nonverbally regardless of whether they are together in virtual or physical space.

Of particular interest to researchers is the question of whether CMC—in particular, the type provided by online social networking and dating sites—has helped or hindered people's chances for romantic success. As of now, the answer is unclear. On the one hand, online forums afford greater *access* to potential dates or mates and provide a setting that minimizes the social risks inherent in face-to-face interactions. This is especially beneficial for people who have few opportunities to meet potential partners, who possess various stigmatizing characteristics that make it difficult for them to initially attract others (e.g., stuttering or vocal difficulties, lower levels of physical attractiveness), or who find the process of interpersonal communication challenging due to shyness or social anxiety (e.g., Lawson & Leck, 2006; Ward & Tracey, 2004). As noted in recent reviews of the literature (see Finkel, Eastwick, Karney, Reis, & Sprecher, 2012; McKenna, 2008; Sprecher, 2009), online interactions also allow a person a greater degree of *anonymity and control* than do face-to-face conversations. In an online setting, for instance, people can choose what personal information they reveal, and they do not have to respond immediately to another individual in the way they would have to during a face-to-face interaction. Additionally, by following another person's posts on social networking sites such as Facebook or Instagram, or by reading someone's profile on a dating website prior to initiating contact, individuals can gain much more *information* about him or her than would normally be possible in traditional face-to-face settings. The anonymity, control, and increased knowledge that are afforded by online forums are likely to result in greater freedom of expression and intimacy between the potential partners during their initial online interactions; this, in turn, may increase the likelihood that they will become romantically involved and that their relationship will eventually move offline.

On the other hand, there are some dangers inherent in seeking a mate online. Many men and women worry about deception and personal safety when considering an online romance; in particular, they fear that the people they meet on the Internet will lie and misrepresent themselves and they believe that they will have to be even more careful about their safety when meeting someone online than when meeting someone in person (Donn & Sherman, 2002). There is solid evidence that these fears are justified: People do lie about their personal attributes as well as their intentions, and some even sexually harass or "cyberstalk" other Internet users (Huang & Yang, 2013; Toma, Hancock, & Ellison, 2008; Valkenburg & Peter, 2011; Whitty & Carr, 2003, 2006). Consider the example below:

> *The day I put my profile on Plenty of Fish, I had over two dozen responses. There were about four or five guys in my age group who seemed really interesting, had travelled, shared my interests, and were quite good looking. So I started going on coffee dates and . . . every one of them had lied on his profile. The guy I met on my first date was married, even though he'd said he was single. He had a tan line on his ring finger, and when I pointed this out, he tried to laugh it off and said he hoped I was "open" to dating a married man. I wasn't, so that ended quickly. On my last date, I met up with a police chief who said he was 50 and who posted a picture of himself rock climbing. Well, when he showed up, he looked nothing like his photo. Turns out he was 68! The photo he posted was more than 20 years old! Did he think I wouldn't notice? I'm okay with someone not being perfect. I'm not okay with gross misrepresentation and dishonesty. When I asked him why he'd lied, he said, "Oh, but I'm a YOUNG 68." And he seemed surprised that I looked exactly like my photo. Whatever. I'm done with dating sites.*
>
> —48-year-old woman interviewed by the author

In addition, although online dating sites are specifically designed to help people find a suitable mate, their very nature actually may hinder people's chances of achieving that goal. For example, Internet dating sites allow their users access to a greater array of eligible partners than they would normally meet in their day-to-day lives; these sites quickly and efficiently expand an individual's pool of possible mates (a seeming benefit). However, no dating site can guarantee that any of those potential partners will, in fact, be receptive to the individual's overtures or agree to be available for interaction. In fact, having a wider selection of possible mates to consider may ultimately prove damaging should none or only a very few respond positively (e.g., a person who "winks" at 20 possible matches on Match.com, and receives no "winks" in return, is likely to experience some degree of psychological distress). Online dating sites make it easy for users to identify, select, and indicate interest to potential mates; by the same token, these sites make it equally easy for those they approach to reject them.

Moreover, the browsing process itself at most online dating sites encourages people to make selections and evaluate other users' profiles quickly, superficially, and judgmentally (by comparing them against one another) rather than individually, deliberately, and holistically. This, in turn, may actually lower the likelihood of a successful, mutually positive experience when interaction eventually occurs. As noted by Finkel and colleagues (2012) in their detailed review of the online dating literature:

> The ways online dating sites typically implement the services of access, communication, and matching do not always improve romantic outcomes; indeed, they sometimes undermine such outcomes. Regarding access, encountering potential partners via online dating profiles reduces three-dimensional people to two-dimensional displays of information, and these displays fail to capture those experiential aspects of social interaction that are essential to evaluating one's compatibility with potential partners. In addition, the ready access to a large pool of potential partners can elicit an evaluative, assessment-oriented mindset that leads online daters to objectify potential partners and might even undermine their willingness to commit to one of them. It can also cause people to make lazy, ill-advised decisions when selecting among the large array of potential partners. (p. 3)

There is much still to be learned about online romance, and this area promises to be an important topic of future research.

## ❖ THE FIRST DATE

After an initial face-to-face or online encounter or series of encounters, and assuming the successful communication of romantic interest, two people may further their relationship by embarking on an "official" romantic interaction—the *first date*. Given the existence of the traditional (heterosexual) sexual script (see Chapter 12), it is not surprising that both men and women feel that it is more socially appropriate for a man to initiate a date than for a woman to do so (Green & Sandos, 1983). Compared with women, men also report a greater willingness to initiate dates and a higher frequency of actual relationship initiations (Clark, Shaver, & Abrahams, 1999; Eaton & Rose, 2012; Green & Sandos, 1983; McNamara & Grossman, 1991; Spreadbury, 1982).

These results notwithstanding, there is some evidence that many heterosexual men would like women to take a more active role in relationship initiation than the traditional script would seem to allow. In one survey (Muehlenhard & Miller, 1988), for example, more than 200 undergraduate men indicated their preferences with regard to three different approaches a woman might make to initiate a date: *asking directly* for a date, *hinting* for a date, and simply *waiting* for the man to ask her out. The majority preferred the more direct approaches. Specifically, 44% said that they preferred a woman to ask for a date, and 53% indicated that they preferred a woman to hint for a date. Only 3% of the men surveyed stated that they preferred a woman to adopt the passive and indirect approach of simply waiting to be asked out. In addition, provided that they liked the woman, nearly all of the men believed that the strategies of directly asking (99%) and hinting (93%) would result in a date. Few men (4%) believed that waiting would result in a date, even if they liked the woman and wanted to go out with her. The initiation of a dating relationship clearly requires active efforts on the part of both individuals.

So what prevents men—and women, for that matter—from pursuing dates with individuals to whom they are attracted? One of the primary reasons why people fail to initiate dating relationships concerns their fear of being rebuffed by the objects of their affection. Jacquie Vorauer and Rebecca Ratner (1996) asked a sample of 291 men and women whether a fear of rejection had ever been a "significant obstacle" to their pursuit of a romantic relationship with another individual. The majority (76%) responded affirmatively, suggesting that the experience of fearful inhibition is quite common. The researchers then asked a second set of participants to imagine themselves in the following situation:

> You are at a party; currently, you are not seriously romantically involved with anyone. Early in the evening, you are introduced to a single person who could be a potential romantic partner. You learn

from a brief conversation that you have a lot in common. In your opinion, the two of you are equally physically attractive. Toward the end of the evening, you find yourself alone in the kitchen with the person. You talk with each other for a while. Neither of you explicitly expresses a romantic interest in the other or an interest in seeing the other again. You head back to join the group in the living room. (pp. 491–492)

After reading the scenario, men and women indicated which of two possible alternatives explained their own and the other person's inaction: lack of romantic interest or fear of being rejected. Interestingly, the results provided strong evidence for *pluralistic ignorance,* a phenomenon in which people observe others behaving similarly to themselves but attribute their own behavior and that of the others to very different underlying causes. In this case, participants attributed their own failure to make a romantic overture to fear of rejection (74%); however, they assumed that the other person's inactivity was caused by a lack of interest (71%). This attributional bias may create a dynamic that impedes a potentially rewarding romantic relationship from even starting. The researchers summarized the process as follows:

> Individuals who are romantically interested in one another hesitate to make their feelings explicit because they fear that they will be rejected. However, even though both people are engaging in the same "waiting" behavior, they apply different explanations to their own and the other person's conduct. They see their own failure to take initiatives as stemming from a fear of rejection, but attribute the other person's inaction to a lack of interest. These unwarranted negative inferences about the other person's feelings subsequently exacerbate individuals' hesitation to take the risk of conveying their affection, leading them to give up on the relationship prematurely. (p. 484)

Thus, it is no wonder that women want men to make the first move when it comes to initiating a first date and that men wish that women would make the first move more often!

A more recent series of investigations by Vorauer and her colleagues (Vorauer, Cameron, Holmes, & Pearce, 2003) demonstrated that the fear of being rejected by a potential partner can produce yet another pernicious attributional bias. The *signal amplification bias* occurs when people believe that their social overtures communicate more romantic interest to potential partners than is actually the case and thus fail to realize that they have not adequately conveyed their feelings of attraction. The following scenario illustrates both of the attributional biases that can prevent a romantic relationship from even starting:

> Paul and Jen are two students who know each other casually and who run into each other one day on campus. Paul likes Jen and would like to ask her out and so he decides to strike up a conversation. "Hi, Jen," he says, "How's it going?" "Fine," Jen responds, and the two chat about their classes and various other topics for the next 20 minutes. Finally, Jen looks at her watch and realizes that she's going to be late to her next class. "Listen," she says, "I've got to get going but I'll catch you later, okay?" As she races off to her class, she thinks to herself, "He is such a nice guy. I wish he were interested in going out with me, but it's clear that he isn't. I mean, if he were, he'd certainly have asked me out by now. And there's no way I'm asking him out—he'd probably say no and then I'd die of embarrassment. I've got to move on and meet some other guys." Watching Jen leave, Paul thinks to himself, "Could I have been any more obvious? I was practically falling all over her. She probably thinks I'm acting like some love-sick fool. I have got to get a grip and play it cool the next time we see each other."

In this fictitious scenario, Jen has fallen prey to pluralistic ignorance. She has attributed her own failure to initiate a romance with Paul to her fear of rejection, and she has failed to realize that he might also be afraid of being rejected. Instead, she assumes that Paul's failure to ask her out stems from his lack of romantic interest in her. For his part, Paul has fallen prey to the signal amplification bias. He has grossly overestimated the amount of romantic interest that his actions have conveyed to Jen (in fact, his "romantic" behavior has largely gone unnoticed by her). Unfortunately, the attributional biases exhibited by these two individuals may prevent them from initiating what could eventually develop into a satisfying and stable romantic relationship.

## What Happens During a First Date?

Of course, many people overcome their hesitation or fears of rejection and successfully initiate a first date. What occurs during a "typical" first date? In an effort to answer this question and identify people's *first date scripts*, psychologists John Pryor and Thomas Merluzzi (1985) asked a sample of undergraduate students to list the typical events that occur during a (heterosexual) first date. Both men and women generated the following event sequence:

Step 1: The man arrives to pick up the woman for the date.

Step 2: The woman greets the man at the door.

Step 3: They make conversation.

Step 4: The woman introduces her date to parents/roommates and the two leave the house/apartment/dormitory.

Step 5: They discuss where they will go on their date.

Step 6: The two talk about common interests (i.e., make "small talk").

Step 7: They go to a movie.

Step 8: The man buys refreshments at the movie.

Step 9: They then go get something to eat/drink and continue their conversation.

Step 10: The man takes the woman home.

Step 11: The man walks the woman to her door.

Step 12: They exchange complimentary views of the evening.

Step 13: If interested, the man asks to call again/the woman hopes the man asks to call again.

Step 14: They kiss.

Step 15: They say "good night" and thank each other for the evening.

Step 16: The man returns home.

More recent research indicates that the first date script has remained largely unchanged over time, at least among cohorts of people living in the United States (see Eaton & Rose, 2012; Laner & Ventrone, 2000; Morr Serewicz & Gale, 2008).

Both men and women generally agree about the *sequence* of events that occur during the first date. However, they may hold slightly different expectations about the *type* of events that should occur. For example, although the "good night kiss" remains a fixed feature of this particular social interaction, men often expect greater sexual involvement than do women on a first date (Mongeau, Jacobsen, & Donnerstein, 2007; Mongeau & Johnson, 1995; Mongeau, Morr Serewicz, & Therrien, 2004). Indeed, there is evidence that men and women may pursue different goals when initiating a romantic relationship. In one study (Clark et al., 1999), researchers asked a large sample of undergraduates to describe what goals they had pursued in the initiation of their two most recent successful romantic relationships. The primary goal identified by the researchers concerned love; most men (84%) and women (81%) said that they sought to obtain a loving, caring, serious relationship. Other relatively common goals mentioned by equal numbers of both sexes included fun (cited by 18% of the men and 16% of the women) and learning (e.g., to experience dating, learn more about the other person [cited by 16% of the men and 18% of the women]). Only one sex difference was found. Far more men (30%) than women (8%) identified sexual intimacy—including kissing, intercourse, and just "following hormones"—as the reason why they sought to initiate a dating relationship.

The different expectations that men and women may bring to their initial romantic interactions may result in misunderstanding and miscommunication. For example, a woman who wishes to communicate her feelings of affection for a new dating partner may smile at him and engage in other nonverbal displays. The woman's partner, whose goal may be sexual intimacy, may misinterpret her behavior as indicating sexual attraction. Indeed, women are more likely than men to report having had their friendliness toward someone of the opposite sex mistakenly perceived as a sign of sexual interest (Abbey, 1987). Men also are much more likely than women to perceive a number of common verbal and nonverbal behaviors as signaling an interest in sex (e.g., Abbey, 1982; Abbey & Melby, 1986; Zellman & Goodchilds, 1983)—including maintaining eye contact with, smiling at, or complimenting a man, having dinner with a man or allowing him to pay for dinner, or even simply accepting a man's invitation for a date (Kowalski, 1993). But men are not the only ones who fall prey to perceptual biases with respect to sexual attraction. Women have their own tendency to misperceive interpersonal behavior; specifically, they tend to *underestimate* the extent of their partner's sexual attraction to them (see Koenig, Kirkpatrick, & Ketelaar, 2007). Clearly, knowledge of the different ways in which men and women perceive interpersonal cues, along with direct and open communication of dating goals and desires, is essential between partners during the early stages of a romantic relationship.

## ❖ BEYOND THE FIRST DATE: INITIATING A ROMANTIC RELATIONSHIP

Only a very small portion of the first dates and other initial encounters that we have with potential partners actually will evolve into stable romantic relationships. What strategies do men and women use when trying to move relationships beyond those beginning stages? To explore this question, communication scholar James Tolhuizen (1989) asked men and women who had been or who were involved in a serious dating relationship to describe the things they said or did to intensify their relationship and change it from "one of casual dating to one of serious and exclusive dating" (p. 418). Analysis of participants' free responses revealed that the most common strategy was to *increase contact*; more than 39% of the participants reported increasing the frequency and duration of their contact and interaction with the partner. Another commonly utilized method was *relationship negotiation* or direct discussion of the relationship, feelings between the partners, and the future of the relationship (29%). Participants also sought *social support and assistance* from individuals in their social networks, usually by asking for advice about how to proceed in intensifying the relationship (26%). Other strategies included *increasing the partner's rewards* (18%; e.g., paying compliments, doing favors), *making a direct bid* for a more serious relationship (17%; e.g., directly requesting a more exclusive or serious relationship), giving the partner *tokens of affection* (16%; e.g., giving gifts, cards, or other items that symbolize feelings of affection for the partner), providing *verbal expressions of affection* (14%; e.g., declaring feelings of love, caring, or affection for the partner), and *accepting a direct bid* for a more serious relationship (10%; e.g., agreeing to a direct request from the partner for a more exclusive relationship). Not surprisingly, men and women differed slightly in the types of strategies they reported. Men were significantly more likely to report using verbal expressions of affection and making a direct relationship bid, whereas women were more likely to report using relationship negotiation and accepting a direct relationship bid.

Similar results were reported by Clark and colleagues (1999), who asked a large group of undergraduates to describe the strategies they used when initiating a romantic relationship. Participants reported engaging in a variety of behaviors to propel a relationship through its beginning stages. One of the most common categories of strategy involved *emotional disclosure* (which required increased contact, as in Tolhuizen's [1989] study). For example, the majority of participants said that they talked in person (94%), talked on the phone (54%), and spent time (85%) with the partner. *Direct and forward action* was also mentioned frequently. Specifically, participants reported asking the other person directly to be their girlfriend or boyfriend (63%) and touching the other person (64%; e.g., kissing, hand holding). As in Tolhuizen's (1989) study, participants also clearly used their social networks to promote the relationship. Approximately 86% reported that third parties helped to initiate and intensify the relationship by engaging in such activities as discovering whether a potential partner was available and/or interested, by introducing the two people, and by going out with them as the relationship began to develop.

In sum, men and women enact a number of behaviors as they attempt to shape their initial encounters with a potential date or mate into a more enduring relationship.

## ❖ PATHWAYS TO COMMITMENT

As we noted earlier, many relationships do not stand the test of time despite the best efforts of the couples to promote or intensify their development. Some relationships, however, will survive beyond the initial exchanges and continue along a path toward commitment. Early evidence for how dating relationships progress over time was provided by Charles King and Andrew Christensen (1983), who surveyed a sample of undergraduate student couples about the occurrence of specific events in their relationships. The researchers found that developing romantic relationships are likely to progress through six consecutive stages. First, the partners express mutual attraction and affection and begin to spend an increasing amount of time together. Second, the partners themselves and the people in their social networks begin to view the two of them as "a couple." Third, the partners express feelings of love to one another and establish an exclusive relationship (e.g., they end or avoid other romantic involvements and make the decision to only date the current partner). Fourth, they begin to project their relationship into the future by considering moving in together and/or becoming engaged or getting married. Fifth, they begin to coordinate their time, money, and activities to pursue joint (as opposed to individual) interests. Finally, they make a more permanent commitment to one another through engagement, cohabitation, or marriage.

Although most couples may follow the developmental sequence outlined by King and Christensen (1983), the amount of time they take to pass through the sequence may vary. A number of different courtship patterns or trajectories to commitment have been identified. For example, in one investigation, social scientist Catherine Surra (1985) asked a sample of young newlywed couples to retrospectively report on how the partners' commitment to each other had changed from the time they first met to the day of their wedding. Specifically, husbands and wives were instructed to estimate the chance of marriage (on a scale ranging from 0% to 100%) that they felt characterized their relationship from the date it began, during the subsequent months of courtship, and up until the wedding day (which naturally received a "chance-of-marriage" rating of 100%). These estimated chance-of-marriage values were placed on a graph that provided a pictorial view of each couple's pathway to commitment.

Surra (1985) then coded monthly chance-of-marriage values for each participant and derived a number of additional variables from the graphs, including length of courtship (number of months from the beginning of the relationship to the wedding day), degree of acceleration (number of months it took for the couple to move from a low [25%] to a high [75%] chance of marriage), number of turning points (upturns and downturns in the graph), and length of stage of involvement (number of months the couple spent in the casually dating, seriously dating, and engaged stages of involvement).

Analysis of the monthly chance-of-marriage values and the derived variables revealed four different courtship paths or trajectories to marital commitment. Couples on an *accelerated* courtship trajectory moved rapidly and smoothly to marriage, spent relatively little time dating prior to engagement, and experienced a higher index of upturns (turning points characterized by increased commitment) than did other couple types. *Accelerated-arrested* couples also experienced a high number of upturns, which Surra (1985) hypothesized may provide momentum to the courtship process. The courtship of these couples was characterized by an even more rapid trajectory to marriage. Specifically, accelerated-arrested couples devoted very little time to dating, preferring to become engaged very quickly and then spending most (nearly 60%) of their courtship in this stage. Couples on a *prolonged* trajectory to marital commitment demonstrated the reverse pattern; that is, they spent 65% of their courtship seriously dating and only 22% of it engaged. The *intermediate* courtship type fell somewhere in between the two accelerated types and the prolonged type in the smoothness and the rapidity of its progression toward commitment.

More recent research has revealed additional courtship paths as well as cultural differences in the length of courtship (e.g., Chang & Chan, 2007; Dailey, Brody, LeFebvre, & Crook, 2013). In sum, there is no one path toward permanence; couples move toward and achieve commitment in a variety of ways.

## Summary

Researchers have identified a number of factors that promote romantic attraction and affiliation between potential partners and thus increase the likelihood that they will interact with each other (and thus possibly establish a romantic relationship). During their initial encounters, men and women engage in a number of behaviors designed to convey romantic interest to their potential mate, including eye contact, smiling, interpersonal touch, and other flirtatious behaviors. Increasingly, people are turning to online forums and using computer-mediated communication to identify potential mates, to flirt, and to initiate romantic relationships. Research reveals a host of beneficial and not-so-beneficial consequences of entering cyberspace to fulfill one's romantic goals. Regardless of how they first meet or interact, many individuals eventually choose to further the relationship by embarking on a "real" (offline or face-to-face) first date. Research indicates that a first date often involves a series of scripted behaviors and action sequences, in some instances including the communication of sexual attraction and the willingness to engage in some form of sexual contact (e.g., good night kiss). After a first date or series of initial encounters, one or both partners may attempt to intensify the relationship or propel it to a state of greater permanence through engaging in various affectional and communicative behaviors. Assuming that the relationship does, in fact, endure beyond these beginning stages, a couple may progress along one of several different pathways to commitment. In Chapter 3, we consider theory and research about the actual processes that serve to move couples along their courtship trajectory.

## Key Concepts

Attraction (p. 26)

Physical attractiveness (as a factor in romantic attraction) (p. 26)

Familiarity (as a factor in romantic attraction) (p. 27)

Mere exposure effect (p. 27)

Similarity (as a factor in romantic attraction) (p. 28)

Responsiveness (as a factor in romantic attraction ) (p. 29)

Affiliation (p. 31)

Field of availables (p. 31)

Interaction accessibility (as a factor in romantic affiliation) (p. 31)

Physical proximity (p. 31)

Virtual proximity (p. 32)

E-courtship (p. 32)

Social proximity (p. 32)

Receptivity (as a factor in romantic affiliation) (p. 33)

Flirting behavior (p. 34)

Eyebrow flash (p. 35)

Computer-mediated communication (p. 38)

First date (p. 42)

Pluralistic ignorance (p. 43)

Signal amplification bias (p. 43)

First date script (p. 44)

Accelerated courtship pattern (p. 49)

Accelerated-arrested courtship pattern (p. 49)

Prolonged courtship pattern (p. 49)

Intermediate courtship pattern (p. 49)

## Discussion Questions

1. How did you meet your current romantic partner? (If you are not currently dating someone, think of your last partner or someone else in whom you are currently interested.) What role did accessibility play in your choice of partner? In other words, consider the ways in which the physical, social, and virtual environments made this person accessible to you as a mate or potential mate.

2. Describe the nonverbal behaviors that people use to signal their romantic interest. Does flirting "work"? Has it worked for you? What behaviors seem to be the most effective? Which ones are the least effective?

3. How does computer-mediated communication differ from face-to-face communication? What strategies can people use to convey their attraction to someone in an online forum?

4. Consider the benefits and risks associated with pursuing a romantic relationship online. Has someone you've met online ever misrepresented himself or herself to you? How did you respond to that situation?

   (If you have time, watch the documentary film *Catfish* (2010, directed by Henry Joost and Ariel Schulman), which details the romance that develops between a young man (Schulman's brother) and a woman (actually the fictitious creation of another person) he meets over Facebook. This film serves as a poignant illustration of what happens when virtual and physical realities collide.)

5. In what ways might attributional biases (specifically, pluralistic ignorance and the signal amplification bias) contribute to missed dating opportunities?

6. Create your own "first date" script. How does the typical first date script identified by researchers differ from—or resemble—your own?

## Recommended Readings

This book presents research on cyberflirting, online dating, Internet infidelity, cyberharassment, and other topics related to romantic and sexual relationships that develop online.

Whitty, M. T., & Carr, A. N. (2006). *Cyberspace romance: The psychology of online relationships*. New York, NY: Palgrave Macmillan.

These four articles examine men's and women's expectations about the events that occur during a first date.

Eaton, A. A., & Rose, S. M. (2012). Scripts for actual first date and hanging-out encounters among young heterosexual Hispanic adults. *Sex Roles, 67,* 285–299.

Morr Serewicz, M. C., & Gale, E. (2008). First-date scripts: Gender roles, context, and relationship. *Sex Roles, 58,* 149–164.

Pryor, J. B., & Merluzzi, T. V. (1985). The role of expertise in processing social interaction scripts. *Journal of Experimental Social Psychology, 21,* 362–379.

Rose, S., & Frieze, I. H. (1993). Young singles' contemporary dating scripts. *Sex Roles, 28,* 499–509.

This book explores the topic of courtship, including the events that take place during courtship, the relation between courtship and later relational outcomes (e.g., marriage), and problematic aspects of courtship (e.g., violence).

Cate, R. M., & Lloyd, S. A. (1992). *Courtship.* Newbury Park, CA: Sage.

# 3

# Relationship Development

In Chapter 2, we discussed how initial encounters with potential partners can lead to the establishment of a more permanent relationship.
We also considered the behavioral strategies that men and women use
to communicate romantic interest to a partner and to intensify the relationship and propel it along its developmental trajectory. In this chapter, we review a variety of theories that have been proposed to explain
exactly how romantic relationships progress and develop over time.

## ❖ THE SEQUENCE OF RELATIONSHIP DEVELOPMENT

Early theories of relationship development proposed that couples
move through a sequential series of stages that are characterized by
increasing amounts of commitment and involvement. Each stage was
assumed to revolve around a particular developmental issue whose
resolution propelled the couple into the next stage. Although largely
supplanted by process-oriented theories, these *stage models* represent
an important historical first step toward understanding relationship
progression.

### Filter Theory

Based upon a longitudinal study of the experiences of dating couples,
Alan Kerckhoff and Keith Davis (1962) proposed that various "filtering
factors" operate during the process of mate selection. According to
*Filter Theory*, specific filters come into prominence at different phases of
courtship. First, potential partners are screened or evaluated in terms
of their similarity on *social attributes,* including religion, education, and
social class. People who are deemed to be too different with respect to
these social attributes are filtered out from the field of potential mates.
At that point, possible partners are screened with respect to similarity
of attitudes and values, or *value consensus.* As before, those who are
judged to be too dissimilar are filtered out. Finally, partners are evaluated on *need complementarity* or whether they possess complementary
or compatible traits, behavioral characteristics, or interpersonal styles.

The notion that different aspects of the "fit" between two partners
would become important at different times in their courtship makes
implicit sense. During early courtship stages, demographic similarity
might be of utmost importance in promoting a couple's relational
growth. Later, as the couple begins to enter more committed or
involved stages of courtship, similarity of underlying values and belief

systems, and compatibility with regard to interpersonal styles, might become more important in determining whether or not the relationship continues. However, although Filter Theory is conceptually interesting, subsequent research generally has not supported this model of relationship development (e.g., Levinger, Senn, & Jorgensen, 1970; for a review, see Levinger, 1983).

## Wheel Theory

Sociologist Ira Reiss (e.g., 1960, 1980) also proposed one of the first developmental models of mate selection. According to his *Wheel Theory of Love*, the "mate-selecting process" involves four sequential but highly interrelated phases. During the initial stage, called *rapport*, potential partners assess the extent to which they feel at ease with, understand, and feel free to talk with each other. The process of establishing and feeling rapport is facilitated by similarity; Reiss suggests that we are most able to feel rapport for those who resemble us on key social and cultural variables (e.g., religious upbringing, educational background). Feelings of rapport, in turn, increase the likelihood that individuals will begin a process of mutual *self-revelation*, in which they reveal or disclose varying degrees of information about their values and belief systems to each other. These acts of self-revelation, in turn, contribute to *mutual dependency*, such that each partner becomes dependent on the other to behave in ways that help him or to enact specific habits or obtain certain goals. For example, Reiss (1980) wrote, "One needs the other person as an audience for one's jokes, as a confidant(e) for the expression of one's fears and wishes, as a partner for one's sexual needs, and so forth" (p. 127). When these goals or habits are not fulfilled, the person will experience frustration and loneliness; consequently, these habits tend to perpetuate a relationship. The fourth and final process in the development of love relationships is called *intimacy need fulfillment*. Here, the partners evaluate whether their relationship and their interactions with each other satisfy basic intimacy needs, including love, sympathy, and support. These needs, as they are fulfilled, "express the closeness and privacy of the relationship" (p. 128).

## Stimulus-Value-Role Theory

Another popular early theory of romantic relationship development was proposed by Bernard Murstein (e.g., 1970, 1976). *Stimulus-Value-Role Theory* suggests that couples progress through three stages in mate selection. In the *stimulus* stage, the potential mates perceive each other's external attributes, physical appearance, and behavior, and each also evaluates his or her own attributes in terms of how attractive they might be to the partner. Based upon this comparison, the individuals estimate the likelihood that their attraction will be reciprocated and that future interaction with the other will be rewarding. If this estimate is favorable (i.e., if each believes that the other will like him or her and find his or her attributes desirable, and if each thinks that additional interaction will be rewarding), then the individuals are propelled into the next stage. During the *value* stage, the partners appraise their compatibility on various values and attitudes. This process of value appraisal allows them to continue to assess the potential benefits or rewards of the relationship. During the final *role* stage, the partners evaluate themselves and each other for suitability in various roles (e.g., spouse, parent). These stages are seen as relatively distinct; for example, Murstein (1987) asserted that stimulus information is gathered during the first encounter, that value information is collected during the second to seventh encounters, and that role assessments are made during and after the eighth encounter. However, he also noted that individuals make stimulus, value, and role assessments of each other throughout the entire courtship process; each factor simply becomes more prominent during a particular stage.

Although historically interesting, stage models of relationship development have fallen out of scientific favor for a number of reasons. First, stage theorists do not agree on the number, the sequence, or even the characteristics of the various stages of courtship. Second, not all relationships progress through the same stages. Third, couples differ in the rate at which they pass through particular courtship stages; as we discussed in Chapter 2, some partners move quickly and rapidly toward engagement and marriage, whereas others spend years leisurely moving along the road to commitment. And finally, a number of process models have been developed that seem to more accurately capture the how and why of relationship progression.

## ❖ THE PROCESS OF RELATIONSHIP DEVELOPMENT

The majority of theorists now agree that romantic relationships develop gradually over time rather than by passing through a series of discrete stages. *Process models* suggest that relationship development is fueled by sometimes imperceptible changes in intimacy, self-disclosure, and other interpersonal processes that occur between partners.

## Self-Disclosure and Intimacy

Irwin Altman and Dalmas Taylor (1973) proposed one of the first process models of relationship progression. *Social Penetration Theory* targets *self-disclosure*—the reciprocal exchange of self-relevant information—as the fuel that propels couples along their developmental trajectory. Specifically, romantic partners are believed to become progressively more committed to each other as they increase both the *depth* (degree of intimacy) and *breadth* (number of areas) of their self-disclosure. At first, relationships are characterized by superficial, shallow exchanges in which the partners reveal relatively impersonal information (low depth) along a very few dimensions (low breadth). Meeting for the first time at a college party, for example, Kate and Leo might exchange information about their majors, their musical preferences, and the food being served by the host of the party. If these initial disclosures are rewarding and if each believes that future interactions will also be rewarding, then presumably they will progress to more intimate exchanges in which they reveal increasingly intimate, emotional, and detailed personal information about themselves along a greater number of dimensions. Following their enjoyable conversation at the party, Kate and Leo might begin to meet a few times a week for coffee. During these interactions, Leo might disclose his ambivalent feelings about his parents and their expectations about his future career. Kate, in turn, might reveal the problems she is experiencing with her roommate and her secret desire to spend a year scuba diving in the Yucatan.

Other theorists have subsequently expanded this theory by proposing that it is not only the depth and breadth of self-disclosure that propels a couple's relationship along its courtship path but also how *responsive* each partner is to the other's disclosures. Recall from Chapter 2 that responsiveness may be communicated verbally and nonverbally (also see Prager, 2000; Prager & Roberts, 2004). According to *Intimacy Theory* (Reis, Clark, & Holmes, 2004; Reis & Patrick, 1996; Reis & Shaver, 1988), attentive, supportive responses that leave the partner feeling validated, understood, cared for, accepted, and nurtured promote the growth of intimacy and the subsequent development of the relationship. In the above example, Kate's acknowledgment of Leo's statements about his parents, her expressions of sympathy, her verbal and nonverbal responsiveness and willingness to continue the conversation, and her reciprocal disclosures all serve to communicate that she understands the situation and that she respects Leo's point of view. This, in turn, will increase Leo's sense of trust and security and will promote intimacy and the development of the relationship. To the extent that Kate fails to reciprocate ("Let's talk about something else"), challenges ("I've never had those feelings about my own parents"), or dismisses ("Hey, I didn't come here to listen to you whine about your personal problems") Leo's revelations, intimacy will decrease and the relationship may stall or be compromised. Thus, it is not simply the act of disclosing information or making personal revelations that contributes to relationship development. Rather, *reciprocal and responsive* disclosures that contribute to *feelings of intimacy*—in other words, disclosures that reflect mutual perceptions of understanding, caring, and validation—are what encourage and sustain the growth of romantic relationships.

## *Empirical Evidence*

Many of these theoretical statements have received empirical support. For example, self-disclosure and intimacy appear to be integrally connected with both relationship satisfaction and stability. Research conducted with dating and married couples generally reveals that people who self-disclose, who perceive their partners as self-disclosing, and who believe that their disclosures and confidences are understood by their partners experience greater need fulfillment, satisfaction, and love than people whose relationships contain lower levels of intimacy and disclosure (e.g., Laurenceau, Barrett, & Rovine, 2005; Meeks, Hendrick, & Hendrick, 1998; Prager & Buhrmester, 1998; Rosenfeld & Bowen, 1991). In one study, for example, Susan Sprecher and Susan Hendrick (2004) asked a sample of 101 dating couples to complete measures of their own level of self-disclosure to the partner, their partner's level of self-disclosure to them, their overall satisfaction with the relationship, and the extent of their commitment to the relationship. Correlational analyses revealed strong positive associations between self-disclosure and relationship quality (i.e., satisfaction and commitment) for both men and women. Specifically, participants who believed that they self-disclosed and that their partners also self-disclosed tended also to be very satisfied with and personally committed to the relationship. Similar results were reported more recently by Nathaniel Lambert and his colleagues (2013), who found that when men and women talked with their partners about various "good things" that had happened to them during the week, they experienced subsequent increases in positive affect and life satisfaction (particularly when their partners responded to these disclosures in a supportive, enthusiastic manner). Thus, the act of sharing information about our lives with a responsive and mutually disclosing partner tends to produce positive personal as well as interpersonal outcomes.

Most people seem aware of the importance of self-disclosure in determining relationship quality. Research reveals that individuals often consciously use self-disclosure and expressions of intimacy as strategies for intensifying and maintaining their romantic relationships. Communication researchers Stephen Haas and Laura Stafford (1998) asked a convenience sample of men and women involved in committed (homosexual) romantic relationships to report on the behaviors that they used to maintain their relationships. Although participants generated a number of maintenance strategies, one of the most commonly cited was self-disclosure. Specifically, 57% of the sample specified open and honest communication about thoughts and feelings, including disclosures about the relationship, as an effective way to maintain the romantic relationship. Less "deep" communication, akin to "small talk," was mentioned by close to 25% as a means by which the relationship is maintained. Research conducted with heterosexual samples corroborates these findings (for a review, see Dindia, 2000).

The process of revealing oneself to another, particularly when accompanied by reciprocity and validation, appears to play an essential role in the progression of romantic relationships.

## Social Exchange

Many theories of relationship development are grounded in principles of *social exchange* (e.g., Adams, 1965; Hatfield, Utne, & Traupmann, 1979; Homans, 1961; Walster, Walster, & Berscheid, 1978; for reviews, see Hatfield & Rapson, 2012; Sprecher & Schwartz, 1994). These theories focus on the exchange of rewards and costs that occur between partners in ongoing mating relationships. Although a number of social exchange theories exist, each with its own particular terminology and "take" on the process of relationship development, all share a few basic assumptions (some of which we reviewed in Chapter 1).

### Principle 1: Maximize Rewards, Minimize Costs

The first assumption is that individuals seek to maximize their rewards and minimize their costs in any given relationship. *Rewards* are anything that the individual considers valuable; they can range from the concrete and tangible to the abstract and intangible. For example, Bob's marriage with Vicki may provide him with a number of concrete benefits that he values, including financial security, sex, children, and the social profit that comes from having an attractive and intelligent partner. This relationship also may provide Bob with a variety of less tangible rewards, including love, emotional support, and the fulfillment of life goals involving marriage and fatherhood. *Costs* are those things that the individual considers to be unrewarding or that involve time, effort, compromise, and lost opportunity. In order to maintain his relationship with Vicki, for instance, Bob contributes to the housework, shares parenting tasks, listens supportively to Vicki's complaints about her new coworker, and spends vacations with his (greatly detested) in-laws.

Of course, what is rewarding or costly for one person may not be for another. The affection and emotional support provided by a steady dating partnership might be rewarding to a person with few other relationships but unimportant (or even costly) to someone with an active social life, extended network of friends and family, and stimulating career. The financial security afforded by a marital relationship might be highly rewarding to an unemployed graduate student but meaningless to a successful attorney. In addition, two individuals in a relationship may not agree about the value of a particular reward or cost. For example, Bob may place greater worth than Vicki does on the housework he completes, and Vicki may believe that listening to her work-related complaints is less costly than Bob finds it to be.

### Principle 2: Relationships Are Dynamic

The second assumption shared by social exchange theories is that relationships themselves are dynamic; they change over time. Relational partners are assumed to engage in a continual process of evaluation whereby they assess each other's gains and losses, profits and expenditures, and rewards and costs. This means that a relationship that is seen as equitable and satisfying at one point in time may come to be viewed as less equitable and satisfying (and even as inequitable and dissatisfying) as the gains and losses of each partner change over time. This happens, in part, because of the shifting nature of rewards and costs. A particular event, behavior, or occurrence may become less rewarding and/or more costly as it occurs repeatedly or as the relationship progresses. Two people caught up in the thrill of a new love might find sexual activity to be highly rewarding and not at all costly. Over time, as they become used to each other and the novelty of their passion decreases, they may come to view sexual activity as less rewarding.

*Principle 3: Evaluations Influence Relationship Development*

Third, social exchange theories assume that the result of each partner's cost-benefit evaluation determines the course of the relationship. For example, two strangers might meet at a party. Following their initial contact, each person evaluates the immediate outcomes of that interaction and makes a prediction about the outcomes of future interactions. If these evaluations and predictions are positive ("What a fun conversation; she seemed to really like me and we have so much in common"), then the individuals are likely to continue down the path to romantic involvement. If the evaluations and predictions are negative ("He didn't listen to a thing I said; we have nothing in common, and what's with those clothes?"), then the two are unlikely to maintain anything other than a superficial relationship; they may even cease to interact altogether.

*Principle 4: Equity Is the Key to Relationship Well-being*

A fourth (and related) assumption is that the partners' perceptions of the outcomes they obtain from the relationship are strongly linked with how satisfying and fulfilling they find that relationship to be. Exchange frameworks posit that people will be most satisfied with (and likely to remain committed to) a relationship when they view the relationship as equitable. Romantic partners achieve *equity* (that is, have an *equitable relationship*) when they experience a relatively equal ratio of positive-to-negative outcomes. More formally, equity occurs when the ratio between the benefits (rewards) derived from the relationship and the contributions (costs or investments) made to the relationship is similar for both partners:

$$\frac{\text{Vicki's benefits}}{\text{Vicki's contributions}} = \frac{\text{Bob's benefits}}{\text{Bob's contributions}}$$

It is the ratio of benefits to contributions that determines equity rather than the exact number that each partner receives or makes. Thus, a relationship in which one partner receives more benefits than the other may still be equitable so long as he or she makes a correspondingly higher number of contributions.

According to this theoretical framework, people who find themselves in an *inequitable relationship*—who are under-benefited or over-benefited relative to the partner—will experience distress and seek to restore equity. Equity can be restored to a relationship in a number of ways. For example, a woman who believes that her dating partner contributes much more to the relationship than she does may attempt to restore *actual equity*. She may increase her own contributions (e.g., by making an effort to return his phone calls more promptly, by paying him more compliments, by carving out more time in her schedule to be with him) and/or decrease her own benefits (e.g., by asking him to fix fewer things around her apartment). Alternatively, she can try to restore *psychological equity*. She may, for instance, convince herself that equity actually does exist ("It's not like I'm taking advantage of our relationship; he likes fixing things, and he already owns all the tools"). It is often easier and less costly to restore psychological than actual equity. And finally, if the distress caused by the inequity should prove too great, then she can simply *end the relationship*.

Equity—just like rewards and costs—is to a large extent in the eye of the beholder. You may consider your current romantic relationship to be highly equitable (and, therefore, very satisfying); however, your partner may consider the relationship less equitable (and, therefore, less satisfying). Social exchange theories recognize that such discrepancies are quite common, particularly given the dynamic and ever-changing nature of close relationships and the fact that people generally are much more aware of their own contributions to a relationship than they are of their partners' contributions.

## Empirical Evidence

Many of the principles set forth by social exchange theories have received empirical support. For example, there is evidence that the nature of rewards and costs shifts over time and within relationships. Sociologist Diane Felmlee (e.g., 1995, 1998, 2001a; also see Sprecher & Felmlee, 2008) has conducted research on what she labels "fatal attractions." Her work demonstrates that a partner's attributes that are seen as particularly attractive, rewarding, and valuable at the beginning of a relationship can later come to be viewed as unpleasant, costly, and detrimental to the relationship. For example, a woman who values her lover's "spontaneous and carefree" nature may later perceive that same attribute as an annoying "flightiness" and "lack of reliability." A man who is attracted to his dating partner's "refreshing innocence" may later find that it has become an irritating "immaturity."

We also know that people differ in terms of what they consider costly and/or rewarding; in particular, there appear to be several sex differences. In one study, Constantine Sedikides, Mary Beth Oliver, and Keith Campbell (1994) investigated the perceived benefits and costs of romantic relationships in a sample of heterosexual college students. Participants were reminded that romantic relationships are likely to result in both benefits and costs and then were asked to list the five most important benefits they had enjoyed, and the five most serious costs they had incurred, as a result of all the romantic relationships they had personally experienced. Analysis of these lists revealed a variety of *benefits*, including the following:

- Companionship or affiliation (cited by 60% of the total sample)
- Sexual gratification (46%)
- Feeling loved or loving another (43%)
- Intimacy (42%)
- Relationship expertise or knowledge (40%)
- Self-growth and self-understanding (37%)
- Enhanced self-esteem (32%)
- Exclusivity (32%)
- Feeling secure (28%)
- Social support from the partner's friends or relatives (22%)
- Feelings of happiness or elation (16%)
- Learning about the other sex (12%)

Although men and women reported experiencing similar kinds of benefits from their romantic relationships, significantly more men (65%) than women (26%) cited sexual gratification as a particularly important benefit. Conversely, significantly more women (49%) than men (14%) specified enhanced self-esteem (including higher self-respect and self-confidence) as a romantic relationship benefit.

Participants also generated a number of different *costs*, including the following:

- Loss of freedom to socialize (cited by 69% of the total sample)
- Loss of freedom to date (68%)
- Time and effort investment (27%)
- Nonsocial sacrifices, such as falling grades (24%)
- Loss of identity (22%)
- Feeling worse about oneself (22%)
- Stress and worry about the relationship (20%)

- Fights (16%)
- Increased dependence on the partner (13%)
- Monetary losses (12%)
- Loss of privacy (10%)
- Loss of innocence about relationships and love (9%)

As before, there were sex differences. More men than women cited loss of freedom to socialize (77% vs. 61%) and to date (83% vs. 56%) as particularly heavy costs associated with their romantic relationships, and more men than women specified monetary losses (18% vs. 6%) as a dating burden. More women than men mentioned loss of identity (29% vs. 14%), feeling worse about themselves (29% vs. 14%), and increased dependence on the partner (23% vs. 3%) as important costs they had experienced in their relationships.

In a second study, the authors asked another sample of men and women to rank order the list of benefits and costs generated by the first group of participants in terms of their perceived importance; these results confirmed and extended those of the first study. Specifically, women in the second study viewed intimacy, self-growth and self-understanding, and enhanced self-esteem as more important benefits than did men, whereas men in the second study perceived sexual gratification and learning about the other sex as more important benefits than did women. Also in the second study, women regarded loss of identity, increased dependence on the partner, feeling worse about oneself, and loss of innocence about relationships and love as greater costs to romantic involvement than did men, who considered monetary losses and time and effort investment to be more serious costs than did women.

Other researchers, rather than exploring perceptions of costs and benefits, have tested the theoretical prediction about the association between equity and relationship satisfaction. People clearly *assume* that equity is an important determinant of relationship quality, *expect* to experience distress if confronted by inequity in close relationships, and *believe* that equity should be restored to inequitable relationships (e.g., Canary & Stafford, 1992; Dainton & Stafford, 1993; Haas & Stafford, 1998). In one study (Sprecher, 1992), for example, college students were asked to imagine that they were in a long-term romantic relationship that had recently become inequitable. Participants first imagined that the inequity benefited their partner (i.e., that the relationship was one of *under-benefit* for themselves): "You feel that you are contributing more (in love, effort, time, emotions, tasks) than your partner is. In other words, you feel that you are currently getting a worse deal than your partner is" (p. 60). They then were asked to imagine the opposite situation—a relationship that was inequitable due to *over-benefit* for themselves. For each scenario, participants indicated how they would respond emotionally to the inequity. The results revealed that men and women expected to become distressed—to experience increased anger and depression and decreased happiness, contentment, satisfaction, and love—in response to under-benefiting inequity. In addition, although participants did not expect to experience a great deal of distress in response to over-benefiting inequity, they did expect their feelings of guilt to increase. Clearly, people *believe* that inequity will result in distress and dissatisfaction.

However, there is mixed evidence about whether equity and interpersonal well-being *actually* are associated in ongoing romantic relationships in the precise way predicted by the social exchange framework. On the one hand, there is clear evidence that equity is associated with a higher level of positive relationship outcomes, including satisfaction and commitment, than is inequity (e.g., Demaris, 2007; Weigel, Bennett, & Ballard-Reisch, 2006; for a review, see Sprecher & Schwartz, 1994; also see Kalmijn & Monden, 2011). For example, Susan Sprecher, Maria Schmeeckle, and Diane Felmlee (2006) asked a sample of men and women in dating relationships to report the degree to which they and their partners were emotionally involved in the relationship. Three groups of participants were identified: those who perceived equal involvement, those who viewed the partner as more involved, and those who saw themselves as more involved. All participants then completed a measure of relationship satisfaction. The results revealed that participants who reported that their current romantic relationship was characterized by equal levels of emotional involvement (that is, equity) were more satisfied than were participants in the two groups characterized by unequal emotional involvement (inequity).

On the other hand, not all types of inequity generate dissatisfaction. In particular, and as we might expect from Sprecher's (1992) belief study, over-benefit does not appear as unpleasant as does under-benefit (at least to the person experiencing it). Yoshinori Kamo (1993) examined the relationship between perceived fairness in the allocation of household chores and self-reported marital satisfaction in a sample of American and Japanese couples. Among American couples, being over-benefited (believing that the spouse does more than his or her fair share of tasks around the house) was positively associated with marital satisfaction—for both husbands and wives. The same result was found for Japanese wives; that is, the more that Japanese wives felt that they benefited from the relationship in terms of household task allocation, the more satisfied they were with their marriage. Similar results were reported more recently by Laura Guerrero, Angela La Valley, and Lisa Farinelli (2008), who examined married couples' responses to equity, under-benefiting inequity, and over-benefiting inequity. The results revealed that both equity and over-benefit were associated with greater marital satisfaction than was under-benefit; husbands and wives reported higher levels of marital happiness when they viewed themselves as being treated equitably or as being over-benefited in comparison to being under-benefited.

Overall, then, most of the basic assumptions of the social exchange framework are supported by empirical research (with the exception of people's reactions to over-benefit). These theories thus provide insight into how the exchange of rewards and costs between romantic partners can promote relationship development and continuity.

## Interdependence

We have seen that the exchanges between partners—their disclosures and revelations, their contributions and benefits—can propel a relationship toward increasing closeness (or, alternatively, toward dissatisfaction and dissolution). *Interdependence frameworks* also focus on partners' exchanges, their perceptions of rewards and costs, and the process by which they evaluate and regulate their relationship (see Holmes, 2000). In addition, these models add to our understanding of relationship development in two important ways. First, interdependence models distinguish between *relationship satisfaction* (how the partners feel about the relationship) and *relationship stability* (whether the relationship will be maintained over time). They recognize that a highly satisfying relationship may ultimately prove unstable, and that a deeply unsatisfying one can endure for a lifetime. Second, these frameworks propose that relationship outcomes are affected not only by what happens between the partners but also by external forces that can serve to cement or weaken the partners' bond. For example, sociocultural taboos against divorce may prevent an unhappily married couple from terminating their relationship; legalization of same-sex marriage may enable another couple to publicly acknowledge their commitment to each other; and parental interference may heighten (or extinguish) the passion between two young lovers.

### Interdependence Theory

John Thibaut and Harold Kelley's (1959) *Interdependence Theory* proposes that two people involved in a relationship are interdependent with respect to the outcomes of their behavior; that is, the thoughts, feelings, and actions of one partner influence his or her own outcomes as well as those of his or her partner. Because each partner generally cannot achieve his or her best possible outcome at the same time, some degree of compromise is necessary for both partners to obtain at least minimally satisfactory outcomes. Thus, as their relationship develops, the partners are likely to coordinate their behaviors in order to achieve mutually rewarding outcomes. For example, Helga may wish to spend the weekends walking dogs with her husband at the local animal shelter (her optimal outcome), whereas her spouse, Peter, would prefer that they go out to dinner and a movie (his optimal outcome). Desiring to achieve their own best outcomes, but recognizing the value of the relationship and the importance of each other's goals, the two may work together to find a mutually beneficial solution—perhaps they decide to spend their Saturdays volunteering together at the shelter in the morning, followed by a movie later in the day. This process of coordination is called *transformation of motivation* and is assumed to produce satisfaction and to enhance commitment to the relationship.

The fact that partners experience a transformation of motivation and coordinate their behaviors to achieve beneficial joint outcomes is not enough, however, to guarantee that their union will be satisfying or that it will endure. Interdependence Theory also proposes that relationship partners rely upon two standards when evaluating the outcomes they are receiving from a relationship. The first, called *comparison level* (CL), is the standard against which a partner evaluates the attractiveness of a relationship or how satisfactory it is. The comparison level is determined by the individual's expectations about the level of outcomes (rewards and costs) that the relationship ought to provide, and it is influenced by personal experience as well as general knowledge of outcomes commonly experienced in that type of relationship. To the extent that the outcomes the person actually experiences in the current relationship meet or exceed what is expected (outcomes $\geq$ CL), he or she is likely to view the relationship as attractive and to be satisfied; to the extent that the outcomes fall short of expectations (outcomes $<$ CL), dissatisfaction is likely to result. Thus, it is possible for someone who benefits immensely from a relationship to nonetheless be unhappy—if he or she expects more. Conversely, it is possible for someone who appears to be in a highly unrewarding relationship to be relatively satisfied—if he or she believes things could be worse. Thus, it is the discrepancy between what we are currently receiving in a relationship and what we believe we ought to be receiving that determines satisfaction.

The second standard upon which partners rely when evaluating their interpersonal outcomes is called the *comparison level for alternatives* (CLalt). CLalt is the standard the partners use in determining whether or not to remain in the relationship, and it reflects the outcomes the partners feel that they could obtain from available alternatives to the present relationship (including having no relationship at all). The discrepancy between current outcomes and CLalt influences whether a person is likely to stay or leave. Specifically, if a person's current outcomes meet or exceed his or her expected outcomes in alternative relationships (outcomes ≥ CLalt), then the relationship is likely to endure. If current outcomes fall below perceived alternative outcomes (outcomes < CLalt), however, the relationship will be unstable and may dissolve. Thus, an unhappy relationship may persist if there are no acceptable alternatives, and a blissful union may dissolve in the face of a particularly appealing alternative (see Figure 3.1 for different combinations of outcomes, CL, and CLalt).

In sum, as outlined in Figure 3.2, this theory predicts that the most stable relationships will be those in which partners do not expect a great deal (have a low CL) but actually get quite a lot (receive many positive outcomes) from the relationship (and consequently experience high levels of satisfaction) and have very few attractive alternatives to the relationship (have a low CLalt). These factors work together to produce a high level of *dependence* on the relationship; the partners need the relationship in order to obtain the outcomes they desire, and they have no other viable options for attaining those desired outcomes. Their dependence, in turn, promotes the stability and endurance of their union.

Interdependence Theory reminds us that satisfaction and stability are not necessarily one and the same and that relationships develop as a function of changes in the partners' needs, motives, and expectations as well as shifts in the surrounding social context.

### Extensions of Interdependence Theory: Cohesiveness and Commitment

Other theorists have elaborated upon the basic principles of Interdependence Theory. For example, George Levinger's (e.g., 1965, 1976) *Marital Cohesiveness Model* posits that the strength of the bond between partners is a function of two basic factors: the various inducements to remain in the relationship and the inducements to leave it (see Figure 3.3). *Inducements to remain* include all of the sources of *attractions* to the marriage and the spouse, which range from affectional rewards (e.g., love, companionship, sexual enjoyment), to socioeconomic rewards

**Figure 3.1**      Various Combinations of Outcomes, CL, and CLalt

(a) A *satisfying and stable relationship* is produced when a person's current outcomes exceed his or her expectations and also exceed the outcomes he or she believes are available from alternatives to the relationship.

(b) A *satisfying but unstable relationship* results when a person's current outcomes exceed his or her expectations but do not exceed the outcomes he or she anticipates receiving from available alternatives to the relationship.

(c) An *unsatisfying and unstable relationship* is likely when a person's current outcomes are below his or her expectations and are also below the outcomes he or she believes are available from alternatives to the relationship.

(d) An *unsatisfying but stable relationship* occurs when a person's current outcomes are below what he or she expects to obtain from the relationship but they exceed the outcomes he or she anticipates receiving from available alternatives.

NOTE: How different combinations of outcomes, CL, and CLalt affect satisfaction and stability. According to Interdependence Theory, relationship satisfaction and stability are the product of three factors: (1) the level of outcomes a person actually receives from his or her current relationship (outcomes); (2) the outcomes he or she believes ought to be received from the current relationship (CL); and (3) the outcomes he or she believes could be obtained from alternatives to the current relationship (CLalt). The discrepancy between current outcomes and CL (outcomes vs. CL) determines satisfaction, whereas the discrepancy between current outcomes and CLalt (outcomes vs. CLalt) determines stability.

**Figure 3.2**        Thibaut and Kelley's Interdependence Theory

NOTE: Interdependence Theory predicts that relationships will endure to the extent that the partners are highly dependent on each other and the relationship for desirable outcomes. Dependence is a function of satisfaction with the relationship (which is highest when people's actual outcomes meet or exceed the outcomes they expect to obtain, i.e., their comparison level) and the comparison level for alternatives (or what is believed to be available from other relationships or partners). Thus, both internal (satisfaction) and external (quality and quantity of alternatives) forces determine whether a relationship will continue.

(e.g., income, material possessions, social prestige), to similarity between the spouses on important demographic dimensions. Other inducements to remain in a relationship include the restraints or *barriers* against its dissolution. Barriers derive from the social structure in which people live and from the social contracts into which they enter. For example, feelings of obligation to the partner, the marriage, and existing children; moral proscriptions stemming from religious values; and external pressures from kin, community, and social institutions all may serve as potent barriers to termination. *Inducements to leave* the relationship include the various attractions or rewards that can be obtained from alternative relationships (including no relationship at all). Essentially, this model proposes that "marital strength is a function of bars as well as bonds" (Levinger, 1965, p. 20). Thus, the bond between two people is likely to be cohesive (strong and stable) to the extent that they experience high attraction to the relationship, many barriers to terminating the relationship, and low attraction to alternative relationships.

Another extension of classic Interdependence Theory—and currently the most prominent interdependence-based model—was proposed by Caryl Rusbult (1983; see also Rusbult & Buunk, 1993). Her

*Investment Model* proposes that *commitment,* defined as the individual's feelings of attachment to the partner and his or her intention and desire to remain in the relationship, is a function of three factors: (a) the person's level of *satisfaction* with the relationship, which is a function of rewards and costs (outcomes actually experienced) and comparison level (the level of outcomes people believe they deserve); (b) the perceived *quality of alternatives* to the relationship, or the degree to which the individual believes that important needs could be met outside the relationship (e.g., by specific others, by friendships, by hobbies and other activities, by no relationship at all); and (c) the size of the person's *investment* in the relationship, which refers to the ways he or she is connected to the partner and bound to the relationship. These can be of a direct nature (e.g., time, emotional energy, personal sacrifice) or an indirect nature (e.g., mutual friends, shared memories, shared possessions). Thus, this model proposes that people will feel committed to their relationship to the extent that they feel satisfied (i.e., their relationship provides abundant rewards, does not involve heavy costs, and closely matches their beliefs and assumptions about an ideal partnership), they believe that they have few and/or poor-quality alternatives to the relationship, and they have invested important resources in the relationship that serve as powerful inducements for its continuation. Commitment, in turn, influences whether or not the relationship will endure (see Figure 3.4).

**Figure 3.3**    Levinger's Marital Cohesiveness Model

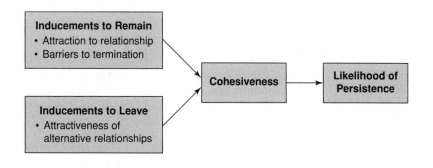

NOTE: Like Interdependence Theory, the Marital Cohesiveness Model proposes that both internal and external factors determine whether a relationship will endure over time. Highly cohesive relationships are the most likely to last. Cohesiveness (the strength of the relational bond between partners) is determined by the level of rewards and costs experienced in the relationship, which produces attraction; by the number of costs associated with terminating the relationship, or barriers; and by the presence or absence of acceptable alternatives to the relationship.

**Figure 3.4**    Rusbult's Investment Model

NOTE: Like Interdependence Theory and the Marital Cohesiveness Model, the Investment Model recognizes that the outcomes an individual obtains in his or her relationship, as well as the perceived quality of alternatives to that relationship, are important contributors to relationship stability. Specifically, this model proposes that people will feel committed to their relationships to the extent that they feel satisfied, believe that they have few good alternatives to the relationship, and have invested important resources in the relationship. This feeling of commitment, in turn, influences whether or not a relationship will last.

### Empirical Evidence

There is strong support for many of the basic propositions just outlined (e.g., Attridge & Berscheid, 1994; Drigotas, Rusbult, & Verette, 1999; Kurdek, 2000; Rusbult, Johnson, & Morrow, 1986; Rusbult, Martz, & Agnew, 1998; for a recent review, see Rusbult, Agnew, & Arriaga, 2012). For example, both Interdependence Theory and the Investment Model propose that relationship satisfaction will be greater to the extent that the partners' actual outcomes meet or exceed their expectations (outcomes $\geq$ CL). Research supports this contention. Marianne Dainton (2000) gave people currently involved in romantic relationships a list of everyday behavioral strategies that can be used to maintain or promote a relationship. These maintenance activities encompassed five general dimensions: *positivity* (e.g., behaving in a cheerful and optimistic manner), *openness* (e.g., engaging in self-disclosure or direct discussion of the relationship), *assurances* (e.g., providing messages stressing commitment to the partner and the relationship), *social networks* (e.g., relying on common friends and affiliations), and *sharing tasks* (e.g., being equally responsible for accomplishing tasks that the couple faces). For each activity, participants were asked to consider their partners' behavior and to indicate the extent to which their current relationships compared, either favorably or unfavorably, with their expectation levels. They also completed a measure of relationship satisfaction. The results revealed a strong and positive correlation between expectation fulfillment and satisfaction; the more an individual perceived his or her partner as using the various maintenance behaviors relative to his or her expectations, the more satisfied the individual was with the relationship.

More recently, psychologists Benjamin Le and Christopher Agnew (2003) conducted a *meta-analysis* to test several of the basic propositions of the Investment Model. (A meta-analysis is a quantitative technique that allows researchers to synthesize the results of many studies testing the same basic hypothesis. Because a meta-analysis uses data from multiple investigations, it usually provides a more reliable test of the hypothesis than would any one individual study.) Le and Agnew first searched the literature for published studies in which the researchers had collected measures of satisfaction, quality of alternatives, investment, and commitment. Overall, 52 studies met these criteria, with data collected from the late 1970s through 1999. The studies included a total of more than 11,000 participants from five countries (the United States, the United Kingdom, the Netherlands, Israel, and Taiwan). Le and Agnew then gathered statistical information from each study and computed the average correlation across all studies between commitment and its proposed bases (satisfaction, quality of alternatives, and investment). Their findings supported the Investment Model: Across the 11,582 participants represented in the 52 studies, satisfaction level, quality of alternatives, and investment size consistently and strongly predicted commitment. Moreover, this result held across ethnic groups, for men and women, and for homosexual and heterosexual respondents alike. The more satisfied with and invested in their relationships participants were, and the lower the perceived quality of their alternatives, the stronger was their commitment to those relationships. Interestingly, because a subset of studies also included information about relationship stability (i.e., whether the partners stayed together or dissolved their relationships), Le and Agnew were able to examine whether commitment predicted relationship persistence as the Investment Model suggests. It did. The higher the participants' commitment levels, the more likely they were to remain in their relationships.

In sum, interdependence models provide a compelling view of relationship development. Both the internal characteristics of a relationship (satisfaction, perceptions of rewards and costs, investment level) and the external forces surrounding the partners (availability and quality of alternatives, presence or absence of societal barriers to divorce) influence the couple's well-being and whether their relationship continues.

## Summary

Recognizing that only a very few relationships survive beyond initial interactions and first dates, social and behavioral scientists have devoted a great deal of time and effort to understanding the how and why of relationship development. In their quest, they have proposed a number of theoretical frameworks. Those who adopt a stage approach have charted the phases or stages of relational progression. Others have focused on the processes—self-disclosure and intimacy, exchange of rewards and costs, interdependence—that occur between partners and that fuel relationship development. Regardless of the framework utilized, researchers and theorists acknowledge that relationships are dynamic entities that fluctuate over time as a result not only of changes in the partners but also of alterations in the social environment and in the properties of the relationship itself.

## Key Concepts

Stage models of relationship development (p. 54)

Filter Theory (p. 54)

Social attributes (p. 54)

Value consensus (p. 54)

Need complementarity (p. 54)

Wheel Theory (p. 55)

Rapport (p. 55)

Self-revelation (p. 55)

Mutual dependency (p. 55)

Intimacy need fulfillment (p. 55)

Stimulus-Value-Role Theory (p. 55)

Stimulus stage (p. 55)

Value stage (p. 56)

Role stage (p. 56)

Process models of relationship development (p. 56)

Social Penetration Theory (p. 57)

Self-disclosure (p. 57)

Depth of disclosure (p. 57)

Breadth of disclosure (p. 57)

Responsiveness (p. 57)

Intimacy Theory (p. 57)

Social exchange theories (p. 59)

Rewards (p. 59)

Costs (p. 60)

Equity (p. 61)

Equitable relationship (p. 61)

Inequitable relationship (p. 61)

Actual equity (p. 62)

Psychological equity (p. 62)

Interdependence frameworks (p. 66)

Relationship satisfaction (p. 66)

Relationship stability (p. 66)

Interdependence Theory (p. 66)

Transformation of motivation (p. 67)

Comparison level (p. 67)

Comparison level for alternatives (p. 68)

Dependence (p. 68)

Marital Cohesiveness Model (p. 68)

Inducements to remain (p. 68)

Attractions (p. 68)

Barriers (p. 70)

Inducements to leave (p. 70)

Cohesiveness (p. 71)

Investment Model (p. 71)                     Quality of alternatives (p. 71)
Commitment (p. 71)                           Investment (p. 71)
Satisfaction (p. 71)                         Meta-analysis (p. 73)

## Discussion Questions

1. What are the basic premises of stage models of relationship development? Why have these models fallen out of favor?

2. Think about your current (or a previous) romantic relationship. Using Social Penetration Theory and Intimacy Theory, explain how your relationship developed as a function of changes in the depth, breadth, and intimacy of self-disclosure between you and your partner.

3. Identify and describe the five basic assumptions of social exchange models of relationship development.

4. Discuss the concept of inequity, and identify the ways in which theorists say that people can restore equity. Have you ever been in an inequitable relationship? How did you respond to the inequity? Does your response support theoretical assumptions or not?

5. Evaluate the following three statements from the perspective of Interdependence Theory:

    Statement 1: "A rewarding marriage is a happy marriage."

    Statement 2: "If he or she were really unhappy, then he or she would leave."

    Statement 3: "A good relationship will last forever."

## Recommended Readings

These reviews present several theories of relationship development, with an emphasis on process models.

Berscheid, E., & Reis, H. T. (1998). Attraction and close relationships. In D. T. Gilbert, S. T. Fiske, & G. Lindzey (Eds.), *The handbook of social psychology* (4th ed., pp. 193–281). New York, NY: McGraw-Hill.

Holmes, J. G. (2000). Social relationships: The nature and function of relational schemas. *European Journal of Social Psychology, 30,* 447–495.

Rusbult, C. E., & Van Lange, P. A. M. (2003). Interdependence, interaction, and relationships. *Annual Review of Psychology, 54,* 351–375.

# 4

# Marriage and Mate Selection

As discussed in Chapter 3, some romantic relationships pass beyond initial attraction and continue to develop over time until they reach a state of relative permanence; the partners become "steady" dates, they move in together, they form a civil union or domestic partnership, or they marry. In this chapter, we examine research on mate choice and on marriage, cohabiting relationships, and other forms of committed, long-term relationship. Because marriage historically has been socially and legally defined as a heterosexual relationship, much of the existing literature—and thus, much of our discussion—is focused on the experiences and outcomes of heterosexual married couples.

## ❖ MATING SYSTEMS ACROSS CULTURES

The norms or general "rules" that govern mate selection and reproduction differ across cultures. Cultural anthropologists, ethnographers, and other social scientists have identified several mating systems that occur (with varying degrees of frequency) in human societies around the world. These include *polygyny*, which literally means "many females" and refers to a mating system in which men marry multiple women; *polyandry* ("many males"), which is defined as a system in which women pair with multiple men; *monogamy*, which encompasses both *monogyny* ("one female") and *monandry* ("one male") and refers to a system in which two individuals pair-bond; and *polygynandry* ("many females and males," also called *cenogamy*), which is defined as group marriage or a system in which husbands and wives share the same spouses (Fisher, 1989; Goodwin, 1999).

Some marriage arrangements are more prevalent than others. One of the most comprehensive sources of cross-cultural information on mating systems is the *Ethnographic Atlas*. The *Atlas* contains data on a variety of sociocultural features (e.g., economy, living arrangement, family organization, mode of marriage, kinship terminology, community size) that characterize more than 1,100 human societies located in Africa, the Mediterranean, Eurasia, the Pacific, North America, and South America. In 1967, ethnologist George Murdock presented information on a subset of 862 of those societies, many of which are no longer in existence today, in a special edition of the journal *Ethnology*. Examination of this information, summarized in Table 4.1, reveals that polyandry historically was much less common than either polygyny or monogamy. For example, only four societies in existence in 1967 (less than 1%) explicitly endorsed a mating system based upon a single woman marrying multiple husbands. Monogamy, either between a man and woman who marry and then live within an extended family or who marry and then form a single independent family, was the predominant mating system in 137 societies (16%). By far, the most socially

**Table 4.1**      Prevalence of Mating Systems Across 862 Human Societies

| Mating System | Number and Percentage of Practicing Societies |
|---|---|
| *Polygyny* | 713 (82.7) |
| General, within extended families | 202 (23.4) |
| General, within independent nuclear families | 177 (20.5) |
| Occasional or limited, within independent nuclear families | 174 (20.2) |
| Occasional or limited, within extended families | 160 (18.6) |
| *Monogamy* | 137 (15.9) |
| Within independent nuclear families | 72 (8.4) |
| Within extended families | 65 (7.5) |
| *Polyandry* | 4 (0.5) |
| Within independent nuclear families | 3 (0.3) |
| Within extended families | 1 (0.1) |
| *Unclassified* | 8 (0.9) |

SOURCE: These frequencies were tabulated by the textbook author from raw data presented in the *Ethnographic Atlas* (Murdock, 1967, pp. 170–231).

endorsed form of marital arrangement was polygyny; a total of 713 (approximately 83%) of the societies included in the *Atlas* permitted this mating arrangement. Polygyny was common in 379 of those societies and was practiced on a limited basis within the remaining 334 societies.

Historically, then, in all but a handful of human societies women practiced monandry; a woman married one man at a time (although in polygynous societies, her spouse may have had multiple wives). Similarly, although the data at first glance suggest a high frequency of polygyny, a closer look reveals that men also tended to practice monogyny; they married one woman at a time. Based on his own analysis of the *Atlas* data, Pierre van den Berghe (1979) reported that only about 10% of the men in polygynous societies actually had more than one wife. Thus, the most frequent type of mating arrangement was (and still is today) that of one man and one woman. As noted by evolutionary scientists Martin Daly and Margo Wilson (1983):

> Polygynous unions remain rarer than monogamous ones . . . even within those societies that permit them. This is hardly surprising given male-male competition for wives and the pressures that are engendered when any substantial number of men are consigned to involuntary celibacy. Hence it is usually only a minority of wealthy, powerful men who have the means to acquire and maintain multiple wives. (pp. 282–283)

In her discussion of human marriage patterns, anthropologist Helen Fisher (1989) also concluded that the formation of a relationship between two individuals (monogamy) is "the primary marriage pattern for both men and women" (p. 333). She went on to suggest—based on an examination of marriage, divorce, and remarriage rates across cultures—that human mate selection and reproduction are perhaps best understood as demonstrating a pattern of *serial pair-bonding* or *serial monogamy* whereby men and women marry successive individual partners over their life spans (as opposed to marrying one partner for the duration of their life spans or many partners at a single time).

Today, monogamy is the only mating system that is both universally practiced and legally permitted. Polygamy is illegal in the majority (approximately 75%) of world nations, including the United States. However, some religious groups in the United States (in particular, members of the Fundamentalist Church of Jesus Christ of Latter-Day Saints [FLDS], many of whom live in two isolated communities along the Utah-Arizona border), practice a system of "plural marriage" or *informal polygyny*. In this mating system, a man legally marries one woman and subsequently informally weds another woman (or women) in a private religious ceremony (see Miller & Karkazis, 2013). Because those additional unions are not legally performed, they are not recognized by the government (and the individuals involved cannot be prosecuted for bigamy). As we will consider in Chapter 5, polygynous unions are fraught with difficulties and often result in negative outcomes, both for the individuals involved (particularly wives) and for their relationship.

So, is one form of mating arrangement "better" or more "natural" than another? In considering this question, Fisher (1992) suggested the following:

> Is monogamy natural? Yes. There certainly are exceptions. Given the opportunity, men often opt for multiple spouses to further their

genetic lines. Polygyny is also natural. Women join harems when the resources they can garner outweigh the disadvantages. Polyandry is natural. But co-wives fight. Co-husbands argue too. Both men and women have to be cajoled by riches to share a spouse. Whereas gorillas, horses, and animals of many other species *always* form harems, among human beings polygyny and polyandry seem to be optional opportunistic exceptions; monogamy is the rule. Human beings almost never have to be cajoled into pairing. Instead, we do this naturally. We flirt. We feel infatuation. We fall in love. We marry. And the vast majority of us marry only one person at a time. Pair-bonding is a trademark of the human animal. (p. 72)

## ❖ THE NATURE OF MARRIAGE

Definitionally, *marriage* is a long-term mating arrangement that is socially sanctioned and that typically involves economic, social, and reproductive cooperation between the partners. Although customs surrounding the marriage ceremony vary widely from culture to culture, all known human societies practice and endorse this type of long-term pairing (Daly & Wilson, 1983; Goodwin, 1999). Thus, marriage is a human universal.

International surveys indicate that marriage rates have declined around the world (Lester, 1996; U.S. Census Bureau, 2012b). The United States, in particular, has experienced a dramatic decrease (U.S. Census Bureau, 1994, 1998). Nationwide surveys indicate that fewer than one half (50%) of all adults currently living in the United States are married, and single people who have never married now constitute one third (33%) of the U.S. adult population (Copen, Daniels, Vespa, & Mosher, 2012; U.S. Census Bureau, 2012a). Nonetheless, most teens and young adults continue to express a desire to marry, expect to marry at some point in their lives, and hold positive attitudes about marriage and married people in general (DePaulo & Morris, 2006; Erchull, Liss, Axelson, Staebell, & Askari, 2010; Hoffnung, 2004; Willoughby, 2010). For example, one team of researchers (Martin, Specter, Martin, & Martin, 2003) assessed the marriage expectations of a large group of adolescent boys and girls, finding that the majority (94%) believed that they would eventually marry (only 6% indicated that they did not anticipate ever getting married). Indeed, despite the increased prevalence of singlehood, marriage remains a relatively common life event for most people, with about two thirds of all men and women destined to marry at least once (U.S. Census Bureau, 2012a).

## The "Rules" of Marriage

As we discussed earlier in this chapter, one of the general norms that characterizes marriage is monogamy: All cultures permit monogamous pair-bonding, and most people do, in fact, marry one person at a time. A second "rule"—albeit an unwritten one—of marriage is the tendency for men and women to marry spouses who resemble them on a number of dimensions. Called *homogamy* or *assortment*, this tendency for similar individuals to pair-bond has been extensively documented. For example, researchers have found positive correlations between marital partners on such characteristics as age, race, ethnicity, education level, socioeconomic status, religion, health status, and physical attractiveness as well as on a host of personality traits and cognitive abilities (Gonzaga, Carter, & Buckwalter, 2010; for reviews, see Berscheid & Reis, 1998; Buss, 1985; Murstein, 1980). The fact that people tend to be attracted to similar others (see Chapter 2) may partly explain this particular marriage "rule."

Another general norm of marriage is *exogamy* or the tendency for people to marry partners outside of their own familial or kinship group. All cultures have some form of *incest taboo* that prohibits sexual intercourse (and, consequently, marriage) between closely related individuals (Fisher, 1992; Frayser, 1989). Many cultures have laws designed to enforce this social norm. In the United States, for example, marriage between parents and their biological children, brothers and sisters, uncles and nieces, and aunts and nephews is illegal. In addition, about half of the states prohibit marriage between first cousins; the rest allow first-cousin marriages or permit them only under special circumstances (e.g., if the individuals are older than 65 years of age, one or both are infertile, or they have received genetic counseling). As in the United States, most other countries also prohibit sexual and/or marital relationships between immediate family members (that is, a person and his or her siblings, parents, grandparents, and aunts and uncles). However, first-cousin marriage is more prevalent in other parts of the world than it is in the United States. For example, recent surveys conducted in Afghanistan and various Middle Eastern countries (such as Oman, Lebanon, Syria, and Turkey) reveal that approximately 20% to 40% of all marriages are between first cousins (e.g., Akbayram et al., 2009; Barbour & Salameh, 2009; El-Kheshen & Saadat, 2013; Islam, 2012; Othman & Saadat, 2009; Saify & Saadat, 2012).

There are also important cross-cultural variations in how violations of the incest taboo are dealt with (Frayser, 1989; Leavitt, 2003). For example, some societies impose milder forms of punishment on transgressors, ranging from social disapproval to temporary ostracism by community members to whipping or other acts that inflict nonpermanent physical damage. Other societies mete out harsher sentences on individuals who violate the incest taboo, including expulsion from the community, mutilation, castration, and even death. As noted by anthropologist Suzanne Frayser (1989) in her seminal cross-cultural investigation of sexual and reproductive relationships, incestuous unions universally are the most "generally prohibited and strongly punished [forms of] relationship" (p. 388).

## Types of Marriage

Social and behavioral scientists have identified a number of dimensions along which marriages can vary. One dimension concerns the amount of personal choice an individual has in selecting a spouse. *Collectivist* cultures (including societies in Asia, the Middle East, and South America) typically limit the amount of freedom a man or woman has in choosing a marriage partner. These cultures are characterized by explicit and firm group boundaries, focus on group loyalty, solidarity, and shared activities, and generally require individual members to subordinate their personal goals to those of the group. Marriage is viewed primarily as a vehicle for maintaining social order and for binding families together rather than as a means of fulfilling personal desires (Goodwin, 1999; Hamon & Ingoldsby, 2003; Hatfield & Rapson, 1996). Given the emphasis placed on group cohesion and social unity, it is not surprising that many collectivist cultures practice (or historically have practiced) *arranged marriages* in which family members or matchmakers choose a mate for the individual. For example, in traditional East Asian and South Asian societies (e.g., Pakistan, India, Nepal), marriage is regarded as one of the most important events in the life cycle as well as a social and cultural duty, and many marriages are arranged or "semiarranged" (see Ghimire, Axinn, Yabiku, & Thornton, 2006; Medora, 2003; Penn, 2011).

*Individualist* cultures (including the United States and Northern and Western European countries) typically allow an individual much greater freedom in the selection of a spouse. In these societies, people are fairly autonomous, group boundaries are flexible, and emphasis is placed on the fulfillment of personal goals in marriage and other life pursuits. Feelings of personal compatibility and mutual attraction between the partners, rather than meeting the needs of families or of society, serve as the primary motivation for marriage, and individuals generally select their own partners. *Free choice marriage* (also called *love-based marriage*) is the norm in those societies.

A second dimension along which marriages vary concerns the allocation of roles and responsibilities between the spouses in the marriage. *Traditional* marriages are those in which the spouses allocate roles and responsibilities on the basis of sex (e.g., Luepnitz, 1988; Rubin, 1976; Turner, 1970). The husband's role encompasses traditional "male" activities and traits. For example, he controls the economic aspects of family life and has the authority to make decisions for the entire family. The wife's role encompasses traditional "female" activities and traits. She is responsible for domestic tasks, including management of the house and children. Traditional relationships often involve little direct or overt expression of emotion between the spouses. Rather, each partner relies on relatives and same-sex friends for companionship and affection (Peplau, 1983). Television sitcoms that were popular in the United States during the late 1950s through the 1970s showcase this type of marriage. *The Donna Reed Show, Father Knows Best, I Love Lucy, All in the Family,* and similar shows depicted marriages in which the husband worked outside the home and functioned as the sole "breadwinner," primary disciplinarian, and decision maker for the family, whereas the wife stayed at home, raised the children, and took care of domestic tasks such as cooking the family meals, shopping, and cleaning.

A quite different type of marriage, and one that is increasingly common (at least among individualist societies), is the *egalitarian, peer,* or *equal-status* marriage (e.g., Gilbert, 1993; Scanzoni, Polonko, Teachman, & Thompson, 1989; Schwartz, 1994). Unlike traditional relationships in which tasks and roles are divided along gender lines, egalitarian marriages are characterized by shared roles and responsibility in all aspects of married life. Both the husband and wife are assumed to be capable of displaying—and expected to contribute to the relationship—social support and caregiving, affection and emotion, sexuality, financial resources, parenting skills, and domestic labor. U.S. television highlighted this kind of union in 1980s programs such as *The Cosby Show* and *Roseanne* and, more recently, in shows like *Medium* (Allison and Joe DuBois), *Friday Night Lights* (Tami and Eric Taylor), *Desperate Housewives* (Lynette and Tom Scavo), *Madame Secretary* (Elizabeth and Henry McCord), *House of Cards* (Claire and Francis Underwood), and *Grimm* (Rosalee Calvert and Monroe). Sociologists Pepper Schwartz and Virginia Rutter (1998) note that true peer marriages are relatively rare: "The potential for power sharing, obligation sharing, and resource sharing in marriage is real, though not commonly enacted. Pairs with the ambition of egalitarianism often fall short, into the 'near peer' category" (p. 157). These "near peer" marriages usually involve a husband who helps with child care and household labor, and a wife who provides financial resources and makes economic decisions, to a greater degree than would be expected in traditional marriages. Although truly egalitarian marriages may still be relatively uncommon, there is some evidence that partners who achieve them experience high levels of companionship and mutual respect as well as low levels of anger and conflict. In sum, "equity has its rewards" (p. 158).

## Division of Labor

Regardless of the type of marriage a (heterosexual) couple has, it is likely that their division of household labor will reflect traditional sex roles. Early studies—those conducted in the 1950s and 1960s—revealed a strict division of labor. Husbands specialized in "outside" tasks, including mowing the lawn, shoveling snow, and maintaining the car, whereas wives specialized in "inside" tasks, including cooking, cleaning, and child care (e.g., Blood & Wolfe, 1960). Subsequent research conducted over the past several decades demonstrates that the same task division continues to characterize modern marriages (Biernat & Wortman, 1991; Coltrane, 2000; Wilkie, Ferree, & Ratcliff, 1998; Zhao, Settles, & Sheng, 2011).

In addition, although both sexes have a tendency to overestimate the amount of time they spend engaged in housework (Lee & Waite, 2005; Press & Townsley, 1998), there is overwhelming evidence that married women spend more time on domestic tasks than do married men (Baxter, 2005; Judkins & Presser, 2008; Solomon, Rothblum, & Balsam, 2004; for a review, see Coltrane & Adams, 2003). Even in *dual-earner marriages* (in which both the husband and wife work and make economic contributions to the family), women average two to three times as many hours per week on housework as do men (Artis & Pavalko, 2003; Bartley, Blanton, & Gilliard, 2005; Blair & Johnson, 1992). As a result, women have fewer hours per day of leisure or "free time" (Robinson, Yerby, Fieweger, & Somerick, 1977). For example, social scientists Darby Saxbe, Rena Repetti, and Anthony Graesch (2011) tracked a sample of dual-earner couples around their homes and recorded their activities for four days. Their results revealed that women engaged in significantly more housework and child care activities than did men (38 vs. 20 tasks, on average), and significantly fewer leisure and personal time activities (11 vs. 20, on average). Indeed, in their comprehensive review of the literature, Scott Coltrane and

Michele Adams (2003) concluded that "the average woman in the United States did about three times as much cooking, cleaning, laundry, and other routine housework in the 1990s as the average married man" (p. 472). And the same holds true today (see Mikula, Riederer, & Bodi, 2012).

Although (heterosexual) marriage might seem to place an unfair burden on women, research indicates that as long as each partner *believes* that the division of labor is fair, he or she is likely to be satisfied with both the division of labor and married life in general (e.g., Frisco & Williams, 2003; Lennon & Rosenfield, 1994; Major, 1993; Mikula et al., 2012).

## ❖ MARITAL SATISFACTION: HOW HAPPY ARE MARRIED COUPLES?

In fact, marriage (or any type of long-term romantic union) usually is associated with personal happiness for both sexes. Married couples often report more happiness, and less loneliness and stress, than unmarried, separated, divorced, or widowed people (e.g., Coombs, 1991; Demo & Acock, 1996; Tornstam, 1992), and married men and women appear equally satisfied (Boerner, Jopp, Carr, Sosinsky, & Kim, 2014; Feeney, Peterson, & Noller, 1994; Jackson, Miller, Oka, & Henry, 2014; Litzinger & Gordon, 2005). For example, Rhonda Faulkner, Maureen Davey, and Adam Davey (2005) analyzed data from a sample of more than 1,500 men and women in first-time marriages who rated their marital satisfaction, the amount of time they spent together talking or sharing an activity, and the likelihood that their marriages would end in divorce. The researchers summed participants' responses to these three items to create an overall measure of marital satisfaction (scores could range from 1 to 21, with 21 indicating the highest level of satisfaction). The results revealed that husbands and wives were extremely (and equally) happy with their marriages: The average score for husbands was 18.5 and the average score for wives was 18.4!

This does not mean that marriage produces a state of perpetual bliss, however. *Longitudinal studies* (in which couples are followed over time and assessed on multiple occasions) generally find that satisfaction declines fairly steadily throughout marriage (e.g., DeMaris, Sanchez, & Krivickas, 2012; Johnson & Bradbury, 1999; Kurdek, 1999, 2002, 2005a; Lavner & Bradbury, 2010; Lavner, Karney, & Bradbury, 2013; Lindahl, Clements, & Markman, 1998). Specifically, most couples begin their married lives with a "honeymoon" period characterized by high amounts of satisfaction and well-being, which then progressively decline (but remain high) during the next several years, stabilize for a period of time (often between the fourth and sixth years of marriage), and then either remain stable or continue to decline, assuming the couple stays together. Husbands and wives show the same progressive changes in marital happiness, although wives appear to experience a more rapid decline in satisfaction.

For example, Ted Huston, Susan McHale, and Ann Crouter (1986) conducted a series of interviews with a sample of newlywed couples over a 1-year period beginning shortly after their wedding and ending around their first anniversary. Couples rated their level of love for each other and completed a 10-item measure of marital satisfaction. In addition, they indicated how satisfied they were with the frequency with which various positive events occurred in the marriage (e.g., partner expressing approval). The results revealed declines in all measures over time. Specifically, both husbands and wives became increasingly dissatisfied with the level of positivity in their relationships, reported lower amounts of marital satisfaction, and felt less love for their spouses after 1 year of married life.

Similar results were reported by psychologists Benjamin Karney and Thomas Bradbury (1997), who conducted a longitudinal study in which they asked a sample of 60 newlywed couples to rate their satisfaction with their marriage, their spouse, and their relationship with their spouse over a 4-year period. Individual differences were evident, such that some spouses initially were clearly happier than others. Despite these differences, the overall satisfaction of both husbands and wives declined linearly over time, with scores decreasing between 3% and 4% per year. Karney and Bradbury (1997) also explored the relationship between participants' satisfaction levels at the start of their marriages and their subsequent changes in satisfaction over time. Interestingly, they found that couples who began their marriages with higher levels of satisfaction experienced smaller reductions in happiness than did couples who entered their marriage with relatively low levels of satisfaction. The researchers posit that very high levels of relational happiness at the very beginning stages of marriage may serve a protective function and allow spouses to maintain positive feelings over time and thus help keep satisfaction levels high.

It might be tempting to conclude from these and related studies that as time passes marriage inevitably produces unhappiness for one or both spouses. Such a conclusion, however, would be erroneous.

In discussing their findings, Huston and colleagues (1986) made the following point:

> The changes in subjective evaluation over the first year of marriage reveal a consistent pattern. Husbands and wives were less satisfied with their patterns of interaction, less in love, more ambivalent, and less satisfied with the married life in general. . . . These results do not mean, however, that these couples were unhappy, disillusioned, and dissatisfied with their lot. After a year of marriage, they were less euphoric than they were shortly after marriage, but their responses still fell on the positive side of the continuum for each variable. (pp. 121–122)

The couples in Karney and Bradbury's (1997) study also remained highly content. Their scores, at each of the assessment times over the 4-year period, were well above average. In fact, subsequent research suggests that it is primarily those couples who begin their marriages with relatively *low* levels of satisfaction who experience dramatic declines in satisfaction (that is, happy newlyweds tend to stay relatively happy over time, whereas unhappy newlyweds tend to become less happy over time; see Lavner & Bradbury, 2010; Lavner, Bradbury, & Karney, 2012). Thus, although happiness may decline during a marriage, it does not inevitably change into *un*happiness for all couples.

In addition to investigating how marital satisfaction changes over time, many researchers have sought to identify the factors that are associated with relational happiness. Part IV of this textbook explores how people's traits, dispositions, and personality attributes may influence both their own marital satisfaction and that of their spouses.

## ❖  HAS MARRIAGE CHANGED OVER TIME?

Modern marriages are a bit different from their historical counterparts. We have already seen some evidence that the traditional division of labor is not quite so strictly upheld by contemporary husbands and wives, and that a new type of egalitarian or peer marriage may be on the rise (or at least available as an option for couples). Another change in the nature of marriage concerns the age at which people marry for the first time. According to data collected by the U.S. Census Bureau (2013), the age at first marriage is rising, with greater numbers of men and women delaying marriage until their late 20s. For example, in 1950, the mean age at first marriage was approximately 23 years for men and 20 years for women. Three decades later, in 1980, the age at first marriage had increased to around 25 for men and 22 for women—a life span delay of 2 full years. By 2000, men were marrying for the first time at around 27, and women were waiting to marry until they were 25. And in 2013, the average age at first marriage had risen even higher, to 29 for men and 27 for women. A similar change is occurring in non-U.S. populations; for example, over the past 30 years, the average age at first marriage in many European and Asian countries has increased by 2 to 4 years (see Williams & Philipguest, 2005; United Nations Economic Commission for Europe, 2014).

Another dramatic change in the nature of marriage concerns the growing emphasis that most men and women place on personal happiness. Love and affection, rather than economic security, reproduction, or any other factor, have become the primary basis for marriage in the United States and other Western cultures. For example, in the late-1960s, social scientist William Kephart (1967) asked a sample of young men and women whether they would marry someone with whom they were not in love if that person possessed all of the other qualities they desired in a spouse. More than one third (35%) of the men and three fourths (76%) of the women responded affirmatively—they were willing to marry without love. However, by the mid-1980s there was evidence of a dramatic shift in attitude. When psychologists Jeffrey Simpson, Bruce Campbell, and Ellen Berscheid (1986) asked a group of young adults the very same question, only 14% of the men and 20% of the women indicated that they would marry someone they did not love if he or she was "perfect" in every other respect. Thus, an overwhelming majority of participants considered love to be an essential prerequisite for marriage.

There is evidence that a similar attitude shift is occurring around the world. About a decade after the study by Simpson and his colleagues (1986), another group of researchers (Levine, Sato, Hashimoto, & Verma, 1995) asked a large sample of adults from 11 countries to answer the question first posed by Kephart (1967): "If a man/woman had all the qualities you desired, would you marry this person if you were not in love with him/her?" Although a greater number of participants from collectivist countries (e.g., India, Pakistan) than from individualist countries (e.g., United States, England) answered the question affirmatively, there was no country in which participants were completely willing to marry in the absence of love. In fact, sizeable numbers of men and women in every country reported that they would not enter a loveless marriage. For example, the percentage of participants who said "no" in response to the question was as follows: United States (86%), England (84%), Mexico (81%), Australia (80%), Philippines (64%), Japan (62%), Pakistan (39%), Thailand (34%), and India (24%).

The increased emphasis given to love as a basis for matrimony has produced other changes in the nature of marriage. In particular, cultures with a strong tradition of arranged marriage increasingly are adopting a matrimonial system that incorporates aspects of love-based marriage, such as personal choice and mutual attraction (for reviews, see Goodwin, 1999; Lieberman & Hatfield, 2006). In these blended or "hybrid" marriages, potential mates are selected by family members or matchmakers, but the final decision rests with the individual partners, who typically base their decisions on attraction, intimacy, and compatibility, and their estimation that these feelings will develop into mutual love (Allendorf, 2013; Netting, 2010). As a result, many collectivist cultures are experiencing a decrease in the number of traditional arranged marriages (and a corresponding increase in the number of love-based or hybrid marriages) that take place. For example, a report by sociologist Fumie Kumagai (1995) revealed that the ratio of arranged (*miai*) to love-based (*renai*) marriages in Japan shifted dramatically over the last half of the 20th century. Specifically, during the World War II era, approximately 70% of new marriages were arranged by parents, whereas 30% were love-based or personal choice matches. By 1988, however, only 23% of new marriages were arranged; the rest either were completely love-based (75%) or reflected a combination of parental arrangement and personal choice (2%). Data collected in the early 1990s revealed an even greater decline in the proportion of traditional arranged marriages: In 1991, the percentage of all new marriages in Japan that could be considered arranged had dropped to 12.7.

Similar changes have been documented in other collectivist countries (e.g., China, Nepal; Ghimire et al., 2006; Xu & Whyte, 1990). Clearly, men and women around the world not only want love in their marriages but also the freedom to choose their own spouses.

## ❖ SAME-SEX MARRIAGE

Like their heterosexual counterparts, most gay men and lesbian women strongly favor "couplehood," value and actively seek to establish committed romantic relationships, and affirm and celebrate their long-term partnerships with ceremonies, anniversaries, and other events that symbolically mark the importance of these unions in their lives (see Clarke, Burgoyne, & Burns, 2013; Lannutti, 2005; Lever, 1994, 1995; Suter, Bergen, Daas, & Durham, 2006). Many choose to marry.

Same-sex marriage is currently legal in about 20 countries in Western Europe, South America, North America, and Oceania, but remains prohibited in most African, Middle Eastern, Asian, and Eastern European countries.

In the United States, the issue of same-sex marriage has been (and continues to be) a hotly debated topic. Prior to 1996, the federal government did not define the nature of marriage. Because the individual states were (and are) allowed to develop their own marriage laws, any marriage recognized by a state was also recognized by the federal government. However, in 1996, the Defense of Marriage Act (DOMA) was passed by Congress and signed into law by then-President Bill Clinton. DOMA defined the concept of marriage (and spouse) for purposes of federal law:

> In determining the meaning of any Act of Congress, or of any ruling, regulation, or interpretation of the various administrative bureaus and agencies of the United States, the word 'marriage' means only a legal union between one man and one woman as husband and wife, and the word 'spouse' refers only to a person of the opposite sex who is a husband or a wife. (Public Law 104-199, Sec. 3. Definition of Marriage, page 110 Stat. 2419, Sep. 21, 1996)

By explicitly defining marriage as a heterosexual union between one man and one woman, DOMA prohibited the federal government from legally recognizing same-sex (or polygamous) marriages, even if those unions were legally recognized by individual states.

DOMA was challenged in 2010 and subsequently struck down in 2013 by the U.S. Supreme Court on the grounds that it violated the Fifth Amendment to the U.S. Constitution. With this decision, the federal government legally recognized same-sex marriages performed by individual states and thus permitted same-sex partners to qualify for spousal benefits established by federal laws and regulations. For example, just like heterosexual married couples, homosexual married couples became able to file joint federal income tax returns (and receive associated tax benefits) and to receive Social Security benefits upon one partner's death. The individual states, though, remained divided with respect to the legality of same-sex marriage. Most states subsequently passed laws allowing same-sex couples to marry, but a handful continued to ban same-sex marriage.

However, on June 26, 2015, the U.S. Supreme Court issued a landmark ruling declaring that same-sex couples have a constitutional right to marry in all states, that individual states must allow same-sex couples to marry, and that each state must recognize marriages performed in other states. In issuing this decision, Justice Anthony Kennedy observed that:

> The ancient origins of marriage confirm its centrality, but it has not stood in isolation from developments in law and society. The history of marriage is one of both continuity and change. That institution— even as confined to opposite-sex relations—has evolved over time. . . .
>
> These considerations lead to the conclusion that the right to marry is a fundamental right inherent in the liberty of the person, and under the Due Process and Equal Protection Clauses of the Fourteenth Amendment couples of the same-sex may not be deprived of that right and that liberty. The Court now holds that same-sex couples may exercise the fundamental right to marry. . . .
>
> It follows that the Court also must hold—and it now does hold—that there is no lawful basis for a State to refuse to recognize a lawful same-sex marriage performed in another State on the ground of its same-sex character.
>
> (*Obergefell v. Hodges*, 576 U.S.—[June 26, 2015])

Many people—including same-sex partners in long-term, committed relationships—remain divided in their attitudes toward same-sex marriage (see Lannutti, 2011). Nonetheless, marriage is now a legal right for all men and women in the United States.

## ❖ COHABITATION: AN ALTERNATIVE TO MARRIAGE

Marriage is not the only option for couples seeking to form a more or less permanent relationship. Other types of long-term romantic commitment exist. For example, *civil unions* or *domestic partnerships* are legally recognized unions that provide (unmarried) heterosexual or homosexual couples with many of the same basic rights, responsibilities, and benefits accorded to married couples. But not all couples choose to formalize their unions. One of the most common (and increasingly popular) alternatives to marriage (and civil unions or domestic partnerships) is *cohabitation*. Cohabitation resembles a marital relationship, civil union, or domestic partnership in that it is essentially a committed pair-bond or monogamous union between two individuals who live together and who coordinate their economic, social, sexual (and sometimes reproductive) activities. Unlike marriage (or civil unions or registered domestic partnerships), however, cohabitation is not legally formalized or sanctioned. Perhaps due in part to more permissive social attitudes regarding premarital sex, rates of cohabitation (at least in the United States) appear to be on the rise. For example, Robert Michael and his colleagues' large national survey revealed that only about 16% of men and 6% of women born between 1933 and 1942 had cohabited prior to marriage (Michael, Gagnon, Laumann, & Kolata, 1994). This number increased to 33% for men and to 24% for women born in the decade between 1943 and 1952. More than half of the men (53%) and nearly half of the women (43%) born between 1953 and 1962 reported having cohabited prior to marriage, and a whopping two thirds of men and women born between 1963 and 1974 had cohabited before marriage. Cohabitation has become so common, in fact, that the researchers concluded the following:

> The path toward marriage, once so straight and narrow, has begun to meander and to have many side paths, one of which is being trodden into a well-traveled lane. That path is the pattern of living together before marriage. Like other recent studies, ours shows a marked shift toward living together rather than marriage as the first union of couples. (p. 96)

According to recent survey data compiled by the U.S. Census Bureau (Lofquist, Lugaila, O'Connell, & Feliz, 2012), there are currently more than 6.8 million opposite-sex and more than 640,000 same-sex "unmarried partner households" in the United States. Cohabitation has seemingly joined marriage as an almost universal life experience.

Research reveals that cohabitation serves a variety of functions in developing relationships (Carmichael & Whittaker, 2007; Murrow & Shi, 2010; Rhoades, Stanley, & Markman, 2009a; Sassler & Miller, 2011; Willoughby, Carroll, & Busby, 2011). For some couples, cohabitation functions as a precursor to marriage; these partners view cohabitation as an important stepping-stone on the path to marriage, and they often decide to cohabit only after they are engaged. For other couples, cohabitation represents a replacement for marriage when marriage is not possible (for example, due to legal or social reasons). Still other couples view cohabitation as simply another phase or stage of commitment in dating relationships; these partners may not have any definite plans to marry, but rather elect to move in together for the sake of convenience and/or because they see cohabitation as a normal development in the lifecycle of a "serious" relationship. Finally, some couples use cohabitation as a "trial run" for marriage, during which they assess their suitability as spouses, explore the logistics of living together and sharing expenses, and test and affirm their commitment. Recently, social scientists have identified a new (and increasingly common) form of cohabitation in which partners frequently stay overnight together but continue to retain separate residences. Called *stayovers, visiting cohabitation,* or *part-time cohabitation,* this type of romantic arrangement seems to function as a convenient, flexible, and less formal alternative to full-time cohabitation, one that is more serious than casual dating but that involves less commitment and involvement (and more personal freedom) than full-time cohabitation (Jamison & Ganong, 2011; Jamison & Proulx, 2013).

The fact that many cohabiters expect to marry their partners (Brown, 2003; Brown & Booth, 1996; Bumpass, Sweet, & Cherlin, 1991; Guzzo, 2009)—and about 40% do, in fact, eventually marry (Copen, Daniels, & Mosher, 2013)—has led some scholars to propose that this form of premarital union provides couples with an opportunity to test their compatibility, iron out their differences, and thus strengthen their relationship before making a formal (and public) commitment via a marriage ceremony. Interestingly, however, existing research does not support this supposition. In actuality, premarital cohabitation appears to be associated with *negative* marital outcomes, including lower levels of satisfaction and commitment, poorer communication and supportive behavior, and greater amounts of conflict (e.g., Amato, Johnson, Booth, & Rogers, 2003; Cohan & Kleinbaum, 2002; Jose, O'Leary, & Moyer, 2010; Kline et al., 2004; Kline Rhoades, Stanley, & Markman, 2006; but see Brown, Sanchez, Nock, & Wright, 2006). For example, Galena Rhoades, Scott Stanley, and Howard Markman (2009b) compared three groups of married couples—those who had lived together before becoming engaged (before-engagement cohabiters), those who moved in together only after becoming engaged (after-engagement cohabiters), and those who did not live together until after getting married (non-premarital cohabiters)—on a number of measures of marital quality. Their results revealed that couples in the before-engagement group reported lower marital satisfaction, less dedication to their relationship, more negative communication, and a greater likelihood of divorce than couples in the other two groups, suggesting that couples who begin cohabiting early in their relationship (i.e., before formalizing their commitment via engagement or marriage) are at greater risk for poor marital outcomes. This finding is so robust, in fact, that relationship scholars have labeled it the *cohabitation effect.*

There is one dimension, however, on which cohabiters seem to experience more beneficial outcomes than their married counterparts: the division of household labor. Cohabitation generally is characterized by a more equal division of household labor than is marriage. Both homosexual and heterosexual cohabiters (as well as heterosexual married couples who cohabited prior to marriage) possess more egalitarian attitudes toward division of household labor and demonstrate a more equitable allocation of household tasks than married couples who did not cohabit (Clarkberg, Stolzenberg, & Waite, 1995; Domínguez-Folgueros, 2013; Goldberg & Perry-Jenkins, 2007; Kurdek, 1993a; for a review, see Kurdek, 2005b).

Despite these differences, research generally indicates that levels of overall satisfaction and well-being are comparable across all types of long-term committed relationship—whether heterosexual or homosexual, married or cohabiting (for reviews, see Kurdek, 2005b; Peplau & Spalding, 2000). Moreover, the same factors that are associated with relational happiness among married heterosexual couples also are correlated with relational happiness among cohabiting heterosexual and homosexual couples (e.g., Kurdek, 2006).

## Summary

Marriage is a cross-cultural universal, with men and women the world over seeking and forming long-term, committed romantic relationships. Although marriages can vary along a number of dimensions, and different types of long-term partnership exist, research generally reveals that most couples are satisfied with the quality of their unions (though they also tend to become less satisfied over time). Significant changes in the nature of marriage have occurred around the world; in particular, there is an increased emphasis on love as the basis for marriage and on personal choice in the selection of a marriage partner.

## Key Concepts

Polygyny (p. 78)

Polyandry (p. 78)

Monogamy (p. 78)

Monogyny (p. 78)

Monandry (p. 78)

Polygynandry (p. 78)

Cenogamy (p. 78)

*Ethnographic Atlas* (p. 78)

Serial pair-bonding or serial
  monogamy (p. 80)

Informal polygyny (p. 80)

Marriage (p. 81)

Homogamy or assortment (p. 82)

Exogamy (p. 82)

Incest taboo (p. 82)

Collectivist cultures (p. 83)

Arranged marriage (p. 83)

Individualist cultures (p. 83)

Free choice or love-based marriage
  (p. 84)

| | |
|---|---|
| Traditional marriage (p. 84) | Civil union (p. 92) |
| Egalitarian, peer, or equal-status marriage (p. 84) | Domestic partnership (p. 92) |
| | Cohabitation (p. 92) |
| Dual-earner marriage (p. 85) | Stayovers (visiting or part-time cohabitation) (p. 94) |
| Longitudinal studies (p. 86) | |
| Defense of Marriage Act (p. 91) | Cohabitation effect (p. 94) |

## Discussion Questions

1. Discuss the various mating systems that occur throughout the world. Find examples of each system, using data from modern or ancient civilizations.

2. There is an old saying that goes something like this:

   *Hogamous, higamous, man is polygamous*

   *Higamous, hogamous, woman is monogamous*

   Evaluate this saying, using evidence from cross-cultural data on mating systems.

3. How would social exchange and evolutionary models of mate selection explain the prevalence of homogamy or assortment?

4. Compare traditional and egalitarian marriages. How have media depictions of married life changed over time? Is one form more prevalent on television, for example, than the other? Find a television sitcom or drama in which one or more marriages are portrayed, and discuss the type of relationship(s) the partners have. Is their marriage similar or different from the types of marriage identified by social scientists?

5. Consider the functions that cohabitation may serve for couples. Do you think that some reasons for cohabiting are more likely than others to result in long-term commitment (e.g., marriage)?

## Recommended Readings

This older but well-written book is designed for a general audience. Fisher is a respected social scientist who presents interesting anecdotes and empirical evidence about the mating arrangements and habits of men and women living in diverse cultures around the world. This book is a fascinating read.

Fisher, H. E. (1992). *Anatomy of love: A natural history of mating, marriage, and why we stray.* New York, NY: Fawcett Columbine.

This article presents an in-depth, nonjudgmental examination of the FLDS polygynous communities in Hildale, Utah, and Colorado City, Arizona. It is an essential read for anyone interested in understanding the lifestyle of this group of individuals, and some of the consequences they experience.

Miller, A. C., & Karkazis, K. (2013). Health beliefs and practices in an isolated polygamist community of southern Utah. *Journal of Religion and Health, 52,* 597-609.

These authors present one of the first (and most widely cited) cross-cultural investigations of marriage and mate selection.

Daly, M., & Wilson, M. (1983). *Sex, evolution, and behavior* (2nd ed.). Belmont, CA: Wadsworth.

These authors review the literature on same-sex unions. Although slightly dated, these review pieces are comprehensive and well written (and the authors are acknowledged experts in the area).

Kurdek, L. A. (2005b). What do we know about gay and lesbian couples? *Current Directions in Psychological Science, 14,* 251–254.

Peplau, L. A., & Spalding, L. (2000). The close relationships of lesbians, gay men and bisexuals. In C. Hendrick & S. S. Hendrick (Eds.), *Close relationships: A sourcebook* (pp. 111–123). Thousand Oaks, CA: Sage.

# 5

# Conflict and Dissolution

Simply because most people actively seek long-term romantic relationships (and eventually form at least one) does not necessarily mean that those relationships will function smoothly or last forever. The process of relationship development is often "bumpy" and tension can easily develop between partners in even the most committed and loving of relationships. In this chapter, we examine the topic of conflict, including the events that occur during conflict and how couples manage conflict. We also consider relationship dissolution—from the sequence of events involved in breakups to the ways in which people commonly respond to the demise of a romantic relationship.

## ❖ CONFLICT

Conflict and disagreement are extremely common occurrences in most romantic relationships. Community surveys, for instance, reveal that nearly all married or cohabiting couples report having differences of opinion, arguments, or "unpleasant disagreements" at least some of the time, with average frequencies ranging from once a day to once a month (Hatch & Bulcroft, 2004; Heimdal, Dørmænen, & Træen, 2008; McGonagle, Kessler, & Schilling, 1992; Papp, Kouros, & Cummings, 2009). In addition, as couples progress from casual dating to more intimate forms of romantic involvement (e.g., steady dating, engagement, marriage), or as they transition through various relational events (e.g., becoming parents), they often experience an increase in the amount of conflict in their relationships (e.g., Braiker & Kelley, 1979). In sum, conflict appears to be part and parcel of most dating and mating relationships.

### What Happens During Conflict? The Role of Attributions

As anyone who has ever had a disagreement with a loved one knows, partners not only act and react to each other during conflict but they also experience emotions and thoughts, express beliefs, form impressions, and come to conclusions. Research now suggests that the *attributions* (explanations for a partner's behavior) that couples make during times of conflict play a crucial role in determining whether they will successfully negotiate and resolve their differences or whether their initial disagreement will escalate to increasingly intense and angry fighting. Two different types of attribution are associated with conflict negotiation versus escalation. *Causal attributions* concern the perceived causes of a partner's behavior. When seeking to understand why the partner acted in a certain way, a person makes a determination about *locus* (the extent to which the cause of the behavior rests in the partner as opposed to the external situation), *stability* (the extent to which the cause of the behavior is likely to change over time), and *globality* (the extent to which the cause of the behavior affects other areas of the relationship). *Responsibility attributions* concern the partner's perceived responsibility or accountability for the behavior. When considering the partner's action, a person also comes to a conclusion about *motivation* (the extent to which the behavior reflects negative or positive, selfish or selfless, and harmful or harmless motives), *intention* (the extent to which the behavior is deliberate, voluntary, and freely chosen), and *blame* (the extent to which the behavior is justified by mitigating circumstances and therefore not worthy of blame). As illustrated in Figure 5.1, conflict is likely to escalate and intensify to the extent that the partner's criticism, rebuff, or other negative behavior is attributed to internal, stable, and global causes and is perceived as intentionally hurtful, motivated by selfish concerns, and blameworthy. Conversely, conflict is likely to proceed smoothly to resolution to the extent that the partner's negative behavior is attributed to external or situational, temporary, and specific causes and is viewed as stemming from unintentional, unselfish, and blameless motives.

Every individual in every relationship makes attributions, and the reality is that even the most well-adjusted partners in even the most idyllic of relationships often form different impressions of (and provide contradictory explanations for) each other's behavior—particularly during times of conflict. In their seminal article on attributional conflict in young couples, social scientists Bruce Orvis, Harold Kelley, and Deborah Butler (1976) identified and explained several basic attributional "facts" about ongoing conflict in close romantic relationships.

The first fact is that during conflict, *attributional processes become activated* as each partner seeks to understand the cause of the conflict and of the other's behavior.

> "I thought he loved me. How could he forget my birthday? He knows how important this day is to me," Julia wonders.

> "Why isn't she speaking to me?" Richard thinks. "What's going on? Did I do something wrong?"

When the relationship is progressing smoothly, partners do not ask why; agreement does not need explaining. It is only when an unpleasant— or unexpected—event occurs that the flow of the relationship is interrupted and partners begin to actively search for an explanation.

The second fact is that *the attribution process is selective and often biased*. During conflict, partners have a tendency to take a positive view of their own behavior. Cognitively, they are able to quickly and easily bring to mind information that serves their personal interests, readily

**Figure 5.1**    Attributions Determine Whether Conflict Intensifies or Resolves

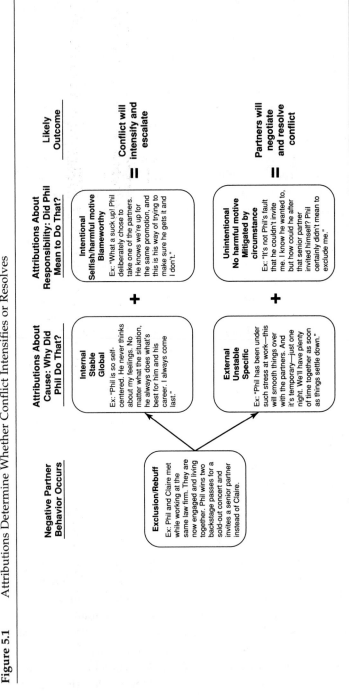

**Negative Partner Behavior Occurs**

**Exclusion/Rebuff**

Ex: Phil and Claire met while working at the same law firm. They are now engaged and living together. Phil wins two backstage passes for a sold-out concert and invites a senior partner instead of Claire.

**Attributions About Cause: Why Did Phil Do That?**

**Internal Stable Global**

Ex: "Phil is so self-centered. He never thinks about my feelings. No matter what the situation, he always does what's best for him and his career. I always come last."

**External Unstable Specific**

Ex: "Phil has been under such stress at work—this will smooth things over with the partners. And it's temporary—just one night. We'll have plenty of time together as soon as things settle down."

**Attributions About Responsibility: Did Phil Mean to Do That?**

**Intentional Selfish/harmful motive Blameworthy**

Ex: "What a suck up! Phil deliberately chose to take one of the partners. He knows we're up for the same promotion, and this is his way of trying to make sure he gets it and I don't."

**Unintentional No harmful motive Mitigated by circumstance**

Ex: "It's not Phil's fault that he couldn't invite me. I know he wanted to, but how could he after that senior partner invited himself? Phil certainly didn't mean to exclude me."

**Likely Outcome**

= **Conflict will intensify and escalate**

= **Partners will negotiate and resolve conflict**

NOTE: Whether a couple's disagreement will reach a satisfactory resolution or will escalate and intensify is partly a function of the attributions that the partners make about each other's behavior. A person who attributes a partner's negative behavior to internal, stable, and global causes, and who concludes that the behavior is intentional, motivated by selfish or hurtful motives, and is not justified or excused by circumstance is likely to become increasingly upset. Conversely, a person who concludes that a partner's negative behavior is the result of external (situational), unstable (not likely to be repeated), and specific (occurring only in this one particular relationship area) causes, and who does not assign high levels of responsibility or blame to the partner, is more likely to attempt to resolve the conflict through direct and calm negotiation.

remembering previous instances of their own "good" behavior. In addition, partners often genuinely believe that they possess an accurate understanding of the causes of each other's behavior and feel that their own behavior is justified.

> "He deserves the silent treatment for not remembering my birthday. I'm constantly doing nice things for him, and I have never once forgotten his birthday or any special occasion. This is my special day and he knows it—it's even circled on the calendar!" Julia fumes.

> "Is she still upset about that comment I made? She knows I was only kidding. How many times do I have to apologize? I hate this silent treatment stuff; it's so childish. I wish she'd just grow up and tell me when she's mad. At least I have the decency to communicate openly about my feelings," Richard sighs with exasperation.

Orvis and his colleagues (1976) noted that attributions can serve conflicting personal interests and still meet the criteria of plausibility because "ordinary events, including interpersonal behavior, readily lend themselves to different interpretations . . . [and] the everyday attributor has great freedom to select from many different kinds of information and causes" (p. 380). In other words, faced with an unpleasant or unexpected relationship event, each partner has at his or her mental fingertips an array of seemingly plausible explanations, any one of which may promote or further his or her own agenda.

The third fact is that *the attributions that partners make during times of conflict can create "attributional conflicts"*—disagreements about the causes of behavior—that usually are irresolvable. Partners often disagree, not only about the ostensible conflict of interest, but also about the reasons for their behavior.

> "I'm so upset with you right now," Julia yells. "How could you forget my birthday? And don't give me any lame excuses; I know how you operate, and I know that this is your way of getting back at me for throwing out that stupid T-shirt."

> "What? You've got to be kidding me. I'm not mad about the T-shirt. I just forgot. You know how crazy work is right now; I'm under a lot of pressure with that new project. The deadline is getting closer and it's sucking up all of my mental energy. I can't believe you think I would deliberately forget your birthday!" Richard argues.

Both partners in our example agree that Richard forgot Julia's birthday (the cause of the conflict). However, they disagree about the reasons for this event (this is attributional conflict). Richard honestly believes that he forgot because he is under extreme pressure at work. Julia just as firmly believes that he forgot because he is upset that she threw out his old T-shirt and therefore is punishing her. As noted by Orvis and his colleagues (1976), the multiple interpretations that can be given to any one behavior (there are many reasons why someone might forget a birthday), the relative inability of each partner to prove that a particular causal explanation is correct (how will Richard ever conclusively prove to Julia that his work-related memory lapse—and not some hidden agenda—is to blame for the forgotten birthday?), and the continuing conflict of interest itself (the missed birthday) all "make it improbable that the actor and the partner can come to see eye-to-eye in the matter" (p. 381). During conflict, then, partners often find themselves with both a source of initial disagreement plus an additional source of conflict regarding attributions. Richard and Julia may end up not only arguing about the forgotten birthday but about the putative reasons for the original conflict.

The fourth fact is that *"meta-attributions" may arise and create additional problems* for the partners. A *meta-attribution* is an evaluation of the explanation that a partner gives for his or her behavior. During conflict, each partner evaluates the credibility and validity of the attributions that are made for a particular behavior (Orvis et al., 1976). When one partner gives a causal explanation that is not credible, that is illogical, or that seems particularly unconvincing, the other partner may wonder why it was given.

> "Wait a minute. He just hired an assistant," Julia thinks. "And his boss said she'd extend the deadline if he needed more time to finish the project. So why would he use that as his excuse for not remembering my birthday? It doesn't make any sense. I know he's still upset about the T-shirt. If he's not, then something else must be going on."

The issue of why a certain attribution was made may raise serious doubts about the giver of the attribution (e.g., his or her candor, trustworthiness, honesty, or perceptiveness) and about the future of the relationship and may become yet another source of conflict between partners.

Investigations of the moment-by-moment thought processes that occur between romantic partners during conflict episodes support many of the observations initially made by Orvis and his colleagues (1976). In one study, for example, married couples visited a "family interaction lab" that was created by researchers Alan Sillars, Linda Roberts, Kenneth Leonard, and Tim Dun (2000). The lab resembled a combination living room and dining room, and each couple spent 15 minutes in this setting discussing one of their current unresolved disagreements. The spouses then went to separate rooms to view the videotape of their interaction. The videotape was designed to stop playing after each 20-second interval; when it did, participants reported into a microphone what they remembered thinking and feeling at the time.

Analysis of these spontaneous thoughts revealed that individuals tended to treat their inferences as objective observations ("He's attacking me"; "She's lying"). They seemed unaware of the possibility that they might be mistaken in their assumptions and/or conclusions. Similarly, participants' thoughts showed little evidence of complex perspective-taking. For example, only 3% of their codable thoughts had a mutual or relational focus (i.e., showed awareness of the interdependence between each partner's behavior), and only 5% of their thoughts focused on how the partner might be interpreting the situation. Furthermore, when participants did attempt to identify or acknowledge the partner's perspective, they tended to view that perspective in simplistic and undifferentiated terms ("He thinks he's right"; "She knows I'm sick of talking about this"). Negative thoughts and feelings also occurred much more frequently than positive ones. And finally, both husbands and wives displayed a tendency to view their own communication during the conflict more favorably than that of their partner. Specifically, both spouses attributed positive acts (e.g., collaboration and cooperation, disclosure and openness, soliciting information, attending to the partner) more often to themselves than to the partner, and both attributed negative acts and intentions (e.g., confrontation, avoidance and withdrawal, topic shifting, stonewalling, lying, insincerity) more often to the partner than to themselves. The researchers concluded,

> A surprisingly high proportion of thoughts were negatively valenced and there was minimal evidence of attention to the inherent complexity and ambiguity that exists in the communicative process. Participants showed a tendency to construe their own and their partner's communicative acts as objectifiable behaviors with unequivocal meaning. Presumably, this is part of the problem that occurs when interaction does not go smoothly—people treat their inferences as objective observations. (Sillars et al., 2000, p. 496)

Taken as a whole, these data suggest that people's perceptions, attributions, and thoughts during conflict often are subjective, simplistic, and self-serving. Knowing this, couples should strive for accuracy, for objectivity, and for empathic understanding of each other's position during times of duress and disagreement.

## How Does Conflict End?

Regardless of the interpretations and impressions that partners form about each other's behavior during an argument, all conflicts eventually end. Relationship scholar Donald Peterson (1983/2002) has provided the most comprehensive taxonomy of the various forms that these endings may take (see Figure 5.2). Some are positive. For example, conflict may produce *structural improvement* in a couple's relationship. Disagreements and differences of opinion provide partners with an opportunity to learn new information about each other's goals, values, and needs as well as the expectations that each has about the relationship. Although such revelations may be disturbing, the new knowledge that the partners gain may allow them to achieve a deeper level of intimacy. Indeed, many dating couples report that their "first big fight" enabled them to clarify their feelings about each other and left them with an increased sense of their degree of commitment (Siegert & Stamp, 1994). Conflict is most likely to result in structural improvement when the partners have high amounts of affection and trust for each other, value and engage in open communication, and make allowances for each other's differences. Another positive outcome is an *integrative agreement*, defined as a solution that simultaneously satisfies both partners' original goals. Peterson (1983/2002) observed that purely integrative agreements are uncommon because it is difficult for two people to reconcile truly divergent interests; rather, what usually happens is that the partners create an alternative that requires one or both to make some slight concessions but that still allows them both to satisfy their major goals. Other conflicts end with *compromise* as each partner reduces his or her wishes until a mutually acceptable alternative is found. Both integrative agreements and compromise require that the partners be willing to cooperate with each other and that they have the flexibility to meet on some middle ground.

Of course, conflict does not always end well. Some disagreements or fights end in conquest or *domination*, with one partner continuing to pursue his or her own personal goals while the other submits or capitulates. Over time, the repeated domination of one partner over another is likely to have a destructive impact on the relationship. In one investigation, Karen Kayser (1993; also see Kayser & Rao, 2006) asked a group of unhappily married individuals to identify the "critical turning points for the worse" in their relationships. Most participants cited

**Figure 5.2**      How Do Conflicts End?

**Conflict Example**

Scott and Meghan have conflicting schedules. She works a night shift and needs to sleep until noon. He works a day shift and likes to get up at 4:30 a.m. to watch the morning news and cook a hearty breakfast. Scott's morning routine interrupts Meghan's sleep; this has become a constant source of conflict for the couple.

**Possible Endings for Scott and Meghan's Conflict**

*Structural Improvement*
Scott and Meghan sit down together and discuss ways to resolve their conflicting schedules. They consider their options, decide what's important to them, and come to a mutually agreeable solution. Their ability to overcome this issue affirms their commitment to each other.

*Integrative Agreement*
Meghan buys a white noise machine and ear plugs to minimize external sound; Scott continues to cook breakfast in the morning but then goes out to the garage to eat and watch his news shows so that he doesn't disturb Meghan.

*Compromise*
Scott agrees to only watch the morning news three times a week; Meghan agrees to sleep in the quieter guest room at the back of the house on those days.

*Domination*
Scott continues to cook and watch TV in the morning (Scott "wins"); Scott agrees to no longer cook and watch TV in the morning (Meghan "wins").

*Separation*
Scott and Meghan decide that their schedules are incompatible. Neither will make any change, and their arguments escalate. Eventually, they terminate their relationship.

NOTE: Psychologist Donald Peterson (1983/2002) has identified five possible endings for conflict. This figure illustrates those five outcomes.

instances in which their partners displayed overly controlling behavior, including unilateral decision making about both minor (e.g., how the participants should dress) and major (e.g., where the couple should live) issues without regard for the participants' opinion and feelings. Domination is related to power imbalances or asymmetries between the partners; the partner with the most resources and the least commitment to the relationship is the one who generally "wins."

The final possible ending identified by Peterson (1983/2002) involves *separation* or the withdrawal of one or both partners without immediate resolution of the conflict. Separation is most likely to occur when partners view their conflict as unmanageable, continue to blame each other, and are unwilling to negotiate. Interestingly, separation actually may be a useful step in attaining later resolution of the conflict, because time apart sometimes allows the partners to cool their tempers and come up with more creative solutions to the problem. Often, however, withdrawal has a damaging effect—the partners become increasingly unhappy and their relationship deteriorates. The results of a study conducted by social scientist Duncan Cramer (2000) revealed a strong correlation between unresolved conflict and relationship satisfaction in dating couples; specifically, the more often that couples reported experiencing conflict that was not resolved, the less satisfied they were with their relationship.

## Conflict Resolution Strategies

Whether conflict ends well or results in additional distress depends, in part, on how the conflict is managed by the partners. For example, research generally reveals that relationship satisfaction is strongly associated with the use of "positive" or constructive conflict resolution strategies. Men and women whose partners employ *reason* (problem solving and the use of rational argument; e.g., presenting alternatives, seeking solutions to the problem), *assertion* (direct expression of opinions or wants; e.g., clearly stating one's position, redirecting the conversation to the issue or topic, emphasizing points by gesture or eye contact), or *partner support* (acknowledgment of the partner's views; e.g., actively listening or questioning, expressing clear agreement with the partner, making compromises or concessions) are happier and more satisfied than individuals whose partners make less use of these strategies (e.g., Noller, Feeney, Bonnell, & Callan, 1994; for a review, see Cupach & Canary, 2003).

"Negative" conflict resolution strategies are associated with interpersonal distress and dissatisfaction (Noller et al., 1994). Negative strategies include *coercion*, defined as seeking control through the use of force (e.g., blame, threats, sarcasm, physical or verbal aggression); *manipulation*, defined as attempting to gain compliance by indirect or false means (e.g., providing misleading information, attempting to make the partner feel guilty or defensive, feigning sincerity or various mood states); and *avoidance*, characterized by a physical and/or emotional retreat from the situation (e.g., changing or avoiding the topic, avoiding eye contact, minimizing the situation by joking).

Another potentially destructive conflict style is the *demand-withdraw pattern* of communication in which one partner desires change and approaches the other about it while the other partner withdraws from the issue or conflict. Across couple types (heterosexual, homosexual, married, cohabiting, dating) the demand-withdraw pattern consistently has been linked with relationship dissatisfaction and instability; that is, the more frequently that couples engage in this interaction pattern, the lower their levels of satisfaction, adjustment, and well-being (e.g., Baucom, McFarland, & Christensen, 2010; Falconier & Epstein, 2011; Heavey, Christensen, & Malamuth, 1995; Uebelacker, Courtnage, & Whisman, 2003; Wegner, 2005). There also is a reliable sex difference with respect to this pattern; although both men and women can and do take on the roles of "demander" and "withdrawer" during conflict, research with both heterosexual and homosexual couples consistently demonstrates that women tend to demand more than men and men tend to withdraw more than women (Christensen & Heavey, 1990; Gottman & Levenson, 1988; also see Eldridge & Christensen, 2002). However, laboratory examinations of actual conflict interactions between couples reveal that it is not so much the sex of the individual partners that predicts the occurrence of demand or withdraw responses but rather whose issue is being discussed and the relative power distribution between partners (e.g., Baucom et al., 2010; Heavey, Layne, & Christensen, 1993; Holley, Sturm, & Levenson, 2010; Sagrestano, Christensen, & Heavey, 1998). Specifically, regardless of his or her sex, the partner whose issue is being discussed or who wants change to occur is the one who typically demands. Thus, men—like women—will adopt a demand orientation when they are discussing issues that are important to them, and women—like men—will avoid or withdraw when the issue is unimportant to them or they wish to maintain the status quo. In addition, the less powerful (and often less satisfied) partner is generally the one who demands change, whereas the more powerful partner is generally the one who attempts to avoid the issue. Since women in (heterosexual) marriages often have less relational power than men, this may explain why women are more likely to demand and men to withdraw in marital relationships. Interestingly, research also has revealed that the seemingly "typical" sex difference in demand-withdraw behavior observed in heterosexual married couples (with wives demanding and husbands withdrawing) actually occurs only in highly distressed relationships (e.g., Eldridge, Sevier, Jones, Atkins, & Christensen, 2007). Happily married couples exhibit much lower frequencies of this destructive conflict style (and each partner, regardless of sex, demands or withdraws at the same low levels).

Is there a secret to resolving conflict? Obviously, no one strategy will work well for all couples. However, we can glean some hints from the available literature. First, successful conflict management requires open and honest communication in which both partners clearly express their opinions, positions, and wants. Second, the partners should remain focused on the issue or situation at hand. Third, each partner must attempt to understand the other's perspective and try to recognize his or her own contribution to the interaction and the partner's responses. Fourth, the partners should try to express positive affect whenever possible and to suppress (or at least not reciprocate) negative feelings and expressions. Finally, the partners' goal should be to reach an equitable solution rather than a win-lose one, and both must be will-ing to compromise and negotiate in service of that goal.

## ❖ RELATIONSHIP DISSOLUTION

Conflict, distress-maintaining attributions, and negative conflict reso-lution strategies certainly can contribute to unhappiness and the demise of a relationship. However, even stable and satisfying relation-ships end. Current nationwide surveys indicate that about 40% of all first marriages and roughly 36% of all remarriages in the United States end in divorce or permanent separation (Aughinbaugh, Robles, & Sun, 2013). Between 1950 and the mid-1980s, the divorce rate rose steadily; since that time, it has remained fairly steady and currently falls at 3.6 divorces per 1,000 people in the population (National Center for Health Statistics, 2013; U.S. Census Bureau, 2007a). Although the United States has one of the highest divorce rates in the world, relatively high divorce rates now characterize many other nations as well (U.S. Census Bureau, 2012b). For example, Japan, France, Germany, Italy, the Netherlands, and Spain all experienced a marked increase in the ratio of divorces to marriages in their populations between the years 1980 and 2000; however, as in the United States, rates in these and other countries (e.g., the United Kingdom, Denmark, Sweden) have stabi-lized in recent years (U.S. Census Bureau, 2007b; 2012b). It is important to recognize that because these estimates do not include information about the termination rates of premarital or cohabiting couples, actual rates of relationship dissolution in general are probably much higher.

Some kinds of committed relationships do appear more prone to dissolution than others. Surveys conducted in the United States and other countries indicate that heterosexual married couples are less likely to end their relationships than are heterosexual and homosexual cohabiting couples (see Blumstein & Schwartz, 1983; Lau, 2012; Moust-gaard & Martikainen, 2009). For example, in one study, psychologist Lawrence Kurdek (2004) compared the rate of relationship dissolution among three groups of participants: cohabiting gay male couples, cohabiting lesbian couples, and heterosexual married couples. His results revealed that significantly more of the cohabiting homosexual couples (19% of the gay male couples and 24% of the lesbian couples) than of the heterosexual married couples (15%) had ended their rela-tionships. In sum, divorce or relationship termination is an increas-ingly common experience in the lives of men and women in the United States and around the world.

## Why Do Relationships End?

Researchers have identified a wide array of factors that are associated with the likelihood of divorce. For example, a number of personality traits and dispositional characteristics are correlated with relationship dissolution. We will examine the association between individual difference variables and marital stability in Chapters 14, 15, and 16. Other factors that are implicated in divorce are demographic. For example, large-scale surveys as well as reviews of the divorce literature (e.g., Copen, Daniels, Vespa, & Mosher, 2012; Rodrigues, Hall, & Fincham, 2006; Røsand, Slinning, Røysamb, & Tambs, 2014; Teachman, Tedrow, & Hall, 2006) indicate that the following variables reliably predict marital dissolution:

- *Age at marriage*: This is one of the most consistent predictors of divorce. Men and women who marry at younger ages have an increased risk of divorce.

- *Education level*: Lower levels of educational attainment are associated with an increased likelihood of marital termination.

- *Race or ethnicity*: Among married couples, Asians and Latinos are less likely to divorce than are other same-race couples (e.g., African Americans, Whites). In addition, there is some limited evidence that divorce is more likely among interracial couples than among same-race couples.

Interpersonal factors are also strongly implicated in relationship dissolution. For example, people often end relationships because they become disillusioned with the partner and disengaged from the relationship. Signs of disillusionment and disengagement include (1) *emotional indifference,* or a lack of strong emotions (positive and negative) felt for the partner; (2) *cognitive disconnection,* including perceiving the partner as detached, unresponsive, and different from oneself, psychologically distancing oneself from the partner, and paying less attention to the partner; and (3) *behavioral distancing,* such as reducing the amount of time spent with the partner, the level of involvement in the partner's life and activities, and the degree of communication with the partner (Barry, Lawrence, & Langer, 2008; Kayser, 1996; Kayser & Rao, 2006). Social scientist Ted Huston and his colleagues (Huston, 2009; Huston, Caughlin, Houts, Smith, & George, 2001) found that divorce was associated with declining feelings of love, lowered rates of affectionate behavior, increasing ambivalence about the marriage, and the growing conviction that one's spouse is not responsive. The various theories we reviewed in Chapter 3 suggest a number of additional interpersonal reasons why relationships might end, including changes in the factors that initially promoted relationship development. For example, self-disclosure can fuel the progression of a romantic relationship as the partners learn new things about each other and experience increased intimacy. Self-disclosure also increases the risk, however, that an individual will reveal something about himself or herself that the other finds unappealing. In addition, researchers find that the disclosure of negative thoughts, feelings, and behaviors may produce unhappiness and contribute to relationship dissolution (Gottman & Levenson, 1992).

In the United States and other countries, a particularly common interpersonal cause for divorce is the unfaithfulness of one of the partners (see Allen & Atkins, 2012; DeMaris, 2013; Qureshi, Charsley, & Shaw, 2014; Scott, Rhoades, Stanley, Allen, & Markman, 2013). Evolutionary scholar Laura Betzig (1989) examined reasons for divorce in a sample of 160 societies around the world. Infidelity or adultery was the most common cause of conjugal dissolution, mentioned in 88 societies (or 55% of the sample). (We will consider the topic of infidelity in greater detail in Chapter 13.) Other frequent causes of divorce or marital dissolution included sterility, usually that of wives (47% of societies); cruelty or maltreatment, primarily by husbands (34%); and "displeasingness" or personality conflicts (32%). Interestingly, polygyny—a husband electing to add another wife to the household— and subsequent co-spouse conflict was the eighth most commonly reported cause of marital dissolution, cited by 16% of societies. As we have seen, polygyny may be an optional form of mate choice in certain cultures, but it is neither common nor does it necessarily produce positive outcomes for the partners. Betzig noted,

> Polygyny in effect legitimizes what would be extramarital sex on the part of a husband. The result is that, to a wife, the most important "other women" are cowives rather than lovers. When a husband has added too many of them or neglected her to favor them, a woman may divorce him. (p. 661)

Other researchers have also found lower rates of marital satisfaction and higher rates of physical and psychological distress among wives in polygynous marriages than among wives in monogamous marriages (Al-Krenawi & Graham, 2006; Al-Krenawi, Graham, & Al Gharaibeh, 2011; Tabi, Doster, & Cheney, 2010); this provides additional evidence that polygyny may not be conducive to optimal personal and interpersonal functioning and thus may contribute to relationship dissolution.

Changes in the social environment may also produce an increased likelihood of relationship dissolution. Several scholars have posited that the increased economic independence of women, the reduction of legal barriers to divorce (e.g., no-fault divorce laws), the reduced social stigma associated with divorce, and other social changes that began in the United States during the 20th century (and that continue today) have made it easier for individuals involved in unhappy marriages to dissolve their unions (see Amato & Irving, 2006; Berscheid & Campbell, 1981). The nature of a person's available alternatives constitutes another social factor that is implicated in relationship termination. Caryl Rusbult and colleagues (Rusbult, Zembrodt, & Gunn, 1982) asked a sample of young adults to think of a time when they became dissatisfied with a romantic relationship and to describe their response to that situation. Their results revealed that men and women who believed that the available alternatives would be "better" and more satisfying than the current partner and relationship were more likely to choose to end that relationship. Other researchers also have found that relationship dissolution is more likely when the existing social environment provides abundant opportunities for "re-partnering" (e.g., Felmlee, 2001b).

These are only a few of the many factors that can contribute to the demise of the association between two people.

## How Do Relationships End?

Several models of romantic relationship termination have been proposed (e.g., Gottman, 1994a, Gottman & Levenson, 1992). For example, relationship scholar Steve Duck (e.g., 1982; Rollie & Duck, 2006) has posited that relationships undergo five interrelated phases of disengagement and dissolution, illustrated in Figure 5.3. Each phase is characterized by different patterns of communication and interaction between the partners. The first phase, the *intrapsychic* phase, begins when one partner (or both partners) crosses a threshold of what Duck calls "unbearable dissatisfaction" with the current state of the relationship. During this phase, the individual privately focuses on the partner's behavior and identifies any causes of dissatisfaction with the partner. In addition, the individual assesses the internal dynamics of the relationship, evaluates the negative aspects of being in the relationship, considers the costs of withdrawing from the relationship, and assesses positive aspects of any available alternatives to the relationship.

This cognitive activity is essentially private and generally is not directly expressed to the partner. In essence, an individual in this beginning phase of relationship dissolution asks himself or herself, "Am I happy? Are things between us okay? Will I be better off by myself or with so-and-so?" Once a person comes to the mental realization that leaving the relationship might be better than staying in it and resolves to confront the partner about this issue, the second phase is engaged.

During the *dyadic* phase, the focus becomes interpersonal. Here, the person must confront the partner with his or her dissatisfaction, express his or her discomfort, and present his or her view of the relationship. The partner, in turn, may question the individual's views, provide alternative explanations for events, present his or her view of the relationship, and so on. This interpersonal process is likely to be difficult and to produce stress and even anger as the two partners face their differences of opinion and negotiate their respective roles. Together, the partners must make a choice between repairing the relationship or allowing its demise; in so doing, they weigh the pros and cons of the relationship and consider alternative forms of the relationship. If the partners decide that the relationship cannot be repaired, then the final steps in the dyadic phase "involve preparation for the post-dissolution state: essentially this means starting to create the 'public story' about the causes and course of the disengagement" (Duck, 1982, p. 24).

The third phase of dissolution, the *social* phase, centers on the public and social repercussions for dissolving the relationship. The partners are faced with the tasks of dealing with their "newly single" status (not an easy situation in a social world that values couplehood) and subsequent doubts about their futures. In addition, they must explain the situation to friends, family, neighbors, and others in the social network and must face the judgment and possible disapproval of those social entities. The social phase concludes when each partner creates and distributes publicly a story about the relationship's demise; these stories attribute blame and provide causal explanations for the breakup and often are used by the partners to save face.

The stories or accounts created during the social phase may be quite different from the ones produced by the ex-partners during the fourth phase, the *grave-dressing* phase. Here, each individual is concerned with coming to terms with the breakup and moving on. As noted by Duck (1982),

> Once the main psychological "work" of dissolving a personal relationship is over, the problem remains of what to do with the memories associated with it. The processes here remind me of grave-dressing: the

**Figure 5.3**    Duck's Model of Relationship Dissolution

**Intrapsychic Phase**
Begins when the person's dissatisfaction exceeds tolerance threshold. Person privately assesses state of relationship, own feelings, and any alternatives.

**Dyadic Phase**
Person communicates his or her own feelings and view of relationship to partner; partner does the same. Together, they choose between relationship repair or dissolution.

**Social Phase**
Partners deal with the public and social repercussions of relationship dissolution. Each creates and distributes publicly his or her story about the end of the relationship.

**Grave-Dressing Phase**
Person retrospectively analyzes the relationship's life history and privately comes to terms with its demise by creating an acceptable personal story about its progression and outcomes.

**Resurrection Phase**
Person fully adapts to the relationship's demise by acknowledging the impact of the loss, gaining self- and relationship-knowledge, and preparing for future romance.

**PROCESS OF DISSOLUTION**

NOTE: Scholar Steve Duck (e.g., 1982; Rollie & Duck, 2006) proposes that relationship dissolution occurs over time as partners pass through five inter-related and often overlapping phases that are characterized by different communication and interaction patterns.

attempt to neaten up the last resting place of the corpse and to erect public statements of its form, contribution, and importance. Much of the activity of getting over a relationship concerns simplification, rationalization, and beautification of the course, themes, and outcomes of the relationship while it still flourished. (p. 27)

Essentially, the persons involved engage in a retrospective analysis of the relationship and its death; this allows them to create an acceptable personal story (as opposed to a public account that attributes blame for the breakup) about the course of the relationship and to tidy up the memories associated with it.

The fifth and final phase, called *resurrection*, centers around the process of adaptation and adjustment to the relationship's termination; here, the individuals confront the loss of what was once a valued union with another person, experience self-growth as they come to view themselves as having "learned" from past relationship mistakes, and ready themselves for future romantic connections.

## Disengagement Strategies

At some point, partners in dissatisfying relationships must choose between repair and dissolution. If the decision is to dissolve the relationship, the partners must then decide how to go about fulfilling that goal. A number of researchers have investigated the means or tactics, called *disengagement strategies*, that people utilize when attempting to end a relationship. A series of studies conducted by Leslie Baxter (1985) suggested that disengagement strategies vary along two basic dimensions. The first, called *indirectness vs. directness*, refers to the extent to which the person's desire to exit the relationship is made clear to the other partner. Direct strategies explicitly make clear the desire to end the relationship, whereas indirect strategies do not. The second dimension is called *other-orientation vs. self-orientation* and indicates the degree to which the disengager (the person attempting to end the relationship) tries to avoid hurting the partner. Other-oriented strategies demonstrate a desire to avoid embarrassing or manipulating the partner; self-oriented strategies display concern for the self at the expense of the partner. These two dimensions combine to form four categories of disengagement strategy, illustrated in Figure 5.4.

The first category encompasses strategies that are *direct and other-oriented*. In using the "state of the relationship talk," one or both partners explicitly acknowledge their dissatisfaction and desire to end the relationship—and they do so in a face-saving context of mutual discussion and agreement to exit: "I'm so glad that we decided to talk things over. We really are in very different places right now. I agree that the best thing is for us to break up." The "negotiated farewell" is a similar strategy that involves an explicit communication that formally ends the relationship and that allows each partner to share responsibility for the breakup: "We went out to dinner and talked about our situation. We came to the conclusion that neither of us is to blame, and we've both made mistakes, and so we decided to end the relationship." Both of these strategies directly and openly express the goal of termination in a manner that saves face both for the disengager and the partner.

The second category contains strategies that are *direct and self-oriented*. Here, the disengager explicitly states his or her desire to end the relationship and makes little to no effort to avoid hurting, embarrassing, or manipulating the partner. Examples of these strategies include "fait accompli" and "attributional conflict." Fait accompli occurs when the disengager declares that the relationship is over with no opportunity for discussion or compromise: "I don't care what you

**Figure 5.4**    Baxter's Model of Disengagement Strategies

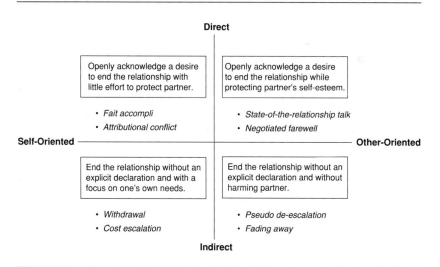

NOTE: Research conducted by Leslie Baxter (1985) suggests that the ways in which people disengage from a relationship vary along two primary dimensions. The *direct/indirect* dimension concerns whether the individual makes his or her desire to end the relationship clear to the partner. The *self-/other-oriented* dimension concerns the degree to which the individual focuses on protecting the self or the partner. These two dimensions combine to form four categories of disengagement strategy.

say. It's over between us. End of discussion." Attributional conflict is a strategy in which both partners wish to end the relationship but cannot agree about why the breakup is necessary and thus blame each other (often bitterly) for its occurrence: "This situation is all your fault!" "No, it's your fault!" People who use these strategies openly call for the termination of the relationship but often accomplish that goal at their partner's expense.

The third category contains those strategies that are considered *indirect and self-oriented*. Here, an individual attempts to end the relationship without explicitly stating that goal and with an overwhelming concern for his or her own feelings and needs (as opposed to those of the partner). "Withdrawal" involves reducing the frequency and/or the intimacy of contact with the partner without telling the partner the real reason for the disengagement (i.e., the desire to end the relationship): "I have a lot of work to do this weekend. I'm going to have to cancel our plans for Saturday, and I don't expect to have much free time on Sunday. In fact, this whole week is going to be really busy. You should just go ahead and make plans without me." A second indirect/self-oriented strategy is "cost escalation," which occurs when the person wishing to exit the relationship attempts to increase the relationship costs of the partner, thereby driving him or her away: "Maybe if I act really mean or pick a fight, my boyfriend/girlfriend will get the hint and break up with me." People who use these strategies avoid any explicit discussion of relationship termination while at the same time focusing on their own needs and feelings—they wish to end the relationship but are unable or unwilling to openly acknowledge this fact and have a direct and honest discussion with their partner. By manipulating the partner into leaving, men and women who use these strategies also allow themselves to play the victim if and when the partner takes action ("I have no idea why he/she broke up with me—I never did anything wrong").

The fourth category contains *indirect and other-oriented* strategies that attempt to accomplish a breakup without an explicit declaration and without excessive harm to either partner. One example is "pseudo de-escalation," when one or both partners (falsely) declare that they desire a transformed but less close relationship rather than a final and complete separation: "It's not like we won't see each other ever again. I mean, we can still be friends." Another is "fading away," when both partners implicitly understand that the relationship is over (but never directly say anything about this state of affairs): "She went back to school yesterday. Neither of us said anything, but I could tell that it's over."

Baxter (1985) pointed out that the process of relationship disengagement is multifaceted and complex and that it is possible for one person to use numerous strategies when attempting to end a specific relationship. In addition, some strategies may be more likely than others to produce beneficial (or at least less distressing) outcomes for the partners. For example, in one recent investigation, Susan Sprecher, Corinne Zimmerman, and Erin Abrahams (2010; also see Fehr, Harasymchuk, & Sprecher, 2014) asked a sample of college students to rate a variety of breakup strategies in terms of their degree of compassion toward the partner. Their results revealed that students found the following other-oriented and direct strategies to be the kindest and most compassionate: emphasizing the good things gained from the relationship, avoiding hurting the partner's feelings or blaming the partner (even if he or she were to blame), openly discussing with the partner the desire to break up, and making an effort to keep from leaving the relationship on a "sour note." Strategies that were considered the least caring and compassionate included such indirect and self-oriented actions as texting, instant messaging, or e-mailing the partner about the breakup, using a third party to inform the partner about the breakup, avoiding contact with the partner, and acting unpleasantly or picking arguments to manipulate the partner into initiating a breakup. In sum, direct strategies that acknowledge the relationship's demise often are easier for individuals to bear than indirect strategies that leave them wondering about their romantic futures. Similarly, strategies that take into consideration the feelings of the person who is being left, and that allow both partners to participate in the breaking up process, are more likely to produce positive outcomes than strategies that do not.

## Accounts: Why Things Turned Out This Way

One of the most common things that people do when faced with the breakup of a romantic relationship is to try to understand what went wrong and why the relationship foundered. In fact, the model of relationship dissolution proposed by Duck (e.g., 1982) and reviewed earlier in the chapter specifically posits that the final stages of breakup occur when the ex-partners achieve a sense of understanding and a feeling of closure about the relationship's end. An important element in this recovery process is the making of *accounts*. Accounts are explanatory scripts that present the plot, introduce the characters and their patterns of interaction, and tell the "why" of the breakup. Like a novel, play, or some other type of dramatic presentation, accounts tell a story—in this case, that of the relationship and its demise.

According to account scholars John Harvey, Ann Weber, and their colleagues (e.g., Harvey & Fine, 2006; Harvey, Weber, Galvin, Huszti, & Garnick, 1986; Weber, 1998), people create accounts for a variety of reasons. First, account making allows individuals to reduce or eliminate the uncertainty and ambiguity that frequently accompany breakups:

> He says, "I know why things didn't work out. It was because I got too wrapped up in work. And so she found someone else. There's no doubt in my mind that this is what killed our marriage."

> She says, "It's not like any one specific thing destroyed our relationship. It was more like a lot of little things that built up over time. I guess eventually I just fell out of love with him."

Accounts are not always accurate, and the individuals involved may create vastly different accounts of the same situation. Nonetheless, accounts allow their creators to clarify their understanding of the breakup, to establish blame or exoneration about an event, and to satisfy their need for control and information.

Second, accounts fulfill what Harvey, Weber, and their colleagues termed a "social-presentational" function that may protect and enhance the individual's self-esteem. During and after a breakup, people often are motivated to present the stories of their relationship to significant others. By influencing the interpretations that others have of the individual and the events of the breakup, accounts may result in social support, help, sympathy, and other beneficial outcomes. Thus, the husband who tells his best friend that he forgives his wife's extramarital affair and that he accepts responsibility for driving her into the arms of another man projects an image of charity and martyrdom that may produce esteem-boosting expressions of admiration and respect from his friend. "You're such a good person," his friend says, "I don't know if I'd have the moral strength to forgive such a thing." The unfaithful wife who confesses her "weakness" and tells her best friend what a "horrible person" she is projects an image of need and dependence that may result in the provision of nurturance, affection, and support: "So you made a mistake," the friend reassures her. "You're only human. You're a good person, and I support you."

And third, accounts serve as a potent vehicle for emotional release. In telling the story of the relationship's demise, individuals may experience a cathartic purging of feelings of guilt, anger, depression, loneliness, insecurity, and confusion: "Here's what happened to me, and here's how I feel about it," the wounded party cries, giving voice to thoughts and pent-up emotions that he or she may not have had the opportunity to express during the breakup itself.

There is empirical evidence that accounts do play a very important role in helping people to adjust to the end of a relationship (e.g., Blackburn, Brody, & LeFebvre, 2014; Doering, 2010). In one investigation, researchers Jody Koenig Kellas and Valerie Manusov (2003) asked a sample of 90 undergraduate students who had experienced the termination of an important romantic relationship to "tell the story" of the breakup in a written narrative. These written narratives were then rated for various aspects of completeness, including the extent to which they were coherent, presented the events in a sequential and episodic manner, attributed responsibility to the characters in the story, evoked and made sense of affect or emotions, and developed characters relevant to the story. Participants also completed a scale that assessed their overall adjustment to the loss of their important love relationship. The researchers found that both the coherence of a participant's narrative and the extent to which he or she segmented the events in a sequential and episodic manner were positively related to overall adjustment. That is, participants whose accounts of relationship dissolution made sense, hung together, were structured in an organized manner, and were supplemented with examples displayed higher levels of adjustment to the loss of their romantic relationships. These findings suggest that the ability to conceptually organize and understand a breakup relates to the process of adjusting to relationship loss.

In sum, assembling one's account of a broken relationship—what happened, why the partnership failed, what went wrong or right—appears to provide the account maker with the tools he or she needs for a successful recovery.

## Reactions to the End of a Relationship

People respond to the demise of a romantic union in a number of ways. How they respond depends to some extent on the nature of the relationship itself. Based on the theories of relationship development we reviewed in Chapter 3, we could predict that people who receive many rewards relative to costs from their partner, who are satisfied with and invested in their relationship, who have been involved with their partner for some time and feel highly committed to him or her, and who believe that they have few viable alternatives to their relationship will experience a great deal of distress at the relationship's demise.

Some research supports this contention. Psychologists Patricia Frazier and Stephen Cook (1993) surveyed 85 men and women who recently had experienced the breakup of a dating relationship. Each participant provided information about the ended relationship and the ex-lover, including relationship *satisfaction* (e.g., how satisfied they were with the partner in a variety of areas), perceived *closeness* of the relationship, and perceived *alternatives* (e.g., how easy it would be to find another partner). In addition, participants indicated how *stressful* the breakup had been for them and the extent to which they felt that they had *recovered* from the breakup, and they completed a 15-item scale of *current emotional adjustment*. They also took a *self-esteem* inventory and a measure of perceived *social support from friends*. The results of the study revealed that individuals who had been more satisfied with their partners, whose relationships had been closer, and who felt that it would be more difficult for them to find another romantic partner reported experiencing greater stress at the breakup. Interestingly, participants' levels of satisfaction, closeness, and perceived alternatives were *not* significantly related to the extent to which they felt they had recovered from the breakup or their current emotional adjustment—but their self-esteem and perceived level of social support were. These results provide a ray of light for men and women experiencing breakups. If the relationships were close and satisfying, then the breakups will probably be painful; however, a positive self-image and a supportive group of friends and family may help to heal the wound and speed the recovery process.

Although depression, anxiety, reduced self-esteem, and other symptoms of psychological distress are common reactions to the end of a close relationship, many people also experience *positive* responses to relationship dissolution. For example, divorced men and women often report beneficial changes in their other relationships (including more frequent and more intimate interaction with friends, family members, and social network members) and themselves (such as personal growth and greater autonomy, self-reliance, and self-esteem) following the dissolution of their marriages (see Tashiro, Frazier, & Berman, 2006). Similar positive responses often occur after the breakup of non-marital romantic relationships. Researchers Ty Tashiro and Patricia Frazier (2003) surveyed 92 men and women who recently had dissolved a dating relationship. Each participant was asked to describe the positive changes (if any) that had occurred as a result of the breakup. On average, participants reported experiencing five positive changes in themselves (e.g., increased self-confidence, self-reliance, independence, and willingness to experience and express emotion), their interpersonal dynamics (e.g., greater relationship knowledge, improved communication skills), and their surrounding social environment (e.g., improved friendships and family relationships).

Not surprisingly, several factors are associated with emotional responses to romantic relationship dissolution. For example, contrary to popular opinion about the pitfalls of "rebound" romance, scientists have discovered that the more quickly people enter a new relationship after ending a prior one, the greater their level of psychological well-being and resolution about the ex-partner (see Brumbaugh & Fraley, 2015). Similarly, among young adults who regularly use social networking sites (e.g., Facebook), those who minimize their online presence and who refrain from breakup-related online activity (such as posting about the breakup, continually checking an ex-partner's profile, etc.) during the breakup process report greater adjustment than those who remain virtually "connected" with the ex-partner (LeFebvre, Blackburn, & Brody, 2015). There also are sex differences with respect to reactions to relationship dissolution. Researchers generally find that women demonstrate greater emotional recovery and adjustment following divorce than do men. This robust finding is commonly attributed to three factors (see Braver, Shapiro, & Goodman, 2006). First, women tend to be more successful than men at accessing and using social support networks that buffer the stresses accompanying divorce. Second, women are less likely than men to rely on harmful or ineffective methods of coping with divorce-related stress (e.g., alcohol, drugs). Third, women are more likely than men to initiate divorce, and the initiating spouse typically experiences high levels of stress in the period leading up to the decision to divorce and then corresponding levels of relief following this decision (whereas the noninitiating spouse—typically the husband—experiences the greatest stress following the decision to divorce).

In addition to exploring reactions to the dissolution of marital and other romantic relationships, scientists have investigated responses and adjustment to the loss of an intimate partner due to death. Shock, helplessness, depression, and other symptoms of emotional distress are among the most common initial responses among individuals who have lost a spouse (Farnsworth, Lund, & Pett, 1989; Stroebe & Stroebe, 1987). Researchers have also found, however, that there is a great deal of variability in the intensity and duration of distress experienced by widowed men and women. Some people recover relatively rapidly from their initial grief, others remain mired in depression for an extended period of time, and still others show little grief at all (Bonanno et al., 2002; Bonanno, Wortman, & Nesse, 2004; Naef, Ward, Mahrer-Imhof, & Grande, 2013). There appears to be no "normal" or "universal" way of responding to a major interpersonal loss—rather, people react to the death of a partner or a relationship in many different ways.

## Summary

Conflict and disagreements are part and parcel of close relationships. Whether a relationship survives conflict (or whether partners survive termination) is, to a large extent, determined by how that conflict (or termination) is managed. People who communicate their needs and feelings clearly and who acknowledge and support those of their partner are more likely to resolve conflict (or accomplish termination) in a manner that benefits both themselves and their partners. There is no single, universal reaction to the loss of a valued romantic relationship; rather, a variety of both positive and negative outcomes and responses are possible.

## Key Concepts

Attributions (p. 100)

Causal attributions (p. 100)

Responsibility attributions (p. 101)

Attributional conflict (p. 103)

Meta-attribution (p. 104)

Structural improvement (as an ending to conflict) (p. 106)

Integrative agreement (as an ending to conflict) (p. 106)

Compromise (as an ending to conflict) (p. 106)

Domination (as an ending to conflict) (p. 106)

Separation (as an ending to conflict) (p. 107)

Positive conflict resolution strategies (p. 108)

Reason (p. 108)

Assertion (p. 108)

Partner support (p. 108)

Negative conflict resolution strategies (p. 108)

Coercion (p. 108)

Manipulation (p. 108)

Avoidance (p. 108)

Demand-withdraw pattern (p. 108)

Emotional indifference (p. 111)

Cognitive disconnection (p. 111)

Behavioral distancing (p. 111)

Phases of relationship dissolution (pp. 113–116)

Intrapsychic phase (p. 113)

Dyadic phase (p. 114)

Social phase (p. 114)

Grave-dressing phase (p. 114)

Resurrection phase (p. 116)

Disengagement strategies (p. 116)

Indirect vs. direct dimension of relationship disengagement (p. 116)

Other vs. self-orientation dimension of relationship disengagement (p. 116)

Accounts (p. 119)

## Discussion Questions

1. Orvis, Kelley, and Butler (1976) identified several attributional events that occur during times of conflict. Using an example from your own life, describe these attributional events.

2. Relationship scholars propose that conflicts may end in five different ways (structural improvement, integrative agreement, compromise, domination, separation). Using specific examples from your own life, illustrate and discuss each possible ending. Which ending did you find to be the most satisfying or beneficial (to you, to your partner, to your relationship)? Which one had the most harmful consequences?

3. Identify three "positive" and three "negative" strategies for managing or resolving conflict. Think of a situation in which you or someone you know has made use of one or more of these strategies. What was the outcome? Was the strategy effective?

4. Many of us hold fairly negative attitudes toward prenuptial agreements— yet partners make these agreements prior to marriage in an effort to estab- lish a set of mutually agreed-upon rules of conduct and thus to avoid future conflict and disagreement. Working together with a classmate or peer, con- struct a prenuptial agreement. You may pretend to be an engaged couple or two attorneys representing the partners' interests. As you draft the agree- ment, consider as many aspects of married life as you can (for example, finances; children—number, care and discipline, education, religion, etc.; family vacations; pets; living arrangements; division of labor/household chores; and so forth).

5. People may dissolve their romantic relationships in a number of different ways, several of which are outlined by Baxter's (1985) model. For this exer- cise, you will need to think of a relationship that you once were involved in but that has now ended. How did that relationship dissolve? Regardless of your own role (i.e., whether you were the leaver or the one who was left), consider whether the ending was primarily other-oriented or self-oriented, and primarily direct or indirect. What specific strategy do you think best exemplifies your situation (e.g., fait accompli, negotiated farewell, with- drawal, fading away)? How did this strategy affect your feelings after the relationship ended?

6. What is an account? Why do people create accounts when experiencing relationship dissolution?

## Recommended Readings

These authors present evidence that the way in which couples think about their own and their partner's behavior is associated with relationship adjustment.

Bradbury, T. N., & Fincham, F. D. (1990). Attributions in marriage: Review and critique. *Psychological Bulletin, 107,* 3–33.

Orvis, B. R., Kelley, H. H., & Butler, D. (1976). Attributional conflict in young couples. In J. H. Harvey, W. J. Ickes, & R. F. Kidd (Eds.), *New directions in attribution research* (Vol. 1, pp. 353–386). Hillsdale, NJ: Erlbaum.

This chapter presents some of the first empirical data gathered on the role of conflict in romantic relationship development.

Braiker, H. B., & Kelley, H. H. (1979). Conflict in the development of close relationships. In R. L. Burgess & T. L. Huston (Eds.), *Social exchange in developing relationships* (pp. 135–168). New York, NY: Academic Press.

This edited book contains chapters focusing on divorce and relationship dissolution, including historical and demographic aspects of relationship termination, causes and underlying processes implicated in divorce, the consequences of divorce, coping with relationship dissolution, relationship termination among understudied groups, and policy issues pertaining to divorce.

Fine, M. A., & Harvey, J. H. (Eds.). (2006). *Handbook of divorce and dissolution.* Mahwah, NJ: Erlbaum.

# 6

# Intervention

There is no doubt that most people value their long-term, committed romantic relationships and invest a good deal of time and energy into making them "work." Nonetheless, as we saw in Chapter 5, many couples will experience decreased satisfaction along with episodes of conflict and tension during the course of their relationships—and many relationships wil' ultimately end. When partners become dissatisfied or realize that their relationship is in trouble, some of them will seek assistance from a professional. In this chapter, we explore the topic of relationship intervention, including the ways therapists identify and treat troubled relationships and whether therapy truly can provide help for couples in distress.

## ❖ IDENTIFYING DISTRESSED RELATIONSHIPS

Before a therapist can effectively intervene in a troubled relationship, he or she must first identify the dysfunctional thoughts, feelings, and behaviors that are contributing to the couple's distress. In Chapter 5, we saw that the way in which partners interpret each other's behavior and how they respond to conflict are strongly associated with the overall health of their relationship. For example, couples whose communication style is characterized by high levels of demand-withdraw behavior and who routinely use negative conflict resolution strategies are more likely to experience long-term distress than are couples who do not fall prey to these dysfunctional processes.

### Unhealthy Attributional Styles

In addition to identifying the attributional processes that occur during conflict (see Chapter 5), researchers also have discovered that particular patterns or characteristic ways of making attributions are associated with relationship well-being. In their exhaustive review of the marital attribution literature, Thomas Bradbury and Frank Fincham (1990) concluded that there is a clear association between a couple's *attributional style,* or characteristic way of interpreting and responding to each other's behavior, and their marital quality. Subsequent research has continued to substantiate this conclusion (see Bradbury, Fincham, & Beach, 2000; Durtschi, Fincham, Cui, Lorenz, & Conger, 2011; Fincham, Paleari, & Regalia, 2002; Karney & Bradbury, 2000; Lavner, Bradbury, & Karney, 2012).

Recall from Chapter 5 that people make both causal and responsibility attributions when attempting to understand the reasons behind a partner's behavior. Research reveals that individuals in nondistressed relationships generally explain the partner's positive behavior as being due to his or her internal disposition and believe that the cause of the behavior will be stable over time and globally influential in a variety of marital situations; moreover, they tend to view the positive behavior as freely chosen and intentional, and therefore worthy of praise (see Figure 6.1). Nondistressed individuals attribute negative partner behavior to external circumstance or the partner's temporary state and believe that these circumstances or states will be unstable over time and specific to that one marital area. They assume that such behavior was unintentional and thus tend not to blame the partner for its occurrence. By enhancing the impact of positive events and minimizing the impact of negative events, this particular attributional pattern promotes relational well-being.

Distressed partners demonstrate the opposite attributional pattern. Specifically, they attribute each other's positive behaviors to situational (rather than dispositional) causes, assume that these causes are unstable and unlikely to be repeated, and believe that these causes are operative in one specific situation rather than in many or all marital situations (see Figure 6.2). Essentially, a distressed spouse views a partner who does something positive as "having acted unintentionally and with less positive and more negative intent, having little control over the cause of the event, being influenced by a temporary state rather than by a persisting trait, behaving involuntarily, being motivated by selfish concerns, being less deserving of praise, and having a less positive attitude toward the respondent" (Bradbury & Fincham, 1990, p. 5). Conversely, negative behaviors are attributed to the partner's enduring dispositional characteristics; these causes are believed to be stable over time and are perceived as globally influential across marital situations rather than as specific to one or a few situations. In addition, the partner is perceived as having acted deliberately and with harmful intent, and consequently as deserving of blame. By discounting positive events and accentuating the impact of negative ones, this unhealthy attributional pattern undermines relationship satisfaction and promotes distress and dysfunction.

## Dysfunctional Interaction Styles

Researchers and clinicians also have identified a number of destructive interaction styles that erode relationship quality and prevent individuals from resolving conflicts and achieving satisfying interpersonal outcomes. Many of these involve the behavior and affect (i.e., feelings, emotions, and sentiments) that the partners display during times of disagreement or tension. Based on extensive observation and analysis of the interaction behavior of happily and unhappily married couples, clinical researcher John Gottman (e.g., 1994b, 1999; Coan & Gottman, 2007) identified four ways of interacting that are particularly corrosive

**Figure 6.1** Happy Couples Make Relationship-Promoting Attributions

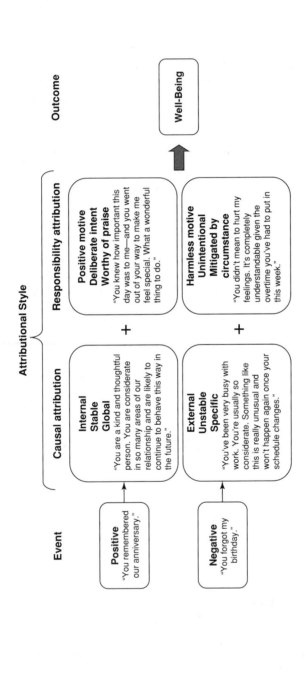

NOTE: After reviewing the marital attribution literature, Thomas Bradbury and Frank Fincham (1990) concluded that there is a clear association between marital satisfaction and attributional styles. People in nondistressed relationships tend to attribute positive partner behaviors to internal, stable, and global causes, and to view the partner as having intentionally acted from selfless and positive motives. They tend to attribute negative partner behaviors to external, unstable, and specific causes, and to perceive the partner as not responsible for the events in question. This healthy attributional pattern enhances the impact of positive events and minimizes the impact of negative ones, and therefore promotes marital function and well-being.

**Figure 6.2**   Distressed Couples Make Relationship-Harming Attributions

**Attributional Style**

**Event**

**Causal attribution**

**Responsibility attribution**

**Outcome**

**Positive**
"You remembered our anniversary."

**External**
**Unstable**
**Specific**
"Well, this is quite a surprise. Your secretary must have reminded you. You're usually not so thoughtful. I'm sure it won't happen again. You never remember other special occasions."

+

**Selfish motive**
**Unintentional**
**Not worthy of praise**
"You normally don't do anything for our anniversary. What's really going on? Are you still trying to get out of going to my parents' for Thanksgiving? You are so manipulative."

**Negative**
"You forgot my birthday."

**Internal**
**Stable**
**Global**
"You are so inconsiderate—of course you forgot my special day. You never remember things that matter to me. This is just one more example of your selfishness."

+

**Harmful motive**
**Deliberate intent**
**Worthy of blame**
"You know how important this day is to me and yet you conveniently "forgot" all about it. Were you trying to upset me? I cannot believe how mean you are."

**Distress**

NOTE: People in distressed marriages demonstrate the opposite attributional pattern. They attribute positive partner behaviors to external, unstable, and specific causes, and view them as unintentional, motivated by selfish concerns, and not worthy of praise. Conversely, they attribute negative partner behaviors to internal, stable, and global causes, and perceive them as stemming from deliberate and harmful motives. This unhealthy attributional pattern diminishes or discounts the impact of positive events and accentuates the impact of negative events, thereby promoting marital distress and dysfunction.

131

to marital happiness: criticism, contempt, defensiveness, and withdrawal. (These behaviors are so lethal to relationship well-being that Gottman called them "The Four Horsemen of the Apocalypse" in reference to the four horsemen that personify Pestilence, War, Famine, and Death in the New Testament's Book of Revelation.)

*Criticism* refers to "supercharged" complaints that attack the partner's character or personality and that are usually accompanied with blame. Unlike complaints about specific actions ("I'm really upset that you accepted that invitation without asking me first"), criticisms involve generalizations about the partner: "You never consult with me before making plans. You always think about yourself and what you want to do. You never think to include me in any decisions that affect us as a couple." Criticism may take a variety of forms, including *blaming*, in which the person assigns fault to the partner along with a personal attack or general accusation ("Now the entire weekend is ruined. This is all your fault—you never check with me before making plans"); *character attacks*, in which the person criticizes the partner's character, personality, or abilities in very general ways ("You are completely selfish. All you do is think about yourself. You are completely incapable of seeing things from anyone else's perspective"); and *kitchen sinking*, in which the person expresses a long list of complaints to showcase the partner's deficiencies ("You never check with me about making plans, and you never ask for my input on weekend activities, and you never take into consideration my feelings, and you always do whatever you want . . ."). According to Gottman (1994b), few couples can completely avoid complaining about things they wish were otherwise or expressing their dissatisfaction with a particular situation. Moreover, the airing of complaints can actually be a healthy activity to the extent that it facilitates open communication and produces positive change in the relationship. (Indeed, we discussed in Chapter 5 how many conflicts, when addressed with open and direct communication, may lead to structural improvement in a couple's relationship.) However, complaints that place blame on the partner or that attack his or her character are not healthy and are likely to negatively impact a couple's union.

If unresolved, criticism is usually followed by *contempt*—statements or actions that are directly intended to insult the partner and inflict psychological damage. Some of the most common signs of contempt include insults and name-calling, hostile humor, mockery, and body language that communicates a lack of respect for the partner (e.g., sneering, rolling one's eyes, curling the upper lip, raising the eyebrows).

He says, sarcastically, "I didn't realize that marriage meant being joined at the hip all the time."

She says, sneering, "And I didn't realize marriage meant I'd be shackled to a narcissistic jerk."

He says, curling his lip, "Better a narcissist than a control freak."

She says, rolling her eyes, "You're such an idiot. I don't know why I ever married you."

Contempt is particularly damaging because once it enters the relationship, the partners experience what Gottman (1994b) called the "immediate decay of admiration" (p. 80)—they find it nearly impossible to remember even one of each other's positive qualities or behaviors. Contempt is so corrosive to a relationship's health that Gottman stated that it ought to be banned from all marital interactions.

When faced with a partner's criticism and contempt, it is difficult for the other partner not to become defensive. *Defensiveness* includes feeling victimized, unfairly treated, or attacked by the partner, particularly during times of disagreement. Forms of defensiveness include *denying responsibility* ("It's not my fault I didn't tell you about the invitation. You never asked"), *making excuses* ("I tried to tell you but I got home too late and you were already asleep"), *cross-complaining* ("Well, you never tell me about invitations we get"), *minimization* ("So what if I didn't tell you before? I'm telling you now. No harm done"), and *aggressive defenses* (vehement, heated denials that come across as childish; "I did tell you!" "No, you didn't!" "Yes, I did!"). In addition, partners who are feeling defensive have a tendency to endlessly reiterate their own positions without truly listening to what the other is saying ("As I said before . . .," "Once again. . . .") and to make what Gottman (1994b) called "yes-but statements," in which they admit to their behavior but then claim that it was morally justified ("Yes, it's true I didn't tell you, but that's because I had to rush out to take your parents to the airport"). There are also nonverbal actions that are frequently associated with defensiveness, such as using a whiny or high-pitched tone of voice, shifting the body from side-to-side, folding the arms across the chest or placing them on the hips, and giving a false smile in which the corners of the mouth rise but the eyes do not change.

The final "horseman" identified by Gottman (1994b) is *withdrawal* or *stonewalling*, which essentially involves removing oneself from the interaction in a way that conveys cold disapproval, icy distance, and smugness. When stonewalling, a person's face typically appears "frozen" or stiff; the jaw may be clenched and the neck muscles strained, or the face may be deliberately calm and composed so as to seem emotionally neutral. Stonewalling or withdrawal often happens while a couple is talking. For example, when faced with a partner's criticism or contempt, an individual may fail to respond or react at all (e.g., by shrugging his or her shoulders, turning away, checking a cell phone, or picking up a book or magazine). He or she may offer monosyllabic responses ("Hmm"), verbally refuse to engage in the interaction ("Whatever," "Yeah, fine"), or display what Gottman calls "active away behaviors" that communicate an unwillingness to pay attention to the partner (e.g., examining or playing with one's hair, cleaning one's fingernails). Or an individual may physically remove himself or herself from the situation by walking away or leaving the room. Because it involves a refusal to communicate, habitual withdrawal is often a sign of a severely dysfunctional relationship.

Clinical research reveals that all four of these interaction styles are associated with marital dissatisfaction. For example, in one early investigation (Gottman & Krokoff, 1989), a sample of married couples completed measures of marital satisfaction and then were videotaped while they discussed an ongoing area of disagreement in their marriage. Observers later examined these videotaped interactions for the presence and amount of the following negative behaviors: (1) *criticism* (e.g., hostile statements expressing unambiguous dislike or disapproval of the partner's behavior and made in an irritated or hostile tone of voice), (2) *contempt* (mockery, sarcasm, insults, ridicule, derision, and other verbal content, tone of voice, facial expressions, gestures, and body movements indicative of contempt), (3) *defensiveness* (e.g., excuse making, denying responsibility), and (4) *withdrawal* (e.g., nonresponsiveness to the partner, not tracking the partner's comments or conversation, turning off or away from the partner, incoherent talk). The results revealed that the frequency with which husbands and wives expressed criticism and contempt during the interaction was negatively correlated both with their own and with their spouses' marital happiness; in other words, the more often that a man criticized or displayed contempt for his wife, or a woman criticized or displayed contempt for her husband, the less satisfied both were with the quality of their marriage. In addition, the more often a wife withdrew from her husband during the interaction, and the more often a husband demonstrated defensiveness toward his wife, the less satisfied both partners were with their marriage. These four interaction styles clearly are associated with marital unhappiness.

## Negative Reciprocity

Unhappy couples also frequently display *negative reciprocity* (also called *negative affect reciprocity*), which is defined as a behavior sequence in which one partner's expression of negativity (verbal or nonverbal) is subsequently reciprocated by the other partner (Baucom, Baucom, & Christensen, 2012; Carstensen, Gottman, & Levenson, 1995; for a review, see Gottman, 1998). The tendency to respond in kind to negative behavior is a hallmark of distressed relationships—unhappy couples appear to be exquisitely sensitive to each other's behavior (in particular, to each other's *negative* behavior). Unfortunately, partners who return each other's negative behavior can find themselves trapped in an extended (and quite destructive) cycle of negativity. For example, consider Steve and Donna, an unhappily married couple. Steve forgets Donna's birthday. She, in turn, "forgets" to remind him about an important doctor's appointment. He then harshly criticizes her in front of their children, and she insults him during dinner with their friends. Steve decides to have an affair, and when Donna finds out she has one as well. And the cycle continues.

Extended cycles of negativity may also develop during the course of one interaction episode:

> "Did you remember to send in the mortgage payment? The late fee we were charged last month really tapped into our savings."

> "Would you get off my back? So I forgot. It was one time. I am sick and tired of you nagging me about it."

> "Nagging? Since when is being responsible the same as nagging? And besides, you're the one who's always complaining about things."

> "Hardly. I didn't say a word about dinner last night, even though you were so late that you missed most of it."

> "You didn't have to say anything—you made your feelings pretty clear when you got up and left the table after I sat down. What a nice 'welcome home' that was for me after a long work day."

> "Well, if you'd taken the time to call and let me know you'd be late, maybe I'd have felt more welcoming. Guess they don't have phones at your office."

Happy couples also sometimes display negative reciprocity in their interactions. Unlike unhappy couples, however, they are able to exit the destructive cycle. One partner simply does not return the other partner's negative behavior, but instead responds positively or neutrally:

> "Did you remember to send in the mortgage payment? The late fee we were charged last month really tapped into our savings."

"Would you get off my back? So I forgot. It was one time. I am sick and tired of you nagging me about it."

"I guess I have mentioned it a lot lately. Sorry about that. I think I've become kind of obsessed about saving for our vacation—I'm so excited about it."

"I'm sorry, too. I shouldn't have snapped at you. We do need to save for our trip—and it's going to be so much fun!"

Both distressed and nondistressed couples often attempt to disrupt negative interactions by using *repair attempts*—humor, distraction, information exchange, appeals to basic values, finding areas of common ground, and other communication processes that are designed to reduce overt negativity and channel the interaction in a more positive direction (Gottman, 1998, 1999). In the examples above, the second partner has attempted to divert the negative flow of the interaction by saying, probably with some irritation or hurt, "Stop bringing [my failure to pay the mortgage last month] up all the time." Repair attempts such as this one generally have two components: an informational component (the content of what is being communicated—in this instance, "Stop bringing this issue up") and an emotional component (the accompanying negative affect—here, irritation or hurt). What seems to separate distressed and nondistressed couples is which part of the repair attempt they focus on. Happy, well-functioning couples attend primarily to the content of what has been said and are able to ignore the negative emotion, so the repair attempt generally works. Conversely, poorly-functioning couples focus primarily on the negative emotion rather than the informational content of the attempt, the repair thus fails, tension continues to rise, and the partners find themselves stuck in their destructive cycle of negativity.

## Ratio of Positive to Negative Behavior

Another factor that clearly distinguishes unhappy from happy couples is the *ratio of positive to negative behavior* that they display during conflict or problem-solving discussions. A series of investigations conducted by Gottman and his colleagues (e.g., Gottman & Levenson, 1992) has consistently revealed that couples in stable, satisfying relationships typically engage in about five positive behaviors for every negative behavior—in other words, they show a 5:1 ratio of positive to negative affect and behavior in their interactions. Couples who are unhappy and prone to divorce, however, show a positive to negative ratio of 0.8:1 (i.e., slightly more negative than positive behavior).

Gottman's research suggests that couples may achieve the 5:1 ratio of positive to negative behavior in several different ways (Gottman, 1993; also see Bodenmann, Gottman, & Backman, 1997). For example, during disagreements, *volatile couples* tend to confront the conflict openly, argue heatedly, and spend most of their time enthusiastically trying to persuade one another about the validity of their own opinion or viewpoint. These couples are passionate and extremely emotionally expressive, and are more likely than other couples to display and to reciprocate both positive (e.g., affection, humor, interest) and negative (e.g., tension, anger) affect. They achieve the 5:1 ratio by engaging in high levels of intensely negative affective behavior and even higher levels of intensely positive affective behavior. The other couple types demonstrate less frequent positive and negative behavior and have more neutral interactions. Like volatile couples, *validating couples* also confront conflict and display emotion openly, but their discussions are characterized by less emotional intensity and greater ease and calm. Recognition and support of—though not necessarily agreement with—the partner's feelings, statements, or description of a problem or issue is a fundamental theme in the interactions of these couples; indeed, in their conversations "there is often the sense that, although there is disagreement between them, they are both working together on a problem" (Gottman, 1993, p. 10). Validators achieve the 5:1 ratio by mixing a moderate amount of positive behavior with a moderate but lower amount of negative behavior. *Avoider couples* demonstrate the lowest levels of expressed emotion and the highest levels of neutral affect, essentially achieving the 5:1 ratio by avoiding negativity. These couples tend to minimize the importance of disagreement, feel that any differences they have are relatively easy to accept or ignore in light of their fundamental similarities, do not have specific conflict resolution strategies (e.g., they prefer to "let things work themselves out"), and make little effort to actively persuade each other or problem solve. Avoiders experience a great deal of calm interaction, but the result is a marriage characterized by some degree of emotional distance between the partners.

On the basis of Gottman's extensive program of research, many clinical researchers and practitioners now believe that the 5:1 ratio is optimal for relationship well-being.

## Failed Bids for Emotional Connection

How couples respond to each other during times of conflict clearly plays an important role in the overall health of their relationship. Interestingly, the seemingly trivial, mundane events that occur during their everyday interactions may be equally important. A growing number of relationship scholars have noted that partners often make an effort to establish intimacy and to connect with each other emotionally as they go about their daily lives and engage in their ordinary interactions (see Gottman & Gottman, 2008; Wile, 1993). For example, after examining hours of videotaped interactions between married couples, John Gottman and Janice Driver (2005) identified a variety of verbal and non-verbal ways in which partners demand emotional involvement from each other. These *bids for emotional connection* include the following:

- Bids for attention—"That's a funny-looking dog over there."
- Bids for interest—"Doesn't your sister's dog look a little bit like that?"
- Bids for enthusiastic engagement—"Hey, maybe we should think about getting a dog."
- Bids for extended conversation—"Have you heard from your sister lately? The last time we saw her she was about to start that new job."
- Bids for play—(reaching out and tickling the partner) "I've been thinking about doing that all day!"
- Bids for humor—"That dog reminds me of a joke I heard. A poodle walks into a bar. . . ."
- Bids for affection—(reaching for the partner's hand, etc.) "I need a hug."
- Bids for emotional support—"I'm still so worried about my job. I hope I don't get laid off."
- Bids for self-disclosure—"What kind of dog did your family have when you were growing up?"

Partners can respond to each other's bids for emotional connection in three basic ways. First, they may display what Gottman and Driver (2005) called "turning toward" responses, in which they react in an appropriate manner to the bid for connection; such responses can range from lower levels of acknowledgment (e.g., a grunt to indicate that they have heard the partner's statement or question) to whole-hearted and enthusiastic replies. Second, partners may respond by "turning away" from the bid for connection. For example, they may simply ignore the other's statements or actions. And finally, partners may engage in "turning against" responses, in which they display an irritable, hostile, or negative reaction to the bid for emotional connection (e.g., "Would you stop bothering me? I'm trying to read").

These everyday exchanges between partners may have important consequences for the health and well-being of their relationship. For example, partners who consistently acknowledge and respond positively to each other's bids for emotional connection may build up a reservoir of positive affect that can help them successfully weather stormy periods in their relationship. Partners with a history of failed bids for connection, however, may not have sufficient positive emotional reserves to fall back on when experiencing a major disagreement and thus may be more likely to use ineffective conflict resolution strategies. Indeed, in a series of studies, Gottman and Driver (2005; Driver & Gottman, 2004) found that the more positive everyday moments that partners shared—for instance, the greater their frequency of playful bids for affection and enthusiastic responses to those bids—the more likely they were to display positive affect and humor during an argument. Conversely, the more often that partners turned away from each other's bids for emotional connection during everyday interactions, the more likely they were to display negative affective and behavioral responses during conflict (including criticism, contempt, defensiveness, and withdrawal). In discussing the results of their studies, the researchers concluded that it is important for relationship therapists to address not just how couples manage conflict but also how they respond to each other in their everyday interactions:

> Clinically, we are suggesting that the therapist specifically look with the couple at *failed bids for emotional connection* that happened during the week as well as conflicts that are upsetting to the couple. This suggests a therapeutic focus beyond the conflict context. . . . The bids and turning unit can help people become more attentive and mindful to this mundane part of their everyday relationship, to the everyday times when they are just "hanging out," when nothing important seems to be happening but when actually very important things are happening. It is our clinical experience that failed bids for connection and subsequent loneliness are a major source of marital conflict. Just helping a couple become mindful of these moments and investigating the "anatomies" of bidding and turning can provide insight that is capable of changing the nature of marital intimacy and the nature of conflict interactions as well. (Gottman & Driver, 2005, p. 76)

## ❖ TREATING DISTRESSED RELATIONSHIPS

Not every couple who enters a therapist's office seeking help will actually receive it. Reputable clinicians and counselors will first take steps to determine whether the treatment approach they offer is likely to provide relief to the couple. In some cases, the answer will be "no" and the couple will be referred to another professional or encouraged to try a different form of treatment. For example, partners who are dealing with a sexual issue may be referred to a sex therapist specializing in that area of function. Couples whose relationships are characterized by alcohol, drug addiction, or physical violence also need immediate treatment from a professional who is trained to deal with those particular issues. And some couples may not wish to repair their relationship but instead enter therapy in hopes of finding a way to end their partnership amicably; in those cases, referral to a legal, family, or mental health professional who specializes in relationship dissolution or divorce mediation is in order. However, assuming that the couple wishes to maintain the relationship and is not dealing with any of the specific problems previously mentioned, there are several different types of therapy available.

## Behavioral Couple Therapy

*Behavioral couple therapy* (BCT) is based on the idea that the rewards and costs that partners experience in their interactions with each other determine how satisfied they are with their relationship (Simpson, Gattis, & Christensen, 2003). The goal of BCT is to modify partners' behavior using principles derived from social learning theory and social exchange theory (Jacobson & Margolin, 1979; for a review, see Gurman, 2013). There are three major components of the typical BCT therapeutic program: *behavior exchange, communication training,* and *problem-solving training.* In behavior exchange, clients are taught to identify the partner behaviors they find desirable or offensive, to monitor their own and their partner's behaviors, to increase their awareness of the consequences of their own behavior, and to show appropriate acknowledgment of their partner's positive behavior. For example, the therapist might ask each partner to create a list of positive behaviors that he or she believes the other would like (such as receiving a compliment, being given a gift, not having to do the dishes, watching a movie, eating out at a favorite restaurant, and so forth). The other partner would then rate each of those behaviors in terms of their desirability. At that point, the therapist is able to generate a list of highly rewarding or positive behaviors for each partner. Then, the therapist encourages the partners to actually engage in those positive actions—either by doing one or more each day or by setting aside a "caring day" to enact multiple behaviors—and provides guidance and support as needed.

BCT also involves teaching couples effective communication skills, including how to develop and make use of active listening skills and how to express themselves without blame and accusation. For example, a distressed couple might be instructed in how to replace statements that express blame and generalizations about the partner's behavior ("You never listen to me") with "I statements" that convey how the partner's behavior makes them feel ("When you don't answer me, it makes me feel as if I'm unimportant to you") and that contain specific requests ("It would make me happy if you would ask me about my day during dinner"). In addition to learning specific communication skills, couples receive training in effective problem solving, including how to clearly and concretely define problems and issues, how to generate possible solutions to those issues, how to negotiate and compromise on possible solutions, how to actually implement the proposed solution, and how to evaluate the effectiveness of the solution.

## Cognitive-Behavioral Couple Therapy

*Cognitive-behavioral couple therapy* (CBCT) grew out of the recognition that it is not just negative behavior that can create discord between relationship partners but also how they interpret that behavior and the meaning they place on it (e.g., Baucom & Boeding, 2013; Baucom & Epstein, 1990; Baucom, Epstein, & Rankin, 1995). In addition to traditional BCT techniques, CBCT uses *cognitive restructuring* to facilitate the partners' ability to recognize, systematically evaluate, and change their maladaptive cognitions, assumptions, and expectations about each other, their relationship, and relationships in general. For example, when clients make sweeping negative generalizations about their partner's behavior ("He never listens to me"), the therapist might ask them to search for exceptions ("Is it true that he really *never* listens to you? Can you think of one instance when he did?"). When clients make negative attributions about their partner's behavior ("I had a bad headache—I just needed some peace and quiet and she had her music blaring even though I was clearly in pain"), the therapist might challenge them to seek an alternative explanation for the same behavior ("Is it possible that she didn't know you had a headache? Did you directly communicate this information to her?"). And the therapist might help clients identify the unrealistic standards and beliefs they hold about relationships—such as the assumptions that "True love means never getting angry with each other" and "Happy couples never argue"—and then assist them in replacing these standards with more realistic expectations ("Conflict occurs in even the most loving and stable of relationships").

## Integrative Behavioral Couple Therapy

The most recent adaptation of BCT is called *integrative behavioral couple therapy* (IBCT). This therapeutic approach was developed by Neil Jacobson and Andrew Christensen (1996; Christensen & Jacobson, 2000; Jacobson, Christensen, Prince, Cordova, & Eldridge, 2000) after they observed that many couples experience issues, problems, or incompatibilities that are difficult to change and that cannot readily be resolved (and indeed often are exacerbated) by traditional BCT and CBCT approaches, which focus on change as the primary mechanism for the reduction of distress. IBCT often is referred to as "acceptance therapy" because it integrates the basic premises and behavioral and cognitive techniques of BCT and CBCT with strategies that are designed to promote the partners' acceptance of each other's entire personality as well as tolerance of each other's behavior. During therapy sessions, partners are asked to remember and to accept the following facts:

> The good qualities you like in your partner may be part of a natural constellation that includes some qualities that you don't like. Your partner's personality is inevitably a "package deal," and you have no "line-item veto" whereby you can cancel some qualities but keep others. (Christensen & Jacobson, 2000, p. 74)

The goal of therapy is not for the partners simply to become resigned to their existing unhappy state of affairs, but rather to learn how to change their expectations about the relationship and the partner, modify their behavior to better meet each other's needs, improve their communication and problem-solving skills, and learn how to better accept and tolerate any differences and issues that are not amenable to change. Consequently, IBCT therapists use traditional behavioral techniques (i.e., behavior exchange, communication skills and problem-solving training) coupled with techniques specifically designed to increase acceptance and tolerance. For example, one *acceptance technique* therapists commonly use is to encourage couples to replace *hard disclosures* that convey anger and resentment and place the speaker in the dominant role (e.g., "You are so selfish. You never ask me how my day went. You think only of yourself. I am sick and tired of this") with *soft disclosures* that express the vulnerability and hurt hiding behind the anger (e.g., "I feel like my needs don't matter in this relationship, that what I do and how I spend my time isn't important. Sometimes I feel completely alone"). By allowing both partners to feel as if they are being heard by one another in an atmosphere of neutrality and empathy rather than one of dominance, blame, and anger, this technique encourages mutual acceptance. Additionally, therapists utilize *tolerance strategies*—including pointing out the positive features of negative partner behavior, having couples practice negative behavior during therapy sessions, and having couples "fake" negative behavior in between therapy sessions—to desensitize the partners to each other's negative behavior and to sensitize them to the impact of their own negative behavior. For example, the therapist might have the couple role play a "just arrived home from a long day at work" scenario (one that typically produces conflict) and deliberately exaggerate their negative responses to one another—in doing so, they might see the impact their actions have, find some humor in the situation, and reduce negative emotion (both in the therapy session itself and later on when the situation arises in real life).

Interestingly, as partners become more tolerant and accepting of each other, and the pressure to change diminishes, they tend to become less emotionally sensitive and reactive to one another's problematic behaviors, and this often prompts the very changes that were initially desired (Dimidjian, Martell, & Christensen, 2008).

## Emotionally Focused Couple Therapy

In contrast to the behavioral therapies previously discussed, *emotionally focused couple therapy* (ECT) is rooted in principles of attachment theory, including the basic premise that all people possess an innate need to form strong, intimate, warm bonds to particular individuals and that failure to meet this need and/or disruption of these bonds will produce distress. (See Chapter 16 for a more detailed discussion of attachment theory.) Developed by Leslie Greenberg and Susan Johnson (1988; Johnson, 2004, 2008, 2009; Johnson & Greenberg, 1995), ECT recognizes that the partner functions as a primary and important attachment figure and that negative relationship events and the emotions that accompany these events thus often reflect the operation of underlying attachment-related issues, such as a fear of abandonment. For example, one of the reasons that people usually respond to a partner's expressions of criticism or contempt with anguish and diminished relational satisfaction is in part because such expressions directly convey that the partner considers them unworthy of love, affection, and care. Similarly, interaction patterns that reflect absence and/or a failure or unwillingness to respond to a partner's needs—such as withdrawal or stonewalling—increase separation distress and threaten attachment security. Other rigid behavioral and cognitive patterns, like negative reciprocity and harmful attributional styles, also maintain feelings of insecurity and make it difficult for the partners to experience emotional bonding.

The goal of ECT is to enable the partners to achieve a secure attachment bond characterized by mutual emotional accessibility and responsiveness. In therapy, partners are encouraged to identify and express their underlying needs, expectations, and emotional experiences (such as their expectations about partner caregiving and fears about partner abandonment). As the therapeutic process progresses, the partners gain valuable information about themselves and each other and are then able, with the help of the therapist, to develop interaction patterns that are more likely to satisfy their underlying attachment needs. For example, the therapist might help Julie, who is angry and hurt because her husband, Jim, has chosen to return to work after years of retirement, recognize and access her underlying fear of abandonment and then express this fear directly to Jim, rather than her surface anger and hurt ("I feel that you don't want to be with me—that your decision to go back to work means that you aren't happy at home. I need reassurance that I matter to you, that you need me, and that you aren't turning away from me. I feel alone in this marriage and that scares me.") Once he recognizes that fear is at the root of Julie's anger and upset, Jim might be able to respond with greater support and caring and less defensiveness and withdrawal ("I do have a tendency to shut you out. I didn't realize that you were lonely and that my returning to work made you feel unloved and abandoned. I just saw you as critical and angry all the time—I didn't see your hurt and sadness. I want to be close to you, but I enjoy working and I need you to understand that it doesn't mean I don't want to be with you."). Together, the two of them may establish a more functional interaction pattern that better meets their basic attachment needs.

## ❖ DOES THERAPY WORK?

Clinical researchers have attempted to address the question of whether couple therapy "works" in a number of ways. The most common method involves comparing distressed couples who receive therapy with distressed couples who do not receive therapy on various measures of well-being and adjustment. If the couples who received therapy (the treatment group) score significantly higher on measures of satisfaction or significantly lower on measures of distress than the couples who did not receive therapy (the no-treatment control group), then the researchers can conclude that therapy is effective. The results of studies that have employed this type of comparison consistently reveal that therapy is better than no therapy at all; that is, treatment couples generally show less distress than control group couples (e.g., Baucom, Hahlweg, & Kuschel, 2003; Shadish & Baldwin, 2005).

However, in their exhaustive review of the marital therapy literature, Andrew Christensen and Christopher Heavey (1999) observed that simply demonstrating that there is a difference between treatment couples and control group couples does not provide conclusive evidence that therapy is effective. For example, it is possible for the couples who received treatment to be less distressed than the couples who did not and yet still show significant levels of dysfunction; in other words, although the therapy has improved their situation relative to the control group, it has not fully alleviated their distress. Consequently, it is important to assess therapeutic effectiveness by evaluating treatment couples against an absolute standard—such as whether they obtain satisfaction, adjustment, or well-being scores in the "normal" range following treatment—rather than by simply comparing their scores to those of a control group.

It is equally essential to assess how long any therapy-induced improvements can be expected to last. Research suggests that most forms of couple therapy—whether behavioral, cognitive-behavioral, integrative-behavioral, or emotionally focused—produce significant and relatively enduring benefits for partners in distressed relationships (e.g., Byrne, Carr, & Clark, 2004; Hahlweg & Markman, 1988; Lebow, Chambers, Christensen, & Johnson, 2012; Shadish & Baldwin, 2005). For example, a meta-analysis of treatment outcome studies conducted by Michael Byrne, Alan Carr, and Marie Clark (2004) revealed that roughly two thirds of couples who received BCT or ECT experienced significant increases in their relationship satisfaction during the treatment period, with 50% to 60% falling in the nondistressed range and about half maintaining those improvements over follow-up periods lasting from two months to several years later. Similar results have been reported for CBCT and IBCT (see Christensen & Heavey, 1999; Lebow et al., 2012; Wesley & Waring, 1996). Of course, in interpreting these findings it is important to recognize that most of the existing research has focused on middle class, heterosexual couples involved in their first marriages. Thus, less is known about the overall effectiveness of couple therapy in other types of relationships.

## Summary

The decision to form a long-term partnership with another individual is one of the most significant decisions that any person will make in the course of his or her life. For this reason, it is essential for couples to be able to find effective treatment when they experience distress. Therapists and clinical researchers have successfully identified a number of dysfunctional behaviors that can adversely impact relationship well-being. In addition, they have developed several different types of therapeutic interventions that may help couples modify their behavior and increase their satisfaction. Although not all couples will benefit from therapy, research generally reveals that most interventions are moderately successful, at least in the short term.

## Key Concepts

Attributional style (p. 128)

Criticism (p. 132)

Contempt (p. 132)

Defensiveness (p. 133)

Withdrawal or stonewalling (p. 133)

Negative reciprocity (p. 134)

Repair attempts (p. 136)

Ratio of positive to negative behavior (p. 136)

Volatile couples (p. 137)

Validating couples (p. 137)

Avoider couples (p. 137)

Bids for emotional connection (p. 138)

Behavioral couple therapy (p. 140)

Behavior exchange (p. 140)

Communication training (pp. 140–141)

Problem-solving training (pp. 140, 141)

Cognitive-behavioral couple therapy (p. 141)

Cognitive restructuring (p. 141)

Integrative behavioral couple therapy (p. 142)

Acceptance techniques (p. 142)

Hard disclosures (p. 142)

Soft disclosures (p. 142)

Tolerance strategies (p. 143)

Emotionally focused couple therapy (p. 143)

## Discussion Questions

1. Partners in even the most satisfying, well-adjusted, healthy relationship sometimes engage in destructive interaction behaviors (particularly during times of conflict). Using one of your own relationships, give a specific example (if you can) of a time in which you or your partner displayed each of the four dysfunctional interaction behaviors identified by Gottman (e.g., 1994b) and described in the textbook.

2. Working alone or with a classmate, come up with specific examples of the various bids for emotional connection outlined in this chapter. What purpose do these bids serve in our close relationships? Think of a time when you made a bid for emotional connection and your partner did not respond in an appropriate or positive manner. How did this make you feel? Think of another time in which your partner did respond positively and appropriately to your bid for emotional connection. How did this make you feel? Compare and contrast those two different experiences.

3. "Every couple in distress should seek treatment. Couple therapy is always the answer." Consider this statement. Is therapy appropriate for all problems and for all couples?

4. If you were involved in a distressed relationship, and you had to choose one and only one type of therapy to enter with your partner, which one would you choose? Why? Discuss your choice with your classmates.

5. Does therapy work? Discuss the different methods that clinical researchers have used in their attempts to answer this question. What do the results of their investigations generally reveal?

## Recommended Readings

John Gottman has written numerous books based on the findings from his research lab. This and more recent books are widely available and present evidence that the way in which couples typically respond to each other during times of disagreement can have profound consequences for the health of their relationship. Gottman also discusses ways to help couples recognize and change their dysfunctional interaction patterns.

Gottman, J. M. (1994). *Why marriages succeed or fail . . . and how you can make yours last*. New York, NY: Simon & Schuster.

This classic review article presents a general overview of the major types of couple therapy and also considers the effectiveness of the different therapeutic interventions that are available for distressed couples. The article also discusses therapies designed to prevent the development of problems.

Christensen, A., & Heavey, C. L. (1999). Interventions for couples. *Annual Review of Psychology, 50*, 165–190.

# Part II

# Love

Most people eagerly seek out love and believe that forming a successful love-based relationship is essential for their personal happiness. Although all of us are likely to experience various types of love and enter into a number of different kinds of love relationships over the course of our lifetimes, social and behavioral scientists have tended to focus on the type of love that occurs in long-term, romantic relationships. This kind of love is linked with a variety of important personal, interpersonal, and societal outcomes, including marriage and other forms of long-term pair-bonding, sex and reproduction, and social support. For example, as we discussed in Chapter 4, most people living in contemporary societies will marry only individuals they love and will leave partners they no longer love. Thus, love—and the relationships it produces and fosters—clearly plays a significant role in human lives.

The following three chapters explore the topic of love. Chapter 7 presents some of the commonly used typologies of love and their associated measurement instruments. Chapter 8 considers the two types of adult romantic love that have received the most intense scrutiny from relationship researchers: passionate and companionate love. Finally, Chapter 9 examines the dark side of love, including unrequited love, obsession and relational stalking, intimate partner violence or relational aggression, and loss of passion.

# Part II

## Love

# 7

# General Theories of Love

Throughout history, scholars from a variety of disciplines have speculated on the nature of love. For example, as early as 1886, German physician and pioneering sexologist Richard von Krafft-Ebing (1886/1945) identified five types of love: *true love, sentimental love, platonic love, friendship,* and *sensual love.* Several decades later, psychotherapist Albert Ellis (1954) proposed additional love varieties: "Love itself . . . includes many different types and degrees of affection, such as conjugal love, parental love, familial love, religious love, love of humanity, love of animals, love of things, self-love, sexual love, obsessive-compulsive love, etc." (p. 101).

One of Ellis's contemporaries, religious theoretician C. S. Lewis (1960/1988), devoted an entire book to a discussion of types of love. Drawing on earlier distinctions made by Greek philosophers, he proposed four main varieties. *Affection* (or *Storge*, pronounced "stor-gay") is based on familiarity and repeated contact and resembles the strong attachment often seen between parents and children. This type of love is experienced for and by a wide variety of social objects, including family members, pets, acquaintances, and lovers. According to Lewis, affectionate love has a "comfortable, quiet nature" (p. 34) and consists of feelings of warmth, interpersonal comfort, and satisfaction in being together. The second variety of love depicted by Lewis is *Friendship* (or *Philias*). Common interests, insights, or tastes, coupled with cooperation, mutual respect, and understanding, form the core of this love type. Lewis argued that Friendship, more than mere companionship, "must be about something, even if it were only an enthusiasm for dominoes or white mice" (p. 66). *Eros*, or "that state which we call 'being in love'" (p. 91), is the third variety of love. Unlike the other love types, Eros contains a mixture of "sweetness" and "terror" as well as a sexual component that Lewis referred to as Venus. Erotic love also is characterized by affection, idealization of and preoccupation with the beloved, and a very short life span. The final love type is *Charity*, a selfless and "Divine Gift-love" that has no expectation of reward and desires only what is "simply best for the beloved" (p. 128).

Contemporary social and behavioral scientists also have proposed taxonomies that specify types or varieties of love (for reviews, see Berscheid, 2010; Hendrick & Hendrick, 1992; Sternberg & Barnes, 1988). Two of the more common classification schemes were developed by psychologist Robert Sternberg (e.g., 1986, 1998) and sociologist John Lee (e.g., 1973, 1988). In developing their theories, both of these scholars not only drew on existing theory and research on love but also conducted large-scale investigations of the self-reported love experiences of men and women.

## ❖ THE TRIANGULAR THEORY OF LOVE

On the basis of a comprehensive review of earlier social psychological work on love, as well as statistical analysis of data collected from people in dating relationships, Sternberg (e.g., 1986, 1998, 2006) proposed that love can be conceptualized in terms of three basic components that form the vertices of a triangle: intimacy, passion, and decision/commitment (see Figure 7.1).

The *intimacy* component is primarily emotional or affective in nature and involves feelings of warmth, closeness, connection, and bondedness in the love relationship. The *passion* component is motivational and consists of the drives that are involved in romantic and physical attraction, sexual consummation, and related phenomena. The *decision/commitment* component is largely cognitive and represents both the short-term decision that one individual loves another and the longer-term commitment to maintain that love over time.

According to Sternberg (1988), these three love components differ with respect to a number of properties, including *stability, conscious controllability,* and *experiential salience.* For example, the elements of intimacy and decision/commitment are usually quite stable in close

**Figure 7.1**      Sternberg's Triangular Model of Love

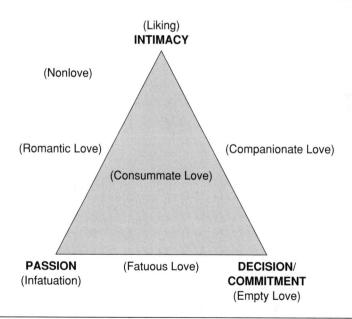

SOURCE: Sternberg, R. J. (1988). Triangulating love. In R. J. Sternberg & M. L. Barnes (Eds.), *The Psychology of Love* (pp. 119–138). New Haven, CT: Yale University Press. Copyright © 1988 by Yale University Press. Adapted with permission.

NOTE: The three components are indicated at the vertices of the triangle. The various types of love produced by different combinations of the components are in parentheses.

relationships (once they occur and become characteristic of a relationship, they tend to endure), whereas passion tends to be less stable and predictable. In addition, whereas people possess a great deal of conscious control over the commitment that they make to a relationship and at least some degree of control over their feelings of intimacy, they actually have very little conscious control over the amount of passion that they experience for their partners (it is difficult to increase or decrease one's level of physical or sexual attraction to a partner). The three components also differ in terms of their experiential salience. Specifically, an individual is usually quite aware of the passion component, but awareness of the intimacy and decision/ commitment components can be extremely variable. For example, a person may experience feelings of intimacy (e.g., closeness, connection, warmth) without explicitly being aware of those feelings or even being able to identify what he or she is feeling. Similarly, a person may not consciously realize the full extent of his or her commitment to the relationship and the partner.

## Types of Love Relationships

The three basic components of love combine to produce eight different love types, summarized in Table 7.1. *Nonlove* (no intimacy, passion, or decision/commitment) describes casual interactions that are characterized by the absence of all three love components. Most of our personal relationships (which are essentially casual associations) can be defined as nonlove. *Liking* (intimacy alone) relationships are essentially friendship. They contain warmth, intimacy, closeness, and other positive emotional experiences but lack both passion and decision/commitment; in other words, we care for the person and enjoy his or her company without feeling any intense passion or sustained commitment to the relationship. *Infatuation* (passion alone) is an intense, "love at first sight" experience that is characterized by extreme attraction and arousal in the absence of any real emotional intimacy and decision/commitment. In *empty love* (decision/commitment alone) relationships, the partners are committed to each other and the relationship but lack an intimate emotional connection and passionate attraction. This type of love is often seen at the end of long-term relationships (or at the beginning of arranged marriages). *Romantic love* (intimacy + passion) consists of feelings of closeness and connection coupled with strong physical attraction. *Companionate love* (intimacy + decision/commitment) is essentially a long-term, stable, and committed friendship that is characterized by high amounts of emotional intimacy, the decision to love the partner, and the commitment to remain in the relationship. This type of love is often seen in "best friendships" that are nonsexual or in long-term marriages in which sexual attraction has waned but deep emotional connection and commitment subsequently have developed. Couples who experience *fatuous love* (passion + decision/commitment) base their commitment to each other on passion rather than deep emotional intimacy. These "whirlwind" relationships are typically unstable and at risk for termination. Finally, *consummate love* (intimacy + passion + decision/commitment) results from the combination of all three components. According to Sternberg, this is the type of "complete" love many individuals strive to attain, particularly in their romantic relationships.

Because the three basic components of love occur in varying degrees within a relationship, most love relationships will not fit cleanly into one particular category but will reflect some combination of categories.

**Table 7.1**    Sternberg's Typology of Love Relationships

| | Love Component | | |
| --- | --- | --- | --- |
| *Kind of Love Relationship* | *Intimacy* | *Passion* | *Decision/ Commitment* |
| Nonlove | Low | Low | Low |
| Liking | High | Low | Low |
| Infatuation | Low | High | Low |
| Empty Love | Low | Low | High |
| Romantic Love | High | High | Low |
| Companionate Love | High | Low | High |
| Fatuous Love | Low | High | High |
| Consummate Love | High | High | High |

NOTE: According to Sternberg (e.g., 1986), the three basic components of love—intimacy, passion, and decision/commitment—combine to produce eight different types of love relationship. For example, infatuation-based relationships are characterized by relatively high levels of passion but relatively low levels of intimacy and commitment, whereas liking relationships are characterized by high levels of emotional intimacy in the absence of much passion or commitment.

## Measurement

Sternberg (1997) developed a 45-item scale to assess the three basic elements of love. The *Intimacy* subscale consists of 15 items designed to reflect feelings of warmth, support, self-disclosure, trust, and other aspects of intimate connection, including the following:

- I feel emotionally close to _____
- I feel that I can really trust _____
- I feel that I really understand _____
- I have a warm relationship with _____
- I share deeply personal information about myself with _____

The 15 items constituting the *Passion* subscale are designed to capture the more intense, physical, and exciting elements of romantic relationships, including:

- Just seeing _____ is exciting for me
- I especially like physical contact with _____
- I find _____ to be very personally attractive
- I adore _____
- I fantasize about _____

The *Decision/Commitment* subscale contains 15 items that assess feelings of stability, commitment, and permanence, including the following:

- I view my commitment to _____ as a solid one
- I have confidence in the stability of my relationship with _____
- I plan to continue in my relationship with _____
- I am certain of my love for _____
- I know that I care about _____

Interestingly, although this scale was designed to measure three distinct aspects of love—intimacy, passion, and decision/commitment—empirical evidence suggests that it may actually measure one general love dimension. For example, psychologists Clyde and Susan Hendrick (1989) administered an early version of the Triangular Love Scale to a large sample of men and women. Their results indicated that the three subscales were highly intercorrelated and also that the items formed a unifactorial scale. In other words, the scale appears to measure one global love dimension rather than three distinct elements or components of love. More recent examinations of the empirical properties of the Triangular Love Scale have produced similar results (see Graham & Christiansen, 2009; Sternberg, 1997). Perhaps for this reason, the scale has not received widespread use among social scientists interested in examining the individual components (i.e., intimacy, passion, decision/commitment) of people's love experiences. However, some researchers (e.g., Graham & Christiansen, 2009) have suggested that the total scale score (sum of the 45 items) may serve as a reliable general measure of the type of love Sternberg (e.g., 1986) identified as consummate love.

## ❖ THE COLORS (STYLES) OF LOVE

Another contemporary theory of love, and one that has produced a widely used measurement instrument, is the typology developed by Lee (e.g., 1977, 1988). In this novel approach, each variety of love is likened to a primary or secondary color (hence the title of Lee's 1973 book, *Colours of Love*). Lee drew heavily on literature and philosophical discourse on the nature of love in developing his theory and, like Sternberg, he also relied on empirical data collected from men and women about their love experiences. The results of Lee's analysis eventually produced a typology consisting of six styles or colors of love, each with characteristic features.

### Primary and Secondary Love Styles

According to Lee (1973), there are three primary colors or styles of loving. The first, *eros*, is an intensely emotional experience that is similar to passionate love. In fact, the most typical symptom of eros is an immediate and powerful attraction to the beloved individual. The erotic lover is "turned on" by a particular physical type, is prone to fall instantly and completely in love with a stranger (that is, experiences "love at first sight"), rapidly becomes preoccupied with pleasant thoughts about that individual, feels an intense need for daily contact with the beloved, and wishes the relationship to remain exclusive. Erotic love also has a strong sexual component. For example, the erotic lover desires the beloved sexually, usually seeks some form of sexual involvement fairly early in the relationship, and enjoys expressing his or her affection through sexual contact. In sum, the erotic lover is "eager to get to know the beloved quickly, intensely—and undressed" (Lee, 1988, p. 50).

The second primary color of love is *ludus* (or game-playing) love. The ludic lover views love as a game to be played with skill and often with several partners simultaneously. The ludic lover has no intention of including the current partner (or partners) in any future life plans or events and worries about any sign of growing involvement, need, or attachment from the partner. As the quintessential commitment-phobe, the ludic lover avoids seeing the partner too often, believes that lies and deception are justified, and expects the partner to remain in control of his or her emotions. In addition, ludic lovers tend to prefer a wide variety of physical types and view sexual activity as an opportunity for pleasure rather than for intense emotional bonding.

*Storge* is the third primary love color. Described by Lee (1973) as "love without fever or folly" (p. 77), storge resembles C. S. Lewis's concept of Affection in that it is stable and based upon a solid foundation of trust, respect, and friendship. Indeed, the typical storgic lover views and treats the partner as an "old friend," does not experience the intense emotions or physical attraction to the partner associated with erotic love, prefers to talk about and engage in shared interests with the partner rather than to express direct feelings, is shy about sex, and tends to demonstrate his or her affection in nonsexual ways. To the storgic lover, love is an extension of friendship.

Like the primary colors, these primary love styles can be combined to form secondary colors or styles of love. The three secondary styles identified by Lee (1973) contain features of the primaries but also possess their own unique characteristics. *Pragma*, a combination of storge and ludus, is "the love that goes shopping for a suitable mate" (p. 124). The pragmatic lover has a practical outlook to love and seeks a compatible lover. He or she creates a shopping list of features or attributes desired in the partner and selects a mate based on how well that individual fulfills the requirements (similarly, he or she will drop a partner who fails to "measure up" to expectations). Pragmatic love is essentially a faster-acting version of storge that has been quickened by the addition of ludus.

*Mania*, the combination of eros and ludus, is another secondary love style. Manic lovers lack the self-confidence associated with eros and the emotional self-control associated with ludus. This obsessive, jealous love style is characterized by self-defeating emotions, desperate attempts to force affection from the beloved, and the inability to believe in or trust any affection the loved one actually does display. The manic lover is eager, even desperate, to fall in love and to be loved. He or she begins immediately to imagine a future with the partner, wants to see the partner daily, tries to force the partner to show love and commitment, distrusts the partner's sincerity, and is extremely possessive. People with a manic approach to love are "irrational, extremely jealous, obsessive, and often unhappy" (Lee, 1973, p. 15).

The last secondary color of love is *agape*, a combination of eros and storge. Agape is similar to C. S. Lewis's concept of Charity, and represents an all-giving, selfless love style that implies an obligation to love and care for others without any expectation of reciprocity or reward. This love style is universal or inclusive in the sense that the typical agapic lover feels that everyone is worthy of love and that loving others is a duty of the mature person. With respect to personal love relationships, an agapic lover will unselfishly devote himself or herself to the partner, even stepping aside in favor of a rival who seems more likely to meet the partner's needs. Although Lee (1973) believed that many lovers respect and strive to attain the agapic ideal, he also believed that the give-and-take that characterizes most romantic relationships precludes the occurrence of purely altruistic love.

## Measurement

Lee's (1973) classification scheme inspired the development of several measurement instruments. The best known and most commonly used is the 42-item Love Attitudes Scale (LAS) designed by the Hendricks and their colleagues (Hendrick & Hendrick, 1986; Hendrick, Hendrick, Foote, & Slapion-Foote, 1984). The LAS appears to reliably measure the six love styles and has subsequently been redesigned so that each of the items refers to a specific love relationship as opposed to more general attitudes about love (Hendrick & Hendrick, 1990). A shorter, 28-item version of the scale is also available (Hendrick, Hendrick, & Dicke, 1998). The complete scale, along with its shorter version, is reproduced in Exhibit 7.1.

## Research on Love Styles

Unlike the Triangular Love Scale, the LAS appears to reliably measure Lee's six love styles; thus, it has been used in numerous scientific investigations. In general, the results of these studies reveal three general findings. First, in accord with other research demonstrating homogamy or assortment in mate selection (see Chapter 4), there is a tendency for people with similar love styles to pair; erotic lovers form relationships

**Exhibit 7.1**   The Love Attitudes Scale

## Instructions

Please answer the following items as honestly and accurately as possible. Whenever possible, answer the questions with your current dating partner in mind. If you are not currently dating anyone, answer the questions with your most recent partner in mind. Otherwise, answer in terms of what you think your responses would most likely be.

*Response Scale*

- 1: strongly disagree
- 2: moderately disagree
- 3: neutral
- 4: moderately agree
- 5: strongly agree

## Items

*Eros*

1. My partner and I were attracted to each other immediately after we first met.
*2. My partner and I have the right physical "chemistry" between us.
3. Our lovemaking is very intense and satisfying.
*4. I feel that my partner and I were meant for each other.
5. My partner and I became emotionally involved rather quickly.
*6. My partner and I really understand each other.
*7. My partner fits my ideal standards of physical beauty/handsomeness.

*Ludus*

8. I try to keep my partner a little uncertain about my commitment to him/her.
*9. I believe that what my partner doesn't know about me won't hurt him/her.
*10. I have sometimes had to keep my partner from finding out about other lovers.
11. I could get over my love affair with my partner pretty easily and quickly.
*12. My partner would get upset if he/she knew of some of the things I've done with other people.
13. When my partner gets too dependent on me, I want to back off a little.
*14. I enjoy playing the "game of love" with my partner and a number of other partners.

*Storge*

15. It is hard for me to say exactly when our friendship turned into love.
16. To be genuine, our love first required *caring* for a while.
17. I expect to always be friends with my partner.
*18. Our love is the best kind because it grew out of a long friendship.
*19. Our friendship merged gradually into love over time.

**Exhibit 7.1**   (Continued)

*20. Our love is really a deep friendship, not a mysterious mystical emotion.
*21. Our love relationship is the most satisfying because it developed from a good friendship.

*Pragma*

22. I considered what my partner was going to become in life before I committed myself to him/her.
23. I tried to plan my life carefully before choosing a partner.
24. In choosing my partner, I believed it was best to love someone with a similar background.
*25. A main consideration in choosing my partner was how he/she would reflect on my family.
*26. An important factor in choosing my partner was whether or not he/she would be a good parent.
*27. One consideration in choosing my partner was how he/she would reflect on my career.
*28. Before getting very involved with my partner, I tried to figure out how compatible his/her hereditary background would be with mine in case we ever had children.

*Mania*

29. When things aren't right with my partner and me, my stomach gets upset.
30. If my partner and I broke up, I would get so depressed that I would even think of suicide.
31. Sometimes I get so excited about being in love with my partner that I can't sleep.
*32. When my partner doesn't pay attention to me, I feel sick all over.
*33. Since I've been in love with my partner, I've had trouble concentrating on anything else.
*34. I cannot relax if I suspect that my partner is with someone else.
*35. If my partner ignores me for a while, I sometimes do stupid things to try to get his/her attention back.

*Agape*

36. I try to always help my partner through difficult times.
*37. I would rather suffer myself than let my partner suffer.
*38. I cannot be happy unless I place my partner's happiness before my own.
*39. I am usually willing to sacrifice my own wishes to let my partner achieve his/hers.
40. Whatever I own is my partner's to use as he/she chooses.
41. When my partner gets angry with me, I still love him/her fully and unconditionally.
*42. I would endure all things for the sake of my partner.

*(Continued)*

---

Exhibit 7.1   (Continued)

## Scoring

Starred items are those included on the short form of the LAS. To find out your love style, add up your ratings for the items in each subscale. You will have scores for the three primary love styles and for the three secondary love styles. Do you have one particular style of love? Or is your orientation to love relationships more complex than that?

SOURCE: Adapted from Hendrick, C., & Hendrick, S. (1990). A relationship-specific version of the Love Attitudes Scale. *Journal of Social Behavior and Personality*, 5, 239–254. Copyright © 1990 by Select Press, Inc. Reprinted with permission.

NOTE: Response options have been reversed from original source. Starred items are included in the short form of the scale from Hendrick, Hendrick, and Dicke (1998).

---

with similarly passionate people, agapic lovers select equally selfless mates, and so forth (Davis & Latty-Mann, 1987; Gana, Saada, & Untas, 2013; Morrow, Clark, & Brock, 1995). Second, certain love styles are strongly associated with relationship well-being; in particular, relationship satisfaction appears to be higher when partners possess an erotic, storgic, or agapic love style, and lower when partners have a ludic or manic orientation to love (Fricker & Moore, 2002; Gana et al., 2013; Goodboy & Myers, 2010; Hendrick, Hendrick, & Adler, 1988; Meeks, Hendrick, & Hendrick, 1998). Third, several individual and group differences in love style have been identified. For example, although sexual orientation does not appear to be associated with love styles (for a review, see Hendrick & Hendrick, 2006), there are fairly robust sex differences. Specifically, researchers commonly find that women score higher on the love styles of storge and pragma than do men, whereas men score higher on ludus (e.g., Dion & Dion, 1993; Hendrick & Hendrick, 1987, 1988, 1995; Hendrick et al., 1984, 1998; Le, 2005; Rotenberg & Korol, 1995; Sprecher & Toro-Morn, 2002). In addition, a number of investigations report higher scores among men than among women on the agapic love style (Hendrick & Hendrick, 2002; Lacey, Reifman, Scott, Harris, & Fitzpatrick, 2004; Lin & Huddleston-Casas, 2005; Neto & Pinto, 2003; Sprecher & Toro-Morn, 2002).

There also are multicultural and cross-cultural differences in love style. Within the United States, Asian American adults often score lower on eros and higher on pragma and storge than White, Latino, and African American adults (e.g., Dion & Dion, 1993; Hendrick & Hendrick, 1986). Latino groups, on the other hand, often score higher on ludus than White groups (e.g., Contreras, Hendrick, & Hendrick, 1996). And cross-cultural comparisons reveal that Chinese adults endorse a more pragmatic approach to love than Americans (Sprecher & Toro-Morn, 2002), and that Americans tend to exhibit higher levels of storge and mania, and lower levels of agape, than the French (e.g., Murstein, Merighi, & Vyse, 1991).

These differences notwithstanding, it is important to keep in mind that not all individuals possess one approach or style of loving. A man or woman may adopt numerous love styles, and a person's love style may change over his or her lifetime or during the course of a given relationship. For example, the preoccupation and intense need associated with a manic love style may occur more often during the beginning stages of a romantic relationship, when the partners are uncertain of their feelings and the future of their association. Over time, however, these feelings may be replaced by more erotic, storgic, or agapic feelings.

## ❖ THE PROTOTYPE APPROACH: MENTAL MODELS OF LOVE

Recall that both Sternberg and Lee created their models of love by reviewing existing theoretical discourse as well as by collecting data directly from men and women about their love experiences. The *prototype approach* to love is also empirically driven; however, prototype researchers focus more specifically on people's knowledge, beliefs, and attitudes—their mental representations—of the concept of love. Researchers who utilize the prototype approach are interested in exploring what people think of when they are asked about love, how they differentiate love from related concepts (e.g., liking), how they form their conceptualizations of love, and how these conceptualizations or mental representations influence their behavior with relational partners.

### The Hierarchy of Love

According to Eleanor Rosch (e.g., 1973, 1975, 1978), an early pioneer in the use of prototype analysis, natural language *concepts* (e.g., *love, dog, apple*) can be viewed as having both a vertical and a horizontal dimension. The former concerns the hierarchical organization of concepts or relations among different levels of concepts. Concepts at one level may be included within or subsumed by those at a higher level. For example, the set of concepts *fruit, apple,* and *Red Delicious* illustrate an abstract-to-concrete hierarchy with superordinate, basic, and subordinate levels.

Using the methods originally developed by Rosch (e.g., 1973, 1975, 1978), some researchers have investigated the hierarchical structure of the concept of love. Psychologist Phillip Shaver and colleagues (Shaver, Schwartz, Kirson, & O'Connor, 1987), for instance, found evidence that *love* is a basic-level concept contained within the superordinate category of *emotion* and subsuming a variety of subordinate concepts that reflect types or varieties of love (e.g., passion, infatuation, liking; see Figure 7.2). That is, most people consider passion, infatuation, and liking to be types of love, which in turn is viewed as a type of emotion.

## The Prototype of Love

Concepts also may be examined along a horizontal dimension. This dimension concerns the differentiation of concepts at the same level of inclusiveness (e.g., the dimension on which such subordinate-level concepts as Red Delicious, Fuji, Gala, and Granny Smith apples vary).

**Figure 7.2**    The Hierarchy of Love and Other Emotions

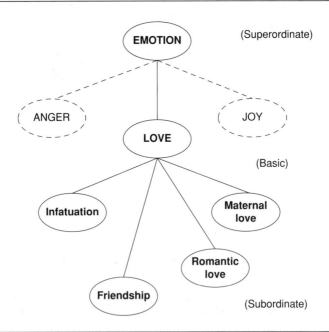

NOTE: Research conducted by Phillip Shaver, Beverley Fehr, and their colleagues (Fehr & Russell, 1991; Fischer, Shaver, & Carnochan, 1990; Shaver, Schwartz, Kirson, & O'Connor, 1987) suggests that love is a basic-level concept contained within the superordinate category of *emotion*. In addition, *love* appears to contain a variety of subordinate concepts that reflect types or varieties of love; of these, *maternal love* is viewed as the most prototypical variety.

According to Rosch (e.g., 1973, 1975, 1978), many natural language concepts or categories have an internal structure whereby individual members of that category are ordered in terms of the degree to which they resemble the prototypic member of the category. A *prototype* is the best and clearest example of the concept (the "appley-est" or the most apple-like apple, e.g., Red Delicious). Individuals use prototypes to help them decide whether a new item or experience belongs or "fits" within a particular concept. For example, in trying to decide whether or not he is in love with his partner, a man might compare the *feelings* ("I'm happy when she's here," "I miss her when she's away," "I'm very attracted to her"), *thoughts* ("I believe she really cares about me," "I wonder if she'd consider moving in with me?", "I think we'd make great parents"), and *behaviors* ("I rearrange my schedule to spend time with her," "We talk every day," "We take vacations together") he's experienced during their relationship with his prototype—his mental model—of "being in love" ("People who are in love miss each other when they're apart, think about each other a lot, imagine a future life together, and spend a lot of time with each other"). If what the man is experiencing "matches" his prototype, he is likely to conclude that he is, in fact, in love with his partner.

The prototype approach has been used to explore the horizontal structure of a variety of relational concepts, including love. Beverley Fehr and James Russell (1991; also see Fehr, 1994), for example, asked men and women to generate as many types of love as they could in a specified time and then asked another sample of individuals to rate these love varieties in terms of prototypicality or "goodness-of-example." Of the 93 subtypes generated, *maternal love* was rated as the best or most prototypical example of love, followed by *parental love, friendship, sisterly love, romantic love, brotherly love,* and *familial love. Infatuation,* along with *sexual love* and *puppy love,* was considered one of the least prototypical examples of love.

Researchers also have identified the prototypic features (as opposed to types) of love. For example, in an earlier demonstration, Fehr (1988) asked one group of participants to list the characteristics of the concept of love and a second group to rate how central each feature was to the concept of love. Features that her participants believed were central or prototypical to love included *trust, caring, honesty, friendship, respect, concern for the other's well-being, loyalty,* and *commitment.* Features that were considered peripheral or unimportant to the concept of love included *see only the other's good qualities, butterflies in stomach, uncertainty, dependency,* and *scary.*

Psychologists Arthur Aron and Lori Westbay (1996) extended Fehr's work by exploring the underlying structure of the prototype of love. Interestingly, these researchers found evidence that the 68 proto-typic love features identified by participants in Fehr's (1988) study could be reduced reliably to three latent dimensions that resembled those included in Sternberg's (1988) triangular theory of love typology: passion, intimacy, and commitment. This suggests that Sternberg's theory is sound; that is, the love experiences of many men and women do, indeed, reflect the three basic dimensions he proposed.

### Do People Share a Common Understanding of Love?

Do people agree about the meaning of love? In North America, the answer to this question is a resounding *yes*. As noted by Fehr (2006) in her comprehensive review of the prototype literature, there is a high degree of consistency across existing studies. Men and women in university and community samples from the west and east coasts of Canada and from the west coast of the United States possess a remarkably similar understanding of love—specifically, they agree that *trust, caring, honesty, friendship,* and *respect* are the most prototypical features of love. In addition, few individual differences in general conceptualizations of love have been identified. Fehr (2006) concluded that "the most striking finding in this literature is the extent of agreement on the prototype of love" (p. 233). However, it is important to note that until additional cross-cultural prototype analyses of love are conducted, we cannot draw any reliable conclusions about whether people around the world share a similar notion of the meaning of love.

## Summary

Social and behavioral scientists, recognizing the important role that love plays in human life, have theorized about its nature. In the process, they have pro-posed a number of typologies or classification schemes that specify types or varieties of love. Other researchers, following a prototype approach, have attempted to delineate the nature of love by examining people's common understandings of love and their love experiences. This body of theoretical and empirical work reveals that many different ways of loving exist. Love truly is a many-splendored—and multifaceted—experience.

## Key Concepts

Storge (p. 152)

Philias (p. 152)

Eros (p. 152)

Charity (p. 152)

Triangular theory of love (p. 152)

Intimacy component (p. 153)

Passion component (p. 153)

Decision/commitment component (p. 153)

Stability property (p. 153)

Conscious controllability property (p. 153)

Experiential salience property (p. 153)

Nonlove (p. 154)

Liking (p. 154)

Infatuation (p. 154)

Empty love (p. 154)

Romantic love (p. 154)

Companionate love (p. 154)

Fatuous love (p. 155)

Consummate love (p. 155)

Erotic love style (p. 157)

Ludic love style (p. 158)

Storgic love style (p. 158)

Pragmatic love style (p. 158)

Manic love style (p. 158)

Agapic love style (p. 159)

Prototype approach (to love) (p. 163)

Concepts (p. 163)

Vertical dimension of the concept of love (p. 163)

Horizontal dimension of the concept of love (p. 164)

Prototype (p. 165)

## Discussion Questions

1. Although philosophers, poets, and writers have speculated on the nature of love for many hundreds of years, the topic of love has only recently begun to receive scientific attention. What do you think might account for this state of affairs?

2. Describe Sternberg's (1988) triangular theory of love. Select two relationships you have seen portrayed in the media (e.g., books, plays, movies, television). Which type of love does each relationship illustrate? Describe each in terms of the three components of love.

3. Define the three primary and three secondary colors of love. What would be the best pairing of love styles? The worst? Why?

4. What is your approach or orientation to love relationships? Complete the Love Attitudes Scale (Exhibit 7.1 in this chapter). Follow the instructions and rate each item, and then sum the ratings you gave for each set of items (each subscale). Look at your total scores on each subscale. On which subscale(s) did you score the highest? Lowest? Do your personal experiences match Lee's descriptions of the different love styles? Perhaps you have similar scores across all of the subscales. If this is the case, then your orientation to love cannot easily be captured by Lee's theory (or this scale); for example, you may be someone who approaches each love relationship differently depending on your partner or your current life situation.

5. What do people think of when they think of the concept of love? This exercise is designed to explore people's mental representations—their prototypes—of love. Find two volunteers. Ask each one to think of the concept of "love" and to write down as many features or attributes of this concept as

possible in two minutes (you'll need to time your volunteers). Then ask each volunteer to look over the features he or she generated and pick the three features that are the most important or central to the concept of love. Once you have collected this information from your participants, take a look at their responses. Do the features they selected match the results reported by Fehr (1988) in her study?

## Recommended Readings

This article, written by one of the foremost experts in the area, provides an outstanding introduction to scientific efforts to understand love. It is available online at: http://www.annualreviews.org/doi/pdf/10.1146/annurev.psych .093008.100318

Berscheid, E. (2010). Love in the fourth dimension. *Annual Review of Psychology, 61*, 1–25.

This delightful book is an excellent example of an "early" love theory. Unlike contemporary scholars, who rely heavily on empirical methods, Lewis draws primarily on literature and philosophical/theological discourse. This book was first published in 1960, but is readily (and inexpensively) available in electronic and paper versions.

Lewis, C. S. (1988). *The four loves.* New York, NY: Harcourt Brace. (Original work published 1960)

In this classic article, the authors examine whether the available love instruments actually measure what they purport to measure.

Hendrick, C., & Hendrick, S. S. (1989). Research on love: Does it measure up? *Journal of Personality and Social Psychology, 56*, 784–794.

This book serves as a wonderful introduction to the author's theory. Although out of print (check the library or a used book store), it is well worth the effort to locate it.

Lee, J. A. (1973). *Colours of love: An exploration of the ways of loving.* Toronto, ON, Canada: New Press.

Both of these edited books are valuable reference tools for anyone interested in understanding social scientific views of love.

Sternberg, R. J., & Barnes, M. L. (Eds.). (1988). *The psychology of love.* New Haven, CT: Yale University Press.
Sternberg, R. J., & Weis, K. (Eds.). (2006). *The new psychology of love.* New Haven, CT: Yale University Press.

# 8

# Passionate and Companionate Love

Most people would probably agree that "being in love" with someone is a very different experience from "loving" that person. However, scientists have been relatively slow to make this same distinction. In fact, it was not until the early 1970s that theorists and researchers began to recognize that passionate love was more than simply an intense or extreme version of liking or loving another (e.g., Berscheid & Walster, 1974; Rubin, 1970, 1973). Now, most social and behavioral scientists agree that love (or more specifically, adult romantic love) comes in at least two distinct forms—a version that is exciting, intense, fleeting, and sexually charged (called passionate love), and a version that is stable, slow to develop, and infused with warmth and intimacy (called companionate love).

## ❖ PASSIONATE LOVE: A "SEXY" KIND OF LOVE

Of all the varieties of love that have been identified by theorists and researchers, *passionate love* (also called erotic or romantic love) has received the lion's share of attention. This particular type of love has assumed special importance in relationships research and in theoretical discourse on love for a number of reasons. First, passionate love appears to be a universal human experience. By young adulthood, most men and women report having been in love at least once (Regan, Durvasula, Howell, Ureño, & Rea, 2004), and researchers have found evidence that passionate love is experienced by people living in all cultures (Jankowiak, 1995; Jankowiak & Fischer, 1992; Sprecher et al., 1994). Second, passionate love has become an essential part of the marriage contract in many human societies—most people say they will not marry without it (Simpson, Campbell, & Berscheid, 1986). Third, the absence or loss of passionate love seems to be a factor in relationship dissolution; many people leave marriages and other romantic relationships when their feelings of passionate love decline or end

(Berscheid, 1985). And fourth—and perhaps most importantly from a scientific perspective—passionate love appears to possess several unique features that differentiate it from other varieties of love (Regan, 1998c, 2000a, 2006).

## Defining Passionate Love

*I hope to hold you in my arms before long, when I shall lavish upon you a million kisses, burning as the equatorial sun.*

—From a letter written by Napoleon Bonaparte
to Josephine, Spring, 1797 (Hall, 1901)

*Marie! Marie! Oh let me repeat that name a hundred times, a thousand times over; for three days now it has lived within me, oppressed me, set me afire. I am not writing to you, no, I am close beside you. I see you, I hear you. . . . Eternity in your arms. . . . Heaven, hell, all is within you and even more than all.*

—From a letter written by Hungarian composer Franz Liszt
to Marie d'Agoult, December, 1834 (Tamplin, 1995)

Early and contemporary love theorists have suggested that passionate love consists of a number of unique features, including a *swift and fairly sudden onset*, a *relatively brief life span*, *idealization* of and *mental preoccupation* with the loved one and the love relationship, *intense and often fluctuating emotions*, *physiological arousal* and its bodily sensations, *sexual attraction*, and *exclusivity* or a focus on one specific individual (see Berscheid & Regan, 2005). Research substantiates most of these theoretical suppositions.

### Idealization and Preoccupation

*I love everything about him—I want him all the time and I think about him all the time. I am so in love with him that I get weak even writing down these words. I can't concentrate, I can't sleep, I don't want to eat.*

—24-year-old woman interviewed by the author

*She's completely amazing. Smart, funny, kind, caring, beautiful, talented . . . if I had to list all of her good qualities, we'd be here forever, trust me. She's the total package. Perfect. When we're together, I'm constantly pinching myself because I can't believe how lucky I am to be with her.*

—20-year-old man interviewed by the author

When people fall passionately in love with someone, they often become so mentally or cognitively preoccupied with thoughts about that individual that they find it difficult to concentrate on anything else (van Steenbergen, Langeslag, Band, & Hommel, 2014). In addition, people who are in love tend to idealize their partners' characteristics as well as the nature of their relationship (e.g., Barelds & Dijkstra, 2009; Barelds, Dijkstra, Koudenburg, & Swami, 2011; Buunk & van der Eijnden, 1997; Murray, Holmes, & Griffin, 1996; Neff & Karney, 2002; Van Lange & Rusbult, 1995). A large body of research reveals that most men and women:

- perceive their own romantic relationships as superior to the relationships of others ("Our relationship is so much better than their relationship," "Our love is stronger than their love")

- view their current partners more favorably than they view other possible partners ("My boyfriend/girlfriend is much more attractive and interesting than that man/woman")

- view their partners more positively than their partners view themselves (He says, "I would say I'm fairly attractive" and she says, "He's the most gorgeous man I've ever seen")

- minimize any seeming faults that their partners possess by miscasting those faults as virtues ("Sure, he can seem kind of opinionated, but that's because he's so direct and refreshingly honest") or by downplaying their significance ("She's not very communicative, but that doesn't really matter. We don't need a lot of words to show our feelings for each other")

- accentuate their partners' positive qualities by emphasizing the beneficial impact of those qualities on the overall relationship ("Because he's so direct and honest, I know I can trust him completely—this is what keeps our relationship strong")

Together, these findings suggest that passionate lovers "see their partners through the filters provided by their ideals, essentially seeing them . . . as they wish to see them" (Murray et al., 1996, p. 86).

## Exclusivity

*She is the one.*

—19-year-old man interviewed by the author

Love theorists have long considered *exclusivity* (a focus on one specific person to the exclusion of all others) to be another important hallmark of passionate love. In his classic work *The American Sexual*

*Tragedy* (1954), psychotherapist Albert Ellis observed that one of the distinguishing features of passionate love was the fact that people fall in love with "one paramount love object" as opposed to multiple other love objects. Existentialist Erich Fromm (1956) similarly noted that an individual's feelings of passionate love are "restricted to one person" and that passionate love is a "completely individual attraction, unique between two specific persons" (p. 57). This view was echoed by C. S. Lewis (1960/1988) in *The Four Loves*: "Eros makes a man really want, not a woman, but one particular woman" (p. 94).

Researchers have found solid evidence in support of these speculations. For example, psychologists Sarah Meyers and Ellen Berscheid (1996) asked a large sample of undergraduate men and women to list the initials of all the people they currently loved and the initials of all those with whom they were currently in love. Their results provided evidence for the exclusive nature of passionate love; specifically, in accord with theoretical supposition, participants listed many people in the "love" category, but generally listed only one person in the "in love" category. This is not surprising given the degree to which passionate lovers are preoccupied with idealized thoughts of their partners and their romantic relationships—it is difficult to notice (let alone fall in love with) someone else when one is engrossed and enraptured by the current partner.

## Emotional Intensity

*When he smiles at me, my heart melts. I am so full of happiness that I feel like a balloon about to burst.*

—18-year-old woman interviewed by the author

*This is my first time being in love and I've felt so many emotions. I've been so down I was practically suicidal. I've been so up I felt like I was high. Sometimes when I think about our love, I feel like I could take on the world. Powerful, joyful, proud. Sometimes I feel scared, because what would I do if he left me?*

—20-year-old man interviewed by the author

Passionate love is an intensely emotional experience. In *The American Sexual Tragedy*, Ellis (1954) noted that "the romantic lover is changeable and frequently goes from one violent passion to another" (p. 102). Two decades later, social psychologists Ellen Berscheid and Elaine Hatfield (then Walster; 1974) applied a well-known theory of emotion to the experience of passionate love in an effort to delineate its essential features. Specifically, these scientists proposed that men and women experience passionate love when a minimum of two conditions occur. First, they are extremely aroused physiologically (an essential ingredient for any strong emotion). Second, they believe that this arousal is caused by the partner and therefore is appropriately labeled "passionate love."

Some indirect empirical support exists for this hypothesis. Psychologists Donald Dutton and Arthur Aron (1974) conducted a now-classic field study in which an attractive woman—a confederate who was working for the researchers—approached men who were walking across two quite different bridges located on the Capilano River in Canada. The Capilano Canyon Suspension Bridge served as the experimental bridge. This narrow, 450-foot-long structure consists of wooden boards attached to wire cables that run across the river. In addition, it possesses several arousal-inducing features, including the following (in the words of the researchers): "(a) a tendency to tilt, sway, and wobble, creating the impression that one is about to fall over the side; (b) very low handrails of wire cable, which contribute to this impression; and (c) a 230-foot drop to rocks and shallow rapids below the bridge" (p. 511). The control bridge, located farther up the river, was constructed of heavy cedar, was considerably wider and sturdier than the experimental bridge, did not tilt or sway, and was suspended a mere 10 feet above a small shallow rivulet that ran into the main body of water. As each male participant crossed his respective bridge, the confederate approached him, introduced herself as a research assistant, and asked whether he would fill out a brief questionnaire. She then gave her phone number to those men who completed the questionnaire and invited them to call her if they had any additional questions about the study and wanted to talk further. The results revealed that fully half (50.0%) of the men who had met the young woman while on the scary experimental bridge called her later, compared with only 12.5% of the men who met her while crossing the sturdy control bridge. What explains this result? The men on the suspension bridge had experienced physiological arousal but had attributed their response to the woman rather than to the life-threatening situation, hence their attraction to her and subsequent interest in pursuing additional contact with her. These results certainly suggest that passion, attraction, and similar experiences are fundamentally "emotional" in nature.

More recent research also demonstrates that passionate love is associated with the experience of deeply positive emotions (and the physiological arousal that is involved in such emotions). For example, men and women in a prototype study were asked to identify the essential features of passionate love, further defined as the state of "being in love" with someone (Regan, Kocan, & Whitlock, 1998).

Among the features they cited as particularly central or important to the concept of passionate love were such emotions as happiness, joy or rapture, closeness, warmth, and tenderness. In addition, they also cited a number of physical sensations that are associated with the experience of intense emotion, including giddiness and a racing heart. Similarly, research with dating couples reveals that the greater the amount of passionate love men and women feel for their partners, the more frequently they experience satisfaction, contentment, joy, and a host of other positive emotions (Sprecher & Regan, 1998). Interestingly, although passionate love seems to be primarily associated with positive emotional experiences, there is one exception—jealousy. Both men and women associate jealousy with the state of being in love (Regan et al., 1998), and those who love passionately also tend to report feeling or having felt jealous (Sprecher & Regan, 1998).

## Sexual Attraction

*I get so excited when I know that I'm going to see him, and then when I do see him, I can't breathe I'm so full of want. When we're together I can't wait for him to touch me, to kiss me, to hold me. And then I want more! This is how I know that I'm really in love—these feelings just keep growing stronger and stronger. This is it!*

—24-year-old woman interviewed by the author

*I want her all the time. You know how people talk about food cravings, like "I have a craving for ice cream"? Well, I have a craving for her. If it were up to me, we'd spend all our time naked in bed.*

—22-year-old man interviewed by the author

As these quotations illustrate, passionate love and sexuality appear to be intricately connected in the eyes of many individuals. Contemporary theorists and researchers also believe that passionate love is a sexually charged experience, and they suggest that *sexual attraction* (the motivational component of human sexuality, also called sexual desire or lust) is the specific sexual ingredient that gives passionate love its unique flavor (e.g., Regan & Berscheid, 1999; Tennov, 1979). For example, Berscheid (1988) wrote,

It is all very well to look down one's nose at Sigmund Freud's cursory analysis of romantic love as repressed, suppressed, or frustrated sexual desire, but, for me at least, Freud seems to have gotten smarter as I've gotten older. And, surely, it is no accident that the wisest of the romantic love theorists, Theodore Reik, entitled his classic book *Of Love and Lust* (1941) (and not, by the way, "Of Love and Liking"). (p. 372)

Research strongly supports this theoretical assumption. Certainly people *believe* that sexual attraction is an essential part of the state of being in love. When Robert Ridge and Ellen Berscheid (1989) asked a sample of undergraduate men and women whether they believed that there was a difference between the experience of being in love with and that of loving another person, most of them (87%) emphatically claimed that there indeed was a difference between the two experiences—and that the difference had to do with feelings of sexual attraction (which they argued was part of the former and not the latter).

Similar results were reported by Regan and her colleagues (1998). These researchers asked a sample of men and women to list in a free response format all of the features that they considered to be characteristic or prototypical of the state of "being in love." Of 119 spontaneously generated features, *sexual desire* received the second-highest frequency rating, cited by 66% (*trust* was first, cited by 80%). In other words, when thinking of passionate love, two thirds of the participants automatically thought of sexual desire. In addition, this feature was viewed as more important to the passionate love concept than such behavioral sexual events as *kissing* (cited by only 10% of participants), *touching/holding* (cited by 18%), and *sexual activity or intercourse* (cited by 25%).

Person perception experiments provide additional support for these prototype results. Person perception experiments are commonly used in social psychological research and essentially involve manipulating people's perceptions of a relationship and then measuring the impact of that manipulation on their subsequent evaluations and beliefs. In the first experiment, Regan (1998b) provided a sample of 60 undergraduate men and women with two self-report questionnaires ostensibly completed by "Rob" and "Nancy," a student couple enrolled at the same university. The members of this couple reported experiencing either no sexual desire for each other or a high amount of sexual desire for each other, and they either were currently engaging in sexual activity with each other or were not sexually active. Participants then estimated the likelihood that the partners experience passionate love as well as a variety of other relationship events. As illustrated in Table 8.1, the results indicated that both men and women believed that dating partners who experience sexual desire for each other are more likely to be passionately in love with each other (as well as more likely to experience a variety of other relationship events) than are dating partners who do not desire each other sexually, regardless of their current level of sexual activity.

A second experiment, a conceptual replication of the first, confirmed these results. Here, 48 men and women received information about the members of a heterosexual, dating "student couple"

**Table 8.1**   What Do a Couple's Sexual Experiences Tell Us About the Nature of Their Relationship?

| How likely is it that Rob and Nancy | "Rob" and "Nancy" report: | | | |
|---|---|---|---|---|
| | High Desire + Intercourse | High Desire + No Intercourse | Low Desire + Intercourse | Low Desire + No Intercourse |
| (1) are passionately in love with each other? | 7.53 | 6.47 | 2.00 | 2.47 |
| (2) like each other? | 8.13 | 8.07 | 4.73 | 6.33 |
| (3) are happy? | 7.73 | 7.40 | 3.60 | 5.60 |
| (4) are satisfied with their relationship? | 7.73 | 7.13 | 2.93 | 5.20 |
| (5) are committed to their relationship? | 7.27 | 7.40 | 5.60 | 5.33 |
| (6) trust each other? | 7.20 | 7.27 | 5.73 | 6.27 |
| (7) love each other? | 6.40 | 5.47 | 3.07 | 3.80 |

SOURCE: Adapted from Regan, P. C. (1998). Of lust and love: Beliefs about the role of sexual desire in romantic relationships. *Personal Relationships, 5,* 139–157.

NOTE: In this study, participants read about a couple (Rob and Nancy) who reported feeling either high or low amounts of sexual attraction for one another and who were either engaging in sexual intercourse or not. After reading about the couple, participants estimated how likely it was that the couple experienced a variety of other feelings, using 1 (not at all likely) to 9 (extremely likely) point scales. As you can see from the results, participants thought that Rob and Nancy were much more likely to be in love with each other (and to like each other and so on) when they sexually desired each other than when they did not sexually desire each other (and it really didn't matter whether or not they were having sex). In other words, people associated sexual desire (and not sexual activity) with passionate love; sexual desire seems to be a "sign" that a couple is in love.

who ostensibly reported that they were currently passionately in love with each other, that they loved each other, or that they liked each other. Participants then estimated the likelihood that the members of the couple experience sexual desire for each other and the amount of desire that they feel for each other. Analyses revealed that participants perceived couples who are passionately in love as more *likely* to experience sexual desire than couples who love each other or who like each other. Similarly, couples who are passionately in love were believed to experience a greater *amount* of sexual desire for each other than couples who love each other or who like each other. Interestingly, sexual desire was believed to be no more likely in a "loving" relationship than in a "liking" relationship, and greater amounts of sexual desire were not believed to occur in loving relationships than in liking relationships. Again, it seems that sexual desire is viewed, at least by young men and women, as an important feature of passionate love relationships—and not of relationships characterized by feelings of loving (i.e., companionate love) and/or liking (i.e., friendship).

Not only do people *believe* that passionate love is characterized by sexual desire, but most men and women report *experiencing* sexual desire for the people with whom they are passionately in love. Regan (2000b) found that the self-reported amount of sexual desire experienced by men and women for their dating partners (and not their level of sexual activity) was significantly positively correlated with the level of passionate love they felt for those individuals. Their feelings of desire were unrelated, however, to the amount of companionate love and liking they experienced for their partners.

In sum, passionate love is a sexualized experience that is strongly associated with feelings of sexual desire or attraction for the partner.

## Fragility

*I was so in love with him. And then one day it went away. I fell out of love. I don't know why my feelings changed but they did.*

—25-year-old woman interviewed by the author

*At the beginning, the whole experience was really exciting. It was sex, romance, passion 24/7. Now it's not like that. We joke that we've become like an old married couple. Are we still in love? I think we are. I guess I don't know. What I do know is that what I feel today is not what I felt before. I'm not complaining—things are just different.*

—25-year-old man interviewed by the author

Another important feature of passionate love is its fragility. In contrast to more durable and lasting types of love, passionate love is viewed by most theorists as an inherently unstable, relatively brief phenomenon. In his discussion of the four general varieties of love, C. S. Lewis (1960/1988) called erotic love "notoriously the most mortal of our loves" and reminded readers that "the world rings with complaints of his fickleness" (p. 113). Fromm (1956), another of the early love theorists, agreed that the "explosive" experience of falling in love with someone is "by its very nature short-lived" (p. 48). This notion has been echoed in more recent discourse. For example, Berscheid (1983) concluded that passionate love, like other intense emotional experiences, has a "swift onset" and is "distressingly fragile." Drawing an analogy to substance addiction, Robert Sternberg (1988) similarly stated that the rapid development of passion is inevitably followed by habituation, so that over time the partner is no longer as "stimulating" or arousing as he or she once was. Once habituation occurs, Sternberg argued, even more time with the loved one is unlikely to provoke the earlier passionate response.

Some cross-sectional and longitudinal research supports the theoretical prediction that passionate love has a fairly brief life span in comparison with other types of love. It is the case that feelings of passionate love initially may increase as a couple progresses from earlier (e.g., casual dating) to later (e.g., steady dating, engaged) courtship stages (e.g., Hatfield & Sprecher, 1986). However, research conducted with married individuals generally finds that passionate love declines over longer periods of time (e.g., Hatfield, Traupmann, & Sprecher, 1984), as well as after major relational transitions (i.e., childlessness to parenthood; Tucker & Aron, 1993). Researchers who have surveyed dating couples find similar results. For example, with a sample of 197 dating couples, Susan Sprecher and Pamela Regan (1998) examined whether the number of months that each couple had been dating was related to the amount of passionate love the partners reportedly felt for each other. These researchers found evidence that passionate love indeed is related to relationship duration; specifically, the longer a couple had been together, the lower the partners' passionate love scores (although scores were high in all couples).

## Measuring Passionate Love

There are two basic ways to assess passionate love: single-item self-report measures and multi-item scales. Single-item measures typically ask respondents to report upon the quantity or the intensity of passionate love for their partner that they experience. Examples of such items are provided in Table 8.2.

Global single-item measures are easy to use and appear to be relatively valid (Sprecher & Regan, 1998). However, many researchers choose to use larger multi-item scales that have been developed

**Table 8.2**    Single-Item Measures of Passionate Love

1. How much passionate love do you feel for _____?

| 1 | 2 | 3 | 4 | 5 | 6 | 7 | 8 | 9 |
|---|---|---|---|---|---|---|---|---|

None                                                    A great deal

2. Rate the intensity of your feelings of passionate love for your current partner.

| 1 | 2 | 3 | 4 | 5 | 6 | 7 | 8 | 9 |
|---|---|---|---|---|---|---|---|---|

Not                                                     Extremely
at all                                                  intense

3. How deeply are you in love with _____?

| 1 | 2 | 3 | 4 | 5 | 6 | 7 | 8 | 9 |
|---|---|---|---|---|---|---|---|---|

Not at                                                  Very deeply
all deeply

4. How strong are your feelings of passionate love for your partner?

| 1 | 2 | 3 | 4 | 5 | 6 | 7 | 8 | 9 |
|---|---|---|---|---|---|---|---|---|

Very weak                                               Very strong

| 1 | 2 | 3 | 4 | 5 | 6 | 7 | 8 | 9 |
|---|---|---|---|---|---|---|---|---|

Not at                                                  Extremely
all strong                                              strong

5. How often do you experience feelings of passionate love for your partner?

| 1 | 2 | 3 | 4 | 5 | 6 | 7 | 8 | 9 |
|---|---|---|---|---|---|---|---|---|

Never                                                   Extremely
                                                        often

_____ times a day
_____ times a week
_____ times a month

6. How often did you experience passionate love in your relationship during the past month?

| 1 | 2 | 3 | 4 | 5 | 6 | 7 | 8 | 9 |
|---|---|---|---|---|---|---|---|---|

Never                      Sometimes                    Extremely
                                                        often

specifically to measure the various theoretically important elements of passionate love. Several different passionate love scales have been constructed over the years (for a review, see Hatfield, Bensman, & Rapson, 2012). The two most commonly used and empirically sound measures are the Erotic subscale of the Love Attitudes Scale (LAS) (see Chapter 7) and the Passionate Love Scale, developed by Elaine Hatfield and Susan Sprecher (1986).

The Passionate Love Scale represents the most valid and reliable measure of passionate love currently available. Drawing upon past theoretical conceptualizations, previously developed measures, and in-depth personal interviews, Hatfield and Sprecher (1986) crafted a series of items designed to assess the various components of the passionate love experience. The complete scale is reproduced in Table 8.3. The items clearly reflect what theorists believe are many of the essential ingredients of passionate love: physiological arousal and its associated bodily sensations ("Sometimes my body trembles with excitement at the sight of _____"), intense emotions ("Since I've been involved with _____, my emotions have been on a roller coaster"), sexual desire ("I possess a powerful attraction for _____"), partner idealization ("For me, _____ is the perfect romantic partner"), and mental preoccupation ("Sometimes I can't control my thoughts; they are obsessively on _____").

**Table 8.3**   The Passionate Love Scale

---

**Instructions**
We would like to know how you feel when you are passionately in love. Some common terms for passionate love are romantic love, infatuation, love sickness, or obsessive love. Please think of the person whom you love most passionately right now. If you are not in love right now, please think of the last person you loved. If you have never been in love, think of the person you came closest to caring for in that way. Try to tell us how you felt at the time when your feelings were the most intense.

### Response Scale

| 1 | 2 | 3 | 4 | 5 | 6 | 7 | 8 | 9 |
|---|---|---|---|---|---|---|---|---|
| Not at all true | | | | Moderately true | | | | Definitely true |

**Items**

1. Since I've been involved with _____, my emotions have been on a roller coaster.

2. I would feel deep despair if _____ left me.

3. Sometimes my body trembles with excitement at the sight of _____.

*(Continued)*

**Table 8.3**      (Continued)

4. I take delight in studying the movements and angles of _____'s body.

5. Sometimes I can't control my thoughts; they are obsessively on _____.

6. I feel happy when I am doing something to make _____ happy.

7. I would rather be with _____ than with anyone else.

8. I'd get jealous if I thought _____ were falling in love with someone else.

9. No one else could love _____ like I do.

10. I yearn to know all about _____.

11. I want _____ physically, emotionally, mentally.

12. I will love _____ forever.

13. I melt when looking deeply into _____'s eyes.

14. I have an endless appetite for affection from _____.

15. For me, _____ is the perfect romantic partner.

16. _____ is the person who can make me feel the happiest.

17. I sense my body responding when _____ touches me.

18. I feel tender toward _____.

19. _____ always seems to be on my mind.

20. If I were separated from _____ for a long time, I would feel intensely lonely.

21. I sometimes find it difficult to concentrate on work because thoughts of _____ occupy my mind.

22. I want _____ to know me—my thoughts, my fears, and my hopes.

23. Knowing that _____ cares about me makes me feel complete.

24. I eagerly look for signs indicating _____'s desire for me.

25. If _____ were going through a difficult time, I would put away my own concerns to help him/her out.

26. _____ can make me feel effervescent and bubbly.

27. In the presence of _____, I yearn to touch and be touched.

28. An existence without _____ would be dark and dismal.

29. I possess a powerful attraction for _____.

30. I get extremely depressed when things don't go right in my relationship with _____.

**Table 8.3**      (Continued)

**Scoring**

To find out your passionate love score, add up the ratings you gave to each item. Divide this total by 30. Is your score average (around 5)? Or are you below average (below 5) or above average (above 5)?

SOURCE: Hatfield, E., & Sprecher, S. (1986). Measuring passionate love in intimate relationships. *Journal of Adolescence, 9*, 383–410. Copyright © 1986 by Academic Press, Inc. Used with permission of Elsevier.

## The Biochemistry of Passion

Recently, scientists have become interested in whether passionate love has a particular biochemical basis. In particular, researchers have focused their attention on three possible correlates of this type of love: pheromones, sex hormones, and brain activity.

### Pheromones

*Pheromones* are chemical secretions that produce unlearned behavioral (often sexual or reproductive) responses from other members of the same species (Karlson & Lüscher, 1959). Because pheromones regulate sexual behavior in many nonhuman mammals (Azar, 1998), and because humans are capable of discriminating among other individuals on the basis of scent (Cernoch & Porter, 1985; Wallace, 1977), it is possible that a human pheromone that stimulates romantic attraction exists. Some researchers have suggested that human skin cells may produce pheromones or process and store pheromonal substances from the bloodstream that are then released when the skin cells die and are sloughed off into the environment (e.g., Berliner, Jennings-White, & Lavker, 1991). Other researchers have noted that men and women possess odor-producing apocrine glands in the underarm, nipple, and genital areas that become active at puberty and that appear to influence some aspects of reproductive behavior (Cohn, 1994). For example, the menstrual cycles of women who engage in heterosexual sexual activity on a regular basis are more regular than the menstrual cycles of women who do not engage in regular sexual activity, perhaps due to their more frequent exposure to male apocrine gland secretions (e.g., Cutler, Preti, Huggins, Erickson, & Garcia, 1985). To date, however, scientists have not conclusively verified the existence of human pheromones that influence passion and other aspects of romantic attraction. (Of course, this does not mean that odor and olfaction are not involved in attraction; for example, people often come to associate a particular scent [e.g., a perfume, cologne, body spray, aftershave, or "natural" body fragrance] with a specific partner. When they smell that particular scent, they are likely to be reminded of that partner and this may provoke feelings of attraction, desire, warmth, intimacy, and other responses. This, however, reflects a learned association and is not a true pheromonal reaction.)

## Sex Hormones

Researchers also have focused on the role that the *sex hormones* (androgens, estrogens, progesterone, and prolactin) play in human attraction. These hormones are produced by several of the glands within the endocrine system, including the adrenal glands, the pituitary gland, the ovaries in women, and the testes in men. Of the various sex hormones, the *androgens* (masculinizing hormones) are the most strongly implicated in the experience of attraction (see Regan, 1999). Scientists interested in the relationship between the androgens and interpersonal attraction have concentrated primarily on *testosterone*, the most potent androgen, and its impact upon sexual attraction. A growing body of evidence indicates that the experience of sexual attraction is at least partially androgen-dependent in both men and women. Reviews of the existing medical, clinical, and social scientific literatures (Davis & Braunstein, 2012; Regan & Bersheid, 1999) reveal the following conclusions:

- Levels of testosterone are positively correlated with self-reported levels of sexual desire and frequency of sexual thoughts in healthy men and women. That is, the higher the level of available (free or active) testosterone in a person's bloodstream, the more sexual desire he or she reports experiencing and the more often he or she indicates having sexual thoughts.

- People who have undergone surgical procedures (e.g., removal of the adrenal glands) that result in a sudden decrease in their levels of testosterone report decreased feelings of sexual desire.

- Treatment with synthetic steroids that suppress the synthesis of testosterone produces diminished sexual desire. This result has been observed in three groups of individuals: (1) male sex offenders who are treated with the anti-androgenic substances cyproterone acetate (CPA) or medroxyprogesterone acetate (MPA), (2) cancer patients who receive anti-androgenic treatment in combination with surgical castration as part of their therapeutic regimen, and (3) people who are given androgen antagonists to treat androgen-dependent hair and skin problems (e.g., acne, alopecia, hirsutism, seborrhea). In all three groups, treatment often is associated with a reduction in sexual desire, fantasies, and urges.

- The administration of testosterone (and other androgens) has been noted to result in an increase in the strength and frequency of sexual desire among three groups of people: (1) otherwise healthy men and women complaining of diminished sexual interest, (2) men with hypogonadism or eugonadism (medical conditions that result in abnormally low levels of testosterone), and (3) women with androgen deficiency syndrome (an androgen deficiency caused by chemotherapy, hysterectomy [removal of the uterus], or oophorectomy [removal of the ovaries]).

These findings suggest that some level of the androgens (and in particular testosterone) may be necessary for the experience of sexual attraction. However, this research does not provide evidence of a direct link between the action of the sex hormones and passionate love. At best, there may be an indirect connection. That is, testosterone is associated with the experience of sexual desire, which in turn is associated with the experience of passionate love. In sum, a series of testosterone injections given to a person with a low level of desire may enhance his or her ability to experience sexual attraction, but the impact will be temporary, general (it may not produce attraction to a specific other person), and certainly not sufficient to produce the state we call "being in love."

## Brain Activity

Other researchers believe that specific *neurotransmitters* (electrochemical messages released by neurons or the cells of the nervous system) are associated with the experience of passionate love (e.g., Fisher, Aron, Mashek, Li, & Brown, 2002; Hawkes, 1992). Although a number of different types of neurotransmitters exist, the monoamines (in particular, *serotonin, dopamine, norepinephrine*) have received the most attention due to their strong relationship with mood and generalized arousal. For example, drawing on the social science literature on passionate love, the neuroscience literature on monoamines, and original empirical research on the properties of passionate love (e.g., Mashek, Aron, & Fisher, 2000), Helen Fisher (e.g., 1998, 2000, 2006) has argued that passionate love is associated primarily with high levels of dopamine and norepinephrine and low levels of serotonin. Evidence that she has cited in support of her hypothesis includes the following:

- People who are in love report focusing on specific events or objects associated with the beloved and remembering and musing over things that the beloved said or did. Increased levels of dopamine are associated with heightened attention, and increased levels of norepinephrine are associated with enhanced memory for new stimuli.

- People in the midst of intense passion report thinking about the loved one obsessively, and low levels of serotonin are implicated in the type of intrusive thinking that is associated with obsessive-compulsive disorder.

- People who are passionately in love often report feelings of euphoria and exhilaration coupled with heightened energy, loss of appetite, and sleeplessness. These same experiences are associated with increased concentrations of dopamine in the brain.

The similarities between the experience of being in love and the psycho-physiological effects of the monoamines may be coincidental. However, one investigation demonstrated that a group of healthy people who were in the early phases of "falling in love" had approximately the same level of serotonin as did a group of people who had been diagnosed with obsessive-compulsive disorder; in addition, the serotonin levels of both of these groups of participants were significantly lower than those of a control group of healthy participants who were not currently in love (Marazziti, Akiskal, Rossi, and Cassano, 1999; also see Kurup & Kurup, 2003). Another study revealed that people who were intensely in love showed increased activity in dopamine-rich areas of the brain when they gazed at a photo of their beloved (Aron et al., 2005; also see Ortigue, Bianchi-Demicheli, Patel, Frum, & Lewis, 2010). Although additional research is needed, these findings suggest that the experience of passionate love may be associated with brain neurochemistry.

## ❖ COMPANIONATE LOVE: A "STURDY" KIND OF LOVE

In their classification schemes, the majority of scientists include not only passionate love but also a type of love called *companionate love*. Variously described as affectionate love, friendship love, true love, attachment, storge, and conjugal love, companionate love reflects "the affection and tenderness we feel for those with whom our lives are deeply entwined" (Hatfield & Rapson, 1993, p. 9).

## Defining Companionate Love

*I hope and pray I shall be able to make you happy and secure during my remaining years, and cherish you my darling one as you deserve, and leave you in comfort when my race is run. What it has been to me to live all these years in yr heart and companionship no phrases can convey. Time passes swiftly, but is it not joyous to see how great and growing is the treasure we have gathered together?*

—From a letter written by Winston Churchill, the British prime minister, to his wife, Clementine, January 23, 1935 (Soames, 1979)

*You have been with me constantly, sweetheart. At Kangerdlooksoah I looked repeatedly at Ptarmigan Island and thought of the time we camped there. At Nuuatoksoah I landed where we were. And on the 11th we passed the mouth of Bowdoin Bay in brilliant weather, and as long as I could I kept my eyes on Anniversary Lodge. We have been great chums dear. . . . In fancy I kiss your dear eyes and lips and cheeks sweetheart; and dream of you and my children, and my home till I come again. Kiss my babies for me.*

—From a letter written by Arctic explorer Robert Peary to his wife, Josephine, August 17, 1908 (Tamplin, 1995)

Companionate love, or the state of "loving" someone, consists of several basic features, including a *relatively slow onset, durability* (permanence or stability), *closeness or interdependence*, and *positive affect* (including feelings of affection, intimacy, and commitment).

### Positive Affect

*My husband is my best friend. I trust him completely. He is kind and caring, he makes me laugh, and I respect him and like him as a person. I can't imagine spending my life with anyone else.*

—29-year-old woman interviewed by the author

In contrast to passionate love's heated and heady emotions, companionate love is assumed to be associated with uniformly positive, and much less intense, emotional experiences. Recall Lewis's (1960/1988) description of affectionate love as "this warm comfortableness, this satisfaction in being together" (p. 32). Relationship scholar Sharon Brehm (1985) described this type of love as built on a solid foundation of respect, admiration, and interpersonal trust and rewards, and Sternberg (1988) similarly depicted companionate love as composed of feelings of emotional intimacy coupled with a firm commitment to the relationship and the partner.

Indeed, research suggests that positive affect is a particularly strong feature of companionate love. Recall that Beverley Fehr's (1988) participants identified warm feelings of *trust, caring, respect, loyalty, supportiveness,* and *friendship* as prototypical features of love; more intense experiences, including *euphoria, heart races, butterflies in stomach,* and other signs of emotional arousal, were not considered to be essential features of this type of love. Similar results were reported by Helmut Lamm and Ulrich Wiesmann (1997), who asked university students to write down how they could tell that they "loved" (as opposed to "liked" or were "in love with") another person. The most common indicator of companionate love generated by the participants was *positive mood* (listed by 53%); distinctive indicators (i.e., elements that were listed significantly more frequently for "love" than for "like" or "in love") included such positive affective experiences as *trust* (41%), *tolerance* (21%), and *relaxedness or calmness* (12%).

The participants in a study conducted by psychologist Donna Castañeda (1993) provided almost identical answers when asked to indicate the qualities and characteristics they believed to be important in a love relationship. Specifically, participants mentioned *trust, mutual respect, communication and sharing, honesty,* and *affection* along with a number of other positive emotions and experiences. Research with dating couples substantiates these survey results. Sprecher and Regan (1998) found that positive emotions (including joy, trust, liking, contentment, satisfaction, and respect) were strongly positively correlated with, and negative emotions (such as anger, hatred, anxiety, and loneliness) were negatively correlated with, the amount of companionate love reported by a sample of romantically involved couples. That is, the more companionate love men and women felt for their partners, the more they experienced positive (and the less they experienced negative) emotions.

### Durability

> I've known my girlfriend since middle school, and we've been together as a couple for the past 8 years. Our relationship is incredibly strong. We come from very different backgrounds, and we've had our share of difficulties. We've both had to make sacrifices and learn how to truly be there for each other. And we've made it. We've stayed together through everything. I can say with 100% honesty that our relationship has only

*gotten stronger over time. I love her with all my heart and I know she feels
the same way about me.*

—26-year-old man interviewed by the author

Unlike passionate love, companionate love is assumed to be relatively impervious to the passage of time. In fact, some theorists speculate that companionate love may grow stronger over time because it is grounded in intimacy processes (including caring, understanding, and attachment) that require time to develop fully (Hatfield & Rapson, 1993). Other scientists propose that romantic relationships may even progress in a linear fashion from passionate love to companionate love. For example, Sternberg (1988) suggested, "Most romantic love relationships that do, in fact, survive eventually turn into companionate love relationships: the passion begins to melt, but the intimacy remains. Passion may be replaced over time by long-term and deeply felt commitment" (p. 127).

A similar proposition was made by theorist Bernard Murstein (1988), who noted,

> With unimpeded access to each other and as a result of habituation, bit
> by bit generalized, overriding passion and longing evaporate and are
> replaced by liking or trust, although in good marriages, passion may
> return on specific occasions. . . . Out of the evolving network of shared
> experiences as a couple—children, family, married life—comes something less ephemeral and more permanent than romantic love. (p. 30)

Certainly, companionate lovers report feeling extremely committed to the partner and desirous of maintaining the relationship; their feelings of companionate love also appear unrelated to the length of their relationship (i.e., time does not appear to have any negative impact on companionate love). Recall that the passionate love scores of the dating couples in Sprecher and Regan's (1998) study were negatively associated with the age of their relationship; specifically, the longer they had been romantically involved with their partners, the less "in love" they reported being with those partners. However, their companionate love scores were not associated with the length of their relationship; that is, regardless of how long they had been together, couples' companionate love scores remained high.

## Closeness

*We love each other. It's a simple statement but it carries a great deal of
meaning. It means that we care about and for each other, we are honest with
each other, we listen to each other respectfully and openly, we take time to be*

*together and we put time and effort into our relationship. We are partners in every sense of the word. It's not me and her, it's us.*

—32-year-old woman interviewed by the author

Closeness is another important feature of companionate love. Love theorists Elaine Hatfield and Richard Rapson (1993) argued that companionate love requires that the partners' lives "must be deeply entwined" (p. 107). Sternberg (1988) similarly suggested that companionate lovers possess mutual understanding, share themselves and their possessions with one another, give and receive emotional support, and demonstrate various other signs of intimate connection and mutuality. A close relationship is defined as one in which the partners' thoughts, emotions, and actions—their lives—are strongly interdependent (Kelley et al., 1983). Companionate love is, in essence, close love; that is, it is characterized by a high degree of interconnection between the two individuals. What one partner says, feels, does, or thinks has a direct impact on the other person.

## Measuring Companionate Love

Companionate love can be measured via single items (e.g., "How much caring, affectionate love do you feel for your partner?") or multi-item scales. For example, Sternberg (1986) defined companionate love as the combination of intimacy and decision/commitment; thus, the 30 items on his scale that reflect those components provide one measure of companionate love. The Storge subscale on the LAS also may assess this type of love. Perhaps the most commonly used measure of companionate love, however, is the 13-item Love Scale created by Zick Rubin (1970). Sprecher and Regan (1998), in an attempt to create an even "purer" measure of companionate love, added an item that assesses interpersonal trust to Rubin's scale and removed several items that reflected a more passionate love experience. The resulting 7-item, adapted Companionate Love Scale is provided in Table 8.4.

## The Biochemistry of Affection

Just as they have with passionate love, scientists have begun to explore the biochemical correlates of affection and attachment. Two peptide hormones, *oxytocin* and *vasopressin,* have been investigated. These substances are released as neurotransmitters (peptides) in the brain and as hormones from the pituitary gland, and they have multiple biological functions involving the kidneys and the cardiovascular and

**Table 8.4**     The Companionate Love Scale

**Instructions**

Companionate love is a stable type of love based on feelings of deep affection and caring. Some common terms for companionate love are *affectionate love, friendship love, true love, attachment,* and *conjugal love*. We would like to know how you feel when you love someone this way. Please think of the person whom you love most companionately *right now*. If you do not love someone right now, please think of the last person you loved. If you have never loved someone, think of the person you came closest to caring for in that way.

**Response Scale**

| 1 | 2 | 3 | 4 | 5 | 6 | 7 | 8 | 9 |
|---|---|---|---|---|---|---|---|---|

Not at all true                Moderately true                Definitely true

**Items**

1. I feel that I can confide in _____ about virtually everything.
2. I find it easy to ignore _____'s faults.
3. I would do almost anything for _____.
4. I would forgive _____ for practically anything.
5. I would greatly enjoy being confided in by _____.
6. I care about _____.
7. I feel that I can trust _____ completely.

**Scoring**

To find out your companionate love score, add up the ratings you gave to each item. Divide this total by 7. How did you score? Were you average (around 5), below average (below 5), or above average (above 5) on the scale?

SOURCE: Sprecher, S., & Regan, P. C. (1998). Passionate and companionate love in courting and young married couples. *Sociological Inquiry, 68,* 163–185. Copyright © 1998 by Blackwell Publishing, Inc. Reprinted with permission.

reproductive systems. For example, vasopressin increases blood pressure and facilitates the flow of blood through the kidneys. Oxytocin, which acts on smooth muscle cells, appears to play a role in various sexual responses including orgasm (in both men and women) and ejaculation (in men). In women, oxytocin also stimulates uterine contractions during childbirth and the release of milk during lactation.

Both vasopressin and oxytocin are associated with a variety of reproductive and caregiving behaviors in nonhuman mammals (see Hiller, 2004; Insel, 1997, 2000; Leckman & Herman, 2002). In addition, decreased levels of oxytocin and other alterations in the endocrine oxytocin and vasopressin systems have been observed in children diagnosed with autism, a developmental disorder characterized by severe social impairment and the inability to form interpersonal connections and lasting emotional attachments (Green et al., 2001). Based on these two lines of research, some scientists have hypothesized that oxytocin and vasopressin may be involved in the ability to form social attachments and to experience feelings of affection, affiliation, and companionate love (Carter, 1998, 2014; Fisher, 2000; Leckman, Hrdy, Keverne, & Carter, 2006). However, preliminary research suggests that elevated levels of oxytocin (in women) and vasopressin (in men) actually are associated with relationship *distress* (see Taylor, Saphire-Bernstein, & Seeman, 2010). Moreover, most current research on the affiliative effects of oxytocin (and other neuropeptides) continues to be conducted on nonhuman mammals (e.g., prairie voles) and is not easily generalizable to humans (for additional discussion, see van Anders, Goodson, & Kingsbury, 2013). Thus, we still have no conclusive evidence about whether neuropeptide levels or activity are associated with the love-related experiences, or affiliative tendencies, of healthy adult men and women.

## Summary

Although most scientists recognize and maintain the distinction between passionate love and companionate love, both types of love are experienced with some frequency by men and women during their lifetimes. Passionate love is an intensely emotional, fragile, and sexualized experience that has become strongly associated with the marriage contract and the establishment of other types of committed, romantic relationship. Companionate love is a more durable, lower-keyed experience that is founded on trust, affection, and respect. Although this type of love has received less attention than its more colorful cousin, it is certainly no less essential to human happiness.

## Key Concepts

Passionate love (p. 170)

Idealization and preoccupation (as features of passionate love) (p. 171)

Exclusivity (as a feature of passionate love) (p. 172)

Emotional intensity (as a feature of passionate love) (p. 173)

Sexual attraction (as a feature of passionate love) (p. 175)

Fragility (as a feature of passionate love) (p. 178)

Single-item measures of passionate love (pp. 179–180)

Passionate Love Scale (p. 181)

Pheromones (p. 183)

Sex hormones (p. 184)

Androgens (p. 184)

Testosterone (p. 184)

Neurotransmitters (p. 185)

Companionate love (p. 186)

Positive affect (as a feature of companionate love) (p. 187)

Durability (as a feature of companionate love) (p. 188)

Closeness (as a feature of companionate love) (p. 189)

Companionate Love Scale (pp. 190, 191)

## Discussion Questions

1. Compare and contrast the experience of passionate and companionate love. If you had to choose, which would you rather feel for a steady dating partner or spouse? Why?

2. Is it possible to feel both types of love—passionate and companionate—for another person?

3. Consider the general theories of love presented in Chapter 7. Which types or styles of love reflect the two varieties discussed in this chapter?

4. Select a movie or television scene that, in your opinion, best illustrates the concept of "passionate" love. Do the same for "companionate" love. Share your examples with the class and discuss the ways in which the scenes exemplify these two types of love.

5. Consider the many ways in which love has been portrayed throughout history and in literature. Is love a "good" thing? A "bad" thing? Use examples to support your conclusion. (Good sources of information include Bartlett's *Familiar Quotations*, any book of proverbs, and *The Oxford Dictionary of Quotations*).

## Recommended Readings

In 1967, Kephart asked a group of men and women whether love was essential for marriage. Twenty years later, Simpson and his colleagues did the same. The results revealed that attitudes about the association between love and marriage had dramatically changed over time, particularly among women.

Kephart, W. M. (1967). Some correlates of romantic love. *Journal of Marriage and the Family, 29*, 470–474.

Simpson, J. A., Campbell, B., & Berscheid, E. (1986). The association between romantic love and marriage: Kephart (1967) twice revisited. *Personality and Social Psychology Bulletin, 12*, 363–372.

Long before most other social scientists, Berscheid recognized that lust (sexual attraction or desire) is one of the essential ingredients of passionate love. In this delightful chapter, she calls for social psychologists to reintegrate sexuality, in particular desire, into their discourse on love.

Berscheid, E. (1988). Some comments on love's anatomy: Or, whatever happened to old-fashioned lust? In R. J. Sternberg & M. L. Barnes (Eds.), *The psychology of love* (pp. 359–374). New Haven, CT: Yale University Press.

This classic article is one of the earliest social psychological commentaries about the nature of love.

Berscheid, E., & Walster, E. (1974). A little bit about love. In T. L. Huston (Ed.), *Foundations of interpersonal attraction* (pp. 355–381). New York, NY: Academic Press.

This article presents an overview of multi-item measures of passionate love.

Hatfield, E., Bensman, L., & Rapson, R. L. (2012). A brief history of social scientists' attempts to measure passionate love. *Journal of Social and Personal Relationships, 29,* 143–164.

# 9

# Love Gone Bad

## *Problematic Aspects of Love*

❖　❖　❖

Love is associated with a variety of positive events. For example, the experience of loving another person may allow us to feel intimacy, contentment, and satisfaction; to experience passion, joy, and excitement; and to provide and receive emotional and social support. All of these experiences, in turn, can enhance and promote our psychological and even our physical well-being. But there is another side to love as well—a dangerous, destructive, and problematic side that is associated with dysfunction, negative emotion, and other harmful outcomes. This chapter examines the "dark" side of love.

## ❖ UNREQUITED PASSIONATE LOVE: WHEN THE ONE WE LOVE DOES NOT LOVE US

*The very first time I fell in love was when I was a freshman in college and it was unrequited—she never knew, or if she did, she probably thought I had a slight crush on her. I never showed my real feelings to her. But I loved her so much. I would spend my day hoping for a glimpse of her, and when I did see her, I would be overcome with these waves of longing. I spent more time daydreaming and creating these elaborate romantic scenarios in my mind than I did studying for all my classes combined. Nothing came of it, but I look back on that experience with great fondness—it was my first love and it was wonderful.*

—40-year-old man interviewed by the author

*In high school, I was friends with a boy who was kind of awkward and unattractive, not very popular. But I was nice to him, because he sat next to me in class and he was smart and actually a pretty decent guy. One day, he passed me a note before class asking me out—he said he loved me, and he listed all the ways I'd shown that I felt the same way about him, and he basically said that because of this I was obligated to go out with him. I was embarrassed and kind of pissed off, because all I had been doing was being nice. I decided to talk with him after class and it was really awkward—I didn't want to hurt his feelings or make him feel bad, but at the same time it's really annoying to have your innocent, friendly behaviors completely misinterpreted and then used against you. I had to work really hard to maintain a friendly relationship with him after that. Overall, it was not a very pleasant experience for me (I'm sure it wasn't fun for him, either, but honestly, I was the one who had to fix things—he did not make it easy for me).*

—27-year-old woman interviewed by the author

Folk wisdom (actually, Victorian poet Alfred Tennyson) tells us that "it is better to have loved and lost than never to have loved at all." And perhaps this is sound advice. After all, love is usually associated with a wonderful and rewarding mix of positive outcomes, events, and feelings. However, passionate love—particularly when it is *unrequited* or not reciprocated by the beloved—has the potential to be just as strongly associated with negative outcomes.

In one of the first studies to attempt to explore the dynamics of unrequited love, Roy Baumeister, Sara Wotman, and Arlene Stillwell (1993) asked 71 people who had been in this situation to write autobiographical accounts of their experiences as would-be suitors and rejectors. The results indicated that unrequited lovers experienced a panoply of both positive and negative emotions. Many (44%) would-be suitors reported that their unreciprocated passion caused them pain, suffering, and disappointment; jealousy and anger (which were usually directed at the loved one's chosen partner); and a sense of frustration. Similarly, 22% experienced worries and fears about rejection. In addition to these unpleasant experiences, however, the lovelorn suitors also reported many pleasant emotional outcomes; in fact, positive feelings far outweighed negative ones in the accounts they gave of their experience. For example, happiness, excitement, the blissful anticipation of seeing the beloved, sheer elation at the state of being in love, and other positive emotions were reported by the majority (98%) of would-be suitors. More than half (53%) also looked back upon their unrequited love experiences with some degree of positive feeling. In explaining this finding, the researchers noted the following:

> Apparently, positive feelings can be remembered in a positive way even if the memory is linked to suffering and disappointment. People remember the warmth of their feelings for another person, and the memory is at least somewhat pleasant. Some of our participants expressed gladness at being able to preserve the friendship that could have been jeopardized if their romantic overtures had become too insistent. Others simply treasured the memory or retained a soft spot in their heart for the one they loved. (Baumeister & Wotman, 1992, p. 60)

When the researchers examined the experiences reported by the rejectors, however, they found little evidence of positive outcomes. Specifically, although roughly one fourth of the rejectors reported feeling flattered by the attention of their potential lovers, the majority also viewed these unwanted advances as annoying (51%), felt uncomfortable about delivering rejection messages (61%), and experienced a host of negative emotions, including anger, frustration, and resentment (70%). In addition, their recollections of the entire experience were far less suffused with warmth, with only 33% indicating any positive affect in retrospect. The researchers concluded:

> Unlike the would-be lover, it was hard for the rejector to feel that his or her life had been enriched by this experience. For many, apparently, it was a useless and pointless set of aggravations. They were forced to

respond to a situation they never wanted, and these responses were difficult for them, bringing uncertainty, guilt, aggravation, all of which went for naught. For some, a valued friendship was destroyed in the bargain. Thus they had plenty to resent and regret. (Baumeister & Wotman, 1992, p. 62)

Other researchers have reported similar findings (e.g., Sinclair & Frieze, 2005). Unrequited love clearly is an emotionally difficult experience for both the rejector and the would-be suitor. Unfortunately, it also is a common event in the lives of adolescents and young adults, particularly men (Hill, Blakemore, & Drumm, 1997), and there is no easy way to recover from romantic rejection. Time is, perhaps, the only cure.

## ❖ RELATIONAL STALKING: WHEN ROMANTIC INTEREST BECOMES OBSESSION

*At first I thought it was sort of cute and romantic that he wanted to be with me all the time. He would ask me to give him a detailed account of my day, all the places I went, the people I talked with, the things I did. . . . I felt flattered that I had a boyfriend who loved me so much. But then it got out of hand. I mean, he wouldn't even let me drive to the store by myself! After we broke up, he began calling me at home, usually several times a night. He also started calling me at work, which made things difficult for me with my boss. So I stopped taking his calls at work and I changed to an unlisted number at home. I think what really made me realize that I needed to take some action and tell people what was going on was when he started spying on me. One morning, I was standing by the window looking outside and I noticed his car. He was just sitting there, watching me. I have no idea how long he had been there, but it really scared me. I felt trapped and violated.*

—32-year-old woman interviewed by the author

*I met a woman I thought I liked. She was attractive, bright, seemed to have a good sense of humor and to be stable and well grounded. We went out on a couple of dates and it turned out that we didn't have that much in common, so I didn't pursue the relationship. No big breakup or anything, we just weren't suited to each other. That should have been the end of it, but it wasn't. She lived about 10 miles from me, and she would drive over to my neighborhood, park in front of my house, and then go jogging around the block for what seemed like hours. I would see her as she passed my house again and again, every single day. She began to eat in the local restaurants I frequented. She called my house and left messages about getting together to "work things out." She was everywhere I went and she did her best to invade every single moment of my day. My friends laughed about it and made jokes about what a lucky guy I was to have this woman chasing after me, but believe me it wasn't funny. Fortunately, I relocated due to my job and I haven't seen her since.*

—46-year-old man interviewed by the author

As we have seen, most people at some time or another become attracted to or fall in love with individuals who do not reciprocate their feelings. And although these experiences often are not pleasant, the majority of men and women manage to deal with them. Sometimes, however, individuals respond to unrequited love or unreciprocated passion with obsessive thinking and inappropriate (and even violent) behavior (Meloy, 1989; Mintz, 1980; Sinclair & Frieze, 2002).

*Relational stalking* is a harmful behavioral syndrome that involves one person (the pursuer or stalker) desiring and actively attempting to create or obtain an intimate relationship with another person (the target or victim) who either does not want this particular kind of relationship or who wants no relationship at all (see Emerson, Ferris, & Gardner, 1998; Spitzberg & Cupach, 2003). This phenomenon also has been called *obsessive relational intrusion* or ORI (Cupach & Spitzberg, 1998), *domestic stalking* (Dunn, 1999), and *intimate partner stalking* (Tjaden & Thoennes, 2000). Relational stalking behavior has three characteristic features: (1) intentional and persistent contact (or attempted contact) by the pursuer that is (2) unwanted and (3) psychologically aversive (unpleasant or offensive) to the recipient. Beginning with California in 1991, every state and district in the United States has enacted antistalking laws designed to protect victims and punish offenders. Although the specifics of these laws vary widely (as does the extent to which they are enforced), relational stalking generally becomes a crime when it poses a credible threat that places the recipient in reasonable fear for his or her safety (see Cupach & Spitzberg, 2004; Meloy, 2007).

Surveys of college and community samples in the United States and other countries (e.g., Italy, Germany) reveal that relational stalking is disturbingly common, with rates ranging from 12% to 40% and with women at greater risk than men for this type of victimization (e.g., Amar & Alexy, 2010; Dressing, Kuehner, & Gass, 2005; Haugaard & Seri, 2003; Logan, Leukefeld, & Walker, 2000; Maran, Varetto, Zedda, & Munari, 2014; Sheridan, Gillett, & Davies, 2002; Spitzberg, Cupach, & Ciceraro, 2010; Turmanis & Brown, 2006). In addition, sizeable numbers of men and women report having been the target of unwanted pursuit or "pre-stalking" behaviors including receiving unwanted letters, notes, phone calls, visits, or gifts, or being followed or watched (Herold, Mantle, & Zemitis, 1979; Jason, Reichler, Easton, Neal, & Wilson, 1984; Leonard et al., 1993; Roscoe, Strouse, & Goodwin, 1994). Most victims of stalking are acquainted with their pursuers; in fact, former romantic partners make up the largest proportion of relational stalkers (Spitzberg & Cupach, 2007).

## Factors Associated With Relational Stalking

What factors contribute to relational stalking? There is some evidence that personality traits (e.g., neuroticism) and disorders (e.g., narcissistic, borderline, and other Cluster B disorders), social skills deficits, and other individual-level factors are associated with an increased likelihood of engaging in unwanted pursuit behavior (Ménard & Pincus, 2012; Tassy & Winstead, 2014; for reviews, see Cupach & Spitzberg, 2008, and Miller, 2012). Relational factors, however, appear to play the most important role. For example, relational stalking may emerge from the normal courtship process—in particular, from the indirect manner in which relationship initiation is typically enacted. Recall from Chapter 2 that most people rely on indirect, nonverbal cues to convey attraction and signal romantic interest to another person. These indirect behaviors—eye contact, smiling, and the like—may pass unnoticed by the target (or may be noticed but not interpreted as a meaningful reflection of romantic interest). Consequently, the target may fail to clearly communicate his or her acceptance or rejection of the overture. And, in the absence of any unequivocal response one way or the other, the pursuer may conclude that the target reciprocates his or her feelings and may persist in (or even escalate) the pursuit behavior. Indeed, research conducted with college student samples reveals that men and women often engage in persistent, unwanted pursuit or "pre-stalking" behaviors during the early stages of courtship (Sinclair & Frieze, 2002; Williams & Frieze, 2005) as well as after the unwanted termination of a romantic relationship (Dutton & Winstead, 2006), and they often fail to accurately perceive the negative impact that their behavior has on the targets of their desire (Sinclair & Frieze, 2005; also see Davis, Ace, & Andra, 2000).

Similarly, pursuers often seek to promote their connection with a target through the same interpersonal processes that characterize normal courtship and relationship development. For example, the development of most romantic relationships is marked by reciprocal and progressively deeper levels of self-disclosure and intimacy, social exchange, interdependence, and commitment (see Chapter 3). During interactions with the target, the pursuer may engage in behaviors that presumably convey and reflect these processes; from the pursuer's perspective, he or she is simply following the path of natural relationship progression. However, in a relational stalking situation, the self-disclosure that occurs typically is one-sided, premature, and excessive (i.e., too much, too personal, too nonreciprocal). Additionally, extreme possessiveness takes the place of closeness, and familiarity and interdependence are created through violations of privacy rather than through the mutual exchanges that characterize normal relationship development. In sum:

> ORI [stalking] relationships are characterized by forms of intimacy that are distorted, exaggerated, accelerated, more intense, and more desperate, compared to the normal prototype for developing intimacy. Although the same dimensions of intimacy that characterize normal relations apply to ORI [stalking] relations, their manifestations are more forced, fabricated, prematurely escalated, and disinhibited. (Spitzberg & Cupach, 2002, p. 206)

The environmental or sociocultural context also may contribute to relational stalking. As discussed in Chapter 2, most men and women believe that it is appropriate for men to initiate dates and actively pursue dating opportunities; given this normative belief, it may be difficult for a man to recognize when his initiation behavior has become inappropriately persistent and threatening. Similarly, a commonly held romantic assumption (and one that is frequently portrayed in movies, literature, and other media) is that "persistence pays." On screen and in the pages of novels, suitors often persist in—and are rewarded for—their efforts to gain attention and affection from a potential mate, and even partners who have ended a relationship sometimes "come around" and renew their love and their commitment to one another (see such early classics as *The Philadelphia Story* [1940] and *His Girl Friday* [1940], as well as a host of more contemporary films including *The Parent Trap* [1961, 1998], *Say Anything* [1989], *Sense and Sensibility* [1995], *Beastly* [2011], and *Chef* [2013], to name a few). Given this state of affairs, it is not surprising that a would-be lover would make repeated attempts to woo a potential or former partner—and would view these actions in a positive light.

By making it difficult for both pursuers and targets to recognize when pursuit behaviors have crossed out of the realm of "normal courtship," these contextual factors—the ambiguity that often surrounds relationship initiation, the occurrence of interpersonal processes that characterize normal relationship progression, and the cultural glorification of persistence in the face of romantic disinterest or rejection—create a situation that is conducive to relational stalking.

## Types of Pursuit or Stalking Behavior

Data gathered by communication scholars William Cupach and Brian Spitzberg (1997, 1998, 2004; Spitzberg & Cupach, 1996, 2002) and others (e.g., Brewster, 2003; Geistman, Smith, Lambert, & Cluse-Tolar, 2013; Turmanis & Brown, 2006) reveal that pursuers use a variety of tactics to promote relationships with their unwilling targets. Some of these strategies are *mildly intrusive and invasive*, including leaving repeated messages, giving gifts and other tokens of affection, unexpectedly "showing up" at places frequented by the target, using third parties to obtain information about the target, and making exaggerated expressions of devotion or affection. Many of these milder forms of pursuit resemble variations of flirting behavior, and most targets consider them annoying but not unduly bothersome or frightening. Examples of *moderately intrusive and invasive* behaviors include surveillance of the target (e.g., following, monitoring, watching, or spying on the target, driving by the target's home or place of work), trespassing, stealing information or property, intentionally sabotaging the target's reputation, and intruding on the target's friends and family. These forms of harassment are much more distressing to the target and often constitute criminal acts (for example, it is illegal to remove mail from a person's mailbox, to steal, damage, or deface someone's private property, and so forth). *Extremely intrusive or invasive* tactics are those that are most likely to induce high levels of fear (in which case the behaviors would legally constitute stalking); examples of these behaviors include threatening to harm the target or his or her loved ones, physically restraining or assaulting the target, injuring or killing the target's pet(s), coercing or forcing the target to engage in sexual activities, damaging the target's property, and invading the target's home or work.

The milder forms of intrusive behavior are the most frequently experienced. For example, approximately 70% of the participants in Spitzberg and Cupach's studies, 75% of the participants in criminologist Mary Brewster's (2003) study, and over 40% of the participants in a recent study conducted by James Geistman and colleagues (2013) reported that their pursuer engaged in the following activities:

- Repeatedly called them on the phone
- Sent letters or gifts
- Asked them if they were seeing someone romantically
- Called and hung up without speaking
- Begged them for another chance

- Watched or stared at them from a distance
- Visited their workplace, school, or university
- Made exaggerated claims about his or her affection
- Gossiped or bragged about the supposed relationship with others

About 10% to 40% of victims reported that their pursuer had engaged in the following less common, but significantly more invasive and threatening, behaviors:

- Threatening to physically or sexually assault the target
- Physically or sexually assaulting the target
- Following the target from place to place
- Damaging or stealing the target's property or possessions
- Trespassing
- Breaking into the target's home or apartment
- Exposing himself or herself to the target
- Taking photos without the target's knowledge or consent
- Recording conversations without the target's consent

## Cyberstalking: A Growing Problem

*I had to remove my Facebook profile because of my ex. I would be at a restaurant or a club, and he would show up. When I'd go online in the morning or late at night, my phone would immediately start ringing and it would be him. It was like he knew where and what I was doing all the time. I finally realized that he was using Facebook to keep track of me. He knew when to call because he could see that I was online, and he knew where I was because I would post something. Even changing my privacy settings didn't work because he was also following my friends.*

—22-year-old woman interviewed by the author

Not surprisingly, given the increased reliance on computer-mediated forms of communication and the proliferation of social networking sites, pursuers are increasingly using online forums to contact, surveil, intrude upon, and attempt to force intimacy from the targets of their obsession. Surveys of college samples reveal that approximately 40% have experienced *cyberstalking* victimization (Reyns, Henson, & Fisher, 2012), and the majority (about 75%) of pursuers report utilizing both face-to-face and online methods of intrusion and invasion (Lyndon, Bonds-Raacke, & Cratty, 2011).

Many of these online methods of pursuit mimic their face-to-face counterparts—and have the advantage (from the pursuers' perspective) of not being limited by physical boundaries. In an analysis of Facebook functionality, for example, researchers Kasey Chaulk and Tim Jones (2011) noted that cyber pursuers can easily engage in a multitude of invasive and intrusive activities, including:

- Leaving unwanted gifts (e.g., using Facebook applications to send presents, flowers, or other unwanted objects)
- Leaving unwanted messages (e.g., using chat to send messages, e-mailing, posting on the target's wall, messaging/e-mailing/posting on the walls of target's friends or family)
- Making exaggerated displays of affection ("poking" the target, sending kisses/hugs/caresses or any other form of intimate contact using Facebook applications)
- Watching and monitoring the target (e.g., joining and visiting the same groups/events as the target, adding the same applications, reading the target's feed and wall conversations, checking the target's profile for updates, using Facebook to keep "tabs" on the target)
- Intruding on the target and his or her friends, family, or coworkers (e.g., sending friend requests, commenting on posts, photos, or conversations)
- Damaging the target's reputation (e.g., posting inappropriate or unflattering pictures of the target, spreading false rumors about the target on various walls or via chat or e-mail)
- Following the target from place to place (e.g., showing up at physical locations or events the target has mentioned or RSVP'd to on Facebook)
- Sending threatening objects (e.g., sending pornographic, bizarre, or sinister gifts, photos, or applications)

These researchers found evidence that Facebook users do, in fact, engage in a significant amount of cyberpursuit. Almost two thirds of their participants (approximately 65%) acknowledged using Facebook to contact, surveil, and seek continued intimacy from their ex-partners (e.g., by sending messages, posting on the ex's wall, visiting groups the ex has joined, checking out the events the ex will be attending and friends the ex has recently added, looking at photos the ex has posted or that have been posted of the ex, reading the ex's mini-feed, sending "friend" requests to the ex).

The ready access to personal information that Facebook and other online social networking sites provide appears to have both positive and negative consequences—on the one hand, such sites allow people to form and maintain healthy connections with loved and valued partners; on the other hand, they provide a fertile ground for surveillance and harassment.

## Responses to Victimization

Given the range of invasive and threatening actions in which pursuers commonly engage, it is hardly surprising that victims of relational stalking often experience a number of negative emotional reactions, including fear, anxiety, paranoia, depression, self-blame, and anger (e.g., Davis, Coker, & Sanderson, 2002; Mullen & Pathé, 1994; Spitzberg, Nicastro, & Cousins, 1998; Wallace & Silverman, 1996). In addition, they may change their lifestyle or activity patterns, develop a heightened distrust of others, and exhibit sleeplessness, illness, and other physical symptoms (Amar, 2006; Spitzberg & Cupach, 2001). Victims often face another difficult challenge—convincing others that they are, in fact, being stalked (see Leitz-Spitz, 2003). Because stalking emerges most commonly from preexisting relationships, other people may blame the victim for contributing to the situation (e.g., by "leading" the stalker on or not sufficiently communicating disinterest), may minimize the extent of the threat, and may disbelieve the victim's claims of harassment (Sheridan, Gillett, Davies, Blaauw, & Patel, 2003). The quotations below illustrate this all-too-common reality:

> My stalker was my ex-boyfriend, and the behavior went on for over a year and got to the point where I ended up with a restraining order against him. The stalking was horrible, but what hurt me the most was the fact that my best friend didn't truly believe me, not deep down. She claimed she did, but she would change the subject, she laughed off the phone calls, texts, gifts, spying, threats, and she even told me once that she thought I'd overreacted and that if I'd just get back together with [name deleted] things would "go back to normal."

—18-year-old woman interviewed by the author

> One of the biggest problems I faced was getting my boss to take the situation seriously. It was only when the person (a coworker) made threats in front of witnesses on multiple occasions and I provided proof of this in the form of

*signed statements and video documentation that he took any action. And the action he took was to simply reassign the person to another department. What a joke. I ended up leaving because the harassment started up again not long after the reassignment.*

—38-year-old man interviewed by the author

Scientists have identified several ways in which targets attempt to deal with relational stalking (Amar & Alexy, 2010; Buhi, Clayton, & Surrency, 2009; de Becker, 1999; Dutton & Winstead, 2011; Pathé, 2002; Spitzberg & Cupach, 1998, 2001). The single most common reaction is *avoidance*—most targets simply ignore the situation or make no response at all. The prevalence of this particular reaction may reflect the fact that many men and women lack a clear script for responding to unwanted romantic attention. According to Baumeister and his colleagues (1993), this "scriptlessness" produces feelings of confusion and self-blame on the part of the target and thus contributes to a passive avoidance of the pursuer or the situation. Research reveals that targets also may employ *direct confrontation*, which includes such actions as admonishing or attempting to reason with the pursuer and requesting that he or she refrain from further contact. *Retaliation* represents a third strategy for dealing with unwanted attention. Retaliatory actions range from verbal threats and attempts to belittle or shame the pursuer to physical violence. Targets may seek *informal support* from friends, family members, counselors, and others who are available to provide guidance, advice, or assistance. And finally, *formal protection* may be sought from law enforcement officials or through administrative channels at work or school (e.g., human resource departments, supervisors, campus police, and workplace safety personnel).

Each of these coping strategies carries a potential cost. For example, because avoidance is an indirect and somewhat ambiguous strategy, the pursuer may fail to interpret it as rejection. Similarly, since the pursuer's goal is to connect with the target, direct confrontation by the target may prove to the pursuer that persistence pays off—that is, that pursuit will eventually bring contact with the object of obsession. Retaliation may demonstrate the target's lack of interest; however, it may also anger the pursuer and push him or her to escalating levels of intrusion and threat. A similar outcome may be associated with formal protection efforts; for example, the seriousness of obtaining a restraining order or having police intervene in the situation may trigger anger and heightened aggression from the pursuer (as well as serve to demonstrate that he or she is finally gaining the target's notice).

So what should a target of obsessive pursuit do? What responses are most effective at minimizing or eliminating intrusive behavior? What strategies can targets employ to reduce their chances of negative outcomes in stalking situations? Some professionals believe that statements and actions that directly and unequivocally convey rejection are most effective at managing unwanted attention (e.g., de Becker, 1999, 2002; Mumm & Cupach, 2010). For example, an individual should refuse gifts and other forms of attention offered by the pursuer, should directly state his or her disinterest, and should cease all further contact and communication with that person. In addition, targets should inform others of the situation, should document all stalking-related incidents, should improve or increase security at home, on campus, or in the workplace, and should devise an escape plan should a threat occur (see Leitz-Spitz, 2003).

Unfortunately, researchers have yet to clearly determine which, if any, of these responses is most effective at managing relational stalking situations. For example, although targets often report that moving away (a form of avoidance) or taking legal action (a type of formal protection) is the most effective way to stop unwanted pursuit, many pursuers state that direct confrontation and retaliation (such as making threats or engaging in assertive or aggressive verbal confrontations) are the most effective methods (Dutton & Winstead, 2011). The effectiveness of the various coping methods also may depend on the nature of the stalking behaviors. One recent survey (Geistman et al., 2013) found that when pursuers were violent, most coping strategies that victims employed either exacerbated the stalking behavior or made no difference at all (in fact, the only strategies that worked were those that involved other people directly confronting or retaliating against the pursuer on behalf of the target). There is still a great deal we do not know about how to effectively manage this particularly problematic syndrome.

## ❖ RELATIONAL AGGRESSION: WHEN LOVE TURNS VIOLENT

*Intimate partner violence*—violence occurring within romantic, marital, family, friend, and other intimate relationships—represents another deeply problematic (and disturbingly common) relational issue. Survey research reveals that minor acts of physical aggression (such as slapping, pushing, or shoving) occur in roughly one third of dating relationships (Hines & Malley-Morrison, 2005). Severe acts of aggression also are quite prevalent among partners in marital or other long-term romantic relationships (U.S. Department of Justice, 2008). Although different types of intimate partner violence can and do occur between partners, the two types that have received the most attention from relationship scientists are situational couple violence and coercive controlling violence (e.g., Johnson, 1999, 2008; Kelly & Johnson, 2008).

## Situational Couple Violence

*One day my girlfriend came over after school and started complaining about something that happened at her work. I was sitting on my bed watching TV and she was standing in the doorway going on and on about the same thing she always complains about. It was irritating so I didn't look at her but kept staring straight ahead at the screen. She got really mad! She started yelling at me and then she came over to the nightstand and picked up the remote control and hurled it at me. It hit me in the face and actually busted my lip wide open.*

—18-year-old man interviewed by the author

*My best friend's boyfriend was physically aggressive to her on multiple occasions. Mostly when she would disagree with him. He would pinch her, grab at her, you know, grab her jacket and pull her up in his face, sort of shove her around. She would tell him to stop but then he'd just laugh and pretend like he didn't really mean it, his temper got the better of him, same old story every time. It was really disturbing. One day, we were all at a restaurant and they were kind of arguing and then she got up to go to the restroom and he reached out and grabbed her hair so hard that she fell back against the table and bruised her arm. I was so happy when they broke up. I hated him.*

—22-year-old woman interviewed by the author

These quotations describe the type of aggression that most typically occurs between romantic partners. *Situational couple violence* (sometimes called *common couple violence* or *conflict-motivated violence*) refers to violent behavior that arises primarily in the context of interpersonal conflict (Ellis & Stuckless, 1996; Kelly & Johnson, 2008). This type of intimate partner violence typically is not accompanied by a chronic pattern of coercion, manipulation, and control; rather, it is associated with poor anger management, communication skill deficits, or ineffective conflict resolution strategies on the part of one or both partners. Situational couple violence typically erupts during a heated argument or disagreement during which one or both partners lose their tempers and impulsively resort to pushing, shoving, or other physical actions to resolve the conflict. Because these lapses of control are situational in nature (i.e., associated only with that particular argument), they tend to result in milder forms of physical aggression and do not commonly recur in the relationship.

Researchers interested in exploring situational couple violence typically use the 12-item Physical Assault Subscale of the revised Conflict Tactics Scale (CTS-2) developed by Murray Straus and his colleagues (Straus, Hamby, Boney-McCoy, & Sugarman, 1996). When responding to the items, participants indicate the frequency with which both they and their partners engaged in various physically violent actions during the past year, including

- throwing something at the partner that could hurt
- twisting the partner's arm or hair
- pushing or shoving the partner
- grabbing the partner
- slapping the partner
- using a knife or gun on the partner
- punching or hitting the partner with something that could hurt
- choking the partner
- slamming the partner against a wall
- beating up the partner
- burning or scalding the partner on purpose
- kicking the partner

The first five items are considered to reflect relatively minor forms of physical aggression, whereas the last seven items are assumed to reflect more severe violence. The CTS-2 also includes an Injury Subscale, which assesses the extent to which individuals are physically injured by their partners' violent behavior (e.g., "I went to a doctor because of a fight with my partner," "I had a sprain, bruise, or small cut because of a fight with my partner," "I had a broken bone from a fight with my partner").

Surveys of nonclinical samples (e.g., community or college student samples) reveal that fairly high (and roughly equal) proportions of men and women engage in situational couple violence (e.g., O'Leary & Williams, 2006; Straus & Ramirez, 2007; but see Archer, 2000). In one investigation, Straus (2004) asked more than 8,000 students from 31 universities located around the world (e.g., Asia, the Middle East, Australia, New Zealand, Europe, South America, Canada, the

United States) to complete the Physical Assault and Injury Subscales of the CTS-2. Although violence rates varied across samples (ranging from a low of 17% in the Braga, Portugal, student sample to a high of 45% in the Louisiana, United States, student sample), a substantial proportion of the participants (almost one third) reported having physically assaulted a dating partner in the previous 12 months. Most of these assaults were minor, such as slapping a partner or shoving a partner in anger; however, the rate of severe violence—ranging from punching, choking, and attacking the partner with weapons—was still disturbingly high (9%). Moreover, 7% of the students indicated that they had inflicted an injury on their dating partners (with men more likely than women to have inflicted severe injuries [e.g., broken bone, head trauma]). Similar results were reported more recently by researchers James McNulty and Julianne Hellmuth (2008), who administered items from the Physical Assault Subscale to a sample of newlywed couples; 36% of couples reporting having experienced at least one act of physical violence during the previous 12 months.

Although both men and women perpetrate situational couple violence, the sexes appear to differ in the type of violence they use. Psychologist John Archer (2002) conducted a meta-analysis using data from 58 previously published studies. Each study provided information on the occurrence of nine of the individual acts of physical violence measured by the original version of the CTS. These nine acts included throwing something; pushing, grabbing, or shoving; slapping; kicking, biting, or punching; hitting with an object; beating; choking or strangling; threatening with a gun or knife; and using a gun or knife. Archer's analysis of the numbers of men and women who inflicted each of these acts on their partners (according to those partners' self-reports) indicated that women were more likely than men to perpetrate acts of minor violence, whereas men were more likely than women to commit acts of severe violence. Specifically, a higher proportion of women than men engaged in four of the five acts of minor violence, including throwing something at the partner, hitting the partner with an object, slapping the partner, and kicking, biting or punching the partner. Conversely, a higher proportion of men than women had perpetrated three of the four acts of severe violence, including beating, choking or strangling, and using a knife or a gun on their partners. Other researchers have found that men are more likely than women to repeatedly aggress against their partners, and that women are more likely than men to suffer physical injury as a result of their partners' aggressive behavior (Breiding, Black, & Ryan, 2008; Morse, 1995; Whitaker, Haileyesus, Swahn, & Saltzman, 2007). Thus, both sexes can be (and often are) aggressive—but the aggression perpetrated by women typically is less severe than that perpetrated by men.

In sum, research on situational couple violence reveals that (minor) violence is a relatively common occurrence in romantic relationships and that both men and women can and do commit a variety of physically aggressive acts against their intimate partners.

## Coercive Controlling Violence

*Coercive controlling violence* (also called *intimate terrorism* and commonly referred to as *domestic violence, spousal abuse,* or *battery*) is the type of intimate partner violence that is encountered most often by workers in agency settings such as hospitals and clinics, domestic violence shelters, public safety or law enforcement departments, and the legal system (Coker, Smith, McKeown, & King, 2000; Frieze & Browne, 1989; Graham-Kevan & Archer, 2003; Johnson, 2006). Unlike situational couple violence, which typically arises in the context of interpersonal conflict and tends to involve minor forms of physical aggression, coercive controlling violence involves physical violence that is associated with a chronic pattern of emotionally abusive intimidation, coercion, and control (e.g., Kelly & Johnson, 2008). Coercively controlling and violent relationships typically involve one partner (the abuser) engaging in a persistent effort to frighten, manipulate, terrorize, hurt, humiliate, injure, and otherwise dominate and control the other partner (the victim). Abusers frequently employ a variety of tactics in their quest for power and control, ranging from physical and emotional abuse, to economic or financial abuse, to isolation and denial (Hines, Brown, & Dunning, 2007; National Domestic Violence Hotline, 2015; Pence & Paymar, 1993; U.S. Department of Justice, 2014). It is important to recognize that coercive controlling individuals do not necessarily use all of these tactics to dominate their partners; rather, they tend to use the combination they believe will be most effective at maintaining their control. For example, in many abusive relationships—particularly those with a history of prior physical violence—the abuser may no longer need to employ physical force to dominate the partner; as a result, coercive controlling violence does not always manifest itself in high levels of physical aggression (see Johnson, 2008).

There is strong evidence of sex asymmetry in coercive controlling violence; that is, among heterosexual couples, abusers are predominantly male and victims are predominantly female. In addition, although physical violence is not always present in high amounts throughout the relationship, it tends to occur with greater frequency than in relationships characterized by other types of intimate partner violence, is likely to escalate over time, and produces more serious consequences in terms of injury (see Johnson, 1999). For example, sociologist Joseph Michalski (2005) analyzed data on intimate partner violence collected as part of a national survey. Over 16,000 men and women involved in romantic relationships were asked whether their partners had ever engaged in acts of physical violence (e.g., "beaten you," "kicked, bit, or hit you with his/her fist," "choked you") and coercive control (e.g., "tried to limit your contact with family or friends," "put you down or called you names," "damaged or destroyed your possessions or property"). The results revealed that domestic violence was relatively infrequent; only 4% of the entire sample reported experiencing physical violence embedded in a pattern of coercive control (indeed, almost 90% of participants reported having never experienced physical aggression or coercive control from their partners). However, although the overall prevalence rate was low, a significantly higher proportion of women (5.2%) than men (3.0%) reported having a violent and coercively controlling partner. Moreover, participants in coercive and controlling relationships experienced twice as many instances of physical violence as other participants, and the violence that occurred was more severe.

Many victims of domestic violence are forced to resort to aggression themselves in order to thwart the actions of their abusers (Henning, Renauer, & Holdford, 2006; Pagelow, 1981; Stuart et al., 2006). Called *violent resistance* (or *resistive/reactive violence*), this type of intimate partner violence is motivated by self-defense. Because most (heterosexual) abusers are male and most victims are female, it is not surprising that violent resistance is primarily enacted by women. For example, 96% of the abused women in one study (Johnson, 1999) had resorted to violence in an effort to protect themselves from injury from their abusive husbands. Unfortunately, self-protective violence may result in additional abuse; faced with physical resistance, an abusive partner may become enraged and perpetrate additional (and more severe) violence (Kelly & Johnson, 2008; Pagelow, 1981). Indeed, Ronet Bachman and Dianne Carmody's (1994) analysis of National Crime Victimization Survey data revealed that women who defended themselves against physical attacks from their intimate partners were twice as likely to sustain injuries as women who did not (also see Bachman, Saltzman, Thompson, & Carmody, 2002).

In addition to physical injury and trauma, victims of domestic violence experience a number of serious and adverse psychological outcomes. Women who are terrorized by their intimate partners often live in a state of chronic fear and anxiety; they also frequently report lowered self-esteem, depression, and symptoms of post-traumatic stress (e.g., Basile, Arias, Desai, & Thompson, 2004; Dobash & Dobash, 1979; Gelles & Harrop, 1989; Golding, 1999; Johnson & Leone, 2005; Tyson, Herting, & Randell, 2007). Although less is known about the consequences of domestic violence for male victims, there is evidence that men who are abused experience the same constellation of physical and psychological outcomes as their female counterparts (for reviews, see Dutton, 2007; Hines & Malley-Morrison, 2005). They may also experience an additional adverse consequence—namely, revictimization by a domestic violence system that is designed to assist female victims and that consequently often does not recognize that men, too, can be abused. When criminal justice scholars Denise Hines, Jan Brown, and Edward Dunning (2007) analyzed calls to a national domestic abuse hotline for men, they discovered that many male victims reported having sought help in the past but having been turned away, laughed at, not taken seriously, and treated as batterers (rather than victims) by agency workers. For many callers, this unfair treatment was as traumatic as the abuse itself.

Relationship scholars have sought to identify the risk factors or correlates of domestic abuse. Comprehensive reviews of the existing literature have revealed the following personal, relational, and environmental correlates (Christopher & Lloyd, 2000; Hines & Malley-Morrison, 2005; Slep, Foran, Heyman, & United States Air Force Family Advocacy Research Program, 2014; Wong & Mellor, 2014):

- Biological sex: As discussed earlier in this chapter, domestic abuse perpetration and victimization demonstrate sex asymmetry, such that the majority of perpetrators are male and the majority of victims are female.

- Age: Intimate partner violence peaks among adults in their 20s and steadily declines in older cohorts.

- Socioeconomic status: Low income, poverty, lower occupational status (e.g., blue collar or working class as opposed to white collar or middle class), and lower educational attainment are among the strongest predictors of domestic violence.

- Immigrant status: There is some evidence within the United States that immigrant women are at greater risk of experiencing domestic violence (evidence linking immigrant status and coercive controlling violence risk is stronger in other countries, in part because the question has received greater empirical attention from researchers employing non-U.S. samples).

- Prior exposure to domestic violence: Women who were exposed to interparental violence growing up are more likely to experience domestic abuse later in their own lives; men who witnessed interparental violence are more likely to be violent toward their female partners.

- Childhood abuse: Women who were psychologically, physically, or sexually abused as children are more likely to be victimized by an intimate partner later in their own lives; men who were abused as children are more likely to perpetrate violence against their romantic partners.

- Attitudes and beliefs: Abusers (and, often, their victims) tend to endorse interpersonal violence and hold highly traditional attitudes toward marriage and sex or gender roles (e.g., they believe that husbands should be the dominant partner in marriage and that it is acceptable for a husband to hit a wife).

- Mental health and psychopathology: Male batterers are more likely than nonbatterers to exhibit symptoms of diminished mental health, as well as a variety of severe clinical disorders ranging from major depression and anxiety to personality disorders (e.g., antisocial, borderline, narcissistic).

- Physical health: Men who perpetrate, and women who experience, domestic abuse report poorer physical health (e.g., greater pain, lower energy, more sleep disturbances) than those who are not in relationships characterized by coercive controlling violence.

- Relationship status: Compared with dating and married couples, couples who cohabit have higher rates of physical assault.

- Relationship satisfaction: Lowered levels of relationship satisfaction are associated with higher likelihood of domestic abuse.

- Alcohol use: Men who abuse alcohol are more likely to assault their romantic partners, and women who abuse alcohol are more likely to be assaulted by an intimate partner.

- Economic pressure: Financial stress is positively correlated with the likelihood of intimate partner violence; the greater the economic pressure a couple is under, the more likely they are to be in a marriage marked by domestic abuse.

- Social isolation: Domestic abuse is more likely to occur when a couple is socially isolated and the partners have few sources of social support.

It is important to recognize that the research in this area is correlational, and researchers thus cannot know with any degree of certainty the extent to which these personal, relational, or environmental risk factors function as true *causes* of intimate partner violence. For example, it is likely that marital conflict or dissatisfaction contributes to a hostile interpersonal climate that is conducive to physical violence; at the same time, it is quite likely that the occurrence of physical abuse leads to marital distress and dissatisfaction. Similarly, individuals with poor mental and physical health may be more likely to perpetrate (or experience) intimate partner violence; yet intimate partner violence itself contributes to difficulties with mental and physical function.

Domestic abuse is among the most pernicious forms of interpersonal violence that can arise in romantic relationships, and additional research on ways to prevent its occurrence and effectively combat its adverse effects is clearly needed.

## ❖ LOSS OF PASSION: WHEN ATTRACTION FADES

*It's not that I don't desire him anymore, it's simply that I don't desire him as much. In a way, our relationship is stronger now, built more solidly on other, less sexual feelings. But there are times when I have to admit I become a bit nostalgic for the passion that we've lost. It used to be that I would glimpse him making a certain gesture, or hear his voice on the phone, or catch the scent of his cologne, and I would literally be infused with this feeling of desire, of need, of sheer want. And it was almost indescribable, a mingling of the physical and the emotional. But we've been together for a long time, and somehow, somewhere that feeling just faded. I love him deeply, maybe more than I ever did before, and I know that we'll grow old together, but it's not the same.*

—35-year-old man interviewed by the author

The emotional intensity and feelings of sexual attraction that are associated with passionate love frequently fade over time in romantic relationships (Sprecher & Regan, 1998). To some extent, we owe this occurrence to our biological design; our bodies simply are not equipped to sustain for long periods the physiological arousal associated with passionate love, desire, and other intense emotional experiences. It is definitely the case that a sudden loss of passion or an intense "falling out of love" may indicate that some degree of emotional conflict or interpersonal dysfunction exists in a couple's relationship. However, it may also serve as a sign that the couple has moved into a different, and no less positive, relational phase. In Chapter 8, we reviewed evidence suggesting that as passion and excitement fade within a relationship, they may be replaced by trust, acceptance, respect, fondness, and the other elements of companionate love.

In addition, passion, desire, and excitement may fade or fluctuate because of changes in the physical or psychological state of the individual partners that have nothing to do with larger relationship issues. Some people regularly experience fluctuations in their feelings of passion and desire (Kaplan, 1979; Levine, 1984; Regan, 2015b). Others may find their ability and/or motivation to experience passion impaired by poor health, hormonal imbalances, chronic drug use, depression and other mood disorders, and so on (see Regan & Berscheid, 1999). It is hard to feel passionately enthralled by the beloved when one is ill or otherwise feeling poorly. Thus, the sense that one is "falling out of love" with, or even losing some degree of sexual attraction to, the partner is not necessarily a sign that the relationship is in trouble. It is only when one or both partners disagree about or are troubled by some element of their relationship that professional intervention may be helpful.

## Summary

Although most men and women find their love relationships to be both positive and life affirming, difficulties may arise. Unrequited passionate love, obsession and relational stalking, violence and aggression, and loss of passion all are problematic experiences that may result in extremely negative outcomes. Understanding the types of love that exist, the changes that commonly occur over time in romantic relationships, the signs and symptoms of interpersonal problems, and the coping mechanisms that are available can enable us to effectively alleviate the difficulties that may develop in our love relationships.

## Key Concepts

Unrequited love (p. 196)

Relational stalking (p. 199)

Cyberstalking (p. 203)

Avoidance (p. 206)

Direct confrontation (p. 206)

Retaliation (p. 206)

Informal support (p. 206)

Formal protection (p. 206)

Intimate partner violence (p. 207)

Situational couple violence (p. 208)

Coercive controlling violence (p. 211)

Violent resistance (p. 212)

## Discussion Questions

1. Is being in love always a positive experience? In what ways can passionate love be problematic? Have you ever found yourself in an unrequited love situation, either as the unrequited lover or the unwilling object of affection? If so, how did you feel? How well does your own experience match the experiences reported by the people who participated in Baumeister et al.'s (1993) unrequited love study?

2. Relational stalking has been portrayed in a variety of movies, including *Fatal Attraction* (1987), *Fear* (1996), *Swimfan* (also called *Swimf@n*, 2002), *Enduring Love* (2004), *Obsessed* (2009), and a host of others. Select two movies that depict obsession and relational stalking and watch each one carefully. Using your knowledge of relational stalking, determine how well these cinematic portrayals match the features and characteristics of relational stalking identified by scientific research.

3. Have you or someone you know ever used the Internet to follow, surveil, or find out information about a potential or former romantic partner? Has someone you were not interested in ever used the Internet to follow, surveil, or seek intimacy from you? How did this make you feel? What did you do to manage the situation?

4. Compare and contrast the two primary types of intimate partner violence that relationship scientists have explored. What are the risk factors and the consequences of these experiences (for victims and for perpetrators)?

5. Why does passion seem to inevitably fade over time in most romantic relationships? Is the loss of passion a sign of interpersonal dysfunction?

## Recommended Readings

This book was written for the reading public and presents a nice blend of scientific research and narrative about the experience of unreciprocated love.

Baumeister, R. F., & Wotman, S. R. (1992). *Breaking hearts: The two sides of unrequited love*. New York, NY: Guilford Press.

This is an excellent, if oftentimes terrifying, glimpse into stalking. De Becker discusses his own extensive experiences working with people (including many celebrities) who have been the recipients of unwanted (and sometimes violent) attention from others. Although many of the stories are graphic and intense, the author gives his readers helpful advice on how to avoid and manage these situations. This is an excellent and informative read and is available on Amazon and other websites.

de Becker, G. (1999). *The gift of fear and other survival signals that protect us from violence*. New York, NY: Dell.

This journal issue and these edited books present a collection of pieces written by theorists and researchers who have explored problematic aspects of close relationships, including relational stalking, violence, loss of passion, and other "dark" interpersonal experiences.

Cupach, W. R., & Spitzberg, B. H. (Eds.). (2011). *The dark side of close relationships II*. New York, NY: Routledge.

Davis, K. E., Frieze, I. H., & Maiuro, R. D. (Eds.). (2002). *Stalking: Perspectives on victims and perpetrators*. New York, NY: Springer.

Frieze, I. H. (Ed.). (2012). Issues of gender in stalking research [Special issue]. *Sex Roles, 66*(5–6).

Spitzberg, B. H., & Cupach, W. R. (Eds.). (1998). *The dark side of close relationships*. Mahwah, NJ: Erlbaum.

# Part III

# Sex

Sexuality plays an important role in dating and mating relationships. We already have seen, in Chapter 8, that feelings of sexual desire or attraction are associated with the experience of passionate love. This section of the text focuses on *relational sexuality*—sexual responses that occur within the context of ongoing romantic relationships. Relational sexuality is very different from sex between uncommitted or casual partners. Certainly, relational and casual sex often stem from similar motives, such as the need for physical release or the urge to satiate or express sexual desires. In addition, both types of sex often produce similar outcomes ranging from sheer physical pleasure, to sexual satisfaction, to the positive feeling that one is desirable and sexually attractive. These similarities notwithstanding, however, relational sex has additional interpersonal meanings, purposes, and consequences. For example, relational partners may engage in sexual activity in order to express feelings of love and intimacy, to demonstrate or reaffirm their commitment to each other, or to shift the balance of power or to restore equity in their relationship (see Sprecher & Regan, 2000). Sexual events that occur within a romantic relationship thus have important nonsexual consequences for that relationship.

Chapter 10 explores attitudes about the role of sex in committed relationships. We then discuss sexuality in both beginning (Chapter 11) and established (Chapter 12) relationships. Finally, we explore problematic aspects of relational sex, including sexual disinterest, nonconsensual sex, sexual infidelity, and sexual jealousy (Chapter 13).

# 10

# Sexual Attitudes

In the minds of many individuals, love and sex share an intimate connection. In fact, most men and women view sexual intercourse as most appropriate when it occurs within the context of a committed, long-term, and love-based relationship. As we discuss in this chapter, a large and growing body of research suggests that people are most accepting of sexual activity between engaged or married partners and are least accepting of sex between uncommitted partners or those at very early relationship stages.

## ❖ BELIEFS ABOUT SEX IN DATING RELATIONSHIPS

*Well, I can't speak for anyone else, but for me, the only way I'd have sex with someone was if we were deeply in love. If two people are in love, then sex seems like a natural way to express those feelings.*

—19-year-old woman interviewed by the author

*The decision to have sex is a personal choice that everyone should be free to make. Some people have sex just because they enjoy it, or because they have the chance to do it. That's fine; it's a personal decision. Other people, and I'm one of them, think that sex is best when it's done out of love, with someone you're involved with.*

—20-year-old man interviewed by the author

In one of the first empirical investigations of *sexual standards*, sociologist Ira Reiss (1964) reported that men and women from a national probability sample of the U.S. population, as well as students from five high schools and colleges, were increasingly accepting of premarital sexual intercourse between two people as their relationship became characterized by correspondingly greater amounts of affection and commitment; in other words, as the couple's relationship progressed from relatively little affection to strong affection, and then to love and engagement, people believed that intercourse was more acceptable. Similar results were reported more than 20 years later by sociologists Susan Sprecher, Kathleen McKinney, Robert Walsh, and Carrie Anderson (1988), who found that increasing numbers of men and women viewed sexual intercourse between two people as acceptable as their relationship stage moved from the first date (28%), to casual dating (41%), to serious dating (72%), to pre-engagement (77%), and then to engagement (82%). And more recently, a group of researchers led by John Earle (Earle et al., 2007) observed a similar pattern, finding that men and women surveyed in the year 2000 were increasingly accepting of premarital intercourse between two people when their relationship shifted from casual acquaintance (with 14% indicating that premarital sex was acceptable in this relational situation), to occasional dating (25%), to regular dating (46%), to "serious" involvement (71%), and, finally, to engagement (77%).

Cross-sectional and longitudinal research indicates that American society has generally become more *sexually permissive* over time (see Elias, Fullerton, & Simpson, 2015; Willetts, Sprecher, & Beck, 2004). In particular, although men and women continue to view sex as most appropriate when it occurs between committed relational partners, there is a trend toward greater acceptance of sexual activity in casual dating relationships. Robert Sherwin and Sherry Corbett (1985), for example, examined normative expectations about sexual activity in various types of dating relationships on a college campus. Three groups of students—the first surveyed in 1963, the second in 1971, and the third in 1978—were asked to indicate the extent to which various sexual activities generally were expected to play a part in the relationship between casually dating, steadily dating, and engaged couples. The results provided evidence for increasingly liberal campus sexual norms among both men and women over the 15-year period. For example, none of the men and women in the 1963 sample expected sexual intercourse to occur in a casual dating relationship; by 1978, however, 17% of the men and 9% of the women viewed intercourse as a normal part of casual dating.

A more recent investigation by psychologists Brooke Wells and Jean Twenge (2005) confirmed these results. These researchers first identified 45 individual research studies conducted in the United States between the years 1955 and 1989 that had examined attitudes toward premarital sex. Next, for each study they gathered information on the year of data collection and the proportion of participants who indicated approval of premarital intercourse. The results clearly revealed that attitudes toward premarital sex had become considerably more permissive over time in the United States. Specifically, there was a positive correlation between the year of publication and the percentage of participants endorsing premarital sex. Only 12% of young women surveyed during the mid-to-late 1950s (1955–1959) approved of premarital sex. By the mid-1980s, however, 73% of women approved of premarital sexual intercourse. Young men displayed a similar shift in attitude over time; 40% of men surveyed in the 1950s approved of premarital sex compared to 79% of men surveyed in the 1980s. More recent research, however, indicates that levels of sexual permissiveness peaked among the baby boomer generation (men and women born during the 1950s) and have since stabilized (see Elias et al., 2015); in other words, individuals born during the 1980s, 1990s, and 2000s (often called millennials) are no more permissive than their baby boomer and generation X counterparts.

There is evidence that other countries around the world are also experiencing a similar shift in attitude toward increased sexual permissiveness (e.g., Herlitz & Ramstedt, 2005; Widmer, Treas, & Newcomb, 1998). For example, one group of researchers (Le Gall, Mullet, & Shafighi, 2002) surveyed the sexual attitudes of a large sample of French men and women who represented four different age groups: *young adults* between the ages of 18 and 29, *adults* between the ages of 30 and 49, *middle-aged adults* between the ages of 50 and 64, and *older adults* between the ages of 65 and 89. All of the participants answered a series of questions designed to measure sexual permissiveness (e.g., "Casual sex is acceptable"). The researchers discovered that the two younger cohorts (young adults and adults) were significantly more permissive in their sexual attitudes than the two older cohorts (middle-aged and older adults)—and this difference was found for both men and women. Today, sexual intercourse clearly is considered a more acceptable part of the premarital interactions of men and women than it was in earlier generations.

## The Role of Biological Sex

One of the most potent correlates of attitudes toward premarital sex is biological sex. For example, men tend to hold more permissive or positive attitudes toward uncommitted or casual sexual activity than do women (for reviews, see Oliver & Hyde, 1993; Petersen & Hyde, 2010, 2011). This sex difference is robust and has been documented in a number of different world cultures (e.g., Do & Fu, 2010; Mwaba & Naidoo, 2005; Odimegwu, 2005; Zuo et al., 2012) and in various ethnic groups living in the United States (e.g., Eisenman & Dantzker, 2006; Hendrick, Hendrick, & Reich, 2006). Men also are less likely than women to associate the occurrence of sexual intercourse with love, commitment, and intimacy. When Ira Robinson, James Balkwell, and Dawn Ward (1980) asked a sample of college students to write down their first five responses to the stimulus word *sex*, fewer men (42%) than women (71%) responded with words indicative of love, and fewer men (16%) than women (43%) provided words reflective of marriage or commitment. Similar results were reported by Susan Hendrick, Clyde Hendrick, Michelle Slapion-Foote, and Franklin Foote (1985), who surveyed a group of undergraduates about various sexual attitudes. These researchers found strong sex differences; for example, men were more likely than women to agree that sexual relations with another person did not require commitment to that person, whereas women were more likely than men to agree that sex without love is meaningless.

More recently, sociologists John Roche and Thomas Ramsbey (1993) asked a large sample of college students to indicate how appropriate they thought sexual intercourse would be between partners at five different stages of dating: dating with no particular affection (Stage 1), dating with affection but not love (Stage 2), dating and being in love (Stage 3), dating one person only and being in love (Stage 4), and engaged (Stage 5). Equally high numbers of men (76%) and women (67%) believed that sexual intercourse was appropriate between engaged partners (Stage 5), and equally low numbers (3% of the men, 0% of the women) felt that it was acceptable in the complete absence of commitment and affection (Stage 1). However, men and women clearly diverged in their attitudes about the role of sex in dating relationships in the other relationship stages. For example, 17% of the men, compared to only 1% of the women, believed that intercourse was appropriate when dating partners felt affection but not love (Stage 2). Similarly, many more men (44%) than women (15%) felt that sexual intercourse was acceptable when partners were dating and in love (Stage 3). Thus, both sexes viewed intercourse as increasingly acceptable as a dating relationship became characterized by greater amounts of commitment and affection. However, men felt that sex was appropriate at earlier relationship stages than did women (in fact, more men than women simply believed that sex was appropriate— regardless of relationship stage).

In addition, both sexes seem to know that women are more likely than men to associate sex with love and intimacy. For instance, participants in one study (Regan & Berscheid, 1995) were asked to specify the causes of male and female sexual desire. More than 40% stated that love caused women to experience a desire for sexual activity, whereas fewer than 10% believed that love caused men to want sex. One male respondent mentioned "thoughts of love and romance" as playing an important role in female sexual interest, another noted that "a woman tends to be in love when she feels desire or has sexual intercourse," and one female respondent stated that "often the words 'I love you' will cause sexual desire in a woman."

Based on these results, it might be tempting to conclude that women simply do not experience as much sexual interest as do men for their dating partners or that women just desire less sexual involvement than men in general in their romantic relationships. This is not the case, however. For example, surveys of adolescents and young adults reveal that both boys *and* girls, and both men *and* women, report thinking about sex often and experiencing sexual desire frequently (Juhasz, Kaufman, & Meyer, 1986; Regan & Atkins, 2006; Useche, Villegas, & Alzate, 1990). Similarly, over 80% of the high school girls who participated in David Muram and his colleagues' (Muram, Rosenthal, Tolley, Peeler, & Dorko, 1991) study reported being sexually excited by their dating partners, regardless of whether or not they actually engaged in intercourse. Thus, it is not that women are less interested than men in becoming sexually involved with their dating partners, but rather that women generally prefer a greater amount of emotional commitment *prior* to sexual involvement.

The results of one study illustrate this phenomenon. Marita McCabe and John Collins (1984) asked men and women to indicate how much sexual activity they desired at three stages of a romantic relationship: on the first date, after several dates had occurred, and when going steady. The researchers found—as we might expect—that men expressed a desire for a higher level of sexual activity at the earlier relationship stages (i.e., on the first date and after several dates) than did women. However, there was no difference in how much sexual activity men and women wanted at the *later* relationship stage of going steady. In other words, both sexes were willing for sexual activity to occur in a dating relationship, but men wanted this activity to begin earlier in the development of the relationship than did women, who felt that sex should wait until there was some evidence of commitment and emotional involvement.

## The Role of Culture

*Sex outside of marriage is sinful. I am from a traditional family and I was raised to honor my spiritual and cultural upbringing. I will not pollute myself before marriage.*

—18-year-old Pakistani-born man interviewed by the author

*Premarital sex is the norm these days. As long as both people are careful (and consenting!), it's perfectly fine. I'm not a virgin and I don't expect my future wife to be one, either.*

—19-year-old U.S.-born man interviewed by the author

Another important correlate of attitudes toward premarital sexual activity is culture. As noted by cross-cultural psychologist Robin Goodwin (1999), human societies vary considerably in the extent to which they permit premarital sex, and this is partly due to whether they are collectivist or individualist in cultural orientation. Recall from Chapter 4 that collectivist cultures are those in which people are integrated into cohesive groups; marriages link families and are sometimes arranged by those families; group boundaries are explicit and firm; and there is a strong emphasis on group loyalty, solidarity, and shared activity. Individualist cultures reflect the opposite pattern; people are loosely connected and autonomous, group boundaries are flexible, and emphasis is placed upon the fulfillment of personal preferences and goals in romance and other life pursuits. Goodwin's review indicates that young adults in collectivist cultures (e.g., Asia, the Middle East) strongly disapprove of premarital sex, whereas young adults from individualist cultures (e.g., Britain, Belgium, France, Scandinavian countries) tend to hold more permissive attitudes (also see Widmer et al., 1998; Yan, 2006).

Indeed, Susan Sprecher and Elaine Hatfield (1995) asked over 1,500 college students from the United States, Russia, and Japan to indicate how acceptable they thought sexual intercourse was on a first date, when casually dating, when seriously dating, when pre-engaged, and when engaged to be married. Although participants from all three cultures disapproved of sex between uncommitted partners (those who were on a first date or those who were casually dating), American students generally were more tolerant of sexual activity between seriously dating, pre-engaged, and engaged partners than were Russian and Japanese students. In America, sex was deemed acceptable as soon as some evidence of the couple's commitment was present. In Russia and Japan, however, the fact that the couple was seriously involved or even engaged was insufficient justification for sexual activity—a marriage vow was required.

A more recent global survey of premarital sex attitudes conducted by scientists at the Pew Research Center (2014b) provides further evidence that culture is strongly associated with sexual attitudes. When asked whether sex between unmarried adults was morally acceptable, morally unacceptable, or was not a moral issue, 90% or more of adults in traditional, collectivist countries (e.g., Indonesia, Jordan, Pakistan, Turkey, Egypt) expressed the opinion that this behavior was morally unacceptable. However, fewer than 10% of the adults surveyed in individualistic, Western European countries (e.g., Britain, Spain, Germany, France, Italy) agreed; rather, the majority indicated that premarital sex was either morally acceptable or was not a moral issue at all. The United States, with 30% of respondents expressing moral disapproval, was in between these two extremes.

## ❖ BELIEFS ABOUT SEX IN MARITAL RELATIONSHIPS

Although there have been few empirical investigations of attitudes about sexuality in marital relationships, some general conclusions can be gleaned from the available literature. First, sexual intercourse is considered a "normal" part of the marital relationship. Not only do most people view sexual activity as completely acceptable between spouses, but marriage historically has been defined as a socially sanctioned sexual and reproductive relationship. In Western culture, for example, 17th-century church doctrine specified sexual intercourse as a marital duty for both spouses (Leites, 1982), and many non-Western cultures continue to view reproduction as one of the primary goals of the marital relationship (e.g., Hamon & Ingoldsby, 2003).

Second, marital sex is assumed to be exclusive sex. That is, once an individual is married (or involved in any other type of long-term, committed romantic relationship), the general presumption is that he or she will confine sexual activities to that one relationship. Data indicate that most men and women possess strong expectations about fidelity or *sexual exclusivity* (e.g., Wiederman & Allgeier, 1996), disapprove of extramarital or extrarelational sex (e.g., Davis & Smith, 1991; Glenn & Weaver, 1979; Thornton & Young-DeMarco, 2001; Wright, Tokunaga, & Bae, 2014), and express negative beliefs about "cheating spouses" (e.g., Sprecher, Regan, & McKinney, 1998). For example, sex researcher Robert Michael and his colleagues (Michael, Gagnon, Laumann, & Kolata, 1994) asked a U.S. sample of more than 3,400 adults the following question: "What is your opinion about a married person having sexual relations with someone other than the marriage partner—is it always wrong, almost always wrong, sometimes wrong, or not wrong at all?" (p. 287). Their results revealed that 77% of the entire sample felt that extramarital sex was "always wrong"—a strong condemnation indeed.

Similar results were reported in a large cross-cultural investigation conducted by anthropologists Eric Widmer, Judith Treas, and Robert Newcomb (1998). These researchers contacted nationally representative samples of adults from 24 different countries and asked them to indicate whether it was acceptable for a married person to have "sexual relations with someone other than his or her husband or wife" (p. 352). Participants were given four response options: always wrong, almost always wrong, wrong only sometimes, and not wrong at all. Across all 24 countries, the vast majority (87%) of participants agreed that extramarital sex was "always wrong" or "almost always wrong." A mere 4% of the participants indicated they believed that it was "not wrong at all" for married people to engage in sexual relations with another person. Similar results have been reported by other researchers who have collected attitudinal data from cross-cultural and non-U.S. samples (e.g., Haavio-Mannila & Kontula, 2003; Pew Research Center, 2014a; Zhang, Parish, Huang, & Pan, 2012). Moreover, men and women generally do not differ in their (negative) attitudes (see Petersen & Hyde, 2010, 2011). Thus, there is a general consensus among adults around the world that extramarital sex or extrarelational sex is unacceptable.

Interestingly, people also appear to disapprove of extrarelational sex even when the partners are aware of—and have agreed to—its occurrence. *Consensual non-monogamy* is an interpersonal arrangement or agreement in which partners openly engage in sexual, emotional, and/or romantic involvements with others, with all individuals aware of and consenting to the situation (Barker & Langdridge, 2010a, 2010b). Forms of consensual non-monogamy include:

- *Swinging*, in which a married or otherwise committed couple engages in sexual activity with another individual or couple (e.g., a cohabiting couple who attends a swingers event and has a "threesome" with another participant)

- *Open marriages/relationships*, in which members of a committed couple agree that one or both of them may have sexual activity with others outside of their primary relationship (e.g., a husband who does not engage in extramarital sex but who agrees that his wife may do so; a cohabiting couple who have "outside" sexual involvements that both are aware of and informed about)

- *Polyamory or polyamorous relationships*, in which both sexual and emotional involvement is shared among multiple partners (e.g., a husband, wife, and the wife's live-in lover; two mutually committed and involved couples)

In general, research indicates that both men and women hold negative attitudes about all types of consensual non-monogamy (although they appear to disapprove less of polyamorous unions than of swinging or open relationships) and have negative beliefs about individuals who enter into these arrangements (e.g., that they are immoral, selfish, immature, "kinky," unhappy with their relationship, irresponsible) (Conley, Moors, Matsick, & Ziegler, 2013; Matsick, Conley, Ziegler, Moors, & Rubin, 2014; Qaqiesh & Regan, 2004).

A third belief about marital sexuality concerns the relative power accorded to each sex in the making of sexual and reproductive decisions. For many years, both men and women believed that choices and decisions about the sexual part of married life—including when and how to initiate sexual activity, the frequency and amount of sex, the timing and number of children, the use of contraception, and so forth—were the responsibility of the male spouse. Witness the following quotation, excerpted from a popular guide to love, courtship, and marriage published in the United States over a hundred years ago:

> Usually marriage is consummated within a day or two after the ceremony, but this is gross injustice to the bride. In most cases she is nervous, timid, and exhausted by the duties of preparation for the wedding, and in no way in a condition, either in body or mind, for the vital change which the married relation brings upon her. . . . This, then, is the time for all approaches by the husband to be of the most delicate, considerate, and refined description possible. . . . Young husband! Prove your manhood, not by yielding to unbridled lust and cruelty, but by the exhibition of true power in self-control and patience with the helpless being confided to your care! (Jefferis & Nichols, 1896, pp. 202–204)

The authors of this advice manual clearly consider sexual decisions to be a husband's duty and right; he is the one who must demonstrate self-control and guard against yielding to "unbridled lust," who must determine the appropriate time for the wife's initiation into sexual relations, and who must calmly and patiently guide the couple's first and subsequent sexual interactions.

An examination of modern marriage manuals and guides to newlyweds reveals that this particular belief about marital sexuality has undergone significant change during recent years, at least in the United States and Western Europe. Evidence was provided by researchers Martin Weinberg, Rochelle Swensson, and Sue Hammersmith (1983), who analyzed 49 sex manuals published in the United States between 1950 and 1980. During the 1950s and 1960s, writers continued to emphasize differences between male and female sexuality and complementarity in sexual roles (i.e., husband as sexual teacher and wife as sexual learner). By the late 1970s, however, both sexes were depicted as autonomous sexual beings in control of their own sexuality, capable (and desirous) of sexual pleasure, and equally able to enact the parts of sexual teacher and learner. Additional research conducted in the United States also reveals that many husbands and wives—including those whose cultural background is traditionally patriarchal—share decision making about the sexual aspects of their marriages. For example, Marie Harvey and her colleagues (Harvey, Beckman, Browner, & Sherman, 2002) interviewed a sample of couples of Mexican origin and found that both husbands and wives typically shared in the decision making about sexual activities and contraceptive use.

Despite these changes in the United States, in many other world regions—including parts of Africa, Central and South America, the

Middle East, and Asia—men continue to be expected to make the major sexual and reproductive decisions (e.g., Bertrand, Makani, Edwards, & Baughman, 1996; Karra, Stark, & Wolf, 1997; Villasmil Prieto, 1997). For example, Hausa women living in Nigeria have a range of contraceptive methods available to them, but often do not use them due to the culturally supported belief that reproductive decisions are more appropriately made by men (Renne, 1997). The same pattern has been observed in other societies characterized by traditional gender roles and imbalanced power dynamics between men and women—decision making about sexual issues (e.g., family planning, contraceptive use) is largely controlled by men (Agadjanian & Ezeh, 2000; Levinson, Sadigursky, & Erchak, 2004).

## Summary

Researchers have identified a number of beliefs and assumptions about the role of sexuality in dating relationships. For example, although there is a trend toward greater sexual permissiveness or liberalism in many societies, most men and women continue to view sexual activity as most acceptable when it occurs between partners in committed (as opposed to casual or uncommitted) relationships. A number of beliefs also exist about marital sexuality, including the idea that sexual intercourse is a normative part of the marital union and the assumption that spouses (and other committed relationship partners) should confine their sexual activities to the primary relationship. As we discuss in Chapters 11 and 12, many of these beliefs reflect the sexual realities experienced by men and women in their ongoing romantic relationships.

## Key Concepts

Relational sexuality (p. 219)

Sexual standards (p. 222)

Premarital sexual intercourse (p. 222)

Sexual permissiveness (p. 222)

Sexual exclusivity (p. 228)

Consensual non-monogamy (p. 229)

Swinging (p. 229)

Open marriages/open relationships (p. 229)

Polyamory or polyamorous relationships (p. 229)

## Discussion Questions

1. How does relational sex differ from casual or uncommitted sex?

2. Consider the ways in which sexual standards for dating couples have changed over time. Base your answer on empirical evidence gathered from surveys of sexual attitudes.

3. Discuss the ways in which biological sex and culture are associated with sexual standards.

4. What three general conclusions about marital sexual standards can we draw from the available literature?

5. Describe the three forms of consensual non-monogamy. Why do you think most people have negative attitudes about these unions?

## Recommended Readings

This book contains a collection of chapters examining a variety of relational sexuality topics.

Harvey, J. H., Wenzel, A., & Sprecher, S. (Eds.). (2004). *The handbook of sexuality in close relationships*. Mahwah, NJ: Erlbaum.

The first two works explore the ways in which different cultures view sexuality and the sanctions they impose on men and women who violate sociocultural sexual norms and taboos. The Pew Research Center reports are available for download and provide evidence of cultural variation in attitudes toward premarital and extramarital sex.

Frayser, S. G. (1989). Sexual and reproductive relationships: Cross-cultural evidence and biosocial implications. *Medical Anthropology, 11*, 385–407.

Hatfield, E., & Rapson, R. L. (1996). *Love & sex: Cross-cultural perspectives*. Needham Heights, MA: Allyn & Bacon.

Pew Research Center (2014a). *Pew Research Center global attitudes project: Extramarital affairs*. Available from http://www.pewglobal .org/2014/04/15/global-morality/table/extramarital-affairs/

Pew Research Center (2014b). *Pew Research Center global attitudes project: Premarital sex*. Available from http://www.pewglobal.org/2014/04/15/ global-morality/table/premarital-sex/

These authors review research examining sex differences in sexual attitudes and behavior.

Petersen, J. L., & Hyde, J. S. (2010). A meta-analytic review of research on gender differences in sexuality, 1993–2007. *Psychological Bulletin, 136*, 21–38.

# 11

# Sex in Beginning Relationships

❖ ❖ ❖

The beliefs that people hold with respect to the role of sexual activity in dating and marital relationships undoubtedly have implications for their sexual (and nonsexual) interactions with their partners. In this chapter, we examine the role that sexuality plays in the attraction process and in the initial stages of romantic relationships.

## ❖ SEXUALITY AND THE ATTRACTION PROCESS

As we discussed in Chapter 1, there are a number of dispositional attributes or personality characteristics that people find particularly desirable in dates and marriage partners, including intelligence, honesty, a good sense of humor, emotional stability, and interpersonal warmth. Attributes that are related to sexuality, including a potential partner's "sex appeal," sexual history, and amount of sexual experience, also are important determinants of initial attraction.

### Sex Appeal

Although many social scientists have explored the characteristics that people find attractive in potential mates, relatively few have investigated the factors that render someone particularly sexually appealing and that thus prompt initial attraction. In an effort to discover the specific features that create "sex appeal," social psychologists Pamela Regan and Ellen Berscheid (1995) asked a group of men and women to list all the characteristics that would make a man or woman sexually appealing to others. Analysis of participants' responses revealed that a woman's sex appeal was believed to be primarily a function of her appearance (with 90% specifying this attribute), along with such dispositional dimensions as a good overall personality (cited by 23%), self-confidence (cited by 17%), and intelligence (mentioned by 15%). Examples of participants' responses included the following:

> *From a male participant:* I think men want women to be willing, attractive, and interesting. It makes the desire stronger when he knows she wants the same thing, although not being able to get sex from her sometimes will do the same thing. Physically, I think a desirable woman would be soft, yet athletic, not fat, but not overly thin, with lots of curves and a nice face. A woman who is experienced and enjoys sex is more desirable than either an inexperienced, shy woman or else an overly experienced, "easy" woman.

> *From a male participant:* Her appearance. Nothing else is needed. A man can be with any woman as long as he thinks she looks good. The easiest way to get a man interested in a woman is for his friends to say how good the girl looks. I truly feel that besides the body—no other characteristics are needed.

> *From a female participant:* Definitely an attitude that portrays that she wants "it." Flirtation seems to help men become more interested.

A confident characteristic that would suggest that she is good at "it."
Overall attractiveness (skinny, tall, nice smile).

*From a female participant:* Could be very thin with long, thin legs, long
hair, white teeth. Could be voluptuous—I guess what I'm getting
down to is physical attraction.

Male sex appeal was presumed to be a function of a very similar
constellation of features. Again, appearance was the most frequently
mentioned characteristic (cited by 76%), followed by "sensitivity" or a
compassionate, kind disposition (35%), a good overall personality
(24%), and a sense of humor (18%):

*From a male participant:* I think a well-built, strong man would cause
desire as opposed to a sloppy, overweight guy or a really skinny guy.
I think women desire a guy who is open, honest, and is interested in
pleasing them, instead of the opposite. I also think a woman desires
men who appreciate her sexual appetites/preferences over ones who
force their own wishes on her. Physical qualities would probably
include muscles and cleanliness or being well-groomed.

*From a male participant:* Women like men to be funny and caring.
A major thing for women is that they want a man to be sensitive to
their needs as women. Physical attractiveness is important to women,
although they don't tend to show this as much as men do. I wish
I knew more about this question myself—believe me!

*From a female participant:* A great fit body and nice clothes. This doesn't
mean that's all I'm looking for, but to be sexually attracted—yes.

*From a female participant:* Based on physical characteristics I would say
the way a person looks such as his face, eyes, lips, and a well-toned
body. A man must be caring, kind, and gentle. He must be able to
show his feelings and let you know he cares about you.

In addition to overall physical appearance, specific physical features
may be important elements of an individual's sexual attractiveness. For
example, although the superficial facial features (including skin tone
and pigment, eye color, and lip size) that are considered attractive vary
widely across cultures, certain facial characteristics seem to be
universally preferred. Men and women from a variety of cultures rate
"average" faces with symmetrical features as especially desirable
(e.g., Grammer & Thornhill, 1994; Jones & Hill, 1993; Langlois &
Roggman, 1990; Quist et al., 2012; for a review, see Rubenstein, Langlois, & Roggman, 2001). In addition, there are particular configurations
of facial features that most adults find appealing. A series of studies

conducted by Michael Cunningham and his colleagues (e.g., Cunningham, 1986; Cunningham, Barbee, & Pike, 1990) provides evidence that the most attractive male and female faces possess a combination of three types of attribute: neonate or babyish features (e.g., relatively large, wide-set eyes, a smallish nose), features that indicate sexual maturity (prominent cheekbones and thinner cheeks and, in men, a strong chin), and physical features that imply expressiveness (such as eyebrows set relatively high over the eyes). And finally, research has revealed that it is not simply facial structure that influences perceptions of attractiveness, but also facial expression or emotional display. In one investigation, for example, men and women were rated as significantly more attractive when their faces displayed the emotion of "happiness" than when they expressed sadness, surprise, fear, anger, or disgust (Morrison, Morris, & Bard, 2013).

Morphological characteristics, such as body size and shape, also are important determinants of sex appeal. With respect to body size, research reveals that both men and women view normal weight people as more sexually desirable than they do extremely thin or extremely overweight individuals (Regan, 1996; for a review, see Regan & Berscheid, 1999). Body shape, which is a function of muscularity and body fat distribution, also influences perceptions of attractiveness. For men in particular, upper body physique (e.g., size and muscularity of the arms and chest, width of the shoulders, and body build) appears to be an important component of attractiveness (Franzoi & Herzog, 1987). In general, women rate men with a moderate, tapering "V" upper body shape as more attractive than men with a slender physique or with a bulkier or thicker upper body shape (Dixson, Dixson, Bishop, & Parish, 2010; Lavrakas, 1975; Salusso-Deonier, Markee, & Pedersen, 1993). Many men, too, report that muscularity (i.e., having appropriately developed and defined muscles) is an important component of their own (and of other men's) sex appeal (Steinfeldt, Gilchrist, Halterman, Gomory, & Steinfeldt, 2011).

Another aspect of body shape that is related to perceived attractiveness is body fat distribution (which can be measured by computing a ratio of the circumference of the waist to the circumference of the hips, called the *waist-to-hip ratio*). Before puberty, both sexes exhibit a similar waist-to-hip ratio; however, after puberty, women deposit more fat in the gluteofemoral region (buttocks and thighs), and men deposit more fat in the central and upper body regions (shoulders, abdomen, and nape of the neck). Typically, the waist-to-hip ratio ranges from .67 to .80 in healthy, premenopausal women (an hourglass shape), and from .80 to .90 in healthy men (a straighter shape). Research reveals that men and women of different ages, races, and cultural backgrounds assign higher attractiveness ratings to individuals who possess a waist-to-hip ratio that is typical or average for their sex (e.g., Dixson, Grimshaw, Linklater, & Dixson, 2011; Furnham, Tan, & McManus, 1997; Henss, 1995; Singh, 1994, 1995; Singh, Dixson, Jessop, Morgan, & Dixson, 2010; Singh & Luis, 1995).

Thus, although many characteristics can make a person initially attractive and appealing to others, appearance seems to be the most important factor. And the significance people give to appearance is not surprising. In face-to-face first encounters, before two people have even interacted or struck up a conversation, the primary piece of information they have about one another is what they can see—each other's appearance.

## Sexual Passion

Another sexual characteristic that has implications for attraction is sexual passion. Because most adults associate sexual desire with passionate love (see Chapter 8), we might expect men and women to prefer a partner who is capable of both experiencing and expressing feelings of sexual passion. Although few researchers have directly tested this hypothesis, there is some evidence that supports it. For example, Susan Sprecher and Pamela Regan (2002) asked a large sample of men and women to indicate how much "sexual passion" they preferred in a potential dating or marriage partner. Participants were also asked to report how important it was that they obtain a partner with that particular level of sexual passion. No differences were found between men and women or between types of potential partner in the desired amount or importance of this particular sexual attribute. Participants preferred equally high levels (close to 8 on a 9-point scale) of sexual passion from both types of romantic partner, and they placed equal importance on obtaining these desired high levels.

Participants in another study (Regan, Levin, Sprecher, Christopher, & Cate, 2000) used percentiles to indicate where they would like their potential partners to rank on the characteristic "sexually passionate/ high sex drive" relative to other same-sex individuals (e.g., a score of 50% indicated a preference for a partner who was "average" with respect to the characteristic). The results revealed that both men and women desired a romantic partner who ranked well above average. Specifically, men preferred that their potential mate possess more sexual passion and a higher sex drive than 80% of other women, and women preferred that their potential mate score higher on this attribute than 73% of other men. Family studies scholars Bron Ingoldsby, Paul Schvaneveldt, and Claudia Uribe (2003) obtained similar results when they asked a group of Ecuadoran men and women whether they would be willing to marry someone who "is not interested in sexual relations"—the majority (84%) indicated that they would not.

These preferences for a partner who demonstrates sexual passion and expresses an interest in sex make sense in light of the increasing sexual permissiveness that is developing around the world (see Chapter 10). That is, as sexual activity comes to be viewed as a more acceptable component of (premarital) romantic relationships, men and women consequently may prefer partners who possess sufficient sex drive to engage in that activity.

## Sexual History

Sex appeal (and the features it comprises) and sexual passion are not the only sexual characteristics that influence our attraction to another person. An individual's sexual history also influences how we evaluate him or her. In general, research reveals that men and women prefer their potential dates and mates to possess lower, rather than higher, levels of previous sexual experience. When Regan and Berscheid (1997) asked a group of men and women to rank order a list of characteristics in terms of their desirability in a potential romantic partner, "sexually available or 'easy'" was ranked as the *least* desirable attribute. Male participants in study conducted by psychologists David Buss and David Schmitt (1993) also viewed such sexual attributes as "promiscuous" and "sexually experienced" as undesirable in a potential mate.

Person perception experiments (in which participants receive information about, and then evaluate, a target individual they believe is a "real" person) provide support for this general finding. In one such study conducted by Laura Bettor, Susan Hendrick, and Clyde Hendrick (1995), a group of college students read a brief vignette about two target persons who were involved in either a casual or a serious romantic relationship. In the casual relationship vignette, "Bob" and "Cathy" had met recently at a grocery store and exchanged phone numbers, and within a week had gone on their first date, during which they had sex. In the serious relationship condition, the targets were described as meeting a year ago in a grocery store and dating steadily ever since, now feeling that they were in love, and having sex for the first time very recently. After reading the two vignettes, participants were asked to estimate the likelihood that Bob would consider marrying "a girl like Cathy" and that Cathy would consider marrying "a guy like Bob." The results revealed that participants thought that Bob would be much more likely to marry Cathy, and that Cathy would be much more likely to marry Bob, when the relationship was depicted as serious rather than casual. In other words, targets who engaged in sexual intercourse on a first date after they had just met were not considered as "marriageable" as those who waited to have sex until they were in a committed, loving relationship. Similar results were reported by Lucia O'Sullivan (1995), who found that people preferred as dates and spouses targets who were presented as engaging in intercourse within a committed relationship rather than those who were described as having uncommitted casual sex. And more recently, Luis Garcia (2006) asked participants to rate the romantic desirability of a target individual who varied along two dimensions of sexual experience (number of sexual partners, number of different sexual activities). The results revealed that targets with higher levels of sexual experience (e.g., nine vs. three sexual partners, experience with 21 sexual activities including intercourse vs. experience with seven non-intercourse sexual activities) were rated as significantly less desirable as dating partners and spouses than targets with lower levels of sexual experience. In fact, the least preferred target was the one possessing the highest overall degree of sexual experience (i.e., who had engaged in all 21 sexual activities and who had nine previous sexual partners).

When considering a potential partner's sexual history, then, people clearly believe that "less is more" and that any prior sex should have been confined to committed rather than casual relationships.

## Chastity: No Longer Important?

Although most men and women prefer their dates and mates to possess lower rather than higher levels of lifetime sexual experience, this does not necessarily mean that they desire partners with no sexual knowledge whatsoever. Indeed, data collected over the past several decades suggest that *chastity* (complete sexual inexperience) has become increasingly *un*important to both men and women. For example, in one of the earliest mate preference studies (Hill, 1945), men and women received a list of 18 attributes that they ranked in terms of importance in a romantic partner. Chastity, defined as "no previous sexual experience," was ranked 10th in importance—about halfway down the list. A replication study conducted some 20 years later (Hudson & Henze, 1969) revealed that chastity had fallen to 15th in importance as a partner attribute. A decade later, another replication study (Hoyt & Hudson, 1981) indicated that chastity had continued its decline into irrelevance; women now ranked this attribute second to last (17th), and men ranked it dead last (18th), in importance. Thus, complete and total sexual inexperience does not appear to be a highly desirable partner attribute. Men and women apparently want someone with "just enough" sexual knowledge.

Some cultures, however, value chastity more than others. Research suggests that chastity is considered relatively unimportant (or even undesirable) among men and women in a variety of Western European countries (e.g., Belgium, France, Sweden, Italy, Greece, Norway; see Buss, 1989). However, men and women from other cultures—particularly those with collectivist, patriarchal, and sexually traditional orientations—continue to emphasize the value of premarital virginity (especially for women). Cultures that place a high premium on (female) chastity include Iran, Iraq, Egypt, and a host of other Middle Eastern and African nations (Abdelshahid & Campbell, 2015; Al-Obaidi, Jeffry, Al-Obaidi, & Al-Obaidi, 2014; Chubin, 2014; Shaeer & Shaeer, 2013; van Rooyen & Hartell, 2010). Of course, what people say they value and what they themselves do are sometimes quite different. As noted by cross-cultural psychologist Robin Goodwin (1999), premarital sex is relatively common among both men and women in many contemporary cultures, including those with a history of valuing virginity; therefore, although chastity may be considered a desirable trait, it is not necessarily seen as an indispensable one.

## ❖ SEXUALITY IN BEGINNING RELATIONSHIPS

Premarital sexual activity is an increasingly common event in the lives of most adolescents and young adults, and the majority of this activity occurs within the context of dating relationships (see Christopher, 2001). Insofar as many teenagers and college-age adults believe that sex is an appropriate element of committed romantic relationships (Reiss, 1964; Sprecher, McKinney, Walsh, & Anderson, 1988) and feel that sex can bring a couple closer together (Muram, Rosenthal, Tolley, Peeler, & Dorko, 1991), it is perhaps not surprising that most young people have engaged in some form of sexual activity, including intercourse, by the end of high school (e.g., Leitenberg & Saltzman, 2000; Miller & Leavitt, 2003; Regan, Durvasula, Howell, Ureño, & Rea, 2004). This section considers research on the first sexual encounter in beginning relationships, including the factors that are important in the decision to have sex for the first time with a particular partner and the different pathways to sexual involvement that a couple may follow. We also consider the ways in which men and women attempt to influence their sexual interactions with dating partners.

## The First Sexual Encounter

The first sexual encounter is usually a highly significant event in developing relationships. Interview data collected by Leslie Baxter and Connie Bullis (1986) demonstrate that the first sexual activities shared by a couple serve as an important marker signifying a change in the commitment level or developmental stage of their relationship. These researchers asked a sample of 40 dating couples to identify and discuss in detail all of the turning points in their relationship since the time of their first meeting. Thirteen general categories of relationship turning points subsequently were identified. One of these categories, labeled the "passion turning point" by the researchers, included four events—the couple's first kiss, their first episode of sexual intercourse, the first time they said "I love you," and what the researchers describe as the "whirlwind phenomenon" (essentially the experience of falling in love at first sight)—that couples indicated were important markers in influencing or signaling relationship commitment. Additional research by these and other investigators (e.g., Baxter & Pittman, 2001; also see Metts, 2004) further attests to the important role that first sexual events play in the early stages of romantic relationships.

## The Decision to Have Sex for the First Time in a Relationship

What prompts a couple to become sexually active? Research suggests that a number of factors are involved in this decision. The most important reason appears to be interpersonal in nature—specifically, emotional intimacy and closeness. For example, family studies scholars Scott Christopher and Rodney Cate (1984) asked a group of men and women to rate how important various considerations were in their decision to have sex for the first time in a premarital relationship. Their analysis revealed four general reasons underlying this decision. The first and most important reason involved *positive affection and communication*. For instance, people considered how much love they felt for the partner, the possibility that the relationship would result in marriage, and their level of commitment or involvement when deciding whether to have sex with the partner. *Arousal and receptivity*—including their own or the partner's level of sexual arousal immediately prior to intercourse and their receptivity to the partner's sexual advances—also played a role in the decision to have sex. A third factor concerned *obligation and pressure*. For example, feelings of obligation to have sex with the partner, as well as the partner's pressure or insistence on having sex, contributed to individuals' decisions about sexual involvement. Finally, people's sexual decisions were influenced by *circumstance*, ranging from the amount of drugs or alcohol they or their partner had consumed to the "specialness" of that particular date. These results suggest that although a number of factors clearly influence the decision to have sex, feelings of love and intimacy play an extremely important role.

Research on why people *refrain* from having sex with a particular partner also highlights the impact of the relationship's emotional tenor. In one study, Lucia O'Sullivan and Michelle Gaines (1998) surveyed a sample of college students who had the opportunity for sexual activity but had felt unsure or ambivalent about actually engaging in the activity. Participants were asked to describe the incident and to explain in detail their reasons for feeling ambivalent. Analysis of the free responses revealed that the most common reason given by men (35%) and women (49%) for feeling unsure about having sex with someone who clearly wanted them to do so concerned relationship and intimacy issues, including not feeling sufficient levels of commitment and being uncertain about their feelings for the partner.

Although O'Sullivan and Gaines (1998) found no difference in the percentages of men and women who cited relationship factors as causing their ambivalence about sexual participation, other research suggests that emotional intimacy, commitment, and other interpersonal factors may play a greater role in women's than in men's sexual decision making. We have already reviewed evidence, presented in Chapter 10, that women hold less permissive attitudes about uncommitted or casual sex than do men and that women tend to associate sex with love and intimacy more than do men. Similarly, surveys of dating couples reveal that women are more likely than men to specify insufficient commitment as a reason for actually abstaining from sexual intercourse with their current partners (Peplau, Rubin, & Hill, 1977; also see Carroll, Volk, & Hyde, 1985).

## Pathways to Sexual Involvement

At some point in their relationship, most couples do choose to become sexually intimate. This intimacy may take several forms, ranging from kissing and light petting to intercourse. In addition, some couples elect to engage in sexual activity relatively early in their relationship, while others wait until they have been together for a longer period of time and perhaps are engaged or even married.

Two teams of researchers, using different methodologies, have documented the different paths that couples follow as they move toward their first act of sexual intercourse. Anne Peplau and her colleagues (1977) conducted a longitudinal study in which they followed a group of dating couples over a 2-year period and surveyed them periodically about their sexual (and other) experiences. Christopher and Cate (1985) conducted a retrospective study in which they asked a sample of dating couples to think back over their relationship and report about various events and experiences. Despite their differing methods of data collection, the two research teams found strikingly similar results. For example, in both studies, some couples chose to abstain from sexual intercourse entirely and to limit their sexual interactions to non-intercourse activities (e.g., kissing, light petting). These couples, termed *sexually traditional* or *abstaining* by Peplau et al. (1977) and labeled *low involvement* by Christopher and Cate (1985), generally believed that love alone did not serve to justify sexual intercourse, that intercourse should be saved for marriage, and that abstinence from intercourse was a sign of love and respect between the partners. They also tended to hold conservative sexual attitudes and to have lower overall levels of sexual experience than did other couples.

Both research teams also found evidence of the other extreme— that is, couples who elected to engage in intercourse very early in their relationship (sometimes on the first date or after a few dates). *Sexually liberal* (Peplau et al., 1977) or *rapid involvement* (Christopher & Cate, 1985) couples viewed sex without love as acceptable and did not require commitment in order to have and enjoy intercourse. For these couples, the decision to have sexual intercourse stemmed primarily from physical pleasure and arousal motives rather than from any emotional concerns or relationship factors.

Other types of couples were identified as well. For example, Peplau et al. (1977) described a type of couple they termed *sexually moderate* or *later sex*. Partners in sexually moderate relationships were somewhere in between their traditional and liberal counterparts in terms of their attitudes and behavior. Although they generally chose to wait awhile before engaging in sexual intercourse, they also believed that sexual intercourse was acceptable if the two people loved each other— and they did not need a long-term commitment before becoming sexually involved. Love, rather than commitment per se, was sufficient justification for intercourse.

Christopher and Cate (1985) also described other couple types located between the rapid and low involvement extremes. *Gradual involvement* couples engaged in sexual intercourse when they were considering becoming "couples" and demonstrated gradual increases in sexual intimacy as their relationships became progressively more committed. For example, as they moved from casual dating to steady dating, they engaged in correspondingly more intimate forms of sexual expression. *Delayed involvement* couples—the most common couple type identified by the researchers—also clearly associated sexual involvement with the level of commitment in their relationships. However, they held more conservative sexual attitudes than did the gradual involvement couples and demonstrated a very different pattern of sexual interaction. Specifically, delayed involvement couples engaged in extremely low levels of sexual activity until the partners made a commitment to each other and the relationship; once they were in a steady and monogamous union, they increased their level of sexual involvement. As noted by Christopher (2001), these couples "resolutely limit their sexual involvement until making a monogamous dating commitment. This level of commitment serves as a sexual watershed once reached, allowing them to explore their sexual involvement as fully as the other coitally experienced couples" (p. 87).

Recently, scientists have become interested in whether the specific trajectory a couple chooses to follow toward sexual involvement is associated with later outcomes in their relationship. Research suggests that it may be. For example, several researchers (e.g., Busby, Carroll, & Willoughby, 2010; Willoughby, Carroll, & Busby, 2014) have found that partners who delay sexual intercourse (that is, who wait to have sex until after dating for awhile or who elect not to have sex until after marriage) report greater satisfaction with and commitment to their relationships, and indicate engaging in a higher amount of positive communication with each other, than partners who engage in intercourse earlier in their relationship (e.g., before or on their first date, during the first few weeks of dating). Clearly, commitment, emotional intimacy, and other important relational outcomes are intricately connected with sexuality in most romantic relationships.

## Sexual Influence

Peplau et al.'s (1977) and Christopher and Cate's (1985) studies demonstrated that most dating relationships are characterized by some degree of sexual interaction. Sex, however, does not simply happen; rather, it is something that must be negotiated by the members of the couple. As we discuss next, partners often attempt to influence each other in their quest to have—or to avoid—sexual intimacy.

Several researchers have investigated the ways in which men and women initiate sexual activity or attempt to increase their current level of sexual involvement. Although direct requests are sometimes made, it appears that most individuals prefer to use *indirect* techniques, including sitting closer to their partners and touching, snuggling, kissing, or holding hands with them (Jesser, 1978; McCormick, 1979). For example, Timothy Perper and David Weis (1987) asked women college students to describe in an essay the strategies they would use to influence a sexual interaction. Three primary tactics were identified from the respondents' essays. The first included environmental and situational strategies, ranging from dressing in a sexually suggestive or seductive manner, to offering to get the partner a drink, to creating a romantic setting. Verbal strategies were also mentioned, including paying the partner compliments and engaging in romantic or sexually suggestive talk. The third set of strategies was nonverbal; for example, participants wrote about using eye glances, moving close, cuddling, touching, and kissing the partner as a way to initiate a sexual interlude.

More recently, Scott Christopher and Michela Frandsen (1990) asked a group of men and women to think about any sexual encounters that had occurred during their most recent dates and to report about the extent to which they had used a variety of different tactics (identified by the researchers) to influence those encounters. Analysis of participants' responses revealed four general sexual influence strategies. Some participants reported using *antisocial acts,* which involve imposing sexual wishes on a dating partner in socially unacceptable ways. These actions could be direct and overt, such as threatening to use force against the partner, actually using force, ridiculing and insulting the partner, and getting angry. Antisocial behaviors also could be covert, as when a person sulks, pleads, acts ill or helpless, or otherwise attempts to make the partner feel guilty for not giving in to sexual demands. Participants also reported using *emotional and physical closeness* behaviors to influence the partner. Examples include expressing affection or love, doing "something special" for the partner, complimenting or flattering the partner, moving physically closer, dropping hints, and communicating feelings about the importance of the relationship. People also invoked *logic and reason* in an attempt to influence sexual outcomes. These techniques ranged from calmly presenting a list of reasons about why the couple should become sexually intimate, to claiming to be knowledgeable about how sexual the relationship ought to be, to asserting authority or even attempting to compromise with the partner. The final sexual influence strategy involved *pressure and manipulation* and included such tactics as using drugs or alcohol to influence the partner, pressuring the partner, being persuasive, persisting in one's efforts, threatening to end the relationship, ignoring the partner's actions, and lying to the partner.

Although men were more likely to report having used pressure and manipulation tactics, no sex differences were found for the other types of sexual influence strategy. In fact, the most common way that both sexes reported having influenced their sexual encounters was through the use of emotional and physical closeness behaviors. Because this influence strategy was the one most strongly related to the level of sexual activity that actually occurred during the dates, it does appear to be the most successful means of increasing sexual intimacy.

So how do people successfully *avoid* sexual involvement? One method involves simply avoiding sexual situations entirely. Some of the women who participated in Perper and Weis's (1987) study said that they would avoid sex by keeping away from private settings in which sex might occur. Of course, there are times when an intimate setting cannot be avoided and when one partner issues a sexual invitation that the other partner does not wish to accept. In those circumstances, one of the most common ways in which men and women limit the sexual interaction is by simply ignoring the partner's suggestions, cues, or requests. For example, one person might turn away from the other's attempted kiss or pretend not to hear a compliment or sexually suggestive comment. Men and women also frequently employ logic and reasoning strategies ("We really need to think this over before we decide to take our relationship to that level") to defuse sexual situations and limit sexual involvement (Christopher & Frandsen, 1990).

## Summary

Sexuality plays an important role in the attraction process and in the initial stages of romantic relationships. In general, men and women prefer as dates and mates others who possess moderate sexual experience (as opposed to none or extensive sexual experience), and they weigh a number of factors in deciding whether and when to become sexually active with their current partners. Couples follow different pathways to sexual involvement, with some engaging in sex relatively early in their relationships and others preferring to wait until they reach a later stage characterized by high(er) levels of commitment and intimacy. In the process of negotiating the sexual aspects of their relationships, both men and women employ a number of different influence techniques; some are used to increase the level of the partners' sexual involvement, whereas others are used to limit sexual intimacy. In Chapter 12, we turn to a consideration of sexuality as it is experienced by couples in established partnerships, including marital and cohabiting relationships.

## Key Concepts

Sex appeal (p. 234)

Waist-to-hip ratio (p. 236)

Chastity (p. 239)

Sexually traditional or abstaining couples (p. 243)

Low involvement couples (p. 243)

Sexually liberal couples (p. 243)

Rapid involvement couples (p. 243)

Sexually moderate or later sex couples (p. 243)

Gradual involvement couples (p. 244)

Delayed involvement couples (p. 244)

Indirect sexual influence techniques (p. 245)

Antisocial strategies (p. 245)

Emotional and physical closeness strategies (p. 245)

Logic and reason strategies (p. 245)

Pressure and manipulation strategies (p. 246)

## Discussion Questions

1. How does a person's sexuality (e.g., sex appeal, sexual passion, sexual history) affect his or her desirability as a dating partner? Consider your own standards—would you date someone with absolutely no sexual experience whatsoever? Would you date someone with a history of extensive sexual activity?

2. Discuss how attitudes toward chastity have changed over time. How might this change be related to other social changes (e.g., sex education, media depictions of sexuality, social norms about male and female sexuality)?

3. What factors underlie the decision to have or not have sex with a particular partner for the very first time?

4. Discuss the different pathways to sexual involvement that a couple may follow as they progress toward the first sexual encounter. What might explain why some pathways seem to be associated with "better" outcomes later in a relationship than others?

5. Consider the four general strategies men and women use to influence sexual interactions with their partners. Have you ever used any of these strategies to influence a partner's behavior or to control the sexual "temperature" of your relationship? Has a partner ever used these strategies to influence your decisions about sex?

## Recommended Readings

These edited volumes contain chapters exploring a number of relational sex issues, including sexual attitudes, sexual decision making, sexual communication, and so forth.

McKinney, K., & Sprecher, S. (Eds.). (1991). *Sexuality in close relationships.* Hillsdale, NJ: Erlbaum.

McAnulty, R. D. (Ed.). (2012). *Sex in college: The things they don't write home about.* Santa Barbara, CA: Praeger.

This article suggests that women as well as men use various strategies to influence a couple's sexual interactions.

O'Sullivan, L. F., & Byers, E. S. (1993). Eroding stereotypes: College women's attempts to influence reluctant male sexual partners. *The Journal of Sex Research, 30,* 270–282.

This chapter reviews research examining the impact of four sexual characteristics—sex appeal, sexual passion, sexual history or experience, and sexual fidelity—on attraction. The edited volume containing this chapter is also an excellent introduction to research in the area of relational sexuality.

Regan, P. C. (2004). Sex and the attraction process: Lessons from science (and Shakespeare) on lust, love, chastity, and fidelity. In J. H. Harvey, A. Wenzel, & S. Sprecher (Eds.), *The handbook of sexuality in close relationships* (pp. 115–133). Mahwah, NJ: Erlbaum.

# 12

# Sex in Established Relationships

❖　❖　❖

We have seen in previous chapters that men and women around the world view marriage and other committed romantic relationships as an appropriate—in fact, the most appropriate—context for sexual activity. In this chapter, we review research on sexuality as it occurs and is experienced in long-term or established relationships. Specifically, we explore what is known about sexual frequency, sexual practices and preferences, sexual satisfaction, and sexual communication in partnered (that is, married, cohabiting, or dating) heterosexual and homosexual couples. It is important to keep in mind that because more research has been conducted on marital relationships than other kinds of long-term unions, the conclusions we can draw about sexuality are stronger for that particular type of romantic association.

## ❖ SEXUAL FREQUENCY

One topic that has received a great deal of attention concerns the frequency with which spouses (and other partnered individuals) engage in sexual intercourse. Research conducted over the past 60 years suggests that the average amount of sex that couples have has not changed much over time. For example, during the late 1940s and early 1950s, pioneering sex researcher Alfred Kinsey and his colleagues (Kinsey, Pomeroy, & Martin, 1948; Kinsey, Pomeroy, Martin, & Gebhard, 1953) asked more than 11,000 men and women living in the United States to indicate how often they engaged in sexual intercourse. They found that young married couples between 16 and 25 years of age reported having sex between two and three times a week on average; slightly older couples (between 26 and 35 years of age) indicated engaging in intercourse about twice a week on average. Another survey conducted two decades later yielded similar frequencies, with young couples (18–24 years of age) reporting sexual intercourse approximately three times a week (Hunt, 1974).

Couples surveyed during the 1990s resemble couples from earlier decades in terms of their level of sexual activity. Like Kinsey and his colleagues, sex researchers Robert Michael, John Gagnon, Edward Laumann, and Gina Kolata (1994) conducted a national study of the sexual experiences of men and women living in the United States. One of the questions they asked their participants was how often they had engaged in sex during the past 12 months. The possible responses were *not at all, once or twice, about once a month, two or three times a month, about once a week, two or three times a week,* and *four or more times a week.* Although participants were not asked to report the precise amount of sex in which they had engaged during the specified time period, the results were similar to those reported by previous researchers. Specifically, the response option endorsed by the highest percentages of married men (43%) and women (47%) was *two or three times a month.* The next most commonly endorsed option was *two or three times a week,* reported by 36% of married men and 32% of married women.

Very small percentages of married men (1%) and women (3%) said they had absolutely no intercourse at all with their partners in the past year; similarly, few married men (7%) or women (7%) reported extremely high amounts of sexual activity (i.e., four or more times a week). More recent national surveys reveal similar frequency rates among married men and women (e.g., Herbenick et al., 2010; Reece et al., 2010).

Although research in this area has focused primarily on the experiences of heterosexual married couples, homosexual couples engage in about the same amount of sex (defined here as genital contact) as their heterosexual counterparts. For example, one group of Dutch researchers (Deenen, Gijs, & van Naerssen, 1994) asked more than 300 gay men who were currently involved in a committed relationship about their frequency of intercourse. The clear majority of men (43%) reported having sex one to two times per week, with an additional 30% indicating that they had sex about three times per month (or slightly less than once a week). Of the remaining men, 25% said that they had sex three to five times per week and 2% reported having sex six or more times per week. Surveys reveal that lesbian couples demonstrate similar rates of sexual activity (e.g., Peplau, Cochran, & Mays, 1997; Peplau, Cochran, Rook, & Padesky, 1978). In one recent investigation, psychologists Jacqueline Cohen and Sandra Byers (2014) asked a sample of 586 women in committed same-sex relationships how often they and their partner engaged in genital sexual contact (e.g., breast or genital touching, oral sex, vaginal penetration). The results revealed that the majority of participants (about 40%) reported engaging in these activities one to three times a week, with smaller numbers reporting frequencies greater than (34%) or less than (26%) that.

Thus, taken together, the results of research on sexual frequency indicate that—irrespective of the sexual orientation or marital status of the partners—most couples (at least, most younger couples) tend to engage in sexual intercourse approximately one to three times a week.

Before coming to any firm conclusion about sexual frequency in established relationships, however, it is important to recognize that tremendous variability exists both within and across individual couples. For example, various life events (e.g., school- or job-related stress, financial hardship, fatigue, health issues, pregnancy, child care) might temporarily reduce a couple's motivation and ability to engage in sexual activity. Thus, the rate of intercourse exhibited by any one couple is likely to fluctuate over time. In addition, researchers find that some couples tend to engage in high levels of sexual activity, whereas others have sex infrequently, if at all (Donnelly, 1993; Herbenick et al., 2010; Reece et al., 2010). In one study, social scientist Cathy Greenblat

(1983) asked 80 married participants to retrospectively recall how often they had sexual intercourse each month during their very first year of marriage; reports ranged from one (or an average of 12 times during that first year) to 45 (or 540 times that first year). Clearly, some couples have sex more often than others!

In addition, certain *types* of couples engage in sexual activity more frequently than do others. Although most couples have sex about one to three times a week, surveys also reveal that cohabiting heterosexual couples and homosexual male couples tend to have sex (defined as genital contact) more frequently than do married couples, who in turn have sex more frequently than do homosexual female couples (e.g., Blumstein & Schwartz, 1983; Call, Sprecher, & Schwartz, 1995; Kurdek, 2006; Rao & DeMaris, 1995; Solomon, Rothblum, & Balsam, 2005). And all of these couple types seem to engage in greater amounts of sexual activity than do single men and women. Recall that Michael et al. (1994) found that very few married men (1%) and women (3%) reported having no sex at all during the previous 12 months. Similarly, very few of the cohabiting men and women who participated in their study indicated having a sexless past year, but 23% of the single men and 32% of the single women reported engaging in no intercourse during the same time. Similarly, among the 18 to 49-year-old participants in the 2010 National Survey of Sexual Health and Behavior (NSSHB), the vast majority of partnered women (85%) and men (75%) had engaged in intercourse at least once a month over the past 12 months—but 63% of the single women and 49% of the single men had not had sex even once (Herbenick et al., 2010; Reece et al., 2010). Despite what the media may tell us, being single generally does not produce as much sex as does being married or in a committed relationship:

> We find that the critical factor that produces the most sexual activity is being part of a couple, whether it is a marriage or a cohabitation. Even though married life is not seen as very erotic, it is actually the social arrangement that produces the highest rate of partnered sexual activity. . . . What seems to produce the highest rates of partnered sex is an easily accessible partner. (Michael et al., 1994, p. 118)

Essentially, the state of singlehood is not as conducive to sexual activity as is marriage or cohabitation.

## Age and Sexual Activity

Age—both that of the partners and that of their relationship—is intimately connected with a couple's level of sexual activity.

*Cross-sectional studies*, in which individuals from different age groups or ranges are surveyed about their sexual experiences, generally reveal that older couples engage in sexual intercourse less frequently than do younger couples (e.g., Brewis & Meyer, 2005; Herbenick et al., 2010; Karraker, DeLamater, & Schwartz, 2011; Reece et al., 2010; for reviews see Sprecher, Christopher, & Cate, 2006; Willetts, Sprecher, & Beck, 2004). For example, sociologists Vaughn Call, Susan Sprecher, and Pepper Schwartz (1995) examined sexual frequency across the life span using data gathered as part of the National Survey of Families and Households (a large-scale research endeavor consisting of personal interviews conducted with a national probability sample of 13,008 people). Their analyses were based on the 6,785 respondents who were married and had a spouse living with them in the household, and the item of interest concerned how often the participants reported engaging in sexual intercourse with their spouse during the past month. The results revealed that the frequency of marital sex was negatively correlated with age. For example, married men and women from 19 to 24 years of age reported having intercourse approximately 12 times a month. Those in their early to mid-30s engaged in sexual activity close to 9 times a month. Respondents from 50 to 54 years of age indicated having intercourse an average of 5.5 times a month, those in their late 60s reported having sex a little over twice a month, and those who were 75 years of age or older engaged in intercourse less than once a month. Thus, increasing age was associated with decreasing levels of sexual activity. However, the authors also noted that although the older respondents definitely had less sex than their younger counterparts, they were far from asexual. About half of married adults between 65 and 74 of age were still having sex (just not perhaps every month).

The frequency with which a couple has sexual intercourse is associated not only with the partners' chronological ages but also with the age of their relationship. Most studies demonstrate that the longer a couple has been together, the less often the partners have sex (e.g., Cohen & Byers, 2014; Rao & DeMaris, 1995; Samson, Levy, Dupras, & Tessier, 1991). This decline seems to be greatest during the first year or so of a relationship, such that newlyweds or newly-paireds typically experience high rates of sexual activity during the very beginning phases of their unions and then sharp decreases in activity as they settle into life as a committed couple. A longitudinal study conducted by researcher William James (1981) illustrates what has been termed the "honeymoon effect." James analyzed diaries and calendars kept by 21 newlywed couples, finding that couples had intercourse an average of 17 times during their very first month of marriage but only about 8 times a month by the end of the first year.

A similar decline in sexual frequency over time was observed by Laura Stafford, Susan Kline, and Caroline Rankin (2004), who analyzed data from the 1987–1988 and 1992–1994 National Survey of Families and Households. In this longitudinal investigation, three groups of heterosexual couples—couples who were married prior to the first wave of data collection and who were still married at the time of the second survey, couples who were cohabiting at both data collection times, and couples who were cohabiting at the time of the first survey but had married by the time of the second—were asked how often they and their partners had sex "during the past month" (p. 239) at two points in time (during 1987–1988 and then again five years later). The researchers found that there was a significant decrease in sexual frequency over time in all three groups (married couples, cohabiting couples, and cohabiting couples who transitioned to marriage). At the beginning of the study, couples reported engaging in intercourse an average of 11 times per month. Five years later, their frequency of sex had decreased to an average of 6 instances per month.

The lower level of sexual activity seen in older couples (and in older relationships) is undoubtedly due to a number of different factors, including the physical and psychological changes that are associated with the aging process and the loss of sexual novelty that develops from having intercourse with the same partner year after year. Other factors that may contribute to decreased activity over time include pregnancy (and its associated physical changes), fatigue and loss of privacy due to the presence of children and child care activities, and heavy work schedules (Greenblat, 1983; Smith, 2006; Willetts et al., 2004). All of these may conspire to make it difficult for couples to find the time—and the inclination—for sexual activity.

## ❖ SEXUAL PRACTICES

Another question that has sparked researchers' interest concerns sexual practices, or what people do when they are sexually intimate with each other. Michael and colleagues' (1994) national survey revealed that although there are a number of sexual activities from which to choose, the most commonly practiced among heterosexuals is penile-vaginal intercourse, with more than 95% of the heterosexual respondents stating that they engaged in this particular activity the last time they had sex. Oral sex, although less common than penile-vaginal intercourse, was also reported by a sizeable percentage of heterosexual respondents. Specifically, about one third of cohabiting men, and one fifth of cohabiting women, reported either giving or receiving oral sex during their last sexual interaction. The numbers were slightly lower for married individuals, with approximately 24% of married men and 17% of married women reporting having participated in this activity during their last sexual encounter. Other forms of sexual expression occurred far less frequently. For example, only 2% of cohabiting men and women (and even fewer married respondents) reported having engaged in anal intercourse during their last encounter. Researchers who have surveyed samples of adult heterosexual participants from other countries (e.g., Nicholas, 2004; Richters, de Visser, Rissel, & Smith, 2006) as well as multiethnic samples of adults living in the United States (e.g., Cain et al., 2003; Herbenick et al., 2010; Reece et al., 2010) have found similar patterns of sexual behavior among partnered heterosexual men and women.

Homosexual couples practice many of the same sexual activities as heterosexual couples but report higher frequencies of particular behaviors. For example, lesbian couples engage in more kissing, caressing, holding, and breast stimulation during sex than do cohabiting or married heterosexual couples (e.g., Blumstein & Schwartz, 1983; Masters & Johnson, 1979; also see Cohen & Byers, 2014). In addition, oral and anal sex are more commonly used by homosexual couples than by heterosexual couples. Approximately 40% to 50% of gay male and lesbian couples report usually or always engaging in oral sex during lovemaking, compared with 20% to 30% of heterosexual couples, and gay men are more likely to have anal sex than are heterosexual couples (Blumstein & Schwartz, 1983; Lever, 1995; Michael et al., 1994).

The results of two national surveys conducted by sociologist Janet Lever (1994, 1995) suggest that homosexual couples may also be more experimental than their heterosexual counterparts. For example, many of the lesbian respondents—particularly those in their teens, 20s, and early 30s—had incorporated dildos (43%) or food (35%) into their sexual activities, had engaged in bondage or discipline (25%), or had participated in three-way sex (14%). Similarly, 55% of the gay male respondents had used dildos during sex, 48% had engaged in three-way sex, 24% had participated in group sex, and 10% had experienced a sadomasochistic sexual encounter. It is important to note that Lever's question concerned activities during the past 5 years; consequently, we do not know *how often* participants engaged in these particular behaviors. It is possible that these activities were a common part of her respondents' sexual interactions, but it is also possible that they were tried once and then never again. In either case, her results do suggest that some couple types may be more sexually experimental than others.

## ❖ SEXUAL PREFERENCES

In addition to exploring what people actually do sexually with their partners, some researchers have examined what people say they would *like* to do—in other words, their sexual preferences. Of all the possible sexual practices on the heterosexual menu, penile-vaginal intercourse seems to possess the most appeal. For example, participants in the national survey conducted by Michael et al. (1994) were given the following list of possible sexual activities:

- Having sex with more than one person at the same time
- Having sex with someone of the same sex
- Forcing someone to do something sexual that he/she doesn't want to
- Being forced to do something sexual that you don't want to
- Seeing other people do sexual things
- Having sex with someone you don't personally know
- Watching your partner undress or strip
- Vaginal intercourse
- Using a dildo or vibrator
- A partner performing oral sex on you
- Performing oral sex on a partner
- Partner stimulating your anus with his/her fingers
- Stimulating partner's anus with your fingers
- Passive anal intercourse
- Active anal intercourse (only men received this item)

Participants were asked to indicate how appealing they found each of these sexual activities by using a 4-point scale, where 1 represented *very appealing*, 2 represented *somewhat appealing*, 3 represented *not appealing*, and 4 represented *not at all appealing*.

The results indicated that despite the wide variety of acts from which to choose, both sexes found only a small number to be appealing. Specifically, 96% of younger women and 95% of younger men (18–44 years of age) rated vaginal intercourse as either very appealing or somewhat appealing; similarly, 93% of older women and 95% of older men (45–59 years of age) found this particular act to be at least somewhat appealing. In fact, vaginal intercourse was the clear favorite, with all other acts receiving much lower preference ratings. Watching the partner undress was the second most preferred activity, although this particular event was rated as very appealing by more men than women in both the younger (50% vs. 30%) and older (40% vs. 18%) age groups. This was followed by receiving and giving oral sex, with both men and women indicating that it was more appealing to receive than to give this particular sex act. Each of the other behaviors or events seemed to appeal to only a very small percentage of people. For example, less than 5% of women and men said that they found using a dildo or vibrator, watching other people do sexual things, having sex with a stranger, and passive anal intercourse to be very appealing. No respondents indicated that being forced to do something sexual was very appealing, and none of the women and younger men (and only 1% of the older men) rated forcing someone to do something sexual as very appealing.

Although less is known about the sexual preferences of homosexual men and women, Lever's (1994, 1995) national surveys yield some insight. For example, her male respondents said that their favorite bed-room acts included hugging, caressing, and snuggling (endorsed by 85%); deep kissing (74%); receiving oral sex (72%); giving oral sex (71%); masturbating a partner (52%); and being masturbated by a partner (51%). Their biggest sexual turn-offs were insertive anilingus (oral stimulation of the anus; disliked by 26%) and receptive anal intercourse (disliked by 14%). Interestingly, however, many men selected these two particular sex acts as turn-ons; fully 29% said they preferred insertive anilingus, and 43% endorsed receptive anal intercourse. Lever (1994) concluded, "When it comes to anal play, it appears [that gay] men either love it or hate it, and significant numbers are in both camps" (p. 21).

Homosexual women expressed similar sexual preferences. For example, most participants said they "loved" hugging, caressing, and cuddling (91%); French kissing (82%); caressing a partner's breasts (82%); and sucking a partner's nipples (80%). About 75% identified holding hands, touching a partner's genitals, and having their own genitals touched as appealing practices. Like homosexual men (and like the heterosexual men and women in Michael et al.'s 1994 study), more lesbians prefer receiving oral sex (75%) than giving it (70%). Women reported that their least favorite activity is anal stimulation, with more than half expressing a dislike of anilingus (both giving and receiving) and anal penetration.

Thus, although the sexual menu is varied, most men and women—whether married or cohabiting, homosexual or heterosexual—prefer a limited selection of activities and express many of the same likes and dislikes.

## ❖ SEXUAL SATISFACTION

Most paired individuals report that they are satisfied with their sex lives (e.g., Blumstein & Schwartz, 1983; Kurdek, 1991; Lawrance & Byers, 1995; Mark, Herbenick, Fortenberry, Sanders, & Reece, 2014). For example, approximately two thirds of the husbands and wives in one early national survey reported experiencing a great deal or a very great deal of sexual satisfaction (Greeley, 1991). Similarly, more than half of the men and almost half of the women in committed (cohabiting or marital) relationships who participated in Michael at al.'s (1994) survey stated that their relationship was "extremely" physically pleasurable. More recently, psychologists Sandra Byers and Sheila MacNeil (2006) asked a sample of heterosexual men and women involved in long-term marital or cohabiting relationships to rate the sexual component of their relationships using five scales: *good-bad, pleasant-unpleasant, positive-negative, satisfying-unsatisfying,* and *valuable-worthless.* These ratings were summed to create a global measure of sexual satisfaction. Participants made their evaluations at three different times over an 18-month period, and the researchers found that at all three times sexual satisfaction was uniformly high. Research conducted with non-U.S. samples corroborates these findings. For example, a group of Australian scientists (Smith et al., 2011) surveyed a large sample of people in committed heterosexual relationships and found that more than 75% of both men and women reported being "very satisfied" or "extremely satisfied" sexually with their partner. Homosexual men and women appear equally satisfied sexually; more than 40% of the gay men (most of whom were partnered) in Lever's (1994, 1995) studies rated their current sex lives as great or good, and more than 30% of the partnered lesbians indicated that their sex lives were great.

One of the most important factors associated with sexual satisfaction is how often a couple engages in sexual activity. Both heterosexual and homosexual couples who have more frequent sex generally report higher levels of sexual satisfaction than couples who have less frequent sex (e.g., Blumstein & Schwartz, 1983; Call et al., 1995; Cohen & Byers, 2014; Young, Denny, Luquis, & Young, 1998; Yucel & Gassanov, 2010; for reviews see Peplau, Fingerhut, & Beals, 2004; Sprecher & Cate, 2004). For instance, Lever's (1995) survey data revealed a strong relationship between sexual frequency and sexual satisfaction among partnered homosexual women. Nearly all (92%) of the women who had sex 21 to 40 times during the past month rated their sex lives as great, compared with 67% who had sex 11 to 20 times, 44% who had sex 5 to 10 times, and 18% who had sex 2 to 4 times. Basically, the more sex her respondents reported, the more satisfied they were with the quality of their sexual interactions. Similar results were reported more recently by Cohen and Byers (2014), who found that the more frequently their female participants engaged in genital sexual activities with their (same-sex) partners, the higher their degree of sexual satisfaction. Interestingly (though perhaps not surprisingly), there is some evidence that satisfaction is not just associated with the *actual* frequency with which partners have sex but also the extent to which they *agree* about their sexual frequency (see Smith et al., 2011). Specifically, partners whose preferences correspond (i.e., who want the same amount of sex, regardless of what that amount is) tend to feel more satisfied with their sex lives than partners with discrepant desires.

Sexual satisfaction is also associated with other sexual factors in a couple's relationship, including whether the partners experience orgasm (e.g., Haning et al., 2007; Perlman & Abramson, 1982; Pinney, Gerrard, & Denney, 1987; Tracy & Junginger, 2007; Young et al., 1998), when during the sexual interaction the partners reach orgasm (Brody & Weiss, 2011; Darling, Davidson, & Cox, 1991), the ratio of rewards (e.g., emotional intimacy, physical pleasure, feeling sexually desirable) to costs (e.g., time constraints, performance concerns, discrepancy between preferred and actual activities) that partners receive from their sexual relationship (Byers, Demmons, & Lawrance, 1998; Byers & MacNeil, 2006; Kisler & Christopher, 2008), and the duration and quality of post-sex affectionate behaviors that partners display (e.g., cuddling, caressing, shared intimacy; Muise, Giang, & Impett, 2014). In sum, couples tend to experience higher levels of sexual satisfaction when they engage in sex frequently, want the same amount of sex to occur, reach orgasm as a result of their sexual activity and at about the same time, obtain more rewards than costs from their sexual interactions, and engage in mutually affectionate behaviors in the period immediately following sexual activity.

## ❖ SEXUAL COMMUNICATION

*I consider myself very fortunate in that I can talk with my husband about anything, even the most intimate, personal things. We are both really good at listening to each other and being open and honest with our needs, likes, and dislikes in all areas of our relationship, including sex. I am convinced this is why our sex life is so great—we have realistic expectations and a good sense of humor about sex. We listen and are willing to learn and to do the things that each of us likes, and this makes for a pretty awesome sexual partnership (and marriage, by the way!).*

—28-year-old woman interviewed by the author

*My girlfriend and I have never talked about our sex. We do it, but we don't talk about it. I would like to talk with her, to be sure that I'm doing what she likes. Also because I think this might actually bring us closer. But it's too hard. I would be too embarrassed to bring it up.*

—20-year-old man interviewed by the author

Another factor that is closely connected to sexual satisfaction in long-term relationships is sexual communication. *Communicative competence*—that is, the ability to effectively communicate with the partner about one's sexual needs, preferences, expectations, and attitudes—is very important in established relationships. Not only is effective communication necessary for successfully negotiating the amount and type of a couple's sexual involvement, but it is also essential for maintaining the quality of their sexual relationship over time (Cupach & Comstock, 1990; Metts, Sprecher, & Regan, 1998). Research consistently reveals a positive association between open and direct sexual communication and sexual satisfaction. Specifically, the greater the quality (e.g., openness, directness) and quantity of sexual communication between partners, the more satisfied they report being with the sexual aspects of their relationship (see Mark & Jozkowski, 2013; Montesi, Fauber, Gordon, & Heimberg, 2011; Rehman, Rellini, & Fallis, 2011). Conversely, the more that couples refrain from (or actively avoid) discussing sex, the less sexual satisfaction they report experiencing (Theiss, 2011; Theiss & Estlein, 2014).

One aspect of sexual communication that has received a great deal of attention from theorists and researchers is the initiation and refusal of sexual requests. In the traditional heterosexual "sexual script," men are expected to initiate sexual activity, whereas women are expected to then accept or refuse these sexual requests (e.g., Gagnon & Simon, 1973; Reiss, 1981). Research indicates that heterosexual men and women generally follow this script in their actual sexual interactions, with men functioning as the sexual initiators and women serving as the sexual regulators (Blumstein & Schwartz, 1983; Vannier & O'Sullivan, 2011). For example, Shari Dworkin and Lucia O'Sullivan (2005) asked a sample of heterosexual men to describe the pattern of sexual initiation in their current romantic relationships. The most common pattern was male-dominated, with more than half (56%) of the men reporting that their sexual interactions followed the traditional script. Much smaller proportions of men reported an egalitarian pattern in which both partners initiated sex (25%) or a female-dominated pattern in which their partners initiated sex (19%). Interestingly, only one fourth of the men who reported following the traditional male-dominated initiation script wished to sustain this pattern; most (72%) desired to adopt a more egalitarian pattern with both partners equally responsible for initiating sexual activities. Over time, of course, women may become more comfortable initiating sexual activity with their partners; one early study revealed a small yearly increase in the rate of initiations among wives (Brown & Auerbach, 1981).

Regardless of which partner does the initiating, most sexual initiation attempts that occur in long-term relationships are successful; that is, most men and women respond positively to their partner's sexual invitations (Byers & Heinlein, 1989). These positive responses (as well as the initiation attempts) are generally communicated nonverbally and indirectly (Beres, Herold, & Maitland, 2004; Brown & Auerbach, 1981; Byers & Heinlein, 1989; Vannier & O'Sullivan, 2011). It is unusual for individuals to explicitly and verbally request sex from their partners ("Hey, do you want to have sex?"); it is equally unusual for partners to agree to sexual invitations in a verbally explicit manner ("Why yes, I would love to have sex right now"). Rather, a person who desires sexual activity might put on some romantic music, open a bottle of wine, and glance suggestively in the direction of the bedroom. The partner who receives this indirect invitation might smile, put down his or her book, and engage in other nonverbal behaviors that continue the sexual interaction without explicitly acknowledging acceptance (or even awareness) of the initial invitation.

Sexual *refusals*, however, do tend to be communicated verbally and directly ("Honey, I'm just not in the mood right now; I'm kind of stressed about my research report"). As noted by communication scholars William Cupach and Sandra Metts (1991), such directness "seems to fulfill simultaneously the goals of averting unwanted persistence of initiation by the partner and of maintaining the face of the rejected individual by offering an account" (p. 103). So how do couples ultimately resolve situations in which one partner wants sex and the other does not? Research suggests that couples employ several strategies for reaching amicable conclusions to these episodes. For example, they may mutually agree not to have sex ("Yeah, you're right, you really should spend tonight working on that report"), they may agree to postpone sex until a later time ("Since you need to work on your report tonight, how about tomorrow after you turn it in?"), or they may simply agree to disagree ("Well, I still think we have time, but if you're not in the mood, that's okay"). Of course, sometimes even the most reluctant partners change their minds. They may become aroused and therefore more interested in the proposed activity, they may be swayed by the arguments offered by their partner, or they may simply decide to accommodate their partner's wishes (Byers & Heinlein, 1989).

Whether initiations, refusals, and other aspects of sexual negotiation influence a couple's level of sexual satisfaction depends, to a large extent, on the communicative skill of the partners. It is not easy to be an effective sexual communicator. Successful communication about sexuality requires the ability both to *express* information about one's needs, desires, likes, and dislikes and to *solicit and receive* this information in a nonjudgmental and nondefensive manner from the partner (D'Augelli & D'Augelli, 1985; Metts, 2003). This level of disclosure and intimacy requires a great deal of trust and acceptance and may be difficult for couples to achieve. Many couples do, however, manage to express at least some aspects of their sexual feelings. In one study (Rubin, Hill, Peplau, & Dunkel-Schetter, 1980), researchers asked dating couples to report how much self-disclosure they experienced on a number of topics, including "my feelings about our sexual relationship." The majority (about three fourths) of men and women indicated having full disclosure on this topic with their partner. Thus, although open and honest communication about sexuality may seem like a difficult goal for couples to reach, it is certainly not impossible. Effective sexual communication is vital for maintaining the quality of the sexual relationship.

## ❖ SEXUALITY AND RELATIONSHIP SATISFACTION

Not surprisingly, how people feel about their sex lives is related to how they feel about their relationships in general. All of the aspects of sexuality we have considered—sexual frequency, practices and preferences, satisfaction, and communication—are associated with the *non*sexual dimensions of a relationship. For example, the frequency with which a couple has sexual intercourse is related to relationship satisfaction. Specifically, the more often a couple has sex, the more generally satisfied they are with the relationship (e.g., Call et al., 1995; Donnelly, 1993; Regan, 2000b), the more they enjoy spending time together and sharing activities and hobbies (e.g., Blumstein & Schwartz, 1983; Sprecher, Metts, Burleson, Hatfield, & Thompson, 1995), and the more equitable and fair they perceive their relationship to be (Hatfield, Greenberger, Traupmann, & Lambert, 1982).

Similarly, a large (and increasingly multi- and cross-cultural) body of research indicates that there is a strong correlation between sexual satisfaction and relationship satisfaction (e.g., Butzer & Campbell, 2008; Byers & MacNeil, 2006; Henderson-King & Veroff, 1994; Litzinger & Gordon, 2005; MacNeil & Byers, 2005; Mark & Murray, 2012; McNulty & Widman, 2013; Yoo, Bartle-Haring, Day, & Gangamma, 2014). Heterosexual and homosexual couples who are satisfied with their sexual relationship tend also to be satisfied with other areas of their partnership (for reviews, see Christopher & Sprecher, 2000; Kurdek, 1991; Peplau et al., 2004; Sprecher & Cate, 2004). In one study, for example, Kelli-An Lawrance and Sandra Byers (1995) asked close to 250 heterosexual men and women who were currently involved in long-term (mostly marital) relationships to rate their sexual relationships and their overall relationships on five 7-point bipolar scales: *good-bad, pleasant-unpleasant, positive-negative, satisfying-unsatisfying,* and *valuable-worthless.* They found a strong association between these two measures. Specifically, the more satisfied participants were with their sexual relationships (i.e., the more they rated them as good, pleasant, positive, etc.), the more satisfied they were with their relationships in general.

Of course, such correlational findings do not allow us to come to any firm conclusion about causality. That is, does good sex lead to a good relationship, or does a good relationship produce good sex? Although several researchers have attempted to answer this question, their efforts have met with limited success. For example, longitudinal investigations conducted by Sprecher (2002) and Byers (2005) demonstrated that sexual and relationship satisfaction covaried (that is, at any given point in time, people who were satisfied sexually also tended to be satisfied interpersonally) but were unable to conclusively support one particular causal direction. However, at least one longitudinal study suggests that it is sexual satisfaction that contributes to relationship well-being (rather than the reverse). During five assessments spanning a 10-year period, Hsiu-Chen Yeh and colleagues (Yeh, Lorenz, Wickrama, Conger, & Elder, 2006) asked a sample of married couples to indicate how happy and satisfied they were with their marriages (these items were summed to create a measure of marital quality). Participants also completed an eight-item scale that assessed sexual satisfaction (e.g., "My spouse and I have a wonderful sex life," "My spouse is happy with our sex life," "Sex isn't very important to me" [reverse scored]). The results revealed several interesting findings. First, sexual satisfaction was relatively stable over time; couples who were satisfied with their sex lives in 1990 tended to be satisfied a year later in 1991, and the year after that, and so on. (Marital quality proved equally stable.) Second, sexual satisfaction predicted later marital quality for both husbands and wives. Specifically, higher levels of sexual satisfaction at one assessment point (e.g., 1992) predicted an increase in marital quality at the next assessment point (e.g., 1994). However, marital quality did not predict subsequent levels of sexual satisfaction; in other words, participants' ratings of their marital happiness and satisfaction at one point in time were completely unrelated to how satisfied they were with their sex lives at a later point in time. Although additional corroborating longitudinal research is needed, these results suggest that sexual satisfaction influences subsequent relational functioning (and not vice versa)—good sex leads to a good relationship.

Whatever the direction of causality, researchers agree that sexuality and relationship satisfaction are intimately connected.

## Summary

Sexuality is an important part of marital, cohabiting, and other established romantic relationships. The attitudes that partners hold about relational sexuality, the timing and manner of their sexual initiations, the amount of sex that they have, the kinds of sexual activities in which they engage, and how they communicate with each other about their needs, desires, and preferences can have an enormous impact on their level of sexual satisfaction and on their happiness with the relationship in general. In Chapter 13, we examine what happens when couples develop problems with the sexual aspects of their relationships.

## Key Concepts

Sexual frequency (p. 250)
Cross-sectional studies (p. 253)
Honeymoon effect (p. 253)
Sexual satisfaction (p. 258)
Communicative competence (p. 260)

Sexual initiation (p. 261)
Sexual refusal (p. 261)
Traditional (heterosexual) sexual script (p. 261)
Egalitarian sexual script (p. 261)

## Discussion Questions

1. Consider common themes in partnered sexual behavior (e.g., frequency, practices, preferences).

2. Contrary to popular myths about the "swinging single," paired individuals often have more sex than their single counterparts. Why do you think that marriage or cohabitation might be more conducive to sexual expression than singlehood?

3. Explain how time—duration of a relationship and age of the partners—affects sexual frequency.

4. What factors are associated with sexual satisfaction? Why might sexual frequency be associated with sexual satisfaction (and do you think that this relationship holds even for mediocre or bad sex)? What is the relationship between sexual satisfaction and overall relationship satisfaction?

5. Define the traditional heterosexual sexual script. Do you think that this script has changed over time? Why might it change once a relationship has moved beyond beginning phases and become committed and established?

## Recommended Readings

This book presents the results of the authors' large-scale survey of the sexual practices and preferences of men and women in the United States. It was written for the general public and provides insight into the sexual lives of married, cohabiting, and single people. Although more than two decades old, it is easy to find and the results are still relevant (and have been supported by subsequent research).

Michael, R. T., Gagnon, J. H., Laumann, E. O., & Kolata, G. (1994). *Sex in America: A definitive survey*. Boston, MA: Little, Brown.

These four articles provide overviews of the literature on various aspects of relational sexuality in long-term committed heterosexual and homosexual relationships, including sexual frequency, practices, and attitudes.

Christopher, F. S., & Sprecher, S. (2000). Sexuality in marriage, family, and other relationships: A decade review. *Journal of Marriage and the Family, 62,* 999–1017.

Peplau, L. A., Fingerhut, A., & Beals, K. P. (2004). Sexuality in the relationships of lesbians and gay men. In J. H. Harvey, A. Wenzel, & S. Sprecher (Eds.), *The handbook of sexuality in close relationships* (pp. 349–369). Mahwah, NJ: Erlbaum.

Smith, T. W. (2006). Sexual behavior in the United States. In R. D. McAnulty & M. M. Burnette (Eds.), *Sex and sexuality. Vol. 1. Sexuality today: Trends and controversies* (pp. 103–132). Westport, CT: Praeger.

Willetts, M. C., Sprecher, S., & Beck, F. D. (2004). Overview of sexual practices and attitudes within relational contexts. In J. H. Harvey, A. Wenzel, & S. Sprecher (Eds.), *The handbook of sexuality in close relationships* (pp. 57–85). Mahwah, NJ: Erlbaum.

# 13

# Sex Gone Bad

## Problematic Aspects of Relational Sex

In Chapter 12, we considered how partners who engage in frequent and satisfying sexual interactions are likely to experience happiness, feelings of equity and affirmation, and general satisfaction with each other and with the relationship. However, it is important to recognize that there also exists a dark side to relational sexuality. Not only do relational partners often use sex to express their feelings of love and commitment, but they may also withhold, demand, or coerce sex as a way of punishing each other or demonstrating interpersonal power (Christopher & Lloyd, 2000). In sum, sex can serve as both a positive and a negative force in close relationships. In this chapter, we turn to four problematic aspects of sexuality in beginning and established romantic relationships—sexual disinterest, sexual assault, sexual infidelity, and sexual jealousy.

## ❖ SEXUAL DISINTEREST: WHEN THE ONE WE DESIRE DOES NOT DESIRE US

For many people in committed romantic relationships, a partner's sexual disinterest represents a particularly painful form of interpersonal rejection. We have already reviewed research that suggests that sexual activity declines over time in most long-term unions (see Chapter 12). One of the possible reasons for this decline is *sexual disinterest*—one or both partners experience reduced desire to engage in sexual activities with each other. Because many people routinely undergo fluctuations in their general level of sexual desire, and because sexual desire is associated with age, physical and mental health, drug use, hormonal variations, and a host of other personal factors, a reduction in one partner's level of sexual attraction to the other partner does not necessarily indicate that something is "wrong" with their relationship (Regan & Berscheid, 1999).

Sometimes, however, a reduction in sexual interest (particularly if it occurs suddenly and/or is sustained for a long period of time) may signal a decline in the overall health of a couple's relationship. Research with dating and married couples suggests, in fact, that sexual desire functions to some extent as a "thermometer" to relationship quality— that is, partners' sexual interest in each other waxes and wanes as their relationship undergoes various ups and downs. For example, one study conducted with dating couples (Regan, 2000b) found that the more sexual desire that men and women reported feeling for their partners, the more satisfied they were with their current relationship and the less often they actively thought about ending that relationship.

Similar results were obtained by Michael Brezsnyak and Mark Whisman (2004), whose survey of married couples revealed that the amount of sexual desire that husbands and wives felt for each other was strongly positively correlated with their level of relationship satisfaction (also see Davies, Katz, & Jackson, 1999; Willoughby, Farero, & Busby, 2014). Clinical research using samples of adults (usually women) diagnosed with sexual desire disorders provides additional evidence for the association between sexual interest and overall relationship health (e.g., Dennerstein, Koochaki, Barton, & Graziottin, 2006). In one early investigation, Freida Stuart, D. Corydon Hammond, and Marjorie Pett (1987) administered a marital adjustment scale to a sample of married women who were diagnosed with inhibited sexual desire (ISD), married women who reported normal sexual desire, and the spouses of women in both groups. Not only did the women in the ISD group have significantly lower marital adjustment scores than did women in the non-ISD group, but their spouses also reported significantly lower overall adjustment in their marriages than did the spouses of women in the non-ISD group.

There is also evidence that dysfunctional dynamics between partners—including poor social support and conflict resolution strategies, interpersonal anger and hostility, maladaptive communication patterns, and power struggles—can have a corrosive effect on sexual interest (Arnett, Prosen, & Toews, 1986; Kaplan, 1979; Maurice, 2007; McCarthy, Ginsberg, & Fucito, 2006; Pietropinto, 1986; Trudel, 1991). Moreover, even when the relationship is not overtly hostile, if it is not conducive to open communication and emotional support, sexual desire is likely to be affected. In a longitudinal study of married and cohabiting women, Tore Hällström and Sverker Samuelsson (1990) found that those who reported a decrease over time in their level of sexual desire also tended to perceive insufficient emotional support from, and a lack of a confiding relationship with, their partner. It is no surprise that the majority of clinicians now conceptualize reductions in desire as a "couple issue" rather than a "personal problem," focus on the dynamics of the couple's relationship during treatment, and apply therapeutic techniques that involve both partners (such as communication skills training and sexual intimacy exercises; Hartmann, Rüffer-Hesse, Krüger, & Philippsohn, 2012; for reviews and additional discussion, see Leiblum, 2010, and Ullery, Millner, & Willingham, 2002).

Of course, it is important to remember that partners in a healthy, well-adjusted relationship will not always feel a constant level or an intense degree of sexual desire for one another. Not only are feelings of sexual interest quite likely to change over the course of a long-term partnership, but it is even possible for the closeness and intimacy that characterize functional romantic relationships to create a sexual environment that actually dampens desire (for an in-depth discussion, see Ferreira, Narciso, & Novo, 2012). Psychologists Karen Sims and Marta Meana (2010) asked a sample of married women who had lost their feelings of sexual attraction to their husbands to identify the factors that had reduced their desire and were preventing its reinstatement. Interestingly, very few women mentioned relationship problems when explaining their reduction in desire—they perceived their marriages as satisfying and healthy and they valued their husbands and viewed them in a positive light. Rather, these women uniformly pointed to sexual dynamics that had developed over time within their marriages, including (1) sexual habituation and overfamiliarity (i.e., the loss of novelty, adventure, spontaneity, and excitement that had characterized sexual encounters earlier in the relationship, when sex was riskier and less available and consequently more valuable); (2) "mechanical" or monotonous sexual activity (i.e., orgasm-focused sexual interactions that de-emphasized foreplay, creativity, and technique and that had become highly routine and predictable); and (3) sexual advances from the partner that lacked effort, subtlety, tenderness, and ingenuity. As partners grow comfortable and familiar with each other, they may experience a type of sexual stagnation that makes it increasingly difficult for them to sustain a high degree of sexual interest in one another.

At the same time, it is also possible for partners in long-term relationships to experience a heightened motivation to meet each other's sexual needs, along with increased openness about sexuality and ease with sexual communication; this sexual dynamic is likely to have a positive impact on sexual desire (see McCarthy & Farr, 2012; Metts, Sprecher, & Regan, 1998; Muise, Impett, Kogan, & Desmarais, 2013). Indeed, at least one study (Birnbaum, Cohen, & Wertheimer, 2007) found a strong correlation between sexual intimacy and sexual desire in long-term romantic relationships—women whose sexual interactions with their partners were characterized by high levels of intimacy (e.g., affectionate behavioral exchanges) reported experiencing correspondingly high levels of sexual desire for those partners.

In sum, changes in sexual interest are not necessarily a sign that a romantic relationship is in trouble. However, some interpersonal environments are more conducive to the maintenance of desire than others. A relational climate characterized by love, satisfaction, and commitment—and a sexual climate characterized by open, playful, responsive communication and intimate, innovative, partner-oriented interactions—is likely to create and sustain sexual attraction between partners.

## ❖ SEXUAL ASSAULT: WHEN SEX BECOMES NONCONSENSUAL

*I was raped three years ago by my high school boyfriend. It was after prom and he said it was our special night. He got drunk and he took me behind the hotel and raped me. I begged him to stop but he wouldn't. It hurt so much. I was a virgin and I never told anyone, not even my mom.*

—20-year-old woman interviewed by the author

*Sometimes I'm not in the mood for sex and he'll say things like his balls are turning blue or his dick is going to fall off if he doesn't get to use it, or that he's going to trade me in for someone more 'understanding.' There are times when I give in simply because it takes less energy to give him sex than it does to keep arguing about it.*

—22-year-old man interviewed by the author

*My first husband had very strong beliefs about sex and marriage. He believed that a wife had a duty to satisfy her husband's sexual needs, whenever or wherever those needs arose. On two separate occasions following my refusal to have sex with him, I woke up from a deep sleep to find him on top of me having sex. He didn't hurt me, exactly, but I couldn't get him off me and the sex was one-sided and definitely not consensual.*

—50-year-old woman interviewed by the author

Most couples manage to successfully negotiate changes in desire and the various other sexual situations they encounter and achieve satisfactory and mutually agreed-upon sexual outcomes. For some, however, sexual encounters may involve various forms of unwanted, nonconsensual, or even violent behavior. Broadly speaking, *sexual assault* refers to unwanted or nonconsensual sexual contact (see Christopher & Kisler, 2004; Muehlenhard, Goggins, Jones, & Satterfield, 1991; U.S. Department of Justice, 2012). More specifically, sexual assault occurs when a person engages in sexual activity (1) as a result of physical force or the threatened use of physical force (illustrated in the first quotation presented above); (2) as a result of verbal coercion (e.g., verbal or psychological manipulation or pressure; illustrated in the second quotation); or (3) when he or she is unable to consent or resist (e.g., under the influence of alcohol or drugs, asleep or unconscious; this is called physical coercion and is illustrated in the third quotation). In addition, the unwanted or nonconsensual activity not only includes intercourse (vaginal, oral, anal) but also penetration with a foreign object (e.g., finger, bottle) and touching or fondling of a person's breasts, buttocks, or genitals.

For some couples, nonconsensual sex might happen once or twice and not recur. For other couples, however, forced sex is the norm. Scientists who have investigated the dynamics of these sexually violent relationships have identified three distinct patterns of sexual assault, each with its own characteristic features (see Finkelhor & Yllö, 1985; Groth, 1979; Monson & Langhinrichsen-Rohling, 1998; also see Marshall & Holtzworth-Munroe, 2002). The first, *battering rape* (also called *anger rape*), occurs in the context of a coercive and controlling relationship. The victim experiences forced sex coupled with physical violence and coercive control. In some instances, the physical assault precedes the forced sexual activity, whereas in other instances the physical violence occurs during the sexual assault. In these relationships, the perpetrator engages in multiple forms of aggression and often uses sex as a means to express anger and hurt the partner. The second type of sexual assault is *force-only rape* (or *power rape*). Force-only rape typically does not involve severe physical violence—the perpetrator generally is not physically abusive but will use force to obtain sex from an unwilling partner. In these relationships, the perpetrator's intent is not to cause harm (although injury may result from the assault) but rather to exert dominance over the partner and control over the couple's sexual interactions. *Obsessive rape* (also called *sadistic rape*) is less common than the other two forms of relational sexual violence and is motivated by a sadistic desire to sexually torment and mistreat the partner. The perpetrator is obsessed with forcing the partner to engage in degrading, deviant, and painful sexual activities. He or she derives pleasure from the partner's humiliation and is willing to use physical violence to achieve these sexual goals.

## The Prevalence of Nonconsensual Sex in Romantic Relationships

Research conducted over the past half century reveals that nonconsensual (forced or coerced) sex is a relatively common occurrence within dating relationships. An early study of undergraduate men conducted in the 1960s, for example, revealed that 26% reported having made forceful attempts at intercourse while on a date that had, in turn, caused their partners to fight, cry, or scream (Kanin, 1967). Two decades later, 25% of the men in a national survey of college students stated that they had used some form of sexual coercion or force on a dating partner (about 8% admitted having raped or attempted to rape a partner; Koss, Gidycz, & Wisniewski, 1987). Today, these rates appear largely unchanged. Psychologists Christine Gidycz, Jennifer Warkentin, and Lindsay Orchowski (2007) asked 425 undergraduate men to answer a series of questions about their sexual assault history. Three types of assault behavior were assessed: (1) sexual coercion (defined by the researchers as the use of authority, continual arguments, or pressure to coerce a woman into sexual intercourse); (2) sexually aggressive contact (defined as the use of continual arguments, authority, or physical force to make a woman engage in nonintercourse sexual activities); and (3) rape or attempted rape (defined as the use of alcohol, drugs, physical force, or threats of physical force to coerce a woman into vaginal, oral, or anal sex). The results revealed that nearly 18% of the men reported perpetrating at least one of these forms of sexual assault, and almost all (93%) of their victims were dating partners or acquaintances (only 7% were strangers).

Thus, contrary to popular opinion (which typically portrays sexual assault as a violent act perpetrated by strangers lurking in dark alleys), most victims are coerced, pressured, or forced into sex by intimates. Indeed, data from the 2005–2010 National Crime Victim Survey (Planty, Langton, Krebs, Berzofsky, & Smiley-McDonald, 2013) indicated that only 22% of women rape victims were assaulted by a stranger; the rest (78%) were raped by a spouse or romantic partner, friend or acquaintance, or relative. Recent national surveys conducted by the U.S. Centers for Disease Control and Prevention revealed a similar pattern, with most victims (approximately 87%) reporting having been assaulted by current or former romantic partners or by acquaintances (Black et al., 2011; Breiding et al., 2014). Similarly, almost all (96%) of the women surveyed by Robert Michael and his colleagues (Michael, Gagnon, Laumann, & Kolata, 1994) knew or were romantically involved with their attackers (55%, in fact, said that they were in love with or married to these men)—only 4% of the respondents indicated that their male assailants were strangers who were unknown to them. Thus, most of the forced and unwanted sexual interactions reported by women occur within the context of their existing, and oftentimes love-based, relationships.

Although reliable estimates of marital rape are difficult to obtain, survey data from the United States and other world regions indicate that a sizeable proportion of marriages contain sexual violence (e.g., Garcia-Moreno, Jansen, Ellsberg, Heise, & Watts, 2006; Marshall &

Holtzworth-Munroe, 2002). In the United States, for example, about 10% to 14% of married women (and about half of battered wives) have been sexually assaulted by their husbands (see Martin, Taft, & Resick, 2007). Similarly, a survey conducted in Great Britain by criminologists Kate Painter and David Farrington (1998) revealed that 13% of wives had experienced forced sexual intercourse with their husbands. Higher rates of sexual violence were reported by William Parish and his colleagues (Parish, Luo, Laumann, Kew, & Yu, 2007), who examined the prevalence of unwanted sexual activities among a community sample of more than 1,100 married women in China. Almost one third (32%) of the women reported having been forced to have intercourse by their husbands, usually repeatedly and over a period of five or more years; of those women, 40% had experienced physical injury as a result of the rape(s).

Men, too, can be sexually pressured, coerced, and forced by their partners. Prevalence estimates in which the rape victim is male are also difficult to obtain, in part because so few men are willing to report their assaults to the authorities. However, research indicates that approximately 12% to 40% of gay or bisexual men report having been physically forced or coerced into unwanted intercourse, many by a male partner (see Peterson, Voller, Polusny, & Murdoch, 2011). And almost 4% of the men who participated in a recent national survey reported having been physically forced to sexually penetrate a female partner; an additional 5% said that they had been coerced into performing unwanted sexual intercourse with a female partner (Black et al., 2011). Like women, men typically are assaulted by someone they know. About three fourths of male rape victims in one survey were victimized by a current or former romantic partner or by a friend or acquaintance (Breiding et al., 2014).

## The Origins and Consequences of Sexual Assault

The recognition that coercive and/or forced sexual episodes occur with some frequency within dating and other romantic relationships has created an interest in discovering the factors that are associated with this type of interpersonal behavior. One of the most potent correlates is biological sex. Although women can (and sometimes do) coerce or force sex from unwilling partners, and men can be (and sometimes are) coerced or forced to engage in nonconsensual sexual activities by their partners, the reality is that most sexual assault victims are female and most perpetrators are male (Breiding et al., 2014; Michael et al., 1994; Planty et al., 2013). Men and women also differ in their perceptions of sexual assault. For example, when asked to evaluate date rape scenarios, men generally perceive a higher degree of sexual willingness on the part of the female target than do women. In addition, men typically believe the female target is more responsible for the assault—and the male target's behavior is more justified—than do women (for a review, see van der Bruggen & Grubb, 2014).

Certain dispositional characteristics, including the extent to which people subscribe to and enact traditional gender roles, also appear to be associated with rape perceptions and sexually coercive or violent behavior. *Hypermasculinity* and *hyperfemininity* refer to the tendency to endorse and rigidly adhere to exaggerated male or female gender role stereotypes. Men who possess high levels of hypermasculinity believe that violence is manly; view danger and risk taking as exciting; emphasize competition and dominance in their interactions with others; devalue emotion, cooperation, and other stereotypically "feminine" attributes; and endorse calloused sexual attitudes toward women (Burk, Burkhart, & Sikorski, 2004; Corprew, Matthews, & Mitchell, 2014; Mosher & Sirkin, 1984). Women who possess high levels of hyperfemininity define themselves by their ability to attract a man and maintain a heterosexual romantic relationship; hold traditional views of women as socially and economically subordinate to men; view themselves as sexual objects; value traditionally "masculine" behavior on the part of men; and endorse female use of sexuality, physical attributes, and "femininity" to influence men (Murnen & Byrne, 1991; Nowatzki & Morry, 2009). Not surprisingly, perhaps, research indicates that these two forms of *hypergender* are associated with aspects of sexual coercion and assault. For example, hypermasculine men not only have a more positive emotional response to rape depictions (and report a higher likelihood of committing rape in the future), but are more likely actually to have engaged in sexually and physically aggressive behavior toward their partners than men who possess lower levels of this attribute (e.g., Beaver, Gold, & Prisco, 1992; Guerrero, 2009; Mosher & Anderson, 1986; Parrott & Zeichner, 2003; also see Schewe, Adam, & Ryan, 2009; for a review, see Murnen, Wright, & Kaluzny, 2002). Relatedly, hyperfeminine women report experiencing higher amounts of sexual coercion, and have a less negative reaction to coercive sex depictions, than women who score low on hyperfemininity (Maybach & Gold, 1994; McKelvie & Gold, 1994; Murnen & Byrne, 1991; also see Gold, Sinclair, & Balge, 1999).

Interpersonal or relational factors, including communication patterns between partners, also are implicated in nonconsensual sex. As we discussed in Chapter 12, partners do not always communicate adequately or effectively with each other about their sexual preferences and feelings. Recall that very few men and women explicitly and directly ask their partners for sex—instead, they tend to rely on indirect, nonverbal methods that can be misinterpreted or not noticed by the partner. Moreover, people sometimes fail to accurately communicate their true intentions or wishes. Research indicates that over one third of college men and women admit to having engaged in *token resistance* (defined as saying "no" when they meant "yes") during sexual encounters (Muehlenhard & Hollabaugh, 1988; Sprecher, Hatfield, Cortese, Potapova, & Levitskaya, 1994; but see Muehlenhard & Rodgers, 1998). Another form of ambiguous communication that can occur between partners during their sexual interactions is *compliance*, defined as agreeing to sexual intercourse when one does not really want to (Vannier & O'Sullivan, 2010). Between 35% and 55% of college men and women say that they have complied with a partner's sexual request when they did not wish to do so (Shotland & Hunter, 1995; Sprecher et al., 1994). Token resistance, compliance, and other indirect and ambiguous forms of communication may increase the likelihood that partners experience a nonconsensual sexual encounter (see Krahé, Scheinberger-Olwig, & Kolpin, 2000).

A variety of social and cultural factors also may create an environment that is conducive to sexual coercion and violence within romantic relationships (for reviews, see Christopher, 2001; Christopher & Kisler, 2004; Muehlenhard et al., 1991). For example, sexual victimization is more likely to occur in countries with a patriarchal cultural orientation that emphasizes strict gender roles, glorifies male dominance and aggression, and promotes the subservient status of women. Consider marital rape. In the United States, marital rape is a crime in all 50 states and the District of Columbia. Indeed, marital rape is a crime in all North American, South American, and Western European countries. However, some cultures legally and politically endorse the idea that husbands are entitled to have sex with their wives and that wives have no right to refuse their husbands' sexual requests. A man is legally entitled to rape his wife in approximately 40 countries in Africa (e.g., Kenya, Uganda, Nigeria), the Middle East (e.g., Iran, Jordan, Saudi Arabia), and Asia (e.g., Pakistan, Afghanistan, China). Many of these countries also are marked by rigid gender hierarchies and ideas of manhood that center on violence and sexual entitlement. Other social influences (primarily investigated in the United States) that are believed to promote sexually coercive attitudes and behaviors include (1) sex role scripts associated with heterosexual dating situations (e.g., men should control the progression of the relationship and any sexual interactions that occur); (2) the sexual double standard, which encompasses normative beliefs that men are sexual, that male sexuality is an uncontrollable and powerful force, and that women often offer token resistance to sex; (3) socialization processes that foster the acquisition of rape myths; and (4) peer group norms that support and promote exploitative attitudes toward women and the use of coercive sexual strategies (e.g., Burt, 1980; Castañeda & Burns-Glover, 2004; Eaton & Matamala, 2014; Kanin, 1984, 1985; Martin & Hummer, 1989; also see Loh, Orchowski, Gidycz, & Elizaga, 2007).

Regardless of the origins of sexually aggressive behavior, the consequences for the victim are negative and diverse (e.g., Campbell, Dworkin, & Cabral, 2009; Wadsworth & Records, 2013). In their respective reviews of the literature, Karen Calhoun, Jenna McCauley, and Megan Crawford (2006) and Zoë Peterson and Charlene Muehlenhard (2003) identified a host of acute (immediate) physical and psychological responses that victims of assault may experience, including physical trauma and pain; fatigue; nausea; sleep disturbances; disorientation; and feelings of anxiety, fear, shame or embarrassment, guilt, humiliation, and anger. They noted that in addition to these immediate reactions, victims of assault often experience negative long-term outcomes. Some of these are physical in nature and include chronic illness, disease, or unwanted pregnancy. Other consequences are interpersonal; victims often curtail their social activities, develop some sort of sexual dysfunction, become significantly impaired in their ability to function at work or school, and experience disruption in their relationships with friends or family members. The psychological consequences of sexual assault are equally adverse and range from depression, to fear and anxiety, to *post-traumatic stress disorder* or PTSD (a long-term reaction to traumatic events whose symptomatology includes reexperiencing the event mentally through distressing dreams or intrusive recollections; numbing or avoidance of thoughts, feelings, or memories related to the event; and increased arousal or hypervigilance).

Nonconsensual sexual activity does occur between partners in close relationships, and there is a strong and immediate need for additional research on the causes and consequences of this dark side of relational sex.

## ❖ SEXUAL INFIDELITY: WHEN THE ONE WE'VE CHOSEN CHEATS

As we discussed in Chapter 10, one of the primary beliefs that people hold about marital and other long-term, committed relationships is that they should be *sexually exclusive*. That is, the majority of men and women living in cultures around the world expect married or otherwise committed partners to engage in sexual activities only with each other. And most people appear to not only believe this proscription but also to follow it. (An exception is gay men, who tend to hold more permissive attitudes with respect to sexual infidelity and whose romantic relationships are less likely to be sexually exclusive than those of lesbians and heterosexuals; see Peplau, Fingerhut, & Beals, 2004). When Michael et al. (1994) asked participants to indicate how many sex partners they had had in the past year, the responses men and women gave clearly demonstrated "how likely people are to remain faithful to their sexual partners, whether or not they were married" (p. 101). Specifically, 95% of the married men and women, 75% of the never-married but cohabiting men and women, and 82% of the divorced and now cohabiting men and women had engaged in sexual activity with one person (the partner) over the past 12 months. In fact, the people who reported multiple sex partners were, for the most part, single with no primary romantic partner. The researchers concluded, "Despite the popular myth that there is a great deal of adultery in marriage, our data and other reliable studies do not find it. Instead, a vast majority are faithful while the marriage is intact" (p. 89). The results of more recent surveys conducted in the United States and other countries continue to substantiate this basic relational fact (e.g., Knox, Vail-Smith, & Zusman, 2008; Træen & Thuen, 2013; Vail-Smith, Whetstone, & Knox, 2010; Whisman & Snyder, 2007; Zhang, Parish, Huang, & Pan, 2012; for reviews see Smith, 2006; Treas, 2003).

## Factors That Contribute to Infidelity

However, although most people are sexually faithful to their partners, *infidelity* or *extrarelational sex* does occur. There are many reasons why an individual might engage in sexual activities with someone other than his or her primary partner. After reviewing the literature, social scientists Julie Hall and Frank Fincham (2006) and Pepper Schwartz and Virginia Rutter (1998) identified a variety of personal, relational, and environmental factors that are implicated in sexual infidelity. For example, extrarelational sex is associated with biological sex; compared with women, men are more likely to report having engaged in an extramarital encounter (although this sex difference is most commonly found among older cohorts; see Vail-Smith, et al., 2010; Wiederman, 1997). Environmental factors also are clearly linked with infidelity. Frequent travel, greater availability of alternative partners, and living in an urban setting are associated with a higher lifetime incidence of extramarital sex. Other powerful predictors of infidelity are relational, and include emotional or sexual incompatibility between the partners, interpersonal conflict or anger, problematic communication patterns, and lower levels of equity, commitment, and satisfaction (see also Le, Korn, Crockett, & Loving, 2011).

A longitudinal study conducted by Elizabeth Allen and her colleagues (Allen et al., 2008) highlights the association between infidelity and relational factors. During an initial assessment, engaged couples participated in a brief problem-solving task in which they discussed and attempted to resolve two significant areas of conflict in their relationship. These interactions were videotaped and observers coded four aspects of each couple's interpersonal communication behavior: (1) positive communication (e.g., positive affect, support/validation), (2) negative communication (e.g., negative affect, denial), (3) emotional invalidation (e.g., insults, sarcasm), and (4) emotional validation (e.g., agreement, attribution of positive motives to the partner). Following this initial assessment, couples who subsequently married were recontacted at yearly intervals for eight years and asked to report whether or not they had ever been sexually unfaithful to their spouse. The results revealed that premarital communication behavior significantly predicted later marital infidelity. Compared to faithful couples, couples in which either the husband or wife eventually engaged in infidelity displayed lower levels of positive communication and higher levels of negative communication and emotional invalidation at the initial premarital assessment.

General relationship dissatisfaction and other interpersonal factors (e.g., commitment) also appear to serve as precursors to infidelity (e.g., Maddox Shaw, Rhoades, Allen, Stanley, & Markman, 2013; Whisman, Gordon, & Chatav, 2007). Psychologists William Barta and Susan Kiene (2005) asked a group of men and women who had been unfaithful to their romantic partners to identify the reasons underlying their decision to be unfaithful. Participants were given four general categories of infidelity motivations: motives having to do with *dissatisfaction* (e.g., "I had 'fallen out of love with' my steady partner"; "I wasn't sure if my steady partner was the right person for me"), motives involving *neglect* (e.g., "I felt neglected by my steady partner"; "My steady partner was emotionally distant"), motives concerning *sex* (e.g., "I wanted a greater variety of sexual partners"; "I wanted more frequent sex"), and motives involving *anger* (e.g., "I wanted to 'get back at' my steady partner for something he or she did"; "I wanted to prove to my steady partner that other people found me physically attractive"). Very few of the participants indicated that sex or anger motives played a role in their decision to be sexually unfaithful to their partners. Rather, their infidelity primarily stemmed from issues related to emotional compatibility with the partner and unhappiness with the romantic relationship: Dissatisfaction was the most highly rated reason for infidelity among both men and women, followed by neglect from the steady partner.

## Responses to Infidelity

Just as infidelity may stem from a variety of motives and serve a number of different functions in people's lives, it is also associated with a great many outcomes. Affairs, one-night stands, and other forms of extrarelational sexual encounters certainly can produce beneficial outcomes for the individual, including sheer physical pleasure, a feeling of personal growth, a sense of excitement and adventure, and the formation of an intense physical and/or emotional connection with the extrarelational partner (see Bringle & Buunk, 1991).

In general, however, most research indicates that the negative consequences of infidelity far outweigh any potential benefits. For example, the partner who engages in extrarelational sexual activity often experiences guilt and conflict about deceiving the other partner and violating moral or personal standards about exclusivity and fidelity, as well as anxiety and fear about sexually transmitted diseases, pregnancy, getting caught by the other partner, and so on (Bringle & Buunk, 1991; Spanier & Margolies, 1983). Indeed, an investigation conducted by Hall and Fincham (2009) revealed that men and women who had been unfaithful to their dating partners exhibited higher levels of depression and lower levels of general psychological well-being, as well as greater guilt and shame about their behavior, than men and women who had not been unfaithful.

The cheated-on partner also experiences a host of negative emotional outcomes, including jealousy and anger, as well as feelings of rejection, betrayal, self-doubt, and disappointment (Buunk, 1995; Charny & Parnass, 1995). Moreover, the relationship itself may not survive. Not only do people consider infidelity to be one of the most hurtful and destructive events that can occur in romantic relationships (Bachman & Guerrero, 2006; Feeney, 2004), but infidelity is one of the leading causes of relationship dissolution in the United States and other countries around the world (e.g., Afifi, Falato, & Weiner, 2001; Amato & Rogers, 1997; Atkins, Baucom, & Jacobson, 2001; Betzig, 1989; Previti & Amato, 2004). This may explain why individuals who participate in extramarital relationships receive some form of punishment—from their existing spouses or romantic partners, family members or kin, or social authorities—in virtually all human societies (see Frayser, 1989).

For example, a cross-cultural investigation conducted by anthropologists William Jankowiak and M. Diane Hardgrave (2007) revealed that equally high proportions of men and women sought to terminate a spouse's extramarital affair (in other words, both sexes were equally concerned about infidelity), and that the majority relied on physical violence to do so. Specifically, in 88% of the cultures sampled, men responded to infidelity with direct physical confrontation (e.g., beating the spouse or rival, or both); in 64% of cultures, women also responded to infidelity with physical violence. In sum, sexual infidelity is a potent and often quite destructive force in romantic relationships.

## ❖ SEXUAL JEALOUSY: A COMMON RESPONSE TO RELATIONSHIP THREAT

One of the most powerful consequences of infidelity or suspected infidelity is sexual jealousy. *Sexual jealousy* (also called *romantic jealousy*) is defined as a psychological state that arises when a person's primary romantic relationship is threatened by another person (a rival) and that motivates behavior designed to counter the threat (e.g., Daly & Wilson, 1983; White & Mullen, 1989). Anger and fear—including feelings of rage, hostility, anxiety, and worry—are commonly experienced by people who are in the throes of sexual jealousy (Guerrero, Trost, & Yoshimura, 2005).

Researchers who study sexual jealousy often ask participants to imagine their romantic partner engaging in *emotional infidelity* (e.g., forming a deep emotional attachment to or falling in love with someone else) or *sexual infidelity* (e.g., engaging in sexual activities or having intercourse with someone else) and then to indicate which type of infidelity would be the most upsetting. For example, participants in one study received the following instructions:

> Please think of a serious committed relationship that you have had in the past, that you currently have, or that you would like to have. Imagine that you discover that the person with whom you've become seriously involved became interested in someone else. What would distress or upset you more (please circle only one): (A) Imagining your partner forming a deep emotional attachment to that person. (B) Imagining your partner enjoying passionate sexual intercourse with that person. (Buss, Larsen, Westen, & Semmelroth, 1992, p. 252)

When faced with this kind of choice, both men and women usually (but not always) select the first option; that is, they say that their partner's emotional infidelity would be more upsetting than sexual infidelity (e.g., Buss et al., 1999, Study 1; Harris, 2002; Wiederman & Kendall, 1999; for a meta-analytic review, see Carpenter, 2012). However, two sex differences commonly are found. Specifically, although both sexes typically select emotional infidelity as most upsetting, more men than women select sexual infidelity, and more women than men choose emotional infidelity, as the most distressing event. A study conducted by Christine Harris and Nicholas Christenfeld (1996) illustrates this pattern of results. These researchers asked college students to imagine their romantic partners engaging in sexual infidelity (i.e., "trying different sexual positions" with another person) and emotional infidelity (i.e., "falling in love" with another person). When asked which of the two types of infidelity would be most upsetting, the majority of women and men selected the emotional infidelity scenario. However, significantly more women (78%) than men (53%) chose the emotional infidelity scenario, and significantly more men (47%) than women (22%) selected the sexual infidelity scenario, as the most distressing situation.

## Sex Differences in Jealousy: Where Do They Come From and Just How "Real" Are They?

The origin of these differences between men and women in terms of their jealousy responses has been the source of much debate in the scientific community. Evolutionary psychologists argue that sex differences in jealousy are real and reflect the evolved mating psychologies of men and women, which are assumed to differ as a function of the different obstacles to reproductive success faced by ancestral men and women (see Chapter 1). In the words of evolutionary scholars Martin Daly and Margo Wilson (1983),

> The threat to a man's fitness resides in the risk of alien insemination of his adulterous wife, whereas the threat to a woman's fitness lies not so much in her adulterous husband's sexual contacts as in the risk that he will divert resources away from the wife and family. It follows that male jealousy should have evolved to be more specifically focused upon the sexual act, and female jealousy upon the loss of male attention and resources. (p. 294)

What does this mean? As we discussed in Chapter 1, reproductive success for both sexes is measured by the production of offspring who survive to reach reproductive maturity and who then mate and perpetuate the individual's genetic makeup. From this perspective, modern men are more distressed by sexual infidelity than are women because in the evolutionary past that particular kind of infidelity jeopardized a man's ability to successfully reproduce and pass his genetic material into the next generation. Essentially, a man whose partner was sexually unfaithful could have ended up providing resources to and raising another man's children—a genetic dead end. Modern women, on the other hand, are presumed to be more upset by emotional infidelity than are men because that type of infidelity jeopardized a woman's ability to obtain the steady supply of resources that she needed for her own and her children's survival (again, in the ancestral past). An emotionally unfaithful partner was likely to divert those important resources away from her and to the rival and any offspring the rival produced.

The evolutionary framework does not imply that infidelity, in and of itself, is less upsetting to one sex than to the other. On the contrary, we humans are social creatures who possess minds that are adapted for group living and for the formation of long-term, committed, and monogamous romantic relationships. Consequently, *any* kind of behavior that threatens the primary romantic relationship is assumed to be distressing to both men and women (and for sound evolutionary reasons). What the evolutionary framework suggests is that, to the extent that the sexes faced *different* obstacles to reproductive success over the vast expanse of human evolutionary history, they developed different psychological sensitivities to these forms of infidelity.

Other researchers believe that the commonly observed sex differences do not reflect the operation of specific evolved jealousy mechanisms in men and women but instead are primarily a function of *methodological artifact*; that is, they argue that the sex differences are not real but rather are created or magnified by the methods that researchers typically use to study jealousy (see DeSteno, 2010; DeSteno, Bartlett, Braverman, & Salovey, 2002; Harris, 2003; Sabini & Green, 2004). This criticism is valid. Researchers in this area typically employ hypothetical scenarios and a forced-choice methodology, and their study participants usually are very young adults and/or college students (many of whom may never have actually experienced a partner's infidelity). This is problematic for a number of reasons. First, sex differences are much more likely to occur when participants are forced to choose one, and only one, type of infidelity as being the most distressing. Sex differences diminish or disappear when participants are allowed to evaluate each type of infidelity separately using rating scales rather than a *forced-choice response option*. When this method is employed, both men and women evaluate both types of infidelity as highly distressing (e.g., Cann & Baucom, 2004; Leeker & Carlozzi, 2014; Tagler & Gentry, 2011).

Second, when reading a sparsely detailed hypothetical sexual infidelity scenario, men may be more likely than women to conjure up explicit sexual imagery (and thus respond with greater upset as a result of the vividness of the images rather than the infidelity itself). Indeed, sex differences in responses to (sexual) infidelity disappear when women as well as men are induced to use detailed, realistic, and vivid imagery of a partner's sexual infidelity (Kato, 2014). Third, sex differences are smaller among older (non-college-age) participants, as well as among community or nonstudent samples, again suggesting that aspects of research design and methodology play an important role in determining the extent to which response differences between men and women will be obtained (see Harris, 2003; IJzerman et al., 2014; Sagarin et al., 2012). Fourth, it is very likely that what people *say* they would do or feel in response to a hypothetical and imaginary situation may be different from how they *actually* would respond if they were truly faced with the reality of a loved one's sexual or emotional betrayal.

In an interesting study, Margit Berman and Patricia Frazier (2005) set out to test this latter idea. They selected two groups of participants—a group of men and women who had never, to their knowledge, been betrayed by their romantic partners and a group of men and women who actually had been betrayed by unfaithful romantic partners. Participants in the first group received the usual hypothetical scenario and forced-choice response option; they imagined that their current partners had been unfaithful and selected either sexual infidelity (i.e., the partner "enjoying sexual activities" with another person) or emotional infidelity (the partner's "emotional attachment" to another person) as most upsetting. Participants who had actually been betrayed were asked to think about their partner's infidelity and to indicate whether the sexual behavior or the emotional attachment had distressed or upset them most. The response pattern for participants who had never been betrayed was similar to that typically reported by other researchers who use hypothetical scenarios; more men than women reported that knowledge of their partner's sexual activities would be more distressing than knowledge of an outside emotional attachment (and, conversely, more women than men said that emotional infidelity would be more distressing than sexual infidelity). However, participants who had actually experienced infidelity showed no such sex differences in their responses to the forced-choice question: Equal percentages of men and women (53%) reported that the sexual aspect of their partner's infidelity was worse than the emotional aspect, and equal percentages (47%) indicated that the outside emotional attachment that their partners had formed was worse than their extra-relational sexual activities. The researchers concluded, "The findings reported above make clear the stark contrast between what college-aged men and women think they will feel if their romantic partners cheat on them and what they actually feel when such a betrayal occurs" (p. 1623). Similar results have been observed by other scientists (see Tagler, 2010). The hypothetical forced-choice paradigm obviously is seriously flawed, and clearly more research is needed on the nature of sexual jealousy as it occurs in actual ongoing romantic relationships.

Yet a third explanation (often called the *double-shot hypothesis*) for the observed sex differences has been proposed, this one focusing on the ways in which men and women cognitively interpret different types of infidelity. Several researchers (e.g., DeSteno & Salovey, 1996; Harris & Christenfeld, 1996) have noted that people possess different beliefs about the likelihood that the occurrence of one type of infidelity implies the occurrence of the other type for each sex. In Chapters 10 and 11, we reviewed evidence that men generally hold more positive attitudes about sex in the absence of love and commitment than do women; conversely, women, to a greater degree than men, prefer to engage in sexual intercourse only after the relationship is characterized by some degree of commitment and love. Because most people are aware of these existing sex differences in beliefs and preferences, it makes sense that heterosexual men (and homosexual women, for that matter) would be relatively more upset by a female partner's sexual infidelity than by her emotional infidelity, and that heterosexual women (and homosexual men) would demonstrate the reverse pattern (becoming more upset by a male partner's emotional than sexual infidelity). To her partner, a woman's sexual infidelity implies the presence of *both* sexual and emotional involvement (because that partner assumes that women require emotional intimacy prior to entering a sexual relationship); consequently, this type of infidelity should be more disturbing than a woman's emotional infidelity (which implies emotional involvement alone). For a man's partner, the situation is reversed. Women (or homosexual men) may assume that a sexually unfaithful man is not necessarily emotionally involved with his partner but that an emotionally unfaithful man probably is sexually involved. Thus, a man's emotional infidelity (which implies both emotional and sexual involvement) is more upsetting than is his sexual infidelity (which implies only sexual involvement). Essentially, then, the argument is that each sex selects as most upsetting the type of infidelity that implies their partner's greatest degree of extrarelational involvement and that thus poses the greatest overall threat to the relationship. There is some evidence, collected from heterosexual and homosexual samples, in support of this explanation (see Carpenter, 2012).

### The Bottom Line About Sexual Jealousy

The debate among researchers about sex differences in sexual jealousy may never be fully resolved. Nonetheless, we can draw some fairly firm conclusions about sexual jealousy. First, sexual jealousy is a pervasive human response to real, imagined, or implied infidelity. *Both* men and women report experiencing considerable emotional distress (and other negative emotions) when asked to imagine or to recall a romantic partner's infidelity. Second, jealousy is produced by *all* types of infidelity. Very few people remain emotionally unmoved when faced with their partner's real or imagined sexual infidelity, and very few people remain stoic and unaffected by their partner's emotional infidelity (or any other type of infidelity). These issues are not in question.

## Summary

As we have seen in this and previous chapters, sexuality can produce both positive and negative outcomes for romantic partners. Sexual disinterest, assault, infidelity, and jealousy occur with varying degrees of frequency within committed love relationships. Each of these sexual phenomena produces a number of adverse consequences for the partners and their relationship.

## Key Concepts

Sexual disinterest (p. 268)

Sexual assault (p. 271)

Battering or anger rape (p. 272)

Force-only or power rape (p. 272)

Obsessive or sadistic rape (p. 272)

Hypermasculinity (p. 275)

Hyperfemininity (p. 275)

Hypergender (p. 275)

Token resistance (p. 276)

Compliance (p. 276)

Post-traumatic stress disorder (p. 277)

Sexual exclusivity (p. 278)

Infidelity (p. 278)

Extrarelational sex (p. 278)

Sexual (romantic) jealousy (p. 281)

Emotional infidelity (p. 281)

Sexual infidelity (p. 281)

Methodological artifact (p. 283)

Forced-choice response option (p. 283)

Double-shot hypothesis (p. 285)

## Discussion Questions

1. In what ways can sex serve as a positive force in romantic relationships? As a negative force?

2. Evaluate this statement: "Decreased sexual interest between partners is a sign that their relationship is in trouble."

3. Discuss the factors that may encourage sexual coercion or violence in dating and other romantic relationships.

4. Have you ever cheated on (or been cheated on by) a romantic partner? How did this event make you feel? Did your relationship survive? Consider research on responses to infidelity—in what way did your own experience match (or not match) what research tells us about the consequences of infidelity?

5. How "real" are sex differences in sexual jealousy? Consider the evolutionary perspective as well as the methodological limitations of research in this area in your answer.

## Recommended Readings

These works examine the "dark side" of relational sexuality, including sexual coercion and violence.

Christopher, F. S., & Lloyd, S. A. (2000). Physical and sexual aggression in relationships. In C. Hendrick & S. S. Hendrick (Eds.), *Close relationships: A sourcebook* (pp. 331–343). Thousand Oaks, CA: Sage.

Christopher, F. S., Owens, L. A., & Stecker, H. L. (1993). An examination of single men's and women's sexual aggressiveness in dating relationships. *Journal of Social and Personal Relationships, 10,* 511–527.

Muehlenhard, C. L. (1988). "Nice women" don't say yes and "real men" don't say no: How miscommunication and the double standard can cause sexual problems. *Women and Therapy, 7,* 95–108.

Muehlenhard, C. L., Goggins, M. F., Jones, J. M., & Satterfield, A. T. (1991). Sexual violence and coercion in close relationships. In K. McKinney & S. Sprecher (Eds.), *Sexuality in close relationships* (pp. 155–175). Hillsdale, NJ: Erlbaum.

These articles review existing research on sexual jealousy, including the debate over the origins of sex differences in jealousy responses.

Carpenter, C. J. (2012). Meta-analyses of sex differences in response to sexual versus emotional infidelity: Men and women are more similar than different. *Psychology of Women Quarterly, 36,* 25–37.

Sabini, J., & Green, M. C. (2004). Emotional responses to sexual and emotional infidelity: Constants and differences across genders, samples, and methods. *Personality and Social Psychology Bulletin, 30,* 1375–1388.

# Part IV

# Individual Differences

Both the positive and negative events that occur within mating relationships are affected by a variety of factors. Many of these factors are interpersonal in nature and involve the exchanges that happen over time between the two partners; we have seen how reciprocal self-disclosure, the formation of intimate connections, and the giving and receiving of rewards contribute to the quality and stability of romantic partnerships. Some of these factors are produced by the sociocultural context. The presence or absence of alternative romantic and sexual partners, the way in which the relationship is viewed by friends and family members, and the cultural rules that govern sexuality, mate selection, and marriage all work together to influence the outcomes experienced by relational partners. And some of these factors are individual in nature. Each man and woman possesses—and brings to his or her relationships—a host of dispositional characteristics that can have important relational consequences. For example, people with certain traits may have increased opportunities for sexual and/or romantic interaction. A highly extraverted, outgoing person is perhaps more likely to seek out potential partners than is a shy, withdrawn individual. Similarly, a person's disposition may influence how he or she interprets interpersonal events as well as his or her behavior toward relational partners. A secure, psychologically well-adjusted individual may be more able and willing than an emotionally unstable individual to attribute positive motives to the partner and to engage in other relationship-enhancing behavior during times of conflict.

The following three chapters explore the association between a person's enduring dispositional characteristics and his or her romantic opportunities, responses from others, and interpersonal behavior.

Chapter 14 considers the attribute of maleness or femaleness, examining the interpersonal correlates of biological sex and psychological gender. Chapter 15 explores the association between relational events and global personality characteristics. And Chapter 16 examines the ways in which a person's interpersonal belief systems may influence his or her relational experiences.

# 14

# Maleness and Femaleness

```
Chapter Outline

Biological Sex
        Different Cultures or Same World, Different Ability/Motivation?
Psychological Gender and Gender Role Orientation
Summary
```

Perhaps the most fundamental dimension along which we classify ourselves and our mates is that of maleness-femaleness. *Biological sex* refers to whether a person possesses the biological indicators of maleness or femaleness, which include sex chromosomes (XY or XX), sex hormone prevalence (level of androgens or estrogens), gonads (testes or ovaries), and internal and external genitalia (e.g., penis and vas deferens or clitoris and vagina). Thus, a person's sex as "male" or "female" is a biological characteristic. A person's *psychological gender*, on the other hand, is not a biological fact but refers broadly to whether he or she claims a masculine or feminine identity and possesses traits or characteristics that are believed to be associated with, and that are considered socially appropriate for, each biological sex. A related attribute called *gender role (or sex role) orientation* concerns people's beliefs about the appropriate roles that men and women should play (and the behaviors they should enact) in aspects of social life, including their close romantic relationships. Maleness-femaleness is a powerful individual difference variable that influences many aspects of a person's relational world.

## ❖ BIOLOGICAL SEX

We have seen in earlier chapters that men and women often exhibit similar sexual and romantic attitudes and behaviors. For example, they hold many of the same beliefs about love and report many of the same experiences in their love relationships. Both sexes also endorse many of the same sexual standards and express similar sexual preferences. And they tend to prefer the same attributes—kindness, intelligence, honesty, attractiveness, humor—in their potential mates.

However, although the interpersonal events, experiences, and outcomes of men and women are very similar, they are far from identical. As we have discussed in previous chapters, women's experiences in dating and marital relationships are often less overtly positive than those of men. For example, women report higher amounts of discord and conflict—ranging from inequity in housework and amount of "free time" to sexual coercion and violence—in their romantic relationships than do men. In addition, although both men and women attach equal importance to achieving openness and self-disclosure, respect and acceptance, trust, the development of a relational identity (i.e., having an integrated social network, being recognized as a "couple"), and other standards in their romantic relationships, women's needs and expectations in these areas often are fulfilled less completely than are those of men (see Vangelisti & Daly, 1997).

Other sex differences have been documented as well. In her extensive reviews of the literature, communication scholar Julia Wood (e.g., 2000, 2009, 2013) observed that men and women also differ in the way they communicate, self-disclose, and create and maintain intimacy. Specifically,

- Women engage in more "conversational maintenance" than do men; that is, in their conversations, women are more likely than men to invite others to speak, ask questions, encourage elaborations, respond to statements made by others, and display nonverbal behaviors that signal interest and involvement in the conversation.

- Women are more likely than men to maintain conversational equality by including others in the conversation, expressing support (e.g., sympathy, agreement), and demonstrating responsiveness (e.g., eye contact, head nodding).

- Men are more likely than women to maintain conversational dominance by rerouting conversations to their own interests and agendas, interrupting others, and expressing themselves forcefully.

- Women prefer discussing feelings and personal issues, whereas men prefer discussing impersonal topics (for example, politics, sports, or business).

- Women enjoy sharing the details of their daily lives and activities with their romantic partners, whereas men tend to prefer discussing "big events" and "bottom lines."

- Women value talking about the state and internal dynamics of their romantic relationships more than do men.

The origin of these sex differences has been the subject of some debate among the scientific community. Several explanations have been advanced.

## Different Cultures or Same World, Different Ability/Motivation?

According to the *different cultures thesis*, men and women approach relationships from a different cultural perspective and adopt a different set of standards, values, and beliefs with respect to their close relationships (e.g., Maccoby, 1990; Wood, 2007). Scholars who subscribe to this thesis observe that women traditionally are socialized to value interdependence, to establish intimacy through self-disclosure and affective communication, and to pursue communal goals within their close relationships. Conversely, men are socialized to value independence, to establish intimacy through shared activities, and to maintain power and autonomy in their close relationships. (Note the similarities between this perspective and the social context models presented in Chapter 1.) According to sociolinguist Deborah Tannen (e.g., 1990, 2001), for example, men and women inhabit separate worlds:

> *Intimacy* is key in a world of connection where individuals negotiate complex networks of friendship, minimize differences, try to reach consensus, and avoid the appearance of superiority, which would highlight

> differences. In a world of status, *independence* is key, because a primary means of establishing status is to tell others what to do, and taking orders is a marker of low status. Though all humans need both intimacy and independence, women tend to focus on the first and men on the second. It is as if their lifeblood ran in different directions. (1990, p. 26)

This fundamental difference between independence-oriented men and intimacy-oriented women is posited to have significant consequences in many relational domains, including communication and the expression of intimacy and social support. For example, Tannen (1990) suggested that in the world of women, "conversations are negotiations for closeness in which people try to seek and give confirmation and support, and to reach consensus" (p. 25). In the world of men, however, conversations serve a very different purpose; they are "negotiations in which people try to achieve and maintain the upper hand if they can, and protect themselves from others' attempts to put them down and push them around" (pp. 24–25). According to this framework, then, the different experiences that men and women often have in romantic relationships stem from the vastly different worlds they inhabit, and the achievement of satisfying interpersonal outcomes is dependent on the ability of each sex to understand—and perhaps even learn how to effectively use—the other's culture-specific form of communication, intimacy expression, and support provision.

Although still prominent in popular literature and the media, the different cultures thesis has come under serious attack in recent years for a variety of reasons. First, much of the evidence cited by proponents of this framework is based on anecdote and subjective, first-person accounts that are not appropriate for scientifically testing hypotheses about common preferences or behavior patterns among groups of people. Second, a growing body of empirical research demonstrates that sex differences in communication, emotional support, and conceptions of intimacy are actually far fewer in number and much smaller in magnitude than would be predicted by the different cultures thesis. For example, after conducting a detailed review of the existing literature, communication scholar Brant Burleson (2003) concluded,

> Both men and women believe that the explicit elaboration and exploration of feelings is the best way to provide comfort to one another, and are themselves most comforted by such messages. . . . Although some small sex differences have been observed, these differences exist within much more substantial patterns of similarity, with both men and women assigning priority to the management of distressed feelings in support situations. (pp. 13, 16)

Indeed, a series of studies conducted by Erina MacGeorge and her colleagues provides evidence that men and women are more similar than they are different in their provision of, and responses to, supportive communication (MacGeorge, Graves, Feng, Gillihan, & Burleson, 2004). Mature adult participants in the first study read four scenarios describing a same-sex friend who was upset about a personal problem (i.e., being asked for a divorce by his or her spouse, receiving a poor performance evaluation at work, learning of the death of a high school friend, and having to give a speech to a community group). After reading each scenario, participants were asked to respond to the situation as though their friends "were actually there in the room with you" (p. 153). These responses were tape-recorded and the researchers subsequently identified eight different types of communication made by the participants: *giving advice* ("What you could do is practice your speech a couple of times so when you go up there you'll feel more comfortable"), *expressing sympathy* ("I'm so sorry to hear about your friend"; "Hey, if you need a shoulder to cry on, I'm here for you"), *asking questions* ("Do you want to talk about it?" "Have you talked with your boss yet?"), *offering help* ("If you need an audience to practice on, I'm happy to volunteer"), *minimizing the situation* ("You seem to be making it worse than it really is"), *affirming or encouraging the other person* ("You're going to do great; I know it"; "If your boss never told you what was expected, I don't see why you were given such a poor evaluation"), *sharing a similar problem* ("When my dad died, I know it took me a long time to get over the fact that he was gone"), and *assigning blame* ("Well, you had a ton of chances to work things out, but you chose to let the marriage die"). Contrary to the different cultures thesis, the results revealed very few sex differences. Although men gave advice proportionately more often than women and women were proportionately more likely than men to offer affirmation and help, the sexes did not differ in any of the other forms of support. Furthermore, both men and women largely gave support via advice and expressions of sympathy.

In a second study, the researchers explored whether men and women differ in how they respond to supportive messages. College student participants in this study read two scenarios in which a "good friend" was portrayed as experiencing emotional distress over (1) the recently announced divorce of his or her parents and (2) the failure to receive an anticipated academic scholarship. After reading each scenario, participants received a list of comforting messages that varied in their degree of *person-centeredness* (i.e., the extent to which the message explicitly acknowledged, elaborated, and legitimized the feelings and perspective of the friend in distress). They then rated the messages for sensitivity and effectiveness, and these two measures were combined to provide an overall index of perceived message quality. The different cultures thesis would predict strong sex differences in perceptions of the quality of the messages—women, who come from a culture of intimacy, should respond more favorably to messages that focus on the verbalization of feelings and the provision of emotional support (i.e., highly person-centered messages), whereas men, who come from a culture of independence, should prefer messages that avoid the discussion of feelings and focus instead on instrumental solutions to the problem (i.e., less person-centered messages). Contrary to these predictions, the results revealed that both men and women evaluated messages that were highly person-centered much more positively than they did messages that were low in person-centeredness. In discussing these findings, MacGeorge and her colleagues (2004) observed that their results were consistent with those of other researchers who have also discovered more similarities than differences in men's and women's evaluations of supportive behaviors and communication skills, responses to supportive messages, and goals when providing support. They concluded, "At present, then, there appears to be virtually no relevant, credible evidence that supports the claim that men and women constitute different communication cultures or speech communities, especially with respect to supportive communication" (p. 172).

In view of these and other empirical investigations, a number of theorists have suggested that it may be more accurate to view men and women as belonging to the same culture but as possessing differential communicative skill and motivation. The *differential ability/motivation model* has two major components (Burleson et al., 2009). First, the model posits that men and women hold similar views and expectations about communication, intimacy, and social support and approach their romantic relationships with similar goals and values, but that over the course of socialization, women acquire more of the *ability* or *skills* needed to produce behavior that fulfils those expectations and meets those goals (Kunkel & Burleson, 1999). There is strong evidence in support of this part of the model (for a review, see Burleson & Kunkel, 2006). Second, the model proposes that in addition to possessing different communicative abilities, men and women also possess differential *motivation* to engage in emotionally supportive and intimate forms of communication. The model recognizes that the provision of social support in contemporary American society is viewed as a feminine activity by both men and women (Kunkel & Burleson, 1999), and that most people are motivated to behave in accordance with the norms and expectations associated with their social roles (Eagly, 1987; also see Chapter 1). To the extent that emotionally expressive, intimate, person-centered forms of communication and support provision are inconsistent with sociocultural notions of masculinity, men may be less motivated to engage in such behavior than are women—even if they are able to do so. There is also strong support for this part of the model (see Burleson, Holmstrom, & Gilstrap, 2005).

A series of studies conducted by Brant Burleson, Amanda Holmstrom, and Cristina Gilstrap (2005) revealed a number of findings that demonstrate and support the basic premises of the differential ability/ motivation model. First, the researchers found evidence of differential skill or ability—their studies revealed a consistent sex difference such that women were more likely than men to produce highly person-centered messages when comforting another person in distress (regardless of whether that individual was male or female). Second, the researchers found evidence of differential motivation. Although men viewed highly person-centered messages as the most effective and supportive way of helping someone in emotional distress, they also viewed these communicative behaviors as "feminine" and perceived other men who displayed these behaviors as relatively atypical (and they tended not to like them very much). In other words, the men in these studies possessed the knowledge that person-centered communication is the most useful and comprehensive way to provide emotional support, but, at the same time, they considered it to be a nonmasculine way to behave. Burleson and his colleagues also found that men varied their own use of highly person-centered messages according to the sex of the person in distress; specifically, they indicated that they would be (and, in fact, they were) less likely to provide solace and other sensitive and sophisticated person-centered forms of support to another man than to a woman. The fact that their choice of supportive message varied depending on the sex of the target demonstrated that the men in this study possessed at least some ability to alter their communicative displays to fit the context (i.e., displaying "feminine" support behavior with an emotionally distressed woman and electing to display "masculine" support behavior with an emotionally distressed man).

Thus, a combination of differential ability as well as differential motivation—created and sustained by socialization forces and the prevailing sociocultural climate—probably contributes to the sex differences that social scientists have observed in the areas of emotional support behavior, communicative competence, intimacy, satisfaction, equity, and other important interpersonal processes and relationship outcomes.

## ❖ PSYCHOLOGICAL GENDER AND GENDER ROLE ORIENTATION

In addition to their biological makeup, people differ in the extent to which they possess or endorse attributes, behaviors, and roles that stereotypically are associated with each sex. A number of self-report measures of psychological gender or gender role orientation exist (e.g., Gough, 1987; Spence & Helmreich, 1978). The Bem Sex Role Inventory developed by Sandra Bem (1974) is one of the most commonly used instruments. In this 60-item inventory, a person's psychological gender is determined by his or her self-ratings on various attribute dimensions. One third of the dimensions are considered stereotypically male or socially acceptable for men to possess. Examples of these *instrumental* characteristics include the following:

- Self-reliant
- Independent
- Assertive
- Forceful
- Analytical
- Willing to take risks
- Self-sufficient
- Acts as a leader
- Competitive
- Ambitious

One third of the items are considered stereotypically female or socially acceptable for women to possess. Examples of these *expressive* attributes include the following:

- Yielding
- Shy
- Affectionate
- Sympathetic
- Sensitive to the needs of others
- Childlike
- Warm
- Tender

- Eager to soothe hurt feelings
- Gentle

An additional one third of the items consist of neutral characteristics that are considered equally desirable for men and women to possess (e.g., adaptable, friendly, truthful).

Individuals (men or women) who describe themselves as possessing stereotypically male (i.e., instrumental) traits are considered *masculine*. Those who present themselves as possessing stereotypically female (i.e., expressive) traits are considered *feminine*. Men and women who endorse both male and female attributes are classified as *androgynous*, and those who feel that they possess neither male nor female traits are considered *undifferentiated*. Individuals whose biological sex "matches" their psychological gender (i.e., men who endorse instrumental attributes and women who endorse expressive attributes) often are identified as *sex-typed* or *traditional* in their gender orientation.

There is some evidence that the combination of instrumental masculine and expressive feminine attributes characteristic of people with an androgynous gender or gender role may contribute positively to relationship development and maintenance. For example, androgynous men and women generally are more willing to disclose information on a variety of impersonal and personal topics to other people than are sex-typed or undifferentiated individuals (e.g., Bowman, 2008; Lavine & Lombardo, 1984; Sollie & Fischer, 1985). This willingness to self-disclose is likely to create and enhance feelings of intimacy between the androgynous individual and his or her romantic partner; this, in turn, will fuel the development of their relationship.

Androgyny also appears to be associated with a number of positive interpersonal outcomes. For example, Michel Alain and Yvan Lussier (1988) investigated the postdivorce or separation experiences of a sample of androgynous, masculine, feminine, and undifferentiated men and women. Participants responded to a series of questions concerning their level of upset and preoccupation with the ex-partner (e.g., "I'm always thinking about my ex-partner"), their desire for the ex-partner (e.g., "I'm still attracted to my ex-partner"), and their feelings of affliction about the loss of their partner (e.g., being "depressed about one's future"). They also completed measures of psychological and social adaptation (e.g., happiness and going out to social events such as parties), self-satisfaction and adaptation potential (e.g., how much they experience self-blame and report having problems in adapting to their new life), and social skills (e.g., being "at ease with people" and being "sociable"). The results revealed that androgynous men and women reported the highest levels of psychological well-being and social adjustment, as well as self-satisfaction and adaptation potential, following divorce or separation. Undifferentiated participants reported the lowest levels. Interestingly, masculine and androgynous men and women reported significantly less desire for the ex-partner, upset and preoccupation with the ex-partner, and affliction than did feminine or undifferentiated individuals. In general, this pattern of results suggests that individuals who possess both instrumental and expressive attributes, and who therefore have access to a wide array of potential responses, may be better equipped to deal with changes and disruptions in their romantic relationships.

Additional evidence that androgyny is associated with relationship adjustment and positive interpersonal outcomes was provided by a study conducted by psychologist Cynthia Peterson and her colleagues (Peterson, Baucom, Elliott, & Farr, 1989). These researchers assessed gender role orientation and marital adjustment (using a standard self-report scale of global marital satisfaction) in a large sample of married couples. Half of the couples were recruited from a psychology clinic and were seeking marital therapy; the other half were recruited from the community at large. The researchers first classified each husband and wife with respect to gender role orientation (masculine, feminine, androgynous, or undifferentiated) and then tallied the frequency of each possible husband-wife pairing (e.g., androgynous husband-androgynous wife, androgynous husband-masculine wife, androgynous husband-feminine wife, androgynous husband-undifferentiated wife). Next, the researchers compared the gender role distributions of the clinic sample and the nonclinic sample—and discovered a striking difference. Specifically, of the 16 possible husband-wife gender role pairings, androgynous husband-androgynous wife was the *most* frequent pairing among the nonclinic couples and the *least* frequent pairing among the clinic couples. The exact opposite pattern was found when the undifferentiated husband–undifferentiated wife pairing was considered. This was the *most* frequent pattern for clinic couples and the *least* frequent pattern for nonclinic couples. In addition, there was a higher frequency of nonclinic than of clinic couples in each of the six gender role pairings that involved only one androgynous spouse (e.g., androgynous wife–masculine husband, androgynous wife–feminine husband). Thus, androgyny—of one or both partners—seems to characterize married couples who are not seeking therapy, and undifferentiation (and lack of androgyny) seems to be common among clinically distressed married couples.

The researchers also examined the relation between gender role orientation and marital satisfaction and adjustment scores in the total sample of couples. This analysis revealed that adjustment/satisfaction scores were higher for both men and women when the two partners were androgynous than when they demonstrated any other pattern of husband-wife gender role pairing. In fact, with only one exception, men and women who had androgynous spouses achieved higher than average scores on marital well-being—regardless of their own gender role orientation. (The one exception was that undifferentiated women married to androgynous men had lower than average marital adjustment scores.) Femininity, or high levels of expressivity alone, also appeared to be correlated with marital well-being. Specifically, feminine men and women married to feminine spouses (i.e., a feminine husband–feminine wife pairing) demonstrated marital adjustment scores well above average, and average or above-average adjustment was also seen in couples with one feminine partner (except, as before, when the other partner was undifferentiated). The only gender role orientation consistently associated with *lack* of marital well-being was undifferentiation. Men and women married to undifferentiated partners generally scored below average in terms of their levels of marital satisfaction, and the lowest levels of satisfaction and adjustment occurred in pairings involving two undifferentiated individuals or an undifferentiated person married to a masculine one.

More recent research also has revealed an association between androgyny (i.e., high instrumentality coupled with high expressiveness) and better marital adjustment (e.g., Isaac & Shah, 2004; also see Helms, Proulx, Klute, McHale, & Crouter, 2006) as well as a correlation between an undifferentiated gender role orientation and poorer marital adjustment (e.g., Dasgupta & Basu, 2001). Moreover, couples with *traditional gender role attitudes* or *gender ideology* (i.e., who view men and women as occupying separate spheres and who endorse a strict separation between male and female marital roles and responsibilities; see Chapter 4) demonstrate lower marital satisfaction than couples with egalitarian gender role attitudes/ideology (DeMaris, Sanchez, & Krivickas, 2012; Stanik & Bryant, 2012; for a review, see Davis & Greenstein, 2009). Taken as a whole, these results provide additional evidence that gender and gender role orientation (as well as gender attitude/ideology) are important factors in relationship outcomes.

## Summary

Each person possesses a host of characteristics or attributes that can influence both the quantity and the quality of his or her interpersonal interactions and the relationships he or she forms with others. One of the most significant of these attributes is maleness or femaleness. Both biological sex and psychological gender are associated with a variety of relational experiences and outcomes. In Chapter 15, we consider another set of dispositional variables that appear to play a role in the dating and mating experiences of men and women.

## Key Concepts

Biological sex (p. 291)

Psychological gender (p. 291)

Gender (or sex) role orientation (p. 291)

Different cultures thesis (p. 293)

Person-centered messages (p. 295)

Differential ability/motivation model (p. 296)

Bem Sex Role Inventory (p. 298)

Instrumental attributes (p. 298)

Expressive attributes (p. 298)

Masculine gender role (p. 299)

Feminine gender role (p. 299)

Androgynous gender role (p. 299)

Undifferentiated gender role (p. 299)

Sex-typed or traditional gender orientation (p. 299)

Traditional gender role attitude or ideology (p. 301)

## Discussion Questions

1. Evaluate the following statement, using what you know about theories and research on sex differences in men's and women's relationship experiences: "Men and women are from completely different planets."

2. How do the different cultures thesis and the differential ability/motivation model explain sex differences in relationship experience? Consider the evidence in support of each model. Is it possible that both models can explain men's and women's romantic experiences?

3. Find your psychological gender or gender role orientation using the 20 sample items from the Bem Sex Role Inventory included in this chapter. Use the following scale to indicate how well each item describes you:

|   1   |   2   |   3   |   4   |   5   |   6   |   7   |
| :---: | :---: | :---: | :---: | :---: | :---: | :---: |
| Never or |     |     |     |     |     | Always or |
| almost never true |     |     |     |     |     | almost always true |

Add up your total for the 10 instrumental items and divide by 10. This is your masculinity score. Do the same for the 10 expressive items. This is your femininity score. Find your androgyny score by subtracting your femininity score from your masculinity score (or vice versa) and taking the absolute value of the result (i.e., ignore the sign—positive or negative—of the result and just use the actual number you calculated). Androgynous people show relatively equal amounts of both masculine and feminine attributes, and the difference score (the result of the subtraction) will therefore be close to zero. What is your sex role orientation, according to this measure? Do you possess many more expressive or feminine attributes than instrumental or masculine ones? More instrumental/masculine traits than expressive/feminine ones? Relatively equal amounts of both? What role do you think your psychological gender/gender role orientation has played so far in your romantic experiences?

4. Discuss the association between gender and gender role orientation and relational outcomes. Explain why androgyny might produce positive interpersonal outcomes.

## Recommended Readings

This popular press book was reissued in 2007 and exemplifies the "different cultures" perspective. Copies of this and other works by Tannen are widely available online (e.g., Amazon.com).

Tannen, D. (1990). *You just don't understand: Women and men in conversation.* New York, NY: William Morrow.

This chapter discusses the different models that have been used to explain sex differences in communication, emotional support, intimacy, and other interpersonal processes.

Burleson, B. R., & Kunkel, A. W. (2006). Revisiting the different cultures thesis: An assessment of sex differences and similarities in supportive communication. In K. Dindia & D. J. Canary (Eds.), *Sex differences and similarities in communication* (2nd ed., pp. 137–159). Mahwah, NJ: Erlbaum.

# 15

# Personality

In addition to being male or female, and masculine or feminine (or both), each person possesses a distinctive and stable pattern of behaviors, thoughts, and emotions, called *personality* or *temperament*, that appears to have implications for mating relationships. In this chapter, we consider how three personality dimensions—traits, self-monitoring, and sociosexual orientation—are related to people's sexual and romantic experiences.

## ❖ SUPERTRAITS

Meta-analyses of existing empirical investigations of personality generally reveal five basic traits—the "Big Five"—that are heritable, stable across the life span, and culturally universal and that seem to adequately capture much of the variance in human temperament (e.g., McCrae & Costa, 1997; for reviews, see Digman, 1990; Goldberg, 1993; Hampson, 1999; Heine & Buchtel, 2009). These *supertraits* are extraversion, neuroticism, openness to experience, agreeableness, and conscientiousness. Researchers interested in dating and mating relationships have tended to focus on two particular supertraits: extraversion and neuroticism.

## Extraversion

*Extraversion* (also called *positive affectivity* or *positive emotionality*) reflects the degree to which an individual is oriented toward the social environment and experiences pleasant emotional states (Clark, Watson, & Mineka, 1994; Watson, 2002). People high on this personality dimension (often called *extraverts*) possess an active and positive orientation toward the social environment. They seek out others, take pleasure in social interaction, behave in an outgoing and sociable manner, and tend to be cheerful, energetic, and self-confident. People low on extraversion (often called *introverts*) are wary of social interaction, prefer solitary activities, and direct their attention inward to their own thoughts and feelings. Introverts are generally withdrawn, quiet, and reserved and report lower levels of energy, self-confidence, and positive emotional experience.

A great deal of scientific attention has been devoted to examining the association between extraversion and various relationship outcomes. As of yet, the results are not entirely conclusive. For instance, a good many researchers find that extraversion in one or both spouses is associated with *higher* levels of relationship quality (e.g., Claxton, O'Rourke, Smith, & DeLongis, 2012; Donnellan, Conger, & Bryant, 2004; Dyrenforth, Kashy, Donnellan, & Lucas, 2010; Gordon & Baucom, 2009; Nemechek & Olson, 1996; O'Rourke, Claxton, Chou, Smith, & Hadjistavropoulos, 2011; Solomon & Jackson, 2014). In one recent investigation, for example, psychologists Mieke Decuyper, Marleen De Bolle, and Filip De Fruyt (2012) had both members of a large group of heterosexual married, cohabiting, and dating couples complete measures of personality (including extraversion) as well as a multi-item measure of relationship satisfaction. The results revealed the same pattern for both men and women. Specifically, men's and women's level of extraversion was significantly and positively associated with both their own and their partner's relationship satisfaction; that is, the more extraverted a participant was, the more satisfied he or she (and his or her partner) was with the relationship. However, other researchers find that extraversion is correlated with *lower* levels of adjustment and well-being (e.g., Bouchard, Lussier, & Sabourin, 1999; Lester, Haig, & Monello, 1989), and still others find no association at all between extraversion and relationship satisfaction (e.g., Malouff, Thorsteinsson, Schutte, Bhullar, & Rooke, 2010; Neyer & Voigt, 2004; Razeghi, Nikiju, Mujembari, & Masihi, 2011).

The results are also mixed with respect to the association between extraversion and relationship dissolution. Some researchers find that this personality trait is significantly associated with the likelihood of divorce. For example, psychologists Victor Jockin, Matt McGue, and David Lykken (1996) asked a sample of more than 3,000 men and women who had been married at least once to complete a personality inventory that measured their levels of extraversion (called "positive emotionality") and various other traits. Participants also provided information about their marital histories, including whether or not they had ever divorced. The researchers then examined whether the participants' divorce status could be predicted reliably from their extraversion scores. The results indicated that it could be; that is, the higher men and women scored on extraversion, the greater the likelihood they had experienced marital dissolution. Other researchers, however, have not found any direct relationship between this personality trait and relationship termination (e.g., Kurdek, 1993b; Solomon & Jackson, 2014).

It is possible that extraversion does not directly influence relationship stability but rather has an indirect effect by influencing how partners interact with each other. In one study, researchers Carolyn Cutrona, Robert Hessling, and Julie Suhr (1997) assessed the personality traits of a sample of 100 married couples prior to observing each couple in a 10-minute interaction. These interactions took place in a laboratory furnished to resemble a comfortable living room. One partner was randomly chosen by the researchers to play the role of "support recipient." The support recipient was asked to describe a recent personally stressful situation to his or her spouse. The other member of the couple was assigned the role of "support provider." The support provider was instructed to simply listen to his or her partner and then react spontaneously and naturally. The two partners then switched roles and the process was repeated. These interactions were videotaped, and the researchers examined the support providers' verbal behavior for the presence of four types of positive communication: *emotional support* (expressing love, concern, or empathy for the partner), *esteem support* (communicating respect for the partner and confidence in his or her abilities), *informational support* (providing information about the stressful situation or advice about how to deal with it), and *tangible aid* (providing or offering to provide goods, services, or other explicit forms of assistance needed to deal with the stressful situation). The frequencies with which these four types of positive communication occurred during the interaction were summed to create an overall index of support behavior provided by each spouse.

The results revealed that this overall measure was positively correlated with extraversion levels. Specifically, husbands and wives higher in extraversion made more positive supportive statements overall to their support-seeking spouses than did less extraverted individuals—but they did not receive more support themselves from those spouses. In discussing this interesting pattern, Cutrona and her colleagues (1997) concluded,

> The results that emerged for extraversion highlight the importance of considering the personal characteristics of both the individual and his or her primary source of social support. Contrary to prediction, the extraversion of support *recipients* did not directly predict the amount of support they received from the spouse. Rather, the extraversion of support *providers* proved to be most important. Thus, a shy introvert who married a gregarious extravert might be amply supplied with a lifetime of social support, by virtue of his or her partner's interpersonally oriented nature. (p. 390)

Further analyses also revealed that reciprocity of support was evident in the couples' behavior. That is, the more support a husband or wife *provided* during the first interaction, the more support he or she subsequently *received* during the second interaction—regardless of the level of extraversion of either spouse. This result suggests that extraverted people may indirectly affect their own relational outcomes via the support they provide their partners. Specifically, extraverted men and women tend to give their partners a great deal of social support; these positive behaviors, in turn, seem to evoke corresponding supportive reactions from those partners.

Thus, it is possible that the personality attributes—specifically, the extraversion levels—of romantic partners may influence the nature of their interactions. Over time, these interpersonal dynamics may work to either enhance or erode the quality and stability of the relationship.

## Neuroticism

*Neuroticism*, also called *emotional instability* or *negative affectivity* (or emotionality), refers to a person's sensitivity to negative stimuli, propensity to experience negative emotions, and stability of behavior over time (Clark et al., 1994; Tellegen, 1985; Watson & Clark, 1984). Individuals high on neuroticism hold negative, unfavorable views of themselves and the world around them, tend to feel inadequate and dissatisfied, and are prone to frequent and intense negative emotions. They are generally moody, highly strung, sensitive, and touchy. People low on this personality dimension are emotionally stable and much less prone to negative emotional experiences. In general, they are calm, even-tempered, relaxed, and secure. Neuroticism is strongly implicated in several romantic relationship outcomes, including dissolution (e.g., Cramer, 1993; Eysenck, 1980; Solomon & Jackson, 2014; Tucker, Kressin, Spiro, & Ruscio, 1998) and dissatisfaction or maladjustment (e.g., Barelds, 2005; Barelds & Barelds-Dijkstra, 2006; Bouchard et al., 1999; Donnellan et al., 2004; Dyrenforth et al., 2010; Karney & Bradbury, 1997; Razeghi et al., 2011; Solomon & Jackson, 2014; for a meta-analytic review, see Malouff et al., 2010).

In one classic longitudinal investigation, E. Lowell Kelly and James Conley (1987) followed a sample of 249 married couples from the time of their engagement during the 1930s to 1980. The first data collection took place during the period from 1935 to 1941. During these years, and prior to their marriage, the members of each couple were rated by five of their acquaintances on various personality traits, including neuroticism. In addition, after marriage, the spouses provided annual reports about their current levels of marital satisfaction (on a scale ranging from *extraordinarily happy* to *extremely unhappy*); these annual reports were averaged to provide a measure of marital satisfaction in early marriage. The second data collection occurred in 1954–1955, and the third and final collection took place in 1980–1981. During these two periods, husbands and wives were asked how satisfied they were with their marriage, whether they would still marry their spouse if they had their life to live over, whether they had ever regretted their marriage, and whether they had ever considered divorce or separation from their spouse. Responses to these four questions were then summed to create an overall index of marital satisfaction. At each of the various assessment times, the researchers also collected information on each couple's marital status (i.e., whether or not the spouses had gotten divorced).

The results revealed that both marital outcomes—dissolution and satisfaction—were predicted by initial levels of neuroticism. For example, the men and women who divorced had higher premarriage levels of neuroticism than did their still-married counterparts. In addition, their neuroticism seemed to be strongly implicated in the dissolution of their marriages. Specifically, when asked by the researchers why they decided to divorce, more than one third (36%) cited various manifestations of their own or their partner's neuroticism, including "emotional instability," "emotional overreactions," "emotional disorder," "emotional problems," "emotional reactions," "irritability," and "emotional immaturity." Neuroticism was also related to satisfaction among stably married couples (defined as couples who were still married at the time of any given assessment). For both husbands and wives, premarriage neuroticism levels were negatively correlated with concurrent and subsequent satisfaction scores. That is, husbands and wives who were higher in neuroticism at the beginning of the study reported more unhappiness and less satisfaction with their marriages early and later on in their lives than did men and women with lower levels of this trait. These results—along with those of other longitudinal investigations (e.g., Kurdek, 1993b)—provide evidence that neuroticism is associated with both the quality and the stability of romantic relationships.

In recent years, social scientists have sought to discover why this particular personality trait seems to negatively affect an individual's ability to find relational happiness and stability. One possibility they have explored is that neuroticism may contribute to dysfunctional exchanges between romantic partners. Using a procedure very similar to the one utilized by Cutrona and colleagues (1997) and described earlier in this chapter, Lauri Pasch, Thomas Bradbury, and Joanne Davila (1997) examined the relationship between neuroticism and supportive behavior in newlywed couples. Couples completed measures of marital satisfaction and neuroticism and then were audiotaped during two interactions. In the first interaction, one spouse was randomly selected to serve as the "helpee." The helpee was instructed to talk about an important personal characteristic, problem, or issue he or she would like to change about himself or herself (and that was not a source of tension in the marriage). The other spouse served as the "helper." The helper was simply asked to be involved in the discussion and to respond in whatever way he or she wished. The spouses then switched roles so that both had the opportunity to function as helper and helpee.

The verbal behaviors displayed by helpers and helpees were then examined for the presence of various positive and negative features. For example, *positive helpee behaviors* included offering a specific and clear analysis of the problem, expressing feelings related to the problem, and asking for help or stating needs in a useful way. *Positive helper behaviors* included such instrumental acts as making specific suggestions and giving helpful advice as well as emotional acts ranging from providing reassurance, to giving encouragement, to conveying love and esteem to the helpee. *Negative helpee behaviors* ranged from making demands for help, to criticizing the helper, to whining or complaining about the situation. *Negative helper behaviors* consisted of criticizing or blaming the spouse and offering inconsiderate advice.

The analyses revealed that, for husbands, neuroticism was negatively correlated with providing positive instrumental communications to the helpee. The higher a husband scored on neuroticism, the less often he offered specific suggestions and gave helpful advice to his wife. A similar pattern was found among wives. The higher a wife scored on neuroticism, the less often she displayed positive behavior—and the more often she displayed negative behavior—toward the helpee (her husband). Thus, men and women who were high in neuroticism seemed to provide support in a largely negative and unhelpful manner.

The researchers then examined the audiotaped conversations for evidence of "negative reciprocity" of social support behavior—that is, exchanges characterized by reciprocal displays of negative communications (for example, the helpee complains and the helper then criticizes; the helper blames and the helpee then demands help; see Chapter 6). Analysis of these data indicated that husbands who scored high on neuroticism were more likely to reciprocate their wives' negative behavior when the husbands were in the role of helper; the husbands were also more likely to have their negative helper behavior reciprocated by their wives. The wives' level of neuroticism, however, was not related to reciprocity of negative behavior. In discussing their entire set of results, Pasch and her colleagues (1997) concluded,

> Although support provision is associated with negative affectivity [neuroticism] for husbands and wives, it is the husband's negative affectivity that may have the most detrimental effect on actual interactions between husbands and wives. When husbands were in the role of providing support to their wives and when they were high in negative affectivity, social support interactions were characterized by extended sequences involving negative reciprocity. That is, husbands and wives were engaged in a cycle of negative support solicitation and provision to the extent that husbands were high in negative affectivity. These types of behavioral sequences have been shown to be associated with poor marital outcome . . . and it is plausible to assume that negative reciprocity occurring in the context of soliciting and providing social support may have negative consequences for the marriage and the individual. (p. 376)

Other researchers have reported similar results. For example, a longitudinal investigation conducted by M. Brent Donnellan, Dannelle Larsen-Rife, and Rand Conger (2005; also see Hatton et al., 2008) revealed that young adults who were high in neuroticism during their senior year in high school not only were more likely to display negative behavior five years later during an interaction with their romantic partner but also reported lower levels of relationship quality than did their less emotionally negative counterparts. The evidence with respect to neuroticism, then, is clear. High levels of this personality trait are associated with relationship dissatisfaction, disruption, and dissolution. In addition, neuroticism appears to manifest itself in maladaptive behaviors—including a failure to provide positive support and a tendency to engage in and reciprocate negative displays—that are not at all conducive to relational well-being.

## ❖ SELF-MONITORING

In addition to underlying personality traits, individuals also differ in the domain of self-presentation and expressive behavior. *Self-monitoring* refers to the dispositional tendency to monitor or regulate the images that one presents to others (Snyder, 1987). High self-monitors essentially treat their social interactions as dramatic performances that can be used to gain attention, entertain, and make impressions. These "social chameleons" are strongly motivated to modify their self-presentations, are able to present themselves in a variety of ways to different audiences, and are attentive to social cues and the impressions they make on others. Low self-monitors, in contrast, are motivated to convey their authentic feelings, attitudes, and dispositions to others, are more attentive to their own internal states than to the social climate, and behave consistently across situations and audiences.

The difference between high and low self-monitors becomes clearer when we consider some of the items on the original Self-Monitoring Scale developed by social psychologist Mark Snyder (1974):

- When I am uncertain how to act in a social situation, I look to the behavior of others for cues.

- I sometimes appear to others to be experiencing deeper emotions than I actually am.

- In different situations and with different people, I often act like very different persons.

- I'm not always the person I appear to be.

- I may deceive people by being friendly when I really dislike them.

- My behavior is usually an expression of my true inner feelings, attitudes, and beliefs.

- I have trouble changing my behavior to suit different people and different situations.

- I find it hard to imitate the behavior of other people.

- I can only argue for ideas which I already believe.

- I would not change my opinions (or the way I do things) in order to please someone else or win their favor.

High self-monitors tend to agree with the first five statements and believe that they are very self-descriptive; they tend to disagree with the last five statements. Low self-monitors typically demonstrate the opposite pattern; that is, they do not believe that the first five statements apply to them but find the last five to be very self-descriptive.

A number of researchers have explored the association between self-monitoring and ideal romantic partner preferences. Early investigations suggested that high self-monitors pay considerably more attention to the external, physical attributes of potential romantic partners than to their internal, dispositional characteristics and that low self-monitors do the opposite (e.g., Jones, 1993; Snyder, 1987; Snyder, Berscheid, & Glick, 1985). However, more recent research has failed to replicate these findings (e.g., Rowatt, Cunningham, & Druen, 1998; Shaffer & Bazzini, 1997). A possible explanation for these inconsistent results was provided by Wade Rowatt and his colleagues (Rowatt, DeLue, Strickhouser, & Gonzalez, 2001). Specifically, these researchers observed that because men tend to score higher on self-monitoring than do women, and men also tend to emphasize attractiveness more than do women when rating ideal (hypothetical) mates (see Chapter 1), it stands to reason that high self-monitors (who are likely to be male) would prefer physical attractiveness more than low self-monitors (who are likely to be female). That is, the difference between the ideal romantic preferences of high and low self-monitors may actually be accounted for by their biological sex. To test this hypothesis, the researchers administered the Self-Monitoring Scale (Snyder, 1974) to a sample of men and women. Participants also rated the importance of eight varieties of partner characteristic: fidelity (e.g., faithful, loyal, honest), dependability (e.g., responsible, stable personality, attentive to partner's needs), vitality (e.g., charming, exciting), spiritual values (e.g., spiritual, religious, moral), creativity (e.g., creative, open to new experiences), attractiveness (e.g., physically attractive, sex appeal, athletic), good parenting (e.g., good parent, good family background, wants children), and status-wealth (e.g., status seeking, wealthy, good career). As expected, the results revealed that men had higher self-monitoring scores than women. Men also attached greater importance to attractiveness attributes than did women, whereas women placed greater importance on internal partner qualities (e.g., attributes related to loyalty, dependability, and spiritual values). More importantly, after the effect of the participants' biological sex was statistically controlled, no association was found between self-monitoring and preferences for the various partner attributes. In discussing their findings, Rowatt and his colleagues (2001) observed,

> This research also provides support for the idea that the somewhat inconsistent pattern of findings concerning self-monitoring and mate preferences [is] due, in part, to the biological sex of the participant. Before concluding that self-monitoring influences patterns of social behavior, we encourage researchers to include both men and women as participants and to control for the sex-difference in self-monitoring. (p. 953)

Although self-monitoring per se does not appear to be strongly associated with mate preferences, high and low self-monitoring individuals do tend to have different experiences in their romantic relationships. In fact, a small body of research suggests that high self-monitors are less commitment-oriented and tend to have less stable and satisfying relationships, compared with low self-monitors (e.g., Goodwin & Soon, 1994; Leone & Hall, 2003; Öner, 2002). For example, in one early study, Mark Snyder and Jeffry Simpson (1984) surveyed undergraduates (who were previously classified as high or low self-monitors) about aspects of their dating lives. Their results revealed that high self-monitors had dated nearly twice as many different partners in the previous 12 months as had low self-monitors. In addition, among those participants who were currently involved in exclusive dating relationships, high self-monitors reported having been involved in that relationship only half as long as did low self-monitors. The researchers concluded,

> Together these analyses reveal substantial differences in the structural features of the dating lives of individuals high and low in

self-monitoring. For those involved in multiple relationships, it is high self-monitoring individuals who have dated a greater number of different partners, a finding that seems to be another reflection of an uncommitted orientation to dating relationships. For those involved in single relationships, it is low self-monitoring individuals who are involved in relationships of relatively long duration, an occurrence that may be another manifestation of a committed orientation to dating relationships. (p. 1286)

Similar results were reported more than a decade later by Stacy Norris and Richard Zweigenhaft (1999). These researchers asked a sample of heterosexual dating couples to complete both the Self-Monitoring Scale (Snyder, 1974) and a measure of interpersonal trust that assessed participants' perceptions of their partners' predictability (the extent to which their behavior is consistent and stable), dependability (the extent to which they are honest and reliable), and faith (the extent to which they are believed to have a continuing commitment to the relationship). Participants also estimated the likelihood (in percentages) that they would eventually marry their partners. The researchers found a tendency for people with similar self-monitoring scores to pair romantically; within each couple, the self-monitoring scores for the partners were correlated significantly, and in the majority of couples (63%), both partners were either high or low in terms of self-monitoring. (The remaining couples demonstrated a mixed self-monitoring pattern, with one partner relatively high and the other relatively low on this personality dimension.) The results revealed that the partners in low self-monitoring unions scored higher than individuals in high self-monitoring relationships on all three aspects of interpersonal trust: they believed in each other's honesty, reliability, and commitment to the relationship more than did couples consisting of two high self-monitors. In addition, low self-monitoring was associated with a higher estimated likelihood of marriage. Men and women in low self-monitoring relationships believed it was more likely that they would marry their current partners (75% probability) than did men and women in high self-monitoring relationships (51% probability). As noted by the researchers, these perceptions may be quite accurate. High self-monitors do not consider it highly likely that they will make formal, long-term commitments (via marriage) to their current partners, and when asked to evaluate the commitment of their partners (who are typically also high self-monitors and presumably just as commitment-shy as they are themselves), they provide equally low estimates.

Although other researchers have not found a significant direct association between self-monitoring and romantic relationship satisfaction, commitment, or adjustment (see Oyamot, Fuglestad, & Snyder, 2010; Richmond, Craig, & Ruzicka, 1991), the empirical evidence in general seems to indicate that this personality dimension does play at least some role in mating relationships.

## ❖ SOCIOSEXUAL ORIENTATION

*Sociosexual orientation* is another dispositional variable that may have relational consequences. Sociosexuality reflects the extent to which people require emotional intimacy and commitment before becoming sexually involved with a romantic partner (Gangestad & Simpson, 1990). Men and women who possess a *restricted* sociosexual orientation generally are unwilling to engage in sex outside of a committed relationship, and they require greater emotional closeness and commitment before engaging in sexual activity with a romantic partner. Men and women with an *unrestricted* or permissive orientation require substantially less affection or commitment before having sex with a romantic partner. The seven-item Sociosexual Orientation Inventory (SOI) used to measure this personality construct was developed by Jeffry Simpson and Steven Gangestad (1991; for a revised version, see Penke & Asendorpf, 2008). Respondents provide information about various aspects of their *sexual behavior* (e.g., the number of one-time sex partners they have had, the number of different sex partners they have had during the previous year), *sexual cognitions* (e.g., how often they fantasize about having sex with someone other than their current dating partner), and *sexual attitudes* (e.g., the extent to which they agree with the statement "Sex without love is okay").

Sociosexuality is correlated with a number of romantic and sexual experiences. For example, restricted and unrestricted men and women prefer different types of characteristics in their dating partners. Unrestricted individuals tend to focus on external attributes that are related to sexuality, physical appearance, and social status, whereas restricted individuals tend to pay more attention to internal, dispositional features and attitudinal similarity (see Jones, 1998; Sprecher, Regan, McKinney, Maxwell, & Wazienski, 1997). For example, in a study conducted by Simpson and Gangestad (1992), a group of men and women completed the SOI and rated the importance of 15 characteristics according to how much the characteristics influenced their "selection

of a romantic partner." Correlational analyses revealed a strong association between SOI scores and attribute ratings for both men and
women. In general, the more unrestricted a woman was in her sociosexual orientation, the more importance she attached to a romantic
partner's physical attractiveness and sex appeal and the less importance she placed on dispositional attributes (e.g., kindness and understanding, faithfulness and loyalty, similar values and beliefs) and
parenting qualities (e.g., desire for children, qualities of a good parent).
Similarly, the more unrestricted a man was in terms of sociosexuality,
the more importance he placed on a romantic partner's physical attractiveness, sex appeal, social status, and financial resources, and the less
importance he attached to various dispositional and parenting qualities (e.g., kindness and understanding, responsibility, similar values
and beliefs, qualities of a good parent).

In a second investigation, the researchers examined the attributes
actually possessed by the romantic partners of people with differing
sociosexual orientations. Heterosexual dating couples completed a
companionate love scale (a type of love that reflects deep feelings of
affection, caring, and trust; see Chapter 8), a three-item index that
assessed the likelihood that their current relationship would endure
over time (e.g., "What is the likelihood that you will be dating your
current partner one year from now?"), the SOI, and various other measures. In addition, each participant was evaluated by three observers,
who rated his or her physical and sexual attractiveness. The researchers then correlated each participant's SOI score with the love, attractiveness, and other scores of the participant's dating partner. These
analyses indicated that SOI scores for both men and women were significantly associated with the companionate love and relationship
endurance scores of their partners. Specifically, the more unrestricted
men and women were, the less affectionate love their partners felt for
them and the less likely their partners were to believe that the relationship would endure over time. For men, SOI scores were also correlated
with their partner's physical and sexual attractiveness; the more unrestricted the men were, the more attractive their partners were, according to ratings made by observers (this association nearly reached
statistical significance for women). These investigations provide evidence that restricted and unrestricted individuals desire and actually
acquire romantic partners who possess different sets of attributes. Men
and women with an unrestricted sociosexual orientation seek out partners who are more socially visible and physically appealing, whereas
those with a restricted sociosexual orientation prefer and select

partners who demonstrate more kindness, affection, loyalty, and other positive dispositional attributes.

Subsequent research has demonstrated that sociosexuality is associated with a host of other relationship outcomes and experiences, including commitment and infidelity. Research conducted with men and women in heterosexual and homosexual unions reveals that the less permissive (or the more restricted) they are, the more commitment they feel for their partners and their relationships (Hackathorn & Brantley, 2014; Markey & Markey, 2013; Mattingly et al., 2011). Not surprisingly, given their higher level of commitment, restricted/less permissive men and women are also less likely to cheat on their partners. In one study, for example, William Barta and Susan Kiene (2005) asked a sample of college students whether they had ever been involved in dating infidelity (specifically, whether they had made an agreement to be faithful to their partners but had gotten "either sexually or emotionally involved" with someone else anyway). Participants also completed the SOI. The results revealed a clear difference between the individuals who had been faithful and those who had not: faithful men and women had lower (less permissive) sociosexual orientation scores than their unfaithful counterparts.

Still other researchers have found a connection—at least among men—between sociosexuality and another negative experience that can occur within dating and mating relationships; namely, nonconsensual sex. Specifically, men with an unrestricted or permissive sociosexual orientation tend to endorse rape myths and to report having engaged in coercive or aggressive sexual behavior (see Mouilso & Calhoun, 2012; Schatzel-Murphy, Harris, Knight, & Milburn, 2009; Yost & Zurbriggen, 2006).

Sociosexuality, like self-monitoring, appears to have important implications for interpersonal behavior and the maintenance of romantic relationships.

## Summary

This chapter has explored the ways in which a person's global personality traits and dispositional tendencies are related to his or her romantic experiences. Some traits and attributes seem to promote positive interpersonal outcomes. For example, highly extraverted men and women are likely to provide—and to receive—emotional support in times of stress. Low self-monitors and individuals with a restricted sociosexual orientation tend to offer their partners commitment and stability. Other attributes appear detrimental to relational well-being. Emotionally unstable individuals often experience unstable and unsatisfying partnerships. High self-monitors may leave a date or mate if a more attractive alternative presents himself or herself. People with an unrestricted sociosexual orientation tend to become involved in relationships characterized by relatively low levels of affection and love (and are less likely to be faithful). In sum, who we are, to some extent, determines the quality of our relationships.

## Key Concepts

Personality (p. 305)
Temperament (p. 305)
The Big Five (p. 305)
Supertraits (p. 306)
Extraversion (p. 306)
Extraverts (p. 306)
Introverts (p. 306)
Neuroticism (p. 308)

Self-monitoring (p. 312)
High self-monitors (p. 312)
Low self-monitors (p. 312)
Sociosexual orientation (p. 316)
Restricted sociosexual orientation (p. 316)
Unrestricted sociosexual orientation (p. 316)

## Discussion Questions

1. What is extraversion? How is this personality dimension related to relationship experiences and outcomes?

2. In Chapter 1, we reviewed evidence suggesting that men and women around the world prefer mates who are emotionally stable. Does this universal preference make sense? In other words, is emotional stability related to relationship outcomes? Should men and women be concerned about a partner's emotional stability? Why or why not?

3. Using the sample items from the Self-Monitoring Scale included in the chapter, decide whether you are a high or a low self-monitor (or somewhere in the middle). How do you think this disposition is related to romantic relationship events (in general and for you in particular)?

## Recommended Readings

These articles are good introductory reviews of basic personality theory and research. In fact, any relatively recent issue of the journal *Annual Review of Psychology* will provide comprehensive information on work in the field of personality psychology.

Digman, J. M. (1990). Personality structure: Emergence of the five-factor model. *Annual Review of Psychology, 41,* 417–440.

Heine, S. J., & Buchtel, E. E. (2009). Personality: The universal and the culturally specific. *Annual Review of Psychology, 60,* 369–394.

McCrae, R. R., & Costa, P. T., Jr. (1997). Personality trait structure as a human universal. *American Psychologist, 52,* 509–516.

These articles explore the way in which personality may be implicated in ongoing social and interpersonal interaction. Of particular interest are the methodologies used to examine interaction.

Cutrona, C. E., Hessling, R. M., & Suhr, J. A. (1997). The influence of husband and wife personality on marital social support interactions. *Personal Relationships, 4,* 379–393.

Pasch, L. A., Bradbury, T. N., & Davila, J. (1997). Gender, negative affectivity, and observed social support behavior in marital interaction. *Personal Relationships, 4,* 361–378.

These articles provide good summaries of theory and research on self-monitoring and sociosexuality.

Leone, C., & Hawkins, L. B. (2006). Self-monitoring and close relationships. *Journal of Personality, 74,* 739–778.

Simpson, J. A., Wilson, C. L., & Winterheld, H. A. (2004). Sociosexuality and romantic relationships. In J. H. Harvey, A. Wenzel, & S. Sprecher (Eds.), *The handbook of sexuality in close relationships* (pp. 87–112). Mahwah, NJ: Erlbaum.

# 16

# Interpersonal Belief Systems

People bring to relationships not only their own enduring personality traits and dispositional tendencies but also a variety of stable relationship-relevant beliefs and expectations. These mental representations—also called *relational schemata* or *implicit relationship theories*—consist of a rich web of beliefs, attitudes, values, and expectations that are presumed to develop over time and to influence interpersonal behavior and relationship outcomes (Baldwin, 1992, 1995; Fletcher & Thomas, 1996; Knee & Bush, 2008). This chapter explores three of these important belief systems.

## ❖ ATTACHMENT STYLES

John Bowlby (e.g., 1969) originally proposed the evolutionary concept of *attachment* or the innate and adaptive "propensity of human beings to make strong affectional bonds to particular others" (Bowlby, 1977, p. 201). He hypothesized that human infants come into the world essentially predisposed to form relationships and that this innate predisposition manifests itself in behavioral responses (e.g., crying, clinging, smiling) that promote physical proximity between vulnerable infants and their caregivers and thereby enhance the infants' chances of survival. Over time, and as a result of the caregivers' responses to these proximity-seeking behaviors and the nature of the early interactions between caregivers and infants, children are presumed to develop an *internal working model* about relationships—a set of internalized "expectations of the accessibility and responsiveness of attachment figures" (Bowlby, 1973, p. 235)—that serves as a prototype for later relationships and influences subsequent interpersonal outcomes.

Building upon the theoretical foundation laid by Bowlby, social and personality theorists have proposed the concept of *adult attachment style* (Bartholomew & Horowitz, 1991; Collins, 1996; Hazan & Shaver, 1987), which refers to a person's characteristic beliefs, attitudes, and expectations about the self (worthy of love and support vs. not worthy of love and support), other people (available and supportive vs. unavailable and rejecting), and relationships (rewarding vs. punishing). Most attachment researchers and theorists now agree that four adult attachment styles exist, each reflecting the combination of two underlying dimensions (Feeney & Collins, 2003; see Figure 16.1). The *anxiety dimension* refers to the extent to which an individual worries or is concerned about being rejected or unloved by others; the *avoidance dimension* refers to the degree to which an individual actively avoids or approaches intimacy, connection, and closeness with others. Men and women who possess a *secure attachment style* have low levels of attachment-related anxiety and attachment-related avoidance. They believe that they are worthy of love and support and expect to receive these responses from others and they are comfortable with closeness and believe that relationships can be—and often are—highly rewarding. Men and women with a *preoccupied attachment style* (also called an *anxious/ambivalent style*) have a high level of attachment-related anxiety combined with a low level of attachment-related avoidance. These individuals are preoccupied with intimacy issues and have an exaggerated need for closeness with others yet at the same time are intensely anxious about being abandoned or rejected. People who possess a *dismissing-avoidant attachment style* demonstrate the opposite pattern; they have a low level of attachment-related anxiety and a high level of attachment-related avoidance. These self-reliant men and women value independence more than they do the formation of intimate relationships with others. Finally, individuals with a *fearful-avoidant attachment style* are high in both attachment-related anxiety and avoidance; these adults truly desire to form close, intimate bonds with others but at the same time are highly fearful of being rejected. As a result, they protect themselves from potential disappointment by maintaining distance from others and avoiding intimacy (see Figure 16.1).

Research reveals that individual differences in attachment style are associated with qualitative differences in romantic relationship experiences. For example, research on partner preferences (see Chapter 1) reveals that people who possess a secure attachment style generally are preferred as potential romantic partners by both men and women (Chappell & Davis, 1998; Klohnen & Luo, 2003; Latty-Mann & Davis, 1996; for a review, see Holmes & Johnson, 2009). In addition, the experiences that securely attached adults have within their romantic

**Figure 16.1**      Four Adult Attachment Styles

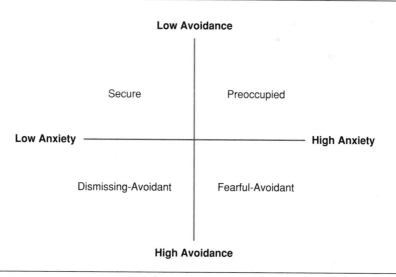

NOTE: Building on earlier work by Cindy Hazan and Phillip Shaver (1987), Kim Bartholomew (e.g., Bartholomew & Horowitz, 1991) created a typology of four adult attachment styles created by two underlying positive-negative dimensions (Model of Self and Model of Other). Subsequent theorists have maintained the four-category framework but have relabeled the underlying dimensions Anxiety and Avoidance (see Feeney & Collins, 2003).

relationships are very different from those reported by insecure (i.e., preoccupied or avoidant) adults. Numerous scholarly reviews (Collins & Feeney, 2004; Collins & Ford, 2010; Feeney & Collins, 2003; Feeney, Noller, & Roberts, 2000; Hadden, Smith, & Webster, 2014; Mikulincer & Shaver, 2009; Simpson & Rholes, 2012) suggest the following general conclusions:

- Compared with avoidant and preoccupied individuals, securely attached men and women report higher levels of satisfaction, trust, intimacy, love, and commitment in their dating and marital relationships.

- Securely attached adults experience lower levels of conflict, interpersonal difficulty, and negative affect than do insecurely attached adults (in fact, the experience of frequent negative emotion is quite common in the relationships of both preoccupied and avoidant men and women).

- Secure individuals exhibit more effective communication styles and display more adaptive and flexible patterns of self-disclosure than their insecure counterparts.

- Compared with insecure individuals, secure individuals provide more responsive and sensitive care to their partners, view social support as more readily available, and are more likely to actively seek support for themselves when needed.

- Compared with avoidant and preoccupied men and women, securely attached adults are more likely to use positive and constructive problem-solving strategies (e.g., compromise, support, validation) for resolving conflict with their partners.

In addition to these qualitative differences in relationship experience, a study conducted by psychologist Nancy Collins (1996) provides evidence that people's attachment orientation biases the way they interpret and explain interpersonal events in their ongoing romantic relationships. Participants who were currently involved in a romantic relationship were asked to imagine that their partner had engaged in four potentially negative behaviors: not responding when the participant wanted to cuddle, not providing comfort when the participant was "feeling down," wanting to spend an evening by himself or herself, and leaving the participant standing alone at a party. After reading about each of these events, participants were asked to write a free-response explanation for the partner's behavior and to rate the extent to which the event would make them feel distressed (e.g., angry, hurt, disappointed, sad, unloved), nervous (e.g., nervous, confused, helpless), and unemotional or indifferent.

Analyses of the free response essays revealed that participants who possessed a preoccupied attachment style explained the event in highly negative and pessimistic ways. Specifically, they were more likely than securely attached (and, in some cases, avoidant) participants to indicate that their partner was unresponsive, unloving, and untrustworthy and that the partner was purposely rejecting them. For example, when asked to explain why the partner would not want to cuddle, some gave responses such as the following: "He feels detached, doesn't want to be close to me," "She doesn't like me anymore," and "He's mad at me and this is his way of punishing me." Securely attached participants were more likely to give explanations that minimized the negative impact of the event. An example was "She just had a bad day and wasn't in the mood to cuddle." This suggests that people with different attachment styles explain and interpret interpersonal events—in this case, potentially negative behavior by a romantic partner—in ways consistent with their internal working models. As Collins (1996) noted,

> Preoccupied individuals were likely to construct explanations that offered much more negative views of their partner and more negative interpretations of events. Consistent with participants' expectations, their explanations were more likely to suggest that their relationship was in jeopardy, and that their partner was unresponsive to their needs, not trustworthy, and purposely rejecting closeness. Their explanations also reflected lower self-worth and self-reliance. In contrast, secure adults provided much more positive explanations. Consistent with their optimistic models of self and others, their explanations were more likely to communicate confidence in their relationship and in their partner's love, they were less likely to view their partner's behavior as purposely rejecting closeness, and overall they tended to construe events in ways that minimized their negative impact and limited their importance for broader issues of relationship stability. (p. 826)

Analysis of the emotional response data provided evidence that men and women with different attachment styles also differ in their affective reactions to potentially negative relationship events. As expected, preoccupied participants reported exaggerated levels of negative emotion. They indicated that they would feel much more emotional distress, helplessness, and nervous confusion in the face of the various partner behaviors than did securely attached participants.

Avoidant participants, on the other hand, reported that they would feel *less* distress than securely attached participants; in fact, the former's primary emotional response was indifference.

Taken altogether, these results suggest that when men and women with insecure (i.e., preoccupied or avoidant) attachment styles are faced with an interpersonal event that lends itself to a potentially negative interpretation, they are likely to respond cognitively and emotionally in ways that are unpleasant for their partner and harmful to the relationship. Craving closeness and validation from their partners—yet feeling unworthy of such responses—preoccupied individuals are only too ready to believe the worst. They assume that the event is caused by the partner's lack of love, concern, and trustworthiness, and they consequently experience overwhelming and excessive distress. Avoidant men and women also readily attribute negative motives to the partners, but their intense need for self-protection produces a very different emotional response—a noncommunicative display of unconcern and stoic indifference. These cognitive and emotional responses are unlikely to produce beneficial outcomes for the partner or the relationship.

In sum, men and women with a secure attachment orientation enter their relationships expecting positive outcomes and then engage in behaviors that seem to promote intimacy and increase the likelihood that they actually will obtain those positive outcomes.

## ❖ REJECTION SENSITIVITY

Another class of beliefs and expectations—having to do specifically with interpersonal rejection—also has clear implications for romantic relationships. Drawing heavily on Bowlby's attachment theory, psychologist Geraldine Downey and her colleagues (e.g., Downey, Bonica, & Rincon, 1999) propose that *rejection sensitivity*—defined as the tendency to anxiously anticipate, readily perceive, and emotionally and behaviorally overreact to rejection from significant others—develops as a self-protective response to parental rejection. Specifically, these theorists suggested the following:

> Our model proposes that when parents tend to meet children's expressed needs with rejection, children become sensitive to rejection. That is, they develop the expectation that when they seek acceptance and support from significant others they will probably be rejected, and they learn to place a particularly high value on avoiding such rejection. They thus experience anticipatory anxiety when expressing

needs or vulnerabilities to significant others. These anxious expectations of rejection make them hypervigilant for signs of rejection.
When they encounter rejection cues, however minimal or ambiguous,
they readily perceive intentional rejection and experience feelings of
rejection. The perceived rejection is then likely to prompt both affective and behavioral overreactions, which may include anger and
hostility, despondency, withdrawal of support, jealousy, and inappropriate attempts to control the significant other's behavior. (Downey &
Feldman, 1996, p. 1328)

Rejection sensitivity is typically assessed by asking individuals to
imagine being in various situations that involve making requests or
asking for assistance from acquaintances, romantic partners, or family
members (e.g., asking a classmate to borrow his or her notes, asking a
boyfriend/girlfriend to cohabit, asking parents for help in deciding
what college programs to apply for). For each situation, participants
are asked whether they would be concerned or anxious about the
response to their request from the person or persons involved and
whether they would expect the other(s) to honor or reject the request.
People who are high in rejection sensitivity usually express anxiety and
concern about the outcome of their request, coupled with an expectation of rejection; those who are low in rejection sensitivity report less
anxiety and concern and express a calm expectation of assistance.

There is growing evidence that rejection sensitive men and women
essentially are primed to perceive rejection in the behavior of others—
even when no rejection is intended. For example, in one study, Geraldine Downey and Scott Feldman (1996) asked a group of college
students, each of whom had recently begun a new romantic relationship, to imagine that their partner had committed three insensitive but
ambiguous actions that conceivably could have occurred for a number
of reasons: had acted cool and distant, had begun to spend less time
with them, and had been intolerant of something the participant did.
Participants then indicated the extent to which they believed that each
action reflected the partner's intentional desire to hurt them. The
results revealed a positive correlation between rejection sensitivity (as
assessed with the multi-item scale) and perceived hurtful intent; the
more sensitive participants were to rejection, the greater the amount of
hurtful intent they perceived in the partner's actions. Thus, it appears
that men and women who anxiously anticipate rejection do actually
"see" rejection in the actions of their intimate partners.

In addition, rejection sensitivity is associated with a number of
negative romantic outcomes. For example, compared with people who
are low in rejection sensitivity, rejection-sensitive people—and their

partners—are less satisfied with their romantic relationships (Downey & Feldman, 1996; Galliher & Bentley, 2010). They are also more likely to be involved in unstable relationships. In one longitudinal study (Downey, Freitas, Michaelis, & Khouri, 1998), dating couples completed a measure of rejection sensitivity and then were contacted one year later and asked to indicate their relationship status (i.e., whether the partners were still together). The results revealed that 44% of the couples who included a rejection-sensitive female partner had broken up, compared with 15% of the couples who included a non-rejection-sensitive female partner. Similarly, 42% of the couples who included a rejection-sensitive male partner had broken up over the 12-month period, compared with 15% of the couples who included a non-rejection-sensitive male partner. Dissolution is a common event in relationships involving at least one rejection-sensitive partner.

Rejection-sensitive men and women also tend to magnify the extent of their partner's dissatisfaction and lack of commitment; in other words, rejection-sensitive people believe that their dating partners are less satisfied and committed than is actually the case. In addition, they often exhibit behavior that can be potentially damaging to their romantic relationships and to their own psychological functioning. For example, research reveals a positive association between rejection sensitivity and the tendency to *self-silence* or inhibit self-expression in intimate relationships (Jack, 1991). A study conducted by psychologists Melinda Harper, Joseph Dickson, and Deborah Welsh (2006) demonstrated that men and women who were high in rejection sensitivity were more likely to report using a host of self-silencing behaviors in their interactions with their romantic partners, including not voicing their feelings if doing so would cause disagreement, rarely expressing anger to their partners, and not expressing opinions or wishes that conflicted with those of their partners. These self-silencing behaviors, in turn, were associated with increased depressive symptoms. These results imply that individuals who are fearful of being rejected by their romantic partners suppress their personal voice and opinions in order to decrease the likelihood of conflict and maintain their relationships; unfortunately, this inhibition of self-expression may damage their own emotional health.

Other research has revealed that rejection-sensitive men and women tend to display hostile, jealous, emotionally unsupportive, and otherwise negative interpersonal behavior (according to their own and their partners' self-reports and laboratory observations of dyadic interaction). Interestingly, there appears to be a sex difference in how rejection-sensitive people manifest their insecurities in close romantic relationships. Specifically, men high in rejection sensitivity are more likely to display jealousy and suspicion and to seek to control their partner's contact with other people, whereas women high in rejection sensitivity are more likely to blame their partner unjustly and to display hostile and unsupportive behavior toward him or her (Downey & Feldman, 1996).

There is also a growing body of evidence that rejection-sensitivity is associated with intimate partner violence and nonconsensual sexual activity. For example, rejection-sensitive adolescent boys and adult men are more likely to engage in aggressive or coercive behaviors toward their dating partners than are non-rejection-sensitive boys and men (Downey, Feldman, & Ayduk, 2000; Galliher & Bentley, 2010), and rejection-sensitive women are more likely to remain in violent or coercive romantic relationships than are less rejection-sensitive women (Young & Furman, 2013). Similarly, rejection sensitivity is positively correlated with an increased likelihood of sexual compliance (e.g., not using a condom, despite one's own desire to do so, in order to satisfy a partner's demands) (Edwards & Barber, 2010). Finally, adolescent girls (and, in some samples, boys) who score high on measures of rejection sensitivity are more likely to report having been sexually victimized by a dating partner or peer than their less rejection-sensitive counterparts (Bekele, van Aken, & Dubas, 2011; Young & Furman, 2008).

In sum, rejection-sensitive people think about and behave toward their partners in ways that appear to undermine the quality of their interactions and limit their chances of developing and maintaining satisfying and stable romantic relationships.

## ❖ ROMANTICISM

In addition to their implicit theories about relationships in general (i.e., that they are rewarding or punishing), men and women possess a subset of beliefs, values, and expectations that are specific to romantic relationships. The *romantic ideal* encompasses five central notions about the nature of love and the characteristic features of romantic unions: the importance of love as a basis for marriage, the idea that love strikes without warning and often at first sight, the belief that there exists only one true love for each person, the idea that true love endures forever, and the notion that love can conquer all obstacles (e.g., Knee, 1998; Sprecher & Metts, 1989).

The most thorough measure of romanticism was created by Susan Sprecher and Sandra Metts (1989), who drew upon previous measurement instruments and theoretical statements about romantic ideology. The Romantic Beliefs Scale contains 15 items that reflect the essential tenets of romanticism (sample items follow):

- *Love Finds a Way:* "If a relationship I have was meant to be, any obstacle can be overcome," "I believe if another person and I love each other we can overcome any differences or problems that may arise."

- *Love at First Sight:* "I am likely to fall in love almost immediately if I meet the right person," "When I find my 'true love' I will probably know it soon after we meet."

- *One and Only:* "There will be only one real love for me," "Once I experience 'true love,' I could never experience it again, to the same degree, with another person."

- *Idealization:* "The relationship I will have with my 'true love' will be nearly perfect," "The person I love will make a perfect romantic partner; for example, he/she will be completely accepting, loving, and understanding."

Romanticism scores decline with age, with older adults less likely to endorse romantic beliefs than teenagers and younger adults (Regan & Anguiano, 2010). In addition, men tend to have higher romanticism scores than do women, at least in college samples (e.g., Sprecher & Metts, 1989, 1999; Weaver & Ganong, 2004). Romanticism also is associated with several relationship experiences, including (not surprisingly) feelings of love for the partner. For example, men and women who strongly endorse the romantic ideal generally report higher levels of passionate love and liking for their partners than do their less romantic counterparts, and the former tend to fall in love with their partners at an earlier stage in their relationships (Sprecher & Metts, 1989). Moreover, highly romantic individuals think about the relationship more during a partner's absence (Cate, Koval, Lloyd, & Wilson, 1995), and they feel higher amounts of satisfaction with and commitment to the partner and the relationship (Sprecher & Metts, 1999; Weaver & Ganong, 2004; but see Metts, 2004). Men and women who subscribe to a generalized romantic ideal may be more likely to feel passion, more eager to commit, and more inclined to view their partners and their relationships in a positive light than are their less overtly romantic counterparts. As noted by Sprecher and Metts (1999), "General positive beliefs about [romantic] relationships tend to be associated with positive feelings and experiences (love, satisfaction, commitment) within a specific relationship" (p. 846).

## Summary

Over time, and as a result of the interpersonal events we experience, each of us develops a host of relationship-relevant beliefs, attitudes, values, and expectations. Like our biological sex, psychological gender, and temperament, these mental representations can influence our interpersonal behavior and the nature of the romantic associations we form with others. Of course, it is important to keep in mind that no single disposition or set of beliefs inevitably determines what happens between partners or the fate of their relationship. Rather, it may be the particular constellation of beliefs, traits, and dispositional features that one person possesses, and how well those attributes mesh with the enduring characteristics of his or her partner, that ultimately proves to have the greatest impact on any given relationship. Thus, an extraverted, securely attached person may experience unhappiness, conflict, and romantic instability, and an emotionally unstable, insecure, rejection-sensitive person may find lasting love and satisfaction. In the realm of dating and mating, anything is possible.

## Key Concepts

Relational schemata (p. 321)
Implicit relationship theories (p. 321)
Attachment (p. 322)
Internal working model (p. 322)
Adult attachment style (p. 322)
Anxiety dimension (p. 322)
Avoidance dimension (p. 322)
Secure attachment style (p. 322)

Preoccupied   (anxious/ambivalent) attachment style (p. 322)
Dismissing-avoidant attachment style (pp. 322–323)
Fearful-avoidant attachment style (p. 323)
Rejection sensitivity (p. 326)
Self-silencing (p. 328)
Romantic ideal (p. 329)

## Discussion Questions

1. Define the concept of relational schemata or implicit relationship theories. In what ways is a prototype (see Chapter 7) similar to these concepts?

2. Identify the four styles of adult attachment. Do you think a person's adult attachment style can change over time?

3. What is rejection sensitivity? Compare this belief system with that of attachment style. How are they similar?

4. Find social scientific research on a phenomenon called "behavioral confirmation" or the "self-fulfilling prophecy." (Hint: Look in any social psychology textbook.) Drawing on this literature, explain how rejection-sensitive people might actually create their own unpleasant interpersonal realities.

5. Define the romantic ideal. In what ways is romanticism related to relationship outcomes? Consider the sample items included in the chapter from the Romantic Beliefs Scale. Using a 7-point rating scale (with 1 = strongly disagree and 7 = strongly agree), rate yourself on the eight sample items. Add up your total score (across all eight items). Assuming that "average" scores are around 32, how romantic are you? Are you above average? Below average? How do you think your level of romanticism has influenced your own relationship experiences and outcomes?

## Recommended Readings

These articles review the ways in which both functional and dysfunctional relationship beliefs can impact interpersonal behavior and relationship outcomes.

Baldwin, M. W. (1995). Relational schemas and cognition in close relationships. *Journal of Social and Personal Relationships, 12,* 547–552.

Knee, C. R., & Bush, A. L. (2008). Relationship beliefs and their role in romantic relationship initiation. In S. Sprecher, A. Wenzel, & J. Harvey (Eds.), *Handbook of relationship initiation* (pp. 471–485). New York, NY: Psychology Press, Inc.

These articles review the concept of adult attachment style and summarize knowledge about the association between different adult attachment styles and relationship experiences and quality.

Feeney, B. C., & Collins, N. L. (2003). Attachment: Couple relationships. In J. J. Ponzetti, Jr. (Ed.), *International encyclopedia of marriage and family* (2nd ed., Vol. 1, pp. 96–103). New York, NY: Macmillan Reference USA.

Feeney, J. A., Noller, P., & Roberts, N. (2000). Attachment and close relationships. In C. Hendrick & S. S. Hendrick (Eds.), *Close relationships: A sourcebook* (pp. 185–201). Thousand Oaks, CA: Sage.

Mikulincer, M., & Shaver, P. R. (2009). An attachment and behavioral systems perspective on social support. *Journal of Social and Personal Relationships, 26,* 7–19.

This early article presents an excellent overview of the concept of attachment and should be required reading for anyone interested in that area.

Karen, R. (1990, February). Becoming attached. *The Atlantic Monthly,* pp. 35–70.

This brief article reviews research on romantic beliefs and explores whether romanticism is correlated with age, sex, and ethnicity in a community sample of men and women.

Regan, P. C., & Anguiano, C. (2010). Romanticism as a function of age, sex, and ethnicity. *Psychological Reports, 107,* 972–976.

# Concluding Remarks

What does it mean to be in love with someone? Are there different ways of loving someone? How long does love last? What characteristics make someone desirable as a romantic partner? What role does sex play in love relationships? What variables influence whether marriages and other romantic relationships endure or dissolve? How can people effectively resolve conflict and other difficulties that may arise in their intimate relationships? Is there a "good" way to end a relationship, or to repair a damaged one? My purpose in writing this text was to address these questions (and, I hope, to provide some answers to them) by considering theories of mate selection, attraction and affiliation, relationship development, love, and relational sexuality, and by reviewing empirical research on these interlinked life experiences.

We have seen that romantic relationships provide people with the opportunity to experience a panoply of positive and affirming events—passion and joy, affection and trust, desire and sexual expression. We have also seen how they can be a source of unhappiness and torment, ranging from incompatibility and dissatisfaction to obsession, coercion, jealousy, and sometimes even violence. Whatever their outcomes, and regardless of the form they take, the mating relationships that we form with others clearly have profound implications for the quality of our lives. I hope that this text has shed some small light on these important and fascinating human experiences.

# References

Abbey, A. (1982). Sex differences in attributions for friendly behavior: Do males misperceive females' friendliness? *Journal of Personality and Social Psychology, 42*, 830–838.

Abbey, A. (1987). Misperceptions of friendly behavior as sexual interest: A survey of naturally occurring incidents. *Psychology of Women Quarterly, 11*, 173–194.

Abbey, A., & Melby, C. (1986). The effects of nonverbal cues on gender differences in perceptions of sexual intent. *Sex Roles, 15*, 283–298.

Abdelshahid, A., & Campbell, C. (2015). 'Should I circumcise my daughter?' Exploring diversity and ambivalence in Egyptian parents' social representations of female circumcision. *Journal of Community & Applied Social Psychology, 25*, 49–65.

Abrahams, M. F. (1994). Perceiving flirtatious communication: An exploration of the perceptual dimensions underlying judgments of flirtatiousness. *Journal of Sex Research, 31*, 283–292.

Adams, J. S. (1965). Inequity in social exchange. In L. Berkowitz (Ed.), *Advances in experimental social psychology* (Vol. 2, pp. 267–299). New York, NY: Academic Press.

Afifi, W. A., Falato, W. L., & Weiner, J. L. (2001). Identity concerns following a severe relational transgression: The role of discovery method for the relational outcomes of infidelity. *Journal of Social and Personal Relationships, 18*, 291–308.

Agadjanian, V., & Ezeh, A. C. (2000). Polygyny, gender relations, and reproduction in Ghana. *Journal of Comparative Family Studies, 31*, 427–441.

Akbayram, S., Sari, N., Akgün, C., Doğan, M., Tuncer, O., Çaksen, H., & Öner, A. F. (2009). The frequency of consanguineous marriage in Eastern Turkey. *Genetic Counseling: Medical, Psychological, and Ethical Aspects, 20*, 207–214.

Alain, M., & Lussier, Y. (1988). Sex-role attitudes and divorce experience. *Journal of Social Psychology, 128*, 143–152.

Al-Krenawi, A., & Graham, J. R. (2006). A comparison of family functioning, life and marital satisfaction, and mental health of women in polygamous and monogamous marriages. *International Journal of Social Psychiatry, 52*, 5–17.

Al-Krenawi, A., Graham, J. R., & Al Gharaibeh, F. (2011). A comparison study of psychological, family function marital and life satisfactions of polygamous and monogamous women in Jordan. *Community Mental Health Journal, 47,* 594–602.

Allen, E. S., & Atkins, D. C. (2012). The association of divorce and extramarital sex in a representative U.S. sample. *Journal of Family Issues, 33,* 1477–1493.

Allen, E. S., Kline Rhoades, G., Stanley, S. M., Markman, H. J., Williams, T., Melton, J., & Clements, M. L. (2008). Premarital precursors of marital infidelity. *Family Process, 47,* 243–259.

Allendorf, K. (2013). Schemas of change: From arranged marriages to eloping for love. *Journal of Marriage and Family, 75,* 453–469.

Al-Obaidi, A. K., Jeffrey, L. R., Al-Obaidi, D., & Al-Obaidi, A. (2014). An Iraqi-specific perspective on adolescent pregnancy. In A. L. Cherry & M. E. Dillon (Eds.), *International handbook of adolescent pregnancy: Medical, psychosocial, and public health consequences* (pp. 379–399). New York, NY: Springer Science & Business Media.

Altman, I., & Taylor, D. A. (1973). *Social penetration: The development of interpersonal relationships.* New York, NY: Holt, Rinehart & Winston.

Amar, A. F. (2006). College women's experiences of stalking: Mental health symptoms and changes in routine. *Archives of Psychiatric Nursing, 20,* 108–116.

Amar, A. F., & Alexy, E. M. (2010). Coping with stalking. *Issues in Mental Health Nursing, 31,* 8–14.

Amato, P. R., & Irving, S. (2006). Historical trends in divorce in the United States. In M. A. Fine & J. H. Harvey (Eds.), *Handbook of divorce and dissolution* (pp. 41–57). Mahwah, NJ: Erlbaum.

Amato, P. R., Johnson, D. R., Booth, A., & Rogers, S. J. (2003). Continuity and change in marital quality between 1980 and 2000. *Journal of Marriage and Family, 65,* 1–22.

Amato, P. R., & Rogers, S. J. (1997). A longitudinal study of marital problems and subsequent divorce. *Journal of Marriage and the Family, 59,* 612–624.

Archer, J. (2000). Sex differences in aggression between heterosexual partners: A meta-analysis. *Psychological Bulletin, 126,* 651–680.

Archer, J. (2002). Sex differences in physically aggressive acts between heterosexual partners: A meta-analytic review. *Aggression and Violent Behavior, 7,* 313–351.

Arnett, J. L., Prosen, H., & Toews, J. A. (1986). Loss of libido due to stress. *Medical Aspects of Human Sexuality, 20,* 140–148.

Aron, A., Fisher, H., Mashek, D. J., Strong, G., Li, H., & Brown, L. L. (2005). Reward, motivation, and emotion systems associated with early-stage intense romantic love. *Journal of Neurophysiology, 94,* 327–337.

Aron, A., & Westbay, L. (1996). Dimensions of the prototype of love. *Journal of Personality and Social Psychology, 70,* 535–551.

Arriaga, X. B., Agnew, C. R., Capezza, N. M., & Lehmiller, J. J. (2008). The social and physical environment of relationship initiation: An interdependence analysis. In S. Sprecher, A. Wenzel, & J. Harvey (Eds.), *Handbook of relationship initiation* (pp. 197–215). New York, NY: Psychology Press.

Artis, J. E., & Pavalko, E. K. (2003). Explaining the decline in women's household labor: Individual change and cohort effects. *Journal of Marriage and Family, 65,* 746–761.

Asendorpf, J. B., Penke, K., & Back, M. D. (2011). From dating to mating and relating: Predictors of initial and long-term outcomes of speed-dating in a community sample. *European Journal of Personality, 25,* 16–30.

Atkins, D. C., Baucom, D. H., & Jacobson, N. S. (2001). Understanding infidelity: Correlates in a national random sample. *Journal of Family Psychology, 15,* 735–749.

Attridge, M., & Berscheid, E. (1994). Entitlement in romantic relationships in the United States: A social exchange perspective. In M. J. Lerner & G. Mikula (Eds.), *Entitlement and the affectional bond: Justice in close relationships* (pp. 117–148). New York, NY: Plenum.

Aughinbaugh, A., Robles, O., & Sun, H. (2013). Marriage and divorce: Patterns by gender, race, and educational attainment. *Monthly Labor Review,* October 2013. Retrieved December 1, 2014 from http://www.bls.gov/opub/mlr/2013/article/marriage-and-divorce-patterns-by-gender-race-and-educational-attainment.htm

Ault, L. K., & Philhower, C. (2001, July). *Allergen avoidance: Qualities in romantic partners that are shunned by lovers and their parents.* Paper presented at the joint conference of the International Network on Personal Relationships and the International Society for the Study of Personal Relationships, Prescott, AZ.

Azar, B. (1998, January). Communicating through pheromones. *APA Monitor, 29,* 1, 12.

Bachman, G. F., & Guerrero, L. K. (2006). Relational quality and communicative responses following hurtful events in dating relationships: An expectancy violations analysis. *Journal of Social and Personal Relationships, 23,* 943–963.

Bachman, R., & Carmody, D. C. (1994). Fighting fire with fire: The effects of victim resistance in intimate versus stranger perpetrated assaults against females. *Journal of Family Violence, 9,* 317–331.

Bachman, R., Saltzman, L. E., Thompson, M. P., & Carmody, D. C. (2002). Disentangling the effects of self-protective behaviors on the risk of injury in assaults against women. *Journal of Quantitative Criminology, 18,* 135–157.

Back, M. J., Penke, L., Schmukle, S. C., Sachse, K., Borkenau, P., & Asendorpf, J. B. (2011). Why mate choices are not as reciprocal as we assume: The role of personality, flirting, and physical attractiveness. *European Journal of Personality, 25,* 120–132.

Baldwin, M. W. (1992). Relational schemas and the processing of social information. *Psychological Bulletin, 112,* 461–484.

Baldwin, M. W. (1995). Relational schemas and cognition in close relationships. *Journal of Social and Personal Relationships, 12,* 547–552.

Barbour, B., & Salameh, P. (2009). Consanguinity in Lebanon: Prevalence, distribution and determinants. *Journal of Biosocial Science, 41,* 505–517.

Barelds, D. P. H. (2005). Self and partner personality in intimate relationships. *European Journal of Personality, 19,* 501–518.

Barelds, D. P. H., & Barelds-Dijkstra, P. (2006). Partner personality in distressed relationships. *Clinical Psychology and Psychotherapy, 13,* 392–396.

Barelds, D. P. H., & Dijkstra, P. (2009). Positive illusions about a partner's physical attractiveness and relationship quality. *Personal Relationships, 16,* 263–283.

Barelds, D. P. H., Dijkstra, P., Koudenburg, N., & Swami, V. (2011). An assessment of positive illusions of the physical attractiveness of romantic partners. *Journal of Social and Personal Relationships, 28,* 706–719.

Barker, M., & Langdridge, D. (Eds.). (2010a). *Understanding non-monogamies.* New York, NY: Routledge.

Barker, M., & Langdridge, D. (2010b). Whatever happened to non-monogamies? Critical reflections on recent research and theory. *Sexualities, 13,* 748–772.

Barry, R. A., Lawrence, E., & Langer, A. (2008). Conceptualization and assessment of disengagement in romantic relationships. *Personal Relationships, 15,* 297–315.

Barta, W. D., & Kiene, S. M. (2005). Motivations for infidelity in heterosexual dating couples: The roles of gender, personality differences, and sociosexual orientation. *Journal of Social and Personal Relationships, 22,* 339–360.

Bartholomew, K., & Horowitz, L. M. (1991). Attachment styles among young adults: A test of a four-category model. *Journal of Personality and Social Psychology, 61,* 226–244.

Bartley, S. J., Blanton, P. W., & Gilliard, J. L. (2005). Husbands and wives in dual-earner marriages: Decision-making, gender role attitudes, division of household labor, and equity. *Marriage & Family Review, 37,* 69–94.

Basile, K. C., Arias, I., Desai, S., & Thompson, M. P. (2004). The differential association of intimate partner physical, sexual, psychological, and stalking violence and posttraumatic stress symptoms in a nationally representative sample of women. *Journal of Traumatic Stress, 17,* 413–421.

Baucom, B. R., & Boeding, S. (2013). The role of theory and research in the practice of cognitive-behavioral couple therapy: If you build it, they will come. *Behavior Therapy, 44,* 592–602.

Baucom, B. R., McFarland, P. T., & Christensen, A. (2010). Gender, topic, and time in observed demand-withdraw interaction in cross- and same-sex couples. *Journal of Family Psychology, 24,* 233–242.

Baucom, D. H., & Epstein, N. (1990). *Cognitive-behavioral marital therapy.* New York, NY: Brunner/Mazel.

Baucom, D. H., Epstein, N., & Rankin, L. A. (1995). Cognitive aspects of cognitive-behavioral marital therapy. In N. S. Jacobson & A. S. Gurman (Eds.), *Clinical handbook of couple therapy* (pp. 65–90). New York, NY: Guilford Press.

Baucom, D. H., Hahlweg, K., & Kuschel, A. (2003). Are waiting-list control groups needed in future marital therapy outcome research? *Behavior Therapy, 34,* 179–188.

Baucom, K. J. W., Baucom, B. R., & Christensen, A. (2012). Do the naïve know best? The predictive power of naïve ratings of couple interactions. *Psychological Assessment, 24,* 983–994.

Baumeister, R. F., & Wotman, S. R. (1992). *Breaking hearts: The two sides of unrequited love.* New York, NY: Guilford Press.

Baumeister, R. F., Wotman, S. R., & Stillwell, A. M. (1993). Unrequited love: On heartbreak, anger, guilt, scriptlessness, and humiliation. *Journal of Personality and Social Psychology, 64,* 377–394.

Baxter, J. (2005). To marry or not to marry: Marital status and the household division of labor. *Journal of Family Issues, 26,* 300–321.

Baxter, L. A. (1985). Accomplishing relationship disengagement. In S. Duck & D. Perlman (Eds.), *Understanding personal relationships: An interdisciplinary approach* (pp. 243–265). London, England: Sage.

Baxter, L. A., & Bullis, C. (1986). Turning points in developing romantic relationships. *Human Communication Research, 12,* 469–493.

Baxter, L. A., & Pittman, G. (2001). Communicatively remembering turning points of relational development in heterosexual romantic relationships. *Communication Reports, 14,* 1–17.

Beaver, E. D., Gold, S. R., & Prisco, A. G. (1992). Priming macho attitudes and emotions. *Journal of Interpersonal Violence, 7,* 321–333.

Bekele, A. B., van Aken, M. A. G., & Dubas, J. S. (2011). Sexual violence victimization among female secondary students in eastern Ethiopia. *Violence and Victims, 26,* 608–630.

Bem, S. L. (1974). The measurement of psychological androgyny. *Journal of Consulting and Clinical Psychology, 42,* 155–162.

Beres, M. A., Herold, E., & Maitland, S. B. (2004). Sexual consent behaviors in same-sex relationships. *Archives of Sexual Behavior, 33,* 475–486.

Berliner, D. L., Jennings-White, C., & Lavker, R. M. (1991). The human skin: Fragrances and pheromones. *Journal of Steroid Biochemistry and Molecular Biology, 39,* 671–679.

Berman, M. I., & Frazier, P. A. (2005). Relationship power and betrayal experience as predictors of reactions to infidelity. *Personality and Social Psychology Bulletin, 31,* 1617–1627.

Berscheid, E. (1983). Emotion. In H. H. Kelley, E. Berscheid, A. Christensen, J. H. Harvey, G. Levinger, E. McClintock, L. A. Peplau, & D. R. Peterson (Eds.), *Close relationships* (pp. 110–168). New York, NY: Freeman.

Berscheid, E. (1985). Interpersonal attraction. In G. Lindzey & E. Aronson (Eds.), *The handbook of social psychology* (3rd ed., Vol. 2, pp. 413–484). New York, NY: Random House.

Berscheid, E. (1988). Some comments on love's anatomy: Or, whatever happened to old-fashioned lust? In R. J. Sternberg & M. L. Barnes (Eds.), *The psychology of love* (pp. 359–374). New Haven, CT: Yale University Press.

Berscheid, E. (2010). Love in the fourth dimension. *Annual Review of Psychology, 61*, 1–25.

Berscheid, E., & Campbell, B. (1981). The changing longevity of heterosexual close relationships. In M. J. Lerner & S. C. Lerner (Eds.), *The justice motive in social behavior* (pp. 209–234). New York, NY: Plenum Press.

Berscheid, E., & Regan, P. (2005). *The psychology of interpersonal relationships.* Mahwah, NJ: Prentice Hall.

Berscheid, E., & Reis, H. T. (1998). Attraction and close relationships. In D. T. Gilbert, S. T. Fiske, & G. Lindzey (Eds.), *The handbook of social psychology* (4th ed., pp. 193–281). New York, NY: McGraw-Hill.

Berscheid, E., & Walster, E. (1974). A little bit about love. In T. L. Huston (Ed.), *Foundations of interpersonal attraction* (pp. 355–381). New York, NY: Academic Press.

Bertrand, J. T., Makani, B., Edwards, M. P., & Baughman, N. C. (1996). The male versus the female perspective on family planning: Kinshasa, Zaire. *Journal of Biosocial Science, 28*, 37–55.

Bettor, L., Hendrick, S. S., & Hendrick, C. (1995). Gender and sexual standards in dating relationships. *Personal Relationships, 2*, 359–369.

Betzig, L. (1989). Causes of conjugal dissolution: A cross-cultural study. *Current Anthropology, 30*, 654–676.

Biernat, M., & Wortman, C. B. (1991). Sharing of home responsibilities between professionally employed women and their husbands. *Journal of Personality and Social Psychology, 60*, 844–860.

Birnbaum, G. E., Cohen, O., & Wertheimer, V. (2007). Is it all about intimacy? Age, menopausal status, and women's sexuality. *Personal Relationships, 14*, 167–185.

Birnbaum, G. E., & Reis, H. T. (2012). When does responsiveness pique sexual interest? Attachment and sexual desire in initial acquaintanceships. *Personality and Social Psychology Bulletin, 38*, 946–958.

Black, M. C., Basile, K. C., Breiding, M. J., Smith, S. G., Walters, M. L., Merrick, M. T., Chen, J., & Stevens, M. R. (2011). *The National Intimate Partner and Sexual Violence Survey (NISVS): 2010 summary report.* Atlanta, GA: National Center for Injury Prevention and Control, Centers for Disease Control and Prevention.

Blackburn, K., Brody, N., & LeFebvre, L. (2014). The I's, we's, and she/he's of breakups: Public and private pronoun usage in relationship dissolution accounts. *Journal of Language and Social Psychology, 33*, 202–213.

Blair, S. L., & Johnson, M. P. (1992). Wives' perceptions of the fairness of the division of household labor: The intersection of housework and ideology. *Journal of Marriage and the Family, 54*, 570–581.

Blau, P. M. (1964). *Exchange and power in social life.* New York, NY: Wiley.

Blood, R. O., Jr., & Wolfe, D. M. (1960). *Husbands and wives: The dynamics of married living.* Glencoe, IL: Free Press.

Blumstein, P., & Schwartz, P. (1983). *American couples.* New York, NY: William Morrow.

Bodenmann, G., Gottman, J. M., & Backman, H. (1997). A Swiss replication of Gottman's couple typology. *Swiss Journal of Psychology, 56,* 205–216.

Boerner, K., Jopp, D. S., Carr, D., Sosinsky, L., & Kim, S.-K. (2014). "His" and "her" marriage? The role of positive and negative marital characteristics in global marital satisfaction among older adults. *Journals of Gerontology, Series B: Psychological Sciences and Social Sciences, 69,* 579–589.

Bonanno, G. A., Wortman, C. B., Lehman, D. R., Tweed, R. G., Haring, M., Sonnega, J., Carr, D., & Nesse, R. M. (2002). Resilience to loss and chronic grief: A prospective study from preloss to 18-months postloss. *Journal of Personality and Social Psychology, 83,* 1150–1164.

Bonanno, G. A., Wortman, C. B., & Nesse, R. M. (2004). Prospective patterns of resilience and maladjustment during widowhood. *Psychology and Aging, 19,* 260–271.

Bornstein, R. F. (1989). Exposure and affect: Overview and meta-analysis of research, 1968–1987. *Psychological Bulletin, 106,* 265–289.

Bouchard, G., Lussier, Y., & Sabourin, S. (1999). Personality and marital adjustment: Utility of the five-factor model of personality. *Journal of Marriage and the Family, 61,* 651–660.

Bowlby, J. (1969). *Attachment and loss, Vol. 1: Attachment.* New York, NY: Basic Books.

Bowlby, J. (1973). *Attachment and loss, Vol. 2: Separation: Anxiety and anger.* New York, NY: Basic Books.

Bowlby, J. (1977). The making and breaking of affectional bonds. *British Journal of Psychiatry, 130,* 201–210.

Bowman, J. M. (2008). Gender role orientation and relational closeness: Self-disclosive behavior in same-sex male friendships. *The Journal of Men's Studies, 16,* 316–330.

Bradbury, T. N., & Fincham, F. D. (1990). Attributions in marriage: Review and critique. *Psychological Bulletin, 107,* 3–33.

Bradbury, T. N., Fincham, F. D., & Beach, S. R. H. (2000). Research on the nature and determinants of marital satisfaction: A decade in review. *Journal of Marriage and the Family, 62,* 964–980.

Braiker, H. B., & Kelley, H. H. (1979). Conflict in the development of close relationships. In R. L. Burgess & T. L. Huston (Eds.), *Social exchange in developing relationships* (pp. 135–168). New York, NY: Academic Press.

Braver, S. L., Shapiro, J. R., & Goodman, M. R. (2006). Consequences of divorce for parents. In M. A. Fine & J. H. Harvey (Eds.), *Handbook of divorce and dissolution* (pp. 313–337). Mahwah, NJ: Erlbaum.

Bredow, C. A., Cate, R. M., & Huston, T. L. (2008). Have we met before? A conceptual model of first romantic encounters. In S. Sprecher, A. Wenzel, & J. Harvey (Eds.), *Handbook of relationship initiation* (pp. 3–28). New York, NY: Psychology Press.

Bredow, C. A., Huston, T. L., & Glenn, N. D. (2011). Market value, quality of the pool of potential mates, and singles' confidence about marrying. *Personal Relationships, 18,* 39–57.

Brehm, S. S. (1985). *Intimate relationships*. New York, NY: Random House.

Breiding, M. J., Black, M. C., & Ryan, G. W. (2008). Prevalence and risk factors of intimate partner violence in eighteen U.S. states/territories, 2005. *American Journal of Preventive Medicine, 34,* 112–118.

Breiding, M. J., Smith, S. G., Basile, K. C., Walters, M. L., Chen, J., & Merrick, M. T. (2014). Prevalence and characteristics of sexual violence, stalking, and intimate partner violence victimization–National Intimate Partner and Sexual Violence Survey, United States, 2011. *Morbidity and Mortality Weekly Report, 63(8),* 1–8. Retrieved November 7, 2014 from http://www.cdc.gov/mmwr/pdf/ss/ss6308.pdf

Brewis, A., & Meyer, M. (2005). Marital coitus across the life course. *Journal of Biosocial Science, 37,* 499–518.

Brewster, M. P. (2003). Power and control dynamics in prestalking and stalking situations. *Journal of Family Violence, 18,* 207–217.

Brezsnyak, M., & Whisman, M. A. (2004). Sexual desire and relationship functioning: The effects of marital satisfaction and power. *Journal of Sex & Marital Therapy, 30,* 199–217.

Bringle, R. G., & Buunk, B. P. (1991). Extradyadic relationships and sexual jealousy. In K. McKinney & S. Sprecher (Eds.), *Sexuality in close relationships* (pp. 135–153). Hillsdale, NJ: Erlbaum.

Brody, S., & Weiss, P. (2011). Simultaneous penile-vaginal intercourse orgasm is associated with satisfaction (sexual, life, partnership, and mental health). *Journal of Sexual Medicine, 8,* 734–741.

Brown, M., & Auerback, A. (1981). Communication patterns in initiation of marital sex. *Medical Aspects of Human Sexuality, 15,* 105–117.

Brown, S. L. (2003). Relationship quality dynamics of cohabiting unions. *Journal of Family Issues, 24,* 583–601.

Brown, S. L., & Booth, A. (1996). Cohabitation versus marriage: A comparison of relationship quality. *Journal of Marriage and the Family, 58,* 668–678.

Brown, S. L., Sanchez, L. A., Nock, S. L., & Wright, J. D. (2006). Links between premarital cohabitation and subsequent marital quality, stability, and divorce. *Social Science Research, 35,* 454–470.

Brumbaugh, C. C., & Fraley, R. C. (2015). Too fast, too soon? An empirical investigation into rebound relationships. *Journal of Social and Personal Relationships, 32,* 99–118.

Buhi, E. R., Clayton, H., & Surrency, H. H. (2009). Stalking victimization among college women and subsequent help-seeking behaviors. *Journal of the American College Health Association, 57,* 419–425.

Bumpass, L. L., Sweet, J. A., & Cherlin, A. (1991). The role of cohabitation in declining rates of marriage. *Journal of Marriage and the Family, 53,* 913–927.

Burgoon, J. K., Buller, D. B., Hale, J. L., & deTurck, M. A. (1984). Relational messages associated with nonverbal behaviors. *Human Communication Research, 10,* 351–378.

Burk, L. R., Burkhart, B. R., & Sikorski, J. F. (2004). Construction and preliminary validation of the Auburn Differential Masculinity Inventory. *Psychology of Men & Masculinity, 5,* 4–17.

Burleson, B. R. (2003). The experience and effects of emotional support: What the study of cultural and gender differences can tell us about close relationships, emotion, and interpersonal communication. *Personal Relationships, 10,* 1–23.

Burleson, B. R., Hanasono, L. K., Bodie, G. D., Holmstrom, A. J., Rack, J. J., Rosier, J. G., & McCullough, J. D. (2009). Explaining gender differences in responses to supportive messages: Two tests of a dual-process approach. *Sex Roles, 61,* 265–280.

Burleson, B. R., Holmstrom, A. J., & Gilstrap, C. M. (2005). "Guys can't say *that* to guys": Four experiments assessing the normative motivation account for deficiencies in the emotional support provided by men. *Communication Monographs, 72,* 468–501.

Burleson, B. R., & Kunkel, A. W. (2006). Revisiting the different cultures thesis: An assessment of sex differences and similarities in supportive communication. In K. Dindia & D. J. Canary (Eds.), *Sex differences and similarities in communication* (2nd ed., pp. 137–159). Mahwah, NJ: Erlbaum.

Burt, M. R. (1980). Cultural myths and supports for rape. *Journal of Personality and Social Psychology, 38,* 217–230.

Busby, D. M., Carroll, J. S., & Willoughby, B. J. (2010). Compatibility or restraint? The effects of sexual timing on marriage relationships. *Journal of Family Psychology, 24,* 766–774.

Buss, D. M. (1985). Human mate selection. *American Scientist, 73,* 47–51.

Buss, D. M. (1989). Sex differences in human mate preferences: Evolutionary hypotheses tested in 37 cultures. *Behavioral and Brain Sciences, 12,* 1–49.

Buss, D. M., Abbott, M., Angleitner, A., Asharian, A., Biaggio, A., Blanco-Villasenor, A., . . . Yang, K.-S. (1990). International preferences in selecting mates: A study of 37 cultures. *Journal of Cross-Cultural Psychology, 21,* 5–47.

Buss, D. M., & Kenrick, D. T. (1998). Evolutionary social psychology. In D. T. Gilbert, S. T. Fiske, & G. Lindzey (Eds.), *The handbook of social psychology* (4th ed., Vol. 2, pp. 982–1026). New York, NY: McGraw-Hill.

Buss, D. M., Larsen, R. J., Westen, D., & Semmelroth, J. (1992). Sex differences in jealousy: Evolution, physiology, and psychology. *Psychological Science, 3,* 251–255.

Buss, D. M., & Schmitt, D. P. (1993). Sexual strategies theory: An evolutionary perspective on human mating. *Psychological Review, 100,* 204–232.

Buss, D. M., Shackelford, T. K., Kirkpatrick, L. A., Choe, J. C., Lim, H. K., Hasegawa, M., Hasegawa, T., & Bennett, K. (1999). Jealousy and the nature of beliefs about infidelity: Tests of competing hypotheses about sex differences in the United States, Korea, and Japan. *Personal Relationships, 6,* 125–150.

Buss, D. M., Shackelford, T. K., Kirkpatrick, L. A., & Larsen, R. J. (2001). A half century of mate preferences: The cultural evolution of values. *Journal of Marriage and Family, 63*, 491–503.

Butzer, B., & Campbell, L. (2008). Adult attachment, sexual satisfaction, and relationship satisfaction: A study of married couples. *Personal Relationships, 15*, 141–154.

Buunk, B. P. (1995). Sex, self-esteem, dependency and extradyadic sexual experience as related to jealousy responses. *Journal of Social and Personal Relationships, 12*, 147–153.

Buunk, B. P., & van der Eijnden, R. J. J. M. (1997). Perceived prevalence, perceived superiority, and relationship satisfaction: Most relationships are good, but ours is the best. *Personality and Social Psychology Bulletin, 23*, 219–228.

Byers, E. S. (2005). Relationship satisfaction and sexual satisfaction: A longitudinal study of individuals in long-term relationships. *The Journal of Sex Research, 42*, 113–118.

Byers, E. S., Demmons, S., & Lawrance, K. (1998). Sexual satisfaction within dating relationships: A test of the interpersonal exchange model of sexual satisfaction. *Journal of Social and Personal Relationships, 15*, 257–267.

Byers, E. S., & Heinlein, L. (1989). Predicting initiations and refusals of sexual activities in married and cohabiting heterosexual couples. *Journal of Sex Research, 26*, 210–231.

Byers, E. S., & MacNeil, S. (2006). Further validation of the interpersonal exchange model of sexual satisfaction. *Journal of Sex & Marital Therapy, 32*, 53–69.

Byrne, D. (1997). An overview (and underview) of research and theory within the attraction paradigm. *Journal of Social and Personal Relationships, 14*, 417–431.

Byrne, D., Ervin, C. R., & Lamberth, J. (1970). Continuity between the experimental study of attraction and real-life computer dating. *Journal of Personality and Social Psychology, 16*, 157–165.

Byrne, M., Carr, A., & Clark, M. (2004). The efficacy of behavioral couples therapy and emotionally focused therapy for couple distress. *Contemporary Family Therapy, 26*, 361–387.

Cain, V. S., Johannes, C. B., Avis, N. E., Mohr, B., Schocken, M., Skurnick, J., & Ory, M. (2003). Sexual functioning and practices in a multi-ethnic study of midlife women: Baseline results from SWAN. *The Journal of Sex Research, 40*, 266–276.

Calhoun, K. S., McCauley, J., & Crawford, M. E. (2006). Sexual assault. In R. D. McAnulty & M. M. Burnette (Eds.), *Sex and sexuality. Vol. 3. Sexual deviation and sexual offenses* (pp. 97–130). Westport, CT: Praeger.

Call, V., Sprecher, S., & Schwartz, P. (1995). The incidence and frequency of marital sex in a national sample. *Journal of Marriage and the Family, 57*, 639–650.

Campbell, R., Dworkin, E., & Cabral, G. (2009). An ecological model of the impact of sexual assault on women's mental health. *Trauma, Violence, & Abuse, 10,* 225–246.

Canary, D. J., & Stafford, L. (1992). Relational maintenance strategies and equity in marriage. *Communication Monographs, 59,* 243–267.

Cann, A., & Baucom, T. R. (2004). Former partners and new rivals as threats to a relationship: Infidelity type, gender, and commitment as factors related to distress and forgiveness. *Personal Relationships, 11,* 305–318.

Carmichael, G. A., & Whittaker, A. (2007). Living together in Australia: Qualitative insights into a complex phenomenon. *Journal of Family Studies, 13,* 202–223.

Carpenter, C. J. (2012). Meta-analyses of sex differences in response to sexual versus emotional infidelity: Men and women are more similar than different. *Psychology of Women Quarterly, 36,* 25–37.

Carroll, J. L., Volk, K. D., & Hyde, J. S. (1985). Differences between males and females in motives for engaging in sexual intercourse. *Archives of Sexual Behavior, 14,* 131–139.

Carstensen, L. L., Gottman, J. M., & Levenson, R. W. (1995). Emotional behavior in long-term marriage. *Psychology and Aging, 10,* 140–149.

Carter, C. S. (1998). Neuroendocrine perspectives on social attachment and love. *Psychoneuroendocrinology, 23,* 779–818.

Carter, C. S. (2014). Oxytocin pathways and the evolution of human behavior. *Annual Review of Psychology, 65,* 17–39.

Castañeda, D., & Burns-Glover, A. (2004). Gender, sexuality, and intimate relationships. In M. A. Paludi (Ed.), *Praeger guide to the psychology of gender* (pp. 69–91). Westport, CT: Praeger Publishers/Greenwood Publishing Group.

Castañeda, D. M. (1993). The meaning of romantic love among Mexican-Americans. *Journal of Social Behavior and Personality, 8,* 257–272.

Cate, R. M., Koval, J., Lloyd, S. A., & Wilson, G. (1995). Assessment of relationship thinking in dating relationships. *Personal Relationships, 2,* 77–95.

Cate, R. M., & Lloyd, S. A. (1992). *Courtship.* Newbury Park, CA: Sage.

Cernoch, J. M., & Porter, R. H. (1985). Recognition of maternal axillary odors in infants. *Child Development, 56,* 1593–1598.

Chang, S., & Chan, C. (2007). Perceptions of commitment change during mate selection: The case of Taiwanese newlyweds. *Journal of Social and Personal Relationships, 24,* 55–68.

Chappell, K. D., & Davis, K. E. (1998). Attachment, partner choice, and perception of romantic partners: An experimental test of the attachment-security hypothesis. *Personal Relationships, 5,* 327–342.

Charny, I. W., & Parnass, S. (1995). The impact of extramarital relationships on the continuation of marriages. *Journal of Sex & Marital Therapy, 21,* 100–115.

Chaulk, K., & Jones, T. (2011). Online obsessive relational intrusion: Further concerns about Facebook. *Journal of Family Violence, 26,* 245–254.

Christensen, A., & Heavey, C. L. (1990). Gender and social structure in the demand/withdraw pattern of marital conflict. *Journal of Personality and Social Psychology, 59,* 73–81.

Christensen, A., & Heavey, C. L. (1999). Interventions for couples. *Annual Review of Psychology, 50,* 165–190.

Christensen, A., & Jacobson, N. S. (2000). *Reconcilable differences.* New York, NY: Guilford Press.

Christensen, H. T. (1947). Student views on mate selection. *Marriage and Family Living, 9,* 85–88.

Christopher, F. S. (2001). *To dance the dance: A symbolic interactional exploration of premarital sexuality.* Mahwah, NJ: Erlbaum.

Christopher, F. S., & Cate, R. M. (1984). Factors involved in premarital sexual decision making. *Journal of Sex Research, 20,* 363–376.

Christopher, F. S., & Cate, R. M. (1985). Premarital sexual pathways and relationship development. *Journal of Social and Personal Relationships, 2,* 271–288.

Christopher, F. S., & Frandsen, M. M. (1990). Strategies of influence in sex and dating. *Journal of Social and Personal Relationships, 7,* 89–105.

Christopher, F. S., & Kisler, T. S. (2004). Sexual aggression in romantic relationships. In J. H. Harvey, A. Wenzel, & S. Sprecher (Eds.), *The handbook of sexuality in close relationships* (pp. 287–309). Mahwah, NJ: Erlbaum.

Christopher, F. S., & Lloyd, S. A. (2000). Physical and sexual aggression in relationships. In C. Hendrick & S. S. Hendrick (Eds.), *Close relationships: A sourcebook* (pp. 331–343). Thousand Oaks, CA: Sage.

Christopher, F. S., Owens, L. A., & Stecker, H. L. (1993). An examination of single men's and women's sexual aggressiveness in dating relationships. *Journal of Social and Personal Relationships, 10,* 511–527.

Christopher, F. S., & Sprecher, S. (2000). Sexuality in marriage, family, and other relationships: A decade review. *Journal of Marriage and the Family, 62,* 999–1017.

Chubin, F. (2014). When my virtue defends your borders: Political justification of nation and order through the rhetorical production of womanhood in the 1979 Islamic revolution of Iran. *Women's Studies International Forum, 42,* 44–55.

Clark, C. L., Shaver, P. R., & Abrahams, M. F. (1999). Strategic behaviors in romantic relationship initiation. *Personality and Social Psychology Bulletin, 25,* 707–720.

Clark, L. A., Watson, D., & Mineka, S. (1994). Temperament, personality, and the mood and anxiety disorders. *Journal of Abnormal Psychology, 103,* 103–116.

Clarkberg, M., Stolzenberg, R. M., & Waite, L. J. (1995). Attitudes, values, and entrance into cohabitational versus marital unions. *Social Forces, 74,* 609–632.

Clarke, V., Burgoyne, C., & Burns, M. (2013). Unscripted and improvised: Public and private celebrations of same-sex relationships. *Journal of GLBT Family Studies, 9,* 393–418.

Claxton, A., O'Rourke, N., Smith, J. Z., & DeLongis, A. (2012). Personality traits and marital satisfaction within enduring relationships: An intra-couple discrepancy approach. *Journal of Social and Personal Relationships, 29,* 375–396.

Coan, J. A., & Gottman, J. M. (2007). The Specific Affect Coding System (SPAFF). In J. A. Coan & J. J. B. Allen (Eds.), *Handbook of emotion elicitation and assessment* (pp. 267–285). New York, NY: Oxford University Press.

Cohan, C. L., & Kleinbaum, S. (2002). Toward a greater understanding of the cohabitation effect: Premarital cohabitation and marital communication. *Journal of Marriage and Family, 64,* 180–192.

Cohen, J. N., & Byers, E. S. (2014). Beyond lesbian bed death: Enhancing our understanding of the sexuality of sexual-minority women in relationships. *Journal of Sex Research, 51,* 893–903.

Cohn, B. A. (1994). In search of human skin pheromones. *Archives of Dermatology, 130,* 1048–1051.

Coker, A. L., Smith, P. H., McKeown, R. E., & King, M. J. (2000). Frequency and correlates of intimate partner violence by type: Physical, sexual, and psychological battering. *American Journal of Public Health, 90,* 553–559.

Collins, N. L. (1996). Working models of attachment: Implications for explanation, emotion, and behavior. *Journal of Personality and Social Psychology, 71,* 810–832.

Collins, N. L., & Feeney, B. C. (2004). An attachment theory perspective on closeness and intimacy. In D. J. Mashek & A. Aron (Eds.), *Handbook of closeness and intimacy* (pp. 163–187). Mahwah, NJ: Erlbaum.

Collins, N. L., & Ford, M. B. (2010). Responding to the needs of others: The caregiving behavioral system in intimate relationships. *Journal of Social and Personal Relationships, 27,* 235–244.

Coltrane, S. (2000). Research on household labor: Modeling and measuring the social embeddedness of routine family work. *Journal of Marriage and the Family, 62,* 1208–1233.

Coltrane, S., & Adams, M. (2003). Division of labor. In J. J. Ponzetti, Jr. (Ed.), *International encyclopedia of marriage and family* (2nd ed., Vol. 1, pp. 470–475). New York, NY: Macmillan Reference USA.

Condon, J. W., & Crano, W. D. (1988). Inferred evaluation and the relation between attitude similarity and interpersonal attraction. *Journal of Personality and Social Psychology, 54,* 789–797.

Conley, T. D., Moors, A. C., Matsick, J. L., & Ziegler, A. (2013). The fewer the merrier?: Assessing stigma surrounding consensually non-monogamous romantic relationships. *Analyses of Social Issues and Public Policy, 13,* 1–30.

Contreras, R., Hendrick, S. S., & Hendrick, C. (1996). Perspectives on marital love and satisfaction in Mexican American and Anglo couples. *Journal of Counseling and Development, 74,* 408–415.

Coombs, R. H. (1991). Marital status and personal well-being: A literature review. *Family Relations, 40,* 97–102.

Cooper, A., & Sportolari, L. (1997). Romance in cyberspace: Understanding online attraction. *Journal of Sex Education and Therapy, 22,* 7–14.

Copen, C. E., Daniels, K., & Mosher, W. D. (2013). First premarital cohabitation in the United States: 2006–2010 National Survey of Family Growth. *National Health Statistics Reports*, No. 64. Hyattsville, MD: National Center for Health Statistics.

Copen, C. E., Daniels, K., Vespa, J., & Mosher, W. D. (2012). First marriages in the United States: Data from the 2006–2010 National Survey of Family Growth. *National Health Statistics Reports*, No. 49. Hyattsville, MD: National Center for Health Statistics.

Corprew, C. S., III, Matthews, J. S., & Mitchell, A. D. (2014). Men at the crossroads: A profile analysis of hypermasculinity in emerging adulthood. *The Journal of Men's Studies, 22,* 105–121.

Cosmides, L., & Tooby, J. (1997). *Evolutionary psychology: A primer.* Retrieved from www.psych.ucsb.edu/research/cep/primer.html

Cramer, D. (1993). Personality and marital dissolution. *Personality and Individual Differences, 14,* 605–607.

Cramer, D. (2000). Relationship satisfaction and conflict style in romantic relationships. *The Journal of Psychology, 134,* 337–341.

Cunningham, M. R. (1986). Measuring the physical in physical attractiveness: Quasi-experiments on the sociobiology of female facial beauty. *Journal of Personality and Social Psychology, 50,* 925–935.

Cunningham, M. R., Barbee, A. P., & Druen, P. B. (1996). Social allergens and the reactions that they produce: Escalation of annoyance and disgust in love and work. In R. M. Kowalski (Ed.), *Aversive interpersonal behaviors* (pp. 189–214). New York, NY: Plenum.

Cunningham, M. R., Barbee, A. P., & Pike, C. L. (1990). What do women want? Facialmetric assessment of multiple motives in the perception of male facial physical attractiveness. *Journal of Personality and Social Psychology, 59,* 61–72.

Cunningham, M. R., Druen, P. B., & Barbee, A. P. (1997). Angels, mentors, and friends: Trade-offs among evolutionary, social, and individual variables in physical appearance. In J. A. Simpson & D. T. Kenrick (Eds.), *Evolutionary social psychology* (pp. 109–140). Mahwah, NJ: Erlbaum.

Cunningham, M. R., Shamblen, S. R., Barbee, A. P., & Ault, L. K. (2005). Social allergies in romantic relationships: Behavioral repetition, emotional sensitization, and dissatisfaction in dating couples. *Personal Relationships, 12,* 273–295.

Cupach, W. R., & Canary, D. J. (2003). Conflict: Couple relationships. In J. J. Ponzetti, Jr. (Ed.), *International encyclopedia of marriage and family* (2nd ed., Vol. 1, pp. 355–360). New York, NY: Macmillan Reference USA.

Cupach, W. R., & Comstock, J. (1990). Satisfaction with sexual communication in marriage: Links to sexual satisfaction and dyadic adjustment. *Journal of Social and Personal Relationships, 7,* 179–186.

Cupach, W. R., & Metts, S. (1991). Sexuality and communication in close relationships. In K. McKinney & S. Sprecher (Eds.), *Sexuality in close relationships* (pp. 93–110). Hillsdale, NJ: Erlbaum.

Cupach, W. R., & Spitzberg, B. H. (1997, February). *The incidence and perceived severity of obsessive relational intrusion behaviors.* Paper presented at the meeting of the Western States Communication Association, Monterey, CA.

Cupach, W. R., & Spitzberg, B. H. (1998). Obsessive relational intrusion and stalking. In B. H. Spitzberg & W. R. Cupach (Eds.), *The dark side of close relationships* (pp. 233–263). Mahwah, NJ: Erlbaum.

Cupach, W. R., & Spitzberg, B. H. (2004). *The dark side of relational pursuit: From attraction to obsession and stalking.* Mahwah, NJ: Erlbaum.

Cupach, W. R., & Spitzberg, B. H. (2008). "Thanks, but no thanks . . ." The occurrence and management of unwanted relationship pursuit. In S. Sprecher, A. Wenzel, & J. Harvey (Eds.), *Handbook of relationship initiation* (pp. 409–424). New York, NY: Psychology Press.

Cupach, W. R., & Spitzberg, B. H. (Eds.). (2011). *The dark side of close relationships II.* New York, NY: Routledge.

Cutler, W. B., Preti, G., Huggins, G. R., Erickson, B., & Garcia, C. R. (1985). Sexual behavior frequency and biphasic ovulatory type menstrual cycles. *Physiology and Behavior, 34,* 805–810.

Cutrona, C. E., Hessling, R. M., & Suhr, J. A. (1997). The influence of husband and wife personality on marital social support interactions. *Personal Relationships, 4,* 379–393.

Dailey, R. M., Brody, N., LeFebvre, L., & Crook, B. (2013). Charting changes in commitment: Trajectories of on-again/off-again relationships. *Journal of Social and Personal Relationships, 30,* 1020–1044.

Dainton, M. (2000). Maintenance behaviors, expectations for maintenance, and satisfaction: Linking comparison levels to relational maintenance strategies. *Journal of Social and Personal Relationships, 17,* 827–842.

Dainton, M., & Stafford, L. (1993). Routine maintenance behaviors: A comparison of relationship type, partner similarity, and sex differences. *Journal of Social and Personal Relationships, 10,* 255–272.

Daly, M., & Wilson, M. (1983). *Sex, evolution, and behavior* (2nd ed.). Belmont, CA: Wadsworth.

Darling, C. A., Davidson, J. K., & Cox, R. P. (1991). Female sexual response and the timing of partner orgasm. *Journal of Sex & Marital Therapy, 17,* 3–21.

Darwin, C. (1859). *On the origin of the species by means of natural selection: Or, preservation of favoured races in the struggle for life.* London, England: J. Murray.

Darwin, C. (1871). *The descent of man, and selection in relation to sex.* London, England: J. Murray.

Dasgupta, S., & Basu, J. (2001). Effects of gender role identity of couples and earning status of the wife on marital quality. *Social Science International, 17,* 16–30.

D'Augelli, A., & D'Augelli, J. F. (1985). The enhancement of sexual skills and competence: Promoting lifelong sexual unfolding. In L. L'Abate & M. A. Milan (Eds.), *Handbook of social skills training and research* (pp. 170–191). New York, NY: Wiley.

Davies, S., Katz, J., & Jackson, J. L. (1999). Sexual desire discrepancies: Effects on sexual and relationship satisfaction in heterosexual dating couples. *Archives of Sexual Behavior, 28,* 553–567.

Davis, D., & Holtgraves, T. (1984). Perceptions of unresponsive others: Attributions, attraction, understandability, and memory of their utterances. *Journal of Experimental Social Psychology, 20,* 383–408.

Davis, D., & Perkowitz, W. T. (1979). Consequences of responsiveness in dyadic interaction: Effects of probability of response and proportion of content-related responses on interpersonal attraction. *Journal of Personality and Social Psychology, 37,* 534–550.

Davis, J. A., & Smith, T. (1991). *General social surveys, 1972–1991.* Storrs: University of Connecticut, Roper Center for Public Opinion Research.

Davis, K. E., Ace, A., & Andra, M. (2000). Stalking perpetrators and psychological maltreatment of partners: Anger-jealousy, attachment insecurity, need for control, and break-up context. *Violence and Victims, 15,* 407–425.

Davis, K. E., Coker, A. L., & Sanderson, M. (2002). Physical and mental health effects of being stalked for men and women. *Violence and Victims, 17,* 429–443.

Davis, K. E., Frieze, I. H., & Maiuro, R. D. (Eds.). (2002). *Stalking: Perspectives on victims and perpetrators.* New York, NY: Springer.

Davis, K. E., & Latty-Mann, H. (1987). Love styles and relationship quality: A contribution to validation. *Journal of Social and Personal Relationships, 4,* 409–428.

Davis, M. (1973). *Intimate relations.* New York, NY: Free Press.

Davis, S. (1990). Men as success objects and women as sex objects: A study of personal advertisements. *Sex Roles, 23,* 43–50.

Davis, S. N., & Greenstein, T. N. (2009). Gender ideology: Components, predictors, and consequences. *Annual Review of Sociology, 35,* 87–105.

Davis, S. R., & Braunstein, G. D. (2012). Efficacy and safety of testosterone in the management of hypoactive sexual desire disorder in postmenopausal women. *Journal of Sexual Medicine, 9,* 1134–1148.

Deaux, K., & Hanna, R. (1984). Courtship in the personals column: The influence of gender and sexual orientation. *Sex Roles, 11,* 363–375.

de Becker, G. (1999). *The gift of fear and other survival signals that protect us from violence.* New York, NY: Dell.

de Becker, G. (2002). I was trying to let him down easy. In J. Boon & L. Sheridan (Eds.), *Stalking and psychosexual obsession: Psychological perspectives for prevention, policing, and treatment* (pp. 35–47). West Sussex, England: Wiley.

Decuyper, M., De Bolle, M., & De Fruyt, F. (2012). Personality similarity, perceptual accuracy, and relationship satisfaction in dating and married couples. *Personal Relationships, 19,* 128–145.

Deenen, A. A., Gijs, L., & van Naerssen, A. X. (1994). Intimacy and sexuality in gay male couples. *Archives of Sexual Behavior, 23,* 421–431.

DeMaris, A. (2007). The role of relationship inequity in marital disruption. *Journal of Social and Personal Relationships, 24,* 177–195.

DeMaris, A. (2013). Burning the candle at both ends: Extramarital sex as a precursor of marital disruption. *Journal of Family Issues, 34,* 1474–1499.

DeMaris, A., Sanchez, L. A., & Krivickas, K. (2012). Developmental patterns in marital satisfaction: Another look at covenant marriage. *Journal of Marriage and Family, 74,* 989–1004.

Demo, D. H., & Acock, A. C. (1996). Singlehood, marriage, and remarriage: The effects of family structure and family relationships on mothers' well-being. *Journal of Family Issues, 17,* 388–407.

Dennerstein, L., Koochaki, P., Barton, I., & Graziottin, A. (2006). Hypoactive sexual desire disorder in menopausal women: A survey of Western European women. *Journal of Sexual Medicine, 3,* 212–222.

DePaulo, B. M., & Morris, W. L. (2006). The unrecognized stereotyping and discrimination against singles. *Current Directions in Psychological Science, 15,* 251–254.

DeSteno, D. (2010). Mismeasuring jealousy: A cautionary comment on Levy and Kelly (2010). *Psychological Science, 21,* 1355–1356.

DeSteno, D., Bartlett, M. Y., Braverman, J., & Salovey, P. (2002). Sex differences in jealousy: Evolutionary mechanism or artifact of measurement? *Journal of Personality and Social Psychology, 83,* 1103–1116.

DeSteno, D. A., & Salovey, P. (1996). Evolutionary origins of sex differences in jealousy? Questioning the "fitness" of the model. *Psychological Science, 7,* 367–372.

Digman, J. M. (1990). Personality structure: Emergence of the five-factor model. *Annual Review of Psychology, 41,* 417–440.

Dijkstra, P., Barelds, D. P. H., Groothof, H. A. K., Ronner, S., & Nauta, A. P. (2012). Partner preferences of the intellectually gifted. *Marriage & Family Review, 48,* 96–108.

Dimidjian, S., Martell, C. R., & Christensen, A. (2008). Integrative behavioral couple therapy. In A. S. Gurman (Ed.), *Clinical handbook of couple therapy* (4th ed., pp. 73–103). New York, NY: Guilford Press.

Dindia, K. (2000). Relational maintenance. In C. Hendrick & S. S. Hendrick (Eds.), *Close relationships: A sourcebook* (pp. 287–299). Thousand Oaks, CA: Sage.

Dion, K. L., & Dion, K. K. (1993). Gender and ethnocultural comparisons in styles of love. *Psychology of Women Quarterly, 17,* 463–473.

Dixson, B. J., Dixson, A. F., Bishop, P. J., & Parish, A. (2010). Human physique and sexual attractiveness in men and women: A New Zealand-U.S. comparative study. *Archives of Sexual Behavior, 39,* 798–806.

Dixson, B. J., Grimshaw, G. M., Linklater, W. L., & Dixson, A. F. (2011). Eye-tracking of men's preferences for waist-to-hip ratio and breast size of women. *Archives of Sexual Behavior, 40,* 43–50.

Do, M., & Fu, H. (2010). Attitudes toward premarital sex in contemporary Vietnam: Findings from a national survey. *International Journal of Sexual Health, 22,* 103–118.

Dobash, R. E., & Dobash, R. P. (1979). *Violence against wives: A case against patriarchy.* New York, NY: Free Press.

Doering, J. (2010). Face, accounts, and schemes in the context of relationship breakups. *Symbolic Interaction, 33,* 71–95.

Domínguez-Folgueros, M. (2013). Is cohabitation more egalitarian? The division of household labor in five European countries. *Journal of Family Issues, 34,* 1623–1646.

Donn, J. E., & Sherman, R. C. (2002). Attitudes and practices regarding the formation of romantic relationships on the Internet. *CyberPsychology & Behavior, 5,* 107–123.

Donnellan, M. B., Conger, R. D., & Bryant, C. M. (2004). The big five and enduring marriages. *Journal of Research in Personality, 38,* 481–504.

Donnellan, M. B., Larsen-Rife, D., & Conger, R. D. (2005). Personality, family history, and competence in early adult romantic relationships. *Journal of Personality and Social Psychology, 88,* 562–576.

Donnelly, D. A. (1993). Sexually inactive marriages. *Journal of Sex Research, 30,* 171–179.

Downey, G., Bonica, C., & Rincon, C. (1999). Rejection sensitivity and adolescent romantic relationships. In W. Furman, B. B. Brown, & C. Feiring (Eds.), *The development of romantic relationships in adolescence* (pp. 148–174). New York, NY: Cambridge University Press.

Downey, G., & Feldman, S. I. (1996). Implications of rejection sensitivity for intimate relationships. *Journal of Personality and Social Psychology, 70,* 1327–1343.

Downey, G., Feldman, S., & Ayduk, O. (2000). Rejection sensitivity and male violence in romantic relationships. *Personal Relationships, 7,* 45–61.

Downey, G., Freitas, A. L., Michaelis, B., & Khouri, H. (1998). The self-fulfilling prophecy in close relationships: Rejection sensitivity and rejection by romantic partners. *Journal of Personality and Social Psychology, 75,* 545–560.

Downey, J. L., & Damhave, K. W. (1991). The effects of place, type of comment, and effort expended on the perception of flirtation. *Journal of Social Behavior and Personality, 6,* 35–43.

Dressing, H., Kuehner, C., & Gass, P. (2005). Lifetime prevalence and impact of stalking in a European population: Epidemiological data from a middle-sized German city. *British Journal of Psychiatry, 187,* 168–172.

Drigotas, S. M., Rusbult, C. E., & Verette, J. (1999). Level of commitment, mutuality of commitment, and couple well-being. *Personal Relationships, 6,* 389–409.

Driver, J. L., & Gottman, J. M. (2004). Daily marital interactions and positive affect during marital conflict among newlywed couples. *Family Process, 43,* 301–314.

Duck, S. (1982). A topography of relationship disengagement and dissolution. In S. Duck (Ed.), *Personal relationships, Vol. 4: Dissolving personal relationships* (pp. 1–30). London, England: Academic Press.

Dunn, J. L. (1999). What love has to do with it: The cultural construction of emotion and sorority women's responses to forcible interaction. *Social Problems, 46,* 440–459.

Durtschi, J. A., Fincham, F. D., Cui, M., Lorenz, F. O., & Conger, R. D. (2011). Dyadic processes in early marriage: Attributions, behavior, and marital quality. *Family Relations, 60*, 421–434.

Dutton, D. G. (2007). Female intimate partner violence and developmental trajectories of abusive females. *International Journal of Men's Health, 6*, 54–70.

Dutton, D. G., & Aron, A. P. (1974). Some evidence for heightened sexual attraction under conditions of high anxiety. *Journal of Personality and Social Psychology, 30*, 510–517.

Dutton, L. B., & Winstead, B. A. (2006). Predicting unwanted pursuit: Attachment, relationship satisfaction, relationship alternatives, and break-up distress. *Journal of Social and Personal Relationships, 23*, 565–586.

Dutton, L. B., & Winstead, B. A. (2011). Types, frequency, and effectiveness of responses to unwanted pursuit and stalking. *Journal of Interpersonal Violence, 26*, 1129–1156.

Dworkin, S. L., & O'Sullivan, L. (2005). Actual versus desired initiation patterns among a sample of college men: Tapping disjunctures within traditional male sexual scripts. *The Journal of Sex Research, 42*, 150–158.

Dyrenforth, P. S., Kashy, D. A., Donnellan, M. B., & Lucas, R. E. (2010). Predicting relationship and life satisfaction from personality in nationally representative samples from three countries: The relative importance of actor, partner, and similarity effects. *Journal of Personality and Social Psychology, 99*, 690–702.

Eagly, A. H. (1987). *Sex differences in social behavior: A social-role interpretation.* Hillsdale, NJ: Erlbaum.

Eagly, A. H., & Wood, W. (2012). Social role theory. In P. A. M. Van Lange, A. W. Kruglanski, & E. T. Higgins (Eds.), *Handbook of theories of social psychology* (Vol. 2, pp. 458–476). Thousand Oaks, CA: Sage.

Eagly, A. H., Wood, W., & Johannesen-Schmidt, M. (2004). Social role theory of sex differences and similarities: Implications for partner preferences of women and men. In A. H. Eagly, A. Beall, & R. J. Sternberg (Eds.), *The psychology of gender* (2nd ed., pp. 269–295). New York, NY: Guilford Press.

Earle, J. R., Perricone, P. J., Davidson, Sr., J. K., Moore, N. B., Harris, C. T., & Cotten, S. R. (2007). Premarital sexual attitudes and behavior at a religiously-affiliated university: Two decades of change. *Sexuality & Culture, 11*, 39–61.

Eastwick, P. W., & Finkel, E. J. (2008). Sex differences in mate preferences revisited: Do people know what they initially desire in a romantic partner? *Journal of Personality and Social Psychology, 94*, 245–264.

Eastwick, P. W., Luchies, L. B., Finkel, E. J., & Hunt, L. L. (2014). The predictive validity of ideal partner preferences: A review and meta-analysis. *Psychological Bulletin, 140*, 623–665.

Eaton, A. A., & Matamala, A. (2014). The relationship between heteronormative beliefs and verbal sexual coercion in college students. *Archives of Sexual Behavior, 43*, 1443–1457.

Eaton, A. A., & Rose, S. M. (2012). Scripts for actual first date and hanging-out encounters among young heterosexual Hispanic adults. *Sex Roles, 67*, 285–299.

Edwards, G. L., & Barber, B. L. (2010). The relationship between rejection sensitivity and compliant condom use. *Archives of Sexual Behavior, 39,* 1381–1388.

Eibl-Eibesfeldt, I. (1975). *Ethology: The biology of behavior* (2nd ed.). New York, NY: Holt, Rinehart & Winston.

Eibl-Eibesfeldt, I. (1989). *Human ethology.* New York, NY: Aldine de Gruyter.

Eisenman, R., & Dantzker, M. L. (2006). Gender and ethnic differences in sexual attitudes at a Hispanic-serving university. *The Journal of General Psychology, 133,* 153–162.

Eldridge, K. A., & Christensen, A. (2002). Demand-withdraw communication during couple conflict: A review and analysis. In P. Noller & J. A. Feeney (Eds.), *Understanding marriage: Developments in the study of couple interaction* (pp. 289–322). New York, NY: Cambridge University Press.

Eldridge, K. A., Sevier, M., Jones, J., Atkins, D. C., & Christensen, A. (2007). Demand-withdraw communication in severely distressed, moderately distressed, and nondistressed couples: Rigidity and polarity during relationship and personal problem discussions. *Journal of Family Psychology, 21,* 218–226.

Elias, V. L., Fullerton, A. S., & Simpson, J. M. (2015). Long-term changes in attitudes toward premarital sex in the United States: Reexamining the role of cohort replacement. *Journal of Sex Research, 52,* 129–139.

El-Kheshen, G., & Saadat, M. (2013). Prevalence of consanguineous marriages among Shi'a populations of Lebanon. *Journal of Biosocial Science, 45,* 675–682.

Ellis, A. (1954). *The American sexual tragedy.* New York, NY: Twayne.

Ellis, D., & Stuckless, N. (1996). *Mediating and negotiating marital conflicts.* Thousand Oaks, CA: Sage.

Emerson, R. M., Ferris, K. O., & Gardner, C. B. (1998). On being stalked. *Social Problems, 45,* 289–314.

Erchull, M. J., Liss, M., Axelson, S. J., Staebell, S. E., & Askari, S. F. (2010). Well . . . she wants it more: Perceptions of social norms about desires for marriage and children and anticipated chore participation. *Psychology of Women Quarterly, 34,* 253–260.

Eysenck, H. J. (1980). Personality, marital satisfaction, and divorce. *Psychological Reports, 47,* 1235–1238.

Falconier, M. K., & Epstein, N. B. (2011). Female-demand/male-withdraw communication in Argentinian couples: A mediating factor between economic strain and relationship distress. *Personal Relationships, 18,* 586–603.

Farnsworth, J., Lund, D. A., & Pett, M. A. (1989). Management and outcomes of loss in later life: A comparison of bereavement and divorce. In D. A. Lund (Ed.), *Older bereaved spouses* (pp. 155–166). Washington, DC: Hemisphere.

Faulkner, R. A., Davey, M., & Davey, A. (2005). Gender-related predictors of change in marital satisfaction and marital conflict. *The American Journal of Family Therapy, 33,* 61–83.

Feeney, B. C., & Collins, N. L. (2003). Attachment: Couple relationships. In J. J. Ponzetti, Jr. (Ed.), *International encyclopedia of marriage and family* (2nd ed., Vol. 1, pp. 96–103). New York, NY: Macmillan Reference USA.

Feeney, J. A. (2004). Hurt feelings in couple relationships: Towards integrative models of the negative effects of hurtful events. *Journal of Social and Personal Relationships, 21,* 487–508.

Feeney, J. A., Noller, P., & Roberts, N. (2000). Attachment and close relationships. In C. Hendrick & S. S. Hendrick (Eds.), *Close relationships: A sourcebook* (pp. 185–201). Thousand Oaks, CA: Sage.

Feeney, J., Peterson, C., & Noller, P. (1994). Equity and marital satisfaction over the family life cycle. *Personal Relationships, 1,* 83–99.

Fehr, B. (1988). Prototype analysis of the concepts of love and commitment. *Journal of Personality and Social Psychology, 55,* 557–579.

Fehr, B. (1994). Prototype-based assessment of layperson's views of love. *Personal Relationships, 1,* 309–331.

Fehr, B. (2006). A prototype approach to studying love. In R. J. Sternberg & K. Weis (Eds.), *The new psychology of love* (pp. 225–246). New Haven, CT: Yale University Press.

Fehr, B., Harasymchuk, C., & Sprecher, S. (2014). Compassionate love in romantic relationships: A review and some new findings. *Journal of Social and Personal Relationships, 31,* 575–600.

Fehr, B., & Russell, J. A. (1991). The concept of love viewed from a prototype perspective. *Journal of Personality and Social Psychology, 60,* 425–438.

Feingold, A. (1990). Gender differences in effects of physical attractiveness on romantic attraction: A comparison across five research paradigms. *Journal of Personality and Social Psychology, 59,* 981–993.

Feingold, A. (1992). Gender differences in mate selection preferences: A test of the parental investment model. *Psychological Bulletin, 112,* 125–139.

Felmlee, D. H. (1995). Fatal attractions: Affection and disaffection in intimate relationships. *Journal of Social and Personal Relationships, 12,* 295–311.

Felmlee, D. H. (1998). Fatal attraction. In B. H. Spitzberg & W. R. Cupach (Eds.), *The dark side of close relationships* (pp. 3–31). Mahwah, NJ: Erlbaum.

Felmlee, D. H. (2001a). From appealing to appalling: Disenchantment with a romantic partner. *Sociological Perspectives, 44,* 263–280.

Felmlee, D. H. (2001b). No couple is an island: A social network perspective on dyadic stability. *Social Forces, 79,* 1259–1287.

Ferreira, L. C., Narciso, I., & Novo, R. F. (2012). Intimacy, sexual desire and differentiation in couplehood: A theoretical and methodological review. *Journal of Sex & Marital Therapy, 38,* 263–280.

Fincham, F. D., Paleari, F. G., & Regalia, C. (2002). Forgiveness in marriage: The role of relationship quality, attributions, and empathy. *Personal Relationships, 9,* 27–37.

Fine, M. A., & Harvey, J. H. (Eds.). (2006). *Handbook of divorce and dissolution.* Mahwah, NJ: Erlbaum.

Finkel, E. J., Eastwick, P. W., Karney, B. R., Reis, H. T., & Sprecher, S. (2012). Online dating: A critical analysis from the perspective of psychological science. *Psychological Science in the Public Interest, 13,* 3–66.

Finkelhor, D., & Yllö, K. (1985). *License to rape: Sexual abuse of wives.* New York, NY: Holt, Rinehart & Winston.

Fischer, K. W., Shaver, P. R., & Carnochan, P. (1990). How emotions develop and how they organize development. *Cognition and Emotion, 4,* 81–127.

Fisher, H. E. (1989). Evolution of human serial pairbonding. *American Journal of Physical Anthropology, 78,* 331–354.

Fisher, H. E. (1992). *Anatomy of love: A natural history of mating, marriage, and why we stray.* New York, NY: Fawcett Columbine.

Fisher, H. E. (1998). Lust, attraction, and attachment in mammalian reproduction. *Human Nature, 9,* 23–52.

Fisher, H. (2000). Lust, attraction, attachment: Biology and evolution of three primary emotion systems for mating, reproduction, and parenting. *Journal of Sex Education and Therapy, 25,* 96–104.

Fisher, H. (2006). The drive to love: The neural mechanism for mate selection. In R. J. Sternberg & K. Weis (Eds.), *The new psychology of love* (pp. 87–115). New Haven, CT: Yale University Press.

Fisher, H. E., Aron, A., Mashek, D., Li, H., & Brown, L. L. (2002). Defining the brain systems of lust, romantic attraction, and attachment. *Archives of Sexual Behavior, 31,* 413–419.

Fisher, R. A. (1958). *The genetical theory of natural selection* (2nd ed.). Oxford, England: Clarendon.

Fletcher, G. J. O., Kerr, P. S. G., Li, N. P., & Valentine, K. A. (2014). Predicting romantic interest and decisions in the very early stages of mate selection: Standards, accuracy, and sex differences. *Personality and Social Psychology Bulletin, 40,* 540–550.

Fletcher, G. J. O., & Thomas, G. (1996). Close relationship lay theories: Their structure and function. In G. J. O. Fletcher & J. Fitness (Eds.), *Knowledge structures in close relationships: A social psychological approach* (pp. 3–24). Mahwah, NJ: Erlbaum.

Franzoi, S. L., & Herzog, M. E. (1987). Judging physical attractiveness: What body aspects do we use? *Personality and Social Psychology Bulletin, 13,* 19–33.

Frayser, S. G. (1989). Sexual and reproductive relationships: Cross-cultural evidence and biosocial implications. *Medical Anthropology, 11,* 385–407.

Frazier, P. A., & Cook, S. W. (1993). Correlates of distress following heterosexual relationship dissolution. *Journal of Social and Personal Relationships, 10,* 55–67.

Fricker, J., & Moore, S. (2002). Relationship satisfaction: The role of love styles and attachment styles. *Current Research in Social Psychology, 7,* 182–204.

Frieze, I. H. (Ed.). (2012). Issues of gender in stalking research [Special issue]. *Sex Roles, 66*(5–6).

Frieze, I. H., & Browne, A. (1989). Violence in marriage. In L. Ohlin & M. Tonry (Eds.), *Family violence* (Vol. 11, pp. 163–218). Chicago, IL: The University of Chicago Press.

Frisco, M. L., & Williams, K. (2003). Perceived housework equity, marital happiness, and divorce in dual-earner households. *Journal of Family Issues, 24,* 51–73.

Fromm, E. (1956). *The art of loving.* New York, NY: Harper & Row.

Furnham, A., Tan, T., & McManus, C. (1997). Waist-to-hip ratio and preferences for body shape: A replication and extension. *Personality and Individual Differences, 22,* 539–549.

Gable, S. L., & Reis, H. T. (2006). Intimacy and the self: An iterative model of the self and close relationships. In P. Noller & J. A. Feeney (Eds.), *Close relationships: Functions, forms and processes* (pp. 211–225). Hove, England: Psychology Press.

Gagnon, J. H., & Simon, W. (1973). *Sexual conduct: The social sources of human sexuality.* Chicago, IL: Aldine.

Galliher, R. V., & Bentley, C. G. (2010). Links between rejection sensitivity and adolescent romantic relationship functioning: The mediating role of problem-solving behaviors. *Journal of Aggression, Maltreatment & Trauma, 19,* 603–623.

Gana, K., Saada, Y., & Untas, A. (2013). Effects of love styles on marital satisfaction in heterosexual couples: A dyadic approach. *Marriage & Family Review, 48,* 754–772.

Gangestad, S. W. (1993). Sexual selection and physical attractiveness: Implications for mating dynamics. *Human Nature, 4,* 205–235.

Gangestad, S. W., & Simpson, J. A. (1990). Toward an evolutionary history of female sociosexual variation. *Journal of Personality, 58,* 69–96.

Gangestad, S. W., & Simpson, J. A. (2000). The evolution of human mating: Trade-offs and strategic pluralism. *Behavioral and Brain Sciences, 23,* 573–587.

Garcia, L. T. (2006). Perceptions of sexual experience and preferences for dating and marriage. *The Canadian Journal of Human Sexuality, 15,* 85–94.

Garcia-Moreno, C., Jansen, H. A. F. M., Ellsberg, M., Heise, L., & Watts, C. H. (2006). Prevalence of intimate partner violence: Findings from the WHO multi-country study on women's health and domestic violence. *The Lancet, 368,* 1260–1269.

Geistman, J., Smith, B., Lambert, E. G., & Cluse-Tolar, T. (2013). What to do about stalking: A preliminary study of how stalking victims responded to stalking and their perceptions of the effectiveness of these actions. *Criminal Justice Studies, 1,* 43–66.

Gelles, R. J., & Harrop, J. W. (1989). Violence, battering, and psychological distress among women. *Journal of Interpersonal Violence, 4,* 400–420.

Ghimire, D. J., Axinn, W. G., Yabiku, S. T., & Thornton, A. (2006). Social change, premarital nonfamily experience, and spouse choice in an arranged marriage society. *American Journal of Sociology, 111,* 1181–1218.

Gidycz, C. A., Warkentin, J. B., & Orchowski, L. M. (2007). Predictors of verbal, physical, and sexual violence: A prospective analysis of college men. *Psychology of Men & Masculinity, 8,* 79–94.

Gilbert, L. (1993). *Two careers/one family.* Newbury Park, CA: Sage.

Givens, D. B. (1978). The nonverbal basis of attraction: Flirtation, courtship, and seduction. *Psychiatry, 41,* 346–359.

Glenn, N. D., & Weaver, N. (1979). Attitudes toward premarital, extramarital, and homosexual relations in the U.S. in the 1970s. *Journal of Sex Research, 15*, 108–119.

Gold, S. R., Sinclair, B. B., & Balge, K. A. (1999). Risk of sexual victimization: A theoretical model. *Aggression and Violent Behavior, 4*, 457–470.

Goldberg, A. E., & Perry-Jenkins, M. (2007). The division of labor and perceptions of parental roles: Lesbian couples across the transition to parenthood. *Journal of Social and Personal Relationships, 24*, 297–318.

Goldberg, L. R. (1993). The structure of phenotypic personality traits. *American Psychologist, 48*, 26–34.

Golding, J. M. (1999). Intimate partner violence as a risk factor for mental disorders: A meta-analysis. *Journal of Family Violence, 14*, 99–132.

Gonzaga, G. C., Carter, S., & Buckwalter, J. G. (2010). Assortative mating, convergence, and satisfaction in married couples. *Personal Relationships, 17*, 634–644.

Goodboy, A. K., & Myers, S. A. (2010). Relational quality indicators and love styles as predictors of negative relational maintenance behaviors in romantic relationships. *Communication Reports, 23*, 65–78.

Goodwin, R. (1999). *Personal relationships across cultures.* London, England: Routledge.

Goodwin, R., & Soon, A. P. Y. (1994). Self-monitoring and relationship adjustment: A cross-cultural analysis. *Journal of Social Psychology, 134*, 35–39.

Goodwin, R., & Tang, D. (1991). Preferences for friends and close relationship partners: A cross-cultural comparison. *Journal of Social Psychology, 131*, 579–581.

Gordon, C. L., & Baucom, D. H. (2009). Examining the individual within marriage: Personal strengths and relationship satisfaction. *Personal Relationships, 16*, 421–435.

Gottman, J. M. (1993). The roles of conflict engagement, escalation, and avoidance in marital interaction: A longitudinal view of five types of couples. *Journal of Consulting and Clinical Psychology, 61*, 6–15.

Gottman, J. M. (1994a). *What predicts divorce? The relationship between marital processes and marital outcomes.* Hillsdale, NJ: Erlbaum.

Gottman, J. M. (1994b). *Why marriages succeed or fail . . . and how you can make yours last.* New York, NY: Simon & Schuster.

Gottman, J. M. (1998). Psychology and the study of marital processes. *Annual Review of Psychology, 49*, 169–197.

Gottman, J. M. (1999). *The marriage clinic: A scientifically-based marital therapy.* New York, NY: W. W. Norton.

Gottman, J. M., & Driver, J. L. (2005). Dysfunctional marital conflict and everyday marital interaction. *Journal of Divorce & Remarriage, 43*, 63–77.

Gottman, J. M., & Gottman, J. S. (2008). Gottman method couple therapy. In A. S. Gurman (Ed.), *Clinical handbook of couple therapy* (4th ed., pp. 138–164). New York, NY: Guilford Press.

Gottman, J. M., & Krokoff, L. J. (1989). Marital interaction and satisfaction: A longitudinal view. *Journal of Consulting and Clinical Psychology, 57*, 47–52.

Gottman, J. M., & Levenson, R. W. (1988). The social psychophysiology of marriage. In P. Noller & M. A. Fitzpatrick (Eds.), *Perspectives on marital interaction* (pp. 182–200). Philadelphia, PA: Multilingual Matters.

Gottman, J. M., & Levenson, R. W. (1992). Marital processes predictive of later dissolution: Behavior, physiology, and health. *Journal of Personality and Social Psychology, 63,* 221–233.

Gough, H. G. (1987). *CPI, California Psychological Inventory: Administrator's guide.* Palo Alto, CA: Consulting Psychologists Press.

Graham, J. M., & Christiansen, K. (2009). The reliability of romantic love: A reliability generalization meta-analysis. *Personal Relationships, 16,* 49–66.

Graham-Kevan, N., & Archer, J. (2003). Intimate terrorism and common couple violence: A test of Johnson's predictions in four British samples. *Journal of Interpersonal Violence, 18,* 1247–1270.

Grammer, K., & Thornhill, R. (1994). Human (homo sapiens) facial attractiveness and sexual selection: The role of symmetry and averageness. *Journal of Comparative Psychology, 108,* 233–242.

Graziano, W. G., Jensen-Campbell, L. A., Todd, M., & Finch, J. F. (1997). Interpersonal attraction from an evolutionary psychology perspective: Women's reactions to dominant and prosocial men. In J. A. Simpson & D. T. Kenrick (Eds.), *Evolutionary social psychology* (pp. 141–167). Mahwah, NJ: Erlbaum.

Greeley, A. M. (1991). *Faithful attraction: Discovering intimacy, love, and fidelity in American marriage.* New York, NY: St. Martin's Press.

Green, L., Fein, D., Modahl, C., Feinstein, C., Waterhouse, L., & Morris, M. (2001). Oxytocin and autistic disorder: Alterations in peptide forms. *Biological Psychiatry, 50,* 609–613.

Green, S. K., & Sandos, P. (1983). Perceptions of male and female initiators of relationships. *Sex Roles, 9,* 849–852.

Greenberg, L. S., & Johnson, S. M. (1988). *Emotionally focused therapy for couples.* New York, NY: Guilford Press.

Greenblat, C. S. (1983). The salience of sexuality in the early years of marriage. *Journal of Marriage and the Family, 45,* 289–299.

Groth, A. N. (1979). Patterns of rape. In A. N. Groth (Ed.), *Men who rape: The psychology of the offender* (pp. 174–180). New York, NY: Plenum Press.

Guerrero, D. A. V. (2009). Hypermasculinity, intimate partner violence, sexual aggression, social support, and child maltreatment risk in urban, heterosexual fathers taking parenting classes. *Child Welfare: Journal of Policy, Practice, and Program, 88,* 135–155.

Guerrero, L. K., La Valley, A. G., & Farinelli, L. (2008). The experience and expression of anger, guilt, and sadness in marriage: An equity theory explanation. *Journal of Social and Personal Relationships, 25,* 699–724.

Guerrero, L. K., Trost, M. R., & Yoshimura, S. M. (2005). Romantic jealousy: Emotions and communicative responses. *Personal Relationships, 12,* 233–252.

Gurman, A. S. (2013). Behavioral couple therapy: Building a secure base for therapeutic integration. *Family Process, 52,* 115–138.

Guzzo, K. B. (2009). Marital intentions and the stability of first cohabitations. *Journal of Family Issues, 30,* 179–205.

Ha, T., van den Berg, J. E. M., Engels, R. C. M. E., & Lichtwarck-Aschoff, A. (2012). Effects of attractiveness and status in dating desire in homosexual and heterosexual men and women. *Archives of Sexual Behavior, 41,* 673–682.

Haas, S. M., & Stafford, L. (1998). An initial examination of maintenance behaviors in gay and lesbian relationships. *Journal of Social and Personal Relationships, 15,* 846–855.

Haavio-Mannila, E., & Kontula, O. (2003). Single and double standards in Finland, Estonia, and St. Petersburg. *The Journal of Sex Research, 40,* 36–49.

Hackathorn, J., & Brantley, A. (2014). To know you is (not) to want you: Mediators between sociosexual orientation and romantic commitment. *Current Psychology: A Journal for Diverse Perspectives on Diverse Psychological Issues, 33,* 89–97.

Hadden, B. W., Smith, C. V., & Webster, G. D. (2014). Relationship duration moderates associations between attachment and relationship quality: Meta-analytic support for the temporal adult romantic attachment model. *Personality and Social Psychology Review, 18,* 42–58.

Hahlweg, K., & Markman, H. J. (1988). Effectiveness of behavioral marital therapy: Empirical status of behavioral techniques in preventing and alleviating marital distress. *Journal of Consulting and Clinical Psychology, 56,* 440–447.

Hall, H. F. (1901). *Napoleon's letters to Josephine, 1796–1812.* London, England: J. M. Dent.

Hall, J. H., & Fincham, F. D. (2006). Relationship dissolution following infidelity. In M. A. Fine & J. H. Harvey (Eds.), *Handbook of divorce and dissolution* (pp. 153–168). Mahwah, NJ: Erlbaum.

Hall, J. H., & Fincham, F. D. (2009). Psychological distress: Precursor or consequence of dating infidelity? *Personality and Social Psychology Bulletin, 35,* 143–159.

Hällström, T., & Samuelsson, S. (1990). Changes in women's sexual desire in middle life: The longitudinal study of women in Gothenburg. *Archives of Sexual Behavior, 19,* 259–268.

Hamon, R. R., & Ingoldsby, B. B. (Eds.). (2003). *Mate selection across cultures.* Thousand Oaks, CA: Sage.

Hampson, S. (1999). State of the art: Personality. *The Psychologist, 12,* 284–288.

Haning, R. V., O'Keefe, S. L., Randall, E. J., Kommor, M. J., Baker, E., & Wilson, R. (2007). Intimacy, orgasm likelihood, and conflict predict sexual satisfaction in heterosexual male and female respondents. *Journal of Sex & Marital Therapy, 33,* 93–113.

Harper, M. S., Dickson, J. W., & Welsh, D. P. (2006). Self-silencing and rejection sensitivity in adolescent romantic relationships. *Journal of Youth and Adolescence, 35,* 459–467.

Harris, C. R. (2002). Sexual and romantic jealousy in heterosexual and homosexual adults. *Psychological Science, 13,* 7–12.

Harris, C. R. (2003). A review of sex differences in sexual jealousy, including self-report data, psychophysiological responses, interpersonal violence, and morbid jealousy. *Personality and Social Psychology Review, 7,* 102–128.

Harris, C. R., & Christenfeld, N. (1996). Gender, jealousy, and reason. *Psychological Science, 7,* 364–366.

Hartmann, U. H., Rüffer-Hesse, C., Krüger, T. H. C., & Philippsohn, S. (2012). Individual and dyadic barriers to a pharmacotherapeutic treatment of hypoactive sexual desire disorders: Results and implications from a small-scale study with bupropion. *Journal of Sex & Marital Therapy, 38,* 325–348.

Harvey, J. H., & Fine, M. A. (2006). Social construction of accounts in the process of relationship termination. In M. A. Fine & J. H. Harvey (Eds.), *Handbook of divorce and dissolution* (pp. 189–199). Mahwah, NJ: Erlbaum.

Harvey, J. H., Weber, A. L., Galvin, K. S., Huszti, H. C., & Garnick, N. N. (1986). Attribution in the termination of close relationships: A special focus on the account. In R. Gilmour & S. Duck (Eds.), *The emerging field of close relationships* (pp. 189–201). Hillsdale, NJ: Erlbaum.

Harvey, J. H., Wenzel, A., & Sprecher, S. (Eds.). (2004). *The handbook of sexuality in close relationships.* Mahwah, NJ: Erlbaum.

Harvey, S. M., Beckman, L. J., Browner, C. H., & Sherman, C. A. (2002). Relationship power, decision making, and sexual relations: An exploratory study with couples of Mexican origin. *The Journal of Sex Research, 39,* 284–291.

Hatch, L. R., & Bulcroft, K. (2004). Does long-term marriage bring less frequent disagreements? Five explanatory frameworks. *Journal of Family Issues, 25,* 465–495.

Hatfield, E., Bensman, L., & Rapson, R. L. (2012). A brief history of social scientists' attempts to measure passionate love. *Journal of Social and Personal Relationships, 29,* 143–164.

Hatfield, E., Greenberger, D., Traupmann, J., & Lambert, P. (1982). Equity and sexual satisfaction in recently married couples. *Journal of Sex Research, 17,* 18–32.

Hatfield, E., & Rapson, R. L. (1993). *Love, sex, and intimacy: Their psychology, biology, and history.* New York, NY: HarperCollins.

Hatfield, E., & Rapson, R. L. (1996). *Love and sex: Cross-cultural perspectives.* Needham Heights, MA: Allyn & Bacon.

Hatfield, E., & Rapson, R. L. (2012). Equity theory in close relationships. In P. A. M. Van Lange, A. W. Kruglanski, & E. T. Higgins (Eds.), *Handbook of theories of social psychology* (Vol. 2, pp. 200–217). Thousand Oaks, CA: Sage.

Hatfield, E., & Sprecher, S. (1986). Measuring passionate love in intimate relationships. *Journal of Adolescence, 9,* 383–410.

Hatfield, E., Traupmann, J., & Sprecher, S. (1984). Older women's perceptions of their intimate relationships. *Journal of Social and Clinical Psychology, 2,* 108–124.

Hatfield, E., Utne, M. K., & Traupmann, J. (1979). Equity theory and intimate relationships. In R. L. Burgess & T. L. Huston (Eds.), *Social exchange in developing relationships* (pp. 99–133). New York, NY: Academic Press.

Hatton, H., Donnellan, M. B., Maysn, K., Feldman, B. J., Larsen-Rife, D., & Conger, R. D. (2008). Family and individual difference predictors of trait aspects of negative interpersonal behaviors during emerging adulthood. *Journal of Family Psychology, 22,* 448–455.

Haugaard, J. J., & Seri, L. G. (2003). Stalking and other forms of intrusive contact after the dissolution of adolescent dating or romantic relationships. *Violence and Victims, 18,* 279–297.

Hawkes, C. H. (1992). Endorphins: The basis of pleasure? *Journal of Neurology, Neurosurgery & Psychiatry, 55,* 247–250.

Haythornthwaite, C., Wellman, B., & Garton, L. (1998). Work and community via computer-mediated communication. In J. Gackenbach (Ed.), *Psychology and the Internet: Intrapersonal, interpersonal, and transpersonal implications* (pp. 29–42). San Diego, CA: Academic Press.

Hazan, C., & Shaver, P. (1987). Romantic love conceptualized as an attachment process. *Journal of Personality and Social Psychology, 52,* 510–524.

Heavey, C. L., Christensen, A., & Malamuth, N. M. (1995). The longitudinal impact of demand and withdrawal during marital conflict. *Journal of Consulting and Clinical Psychology, 63,* 797–801.

Heavey, C. L., Layne, C., & Christensen, A. (1993). Gender and conflict structure in marital interaction: A replication and extension. *Journal of Consulting and Clinical Psychology, 61,* 16–27.

Heimdal, M. R., Dørmænen, A., & Træen, B. (2008). Conflicts among Norwegian couples. *Tidsskrift for Norsk Psykologforening, 45,* 695–703. [English abstract]

Heine, S. J., & Buchtel, E. E. (2009). Personality: The universal and the culturally specific. *Annual Review of Psychology, 60,* 369–394.

Helms, H. M., Proulx, C. M., Klute, M. M., McHale, S. M., & Crouter, A. C. (2006). Spouses' gender-typed attributes and their links with marital quality: A pattern analytic approach. *Journal of Social and Personal Relationships, 23,* 843–864.

Henderson-King, D. H., & Veroff, J. (1994). Sexual satisfaction and marital well-being in the first years of marriage. *Journal of Social and Personal Relationships, 11,* 509–534.

Hendrick, C., & Hendrick, S. S. (1986). A theory and method of love. *Journal of Personality and Social Psychology, 50,* 392–402.

Hendrick, C., & Hendrick, S. S. (1988). Lovers wear rose colored glasses. *Journal of Social and Personal Relationships, 5,* 161–183.

Hendrick, C., & Hendrick, S. S. (1989). Research on love: Does it measure up? *Journal of Personality and Social Psychology, 56,* 784–794.

Hendrick, C., & Hendrick, S. S. (1990). A relationship-specific version of the Love Attitudes Scale. *Journal of Social Behavior and Personality, 5,* 239–254.

Hendrick, C., & Hendrick, S. S. (2006). Styles of romantic love. In R. J. Sternberg & K. Weis (Eds.), *The new psychology of love* (pp. 149–170). New Haven, CT: Yale University Press.

Hendrick, C., Hendrick, S. S., & Dicke, A. (1998). The Love Attitudes Scale: Short Form. *Journal of Social and Personal Relationships, 15,* 147–159.

Hendrick, C., Hendrick, S. S., Foote, F. H., & Slapion-Foote, M. J. (1984). Do men and women love differently? *Journal of Social and Personal Relationships, 1,* 177–195.

Hendrick, C., Hendrick, S. S., & Reich, D. A. (2006). The brief sexual attitudes scale. *The Journal of Sex Research, 43,* 76–86.

Hendrick, S. S., & Hendrick, C. (1987). Love and sex attitudes and religious beliefs. *Journal of Social and Clinical Psychology, 5,* 391–398.

Hendrick, S. S., & Hendrick, C. (1992). *Liking, loving, and relating* (2nd ed.). Pacific Grove, CA: Brooks/Cole.

Hendrick, S. S., & Hendrick, C. (1995). Gender differences and similarities in sex and love. *Personal Relationships, 2,* 55–65.

Hendrick, S. S., & Hendrick, C. (2002). Linking romantic love with sex: Development of the Perceptions of Love and Sex Scale. *Journal of Social and Personal Relationships, 19,* 361–378.

Hendrick, S. S., Hendrick, C., & Adler, N. L. (1988). Romantic relationships: Love, satisfaction, and staying together. *Journal of Personality and Social Psychology, 54,* 980–988.

Hendrick, S. S., Hendrick, C., Slapion-Foote, M. J., & Foote, F. H. (1985). Gender differences in sexual attitudes. *Journal of Personality and Social Psychology, 48,* 1630–1642.

Henning, K., Renauer, B., & Holdford, R. (2006). Victim or offender? Heterogeneity among women arrested for intimate partner violence. *Journal of Family Violence, 21,* 351–368.

Henss, R. (1995). Waist-to-hip ratio and attractiveness: Replication and extension. *Personality and Individual Differences, 19,* 479–488.

Herbenick, D., Reece, M., Schick, V., Sanders, S. A., Dodge, B., & Fortenberry, J. D. (2010). Sexual behaviors, relationships, and perceived health status among adult women in the United States: Results from a national probability sample. *Journal of Sexual Medicine, 7(suppl. 5),* 277–290.

Herlitz, C., & Ramstedt, K. (2005). Assessment of sexual behavior, sexual attitudes, and sexual risk in Sweden (1989–2003). *Archives of Sexual Behavior, 34,* 219–229.

Herold, E. S., Mantle, D., & Zemitis, O. (1979). A study of sexual offenses against females. *Adolescence, 14,* 65–72.

Hill, C. A., Blakemore, J. E. O., & Drumm, P. (1997). Mutual and unrequited love in adolescence and young adulthood. *Personal Relationships, 4,* 15–23.

Hill, R. (1945). Campus values in mate-selection. *Journal of Home Economics, 37,* 554–558.

Hiller, J. (2004). Speculations on the links between feelings, emotions and sexual behaviour: Are vasopressin and oxytocin involved? *Sexual and Relationship Therapy, 19,* 393–412.

Hines, D. A., Brown, J., & Dunning, E. (2007). Characteristics of callers to the Domestic Abuse Hotline for Men. *Journal of Family Violence, 22,* 63–72.

Hines, D. A., & Malley-Morrison, K. (2005). *Family violence in the United States: Defining, understanding, and combating abuse.* Thousand Oaks, CA: Sage.

Hoffnung, M. (2004). Wanting it all: Career, marriage, and motherhood during college-educated women's 20s. *Sex Roles, 50,* 711–723.

Hogben, M., & Byrne, D. (1998). Using social learning theory to explain individual differences in human sexuality. *Journal of Sex Research, 35,* 58–71.

Holley, S. R., Sturm, V. E., & Levenson, R. W. (2010). Exploring the basis for gender differences in the demand-withdraw pattern. *Journal of Homosexuality, 57,* 666–684.

Holmes, B. M., & Johnson, K. R. (2009). Adult attachment and romantic partner preference: A review. *Journal of Personal and Social Relationships, 26,* 833–852.

Holmes, J. G. (2000). Social relationships: The nature and function of relational schemas. *European Journal of Social Psychology, 30,* 447–495.

Homans, G. (1961). *Social behavior: Its elementary forms.* New York, NY: Harcourt, Brace & World.

Hoyt, L. L., & Hudson, J. W. (1981). Personal characteristics important in mate preference among college students. *Social Behavior and Personality, 9,* 93–96.

Huang, C. L., & Yang, S. C. (2013). A study of online misrepresentation, self-disclosure, cyber-relationship motives, and loneliness among teenagers in Taiwan. *Journal of Educational Computing Research, 48,* 1–18.

Hudson, J. W., & Henze, L. F. (1969). Campus values in mate selection: A replication. *Journal of Marriage and the Family, 31,* 772–775.

Hunt, M. (1974). *Sexual behavior in the 1970s.* Chicago, IL: Playboy Press.

Huston, T. L. (1973). Ambiguity of acceptance, social desirability, and dating choice. *Journal of Experimental Social Psychology, 9,* 32–42.

Huston, T. L. (2009). What's love got to do with it? Why some marriages succeed and others fail. *Personal Relationships, 16,* 301–327.

Huston, T. L., Caughlin, J. P., Houts, R. M., Smith, S. E., & George, L. J. (2001). The connubial crucible: Newlywed years as predictors of marital delight, distress, and divorce. *Journal of Personality and Social Psychology, 80,* 237–252.

Huston, T. L., & Levinger, G. (1978). Interpersonal attraction and relationships. *Annual Review of Psychology, 29,* 115–156.

Huston, T. L., McHale, S. M., & Crouter, A. C. (1986). When the honeymoon's over: Changes in the marriage relationship over the first year. In R. Gilmour & S. Duck (Eds.), *The emerging field of personal relationships* (pp. 109–132). Hillsdale, NJ: Erlbaum.

IJzerman, H., Blanken, I., Brandt, M. J., Oerlemans, J. M., Van den Hoogenhof, M. M. W., Franken, S. J. M., & Oerlemans, M. W. G. (2014). Sex differences in distress from infidelity in early adulthood and in later life. *Social Psychology, 45,* 202–208.

Ingoldsby, B., Schvaneveldt, P., & Uribe, C. (2003). Perceptions of acceptable mate attributes in Ecuador. *Journal of Comparative Family Studies, 34,* 171–185.

Insel, T. R. (1997). A neurobiological basis of social attachment. *American Journal of Psychiatry, 154,* 726–735.

Insel, T. R. (2000). Toward a neurobiology of attachment. *Review of General Psychology, 4,* 176–185.

InternetWorldStats.com (2012, June 30). *Internet world stats: Usage and population statistics.* Retrieved July 28, 2014 from http://www.internetworldstats.com/stats.htm

Isaac, R., & Shah, A. (2004). Sex roles and marital adjustment in Indian couples. *International Journal of Social Psychiatry, 50,* 129–141.

Islam, M. M. (2012). The practice of consanguineous marriage in Oman: Prevalence, trends and determinants. *Journal of Biosocial Science, 44,* 571–594.

Jack, D. C. (1991). *Silencing the self: Women and depression.* Cambridge, MA: Harvard University Press.

Jackson, J. B., Miller, R. B., Oka, M., & Henry, R. G. (2014). Gender differences in marital satisfaction: A meta-analysis. *Journal of Marriage and Family, 76,* 105–129.

Jacobson, N. S., & Christensen, A. (1996). *Integrative couple therapy: Promoting acceptance and change.* New York, NY: W. W. Norton & Co.

Jacobson, N. S., Christensen, A., Prince, S. E., Cordova, J., & Eldridge, K. (2000). Integrative behavioral couple therapy: An acceptance-based, promising new treatment for couple discord. *Journal of Consulting and Clinical Psychology, 68,* 351–355.

Jacobson, N. S., & Margolin, G. (1979*). Marital therapy: Strategies based on social learning and behavior exchange principles.* New York, NY: Brunner/Mazel.

James, W. H. (1981). The honeymoon effect on marital coitus. *Journal of Sex Research, 17,* 114–123.

Jamison, T. B., & Ganong, L. (2011). "We're not living together:" Stayover relationships among college-educated emerging adults. *Journal of Social and Personal Relationships, 28,* 536–557.

Jamison, T. B., & Proulx, C. M. (2013). Stayovers in emerging adulthood: Who stays over and why? *Personal Relationships, 20,* 155–169.

Jankowiak, W. (Ed.). (1995). *Romantic passion: A universal experience?* New York, NY: Columbia University Press.

Jankowiak, W., & Hardgrave, M. D. (2007). Individual and societal response to sexual betrayal: A view from around the world. *Electronic Journal of Human Sexuality, 10,* 1–7.

Jankowiak, W. R., & Fischer, E. F. (1992). A cross-cultural perspective on romantic love. *Ethnology, 31,* 149–155.

Jason, L. A., Reichler, A., Easton, J., Neal, A., & Wilson, M. (1984). Female harassment after ending a relationship: A preliminary study. *Alternative Lifestyles, 6,* 259–269.

Jefferis, B. G., & Nichols, J. L. (1896). *Search lights on health. Light on dark corners. A complete sexual science and a guide to purity and physical manhood. Advice to maiden, wife, and mother. Love, courtship and marriage* (18th ed.). Naperville, IL: J. L. Nichols.

Jensen-Campbell, L. A., Graziano, W. G., & West, S. (1995). Dominance, prosocial orientation, and female preferences: Do nice guys really finish last? *Journal of Personality and Social Psychology, 68,* 427–440.

Jesser, C. J. (1978). Male responses to direct verbal sexual initiatives of females. *Journal of Sex Research, 14,* 118–128.

Jockin, V., McGue, M., & Lykken, D. T. (1996). Personality and divorce: A genetic analysis. *Journal of Personality and Social Psychology, 71,* 288–299.

Johnson, M. D., & Bradbury, T. N. (1999). Marital satisfaction and topographical assessment of marital interaction: A longitudinal analysis of newlywed couples. *Personal Relationships, 6,* 19–40.

Johnson, M. P. (1999, November). *Two types of violence against women in the American family: Identifying patriarchal terrorism and common couple violence.* Paper presented at the annual meeting of the National Council on Family Relations, Irvine, CA.

Johnson, M. P. (2006). Conflict and control: Gender symmetry and asymmetry in domestic violence. *Violence Against Women, 12,* 1003–1018.

Johnson, M. P. (2008). *A typology of domestic violence: Intimate terrorism, violent resistance, and situational couple violence.* Boston, MA: Northeastern University Press.

Johnson, M. P., & Leone, J. M. (2005). The differential effects of intimate terrorism and situational couple violence: Findings from the National Violence Against Women survey. *Journal of Family Issues, 26,* 322–349.

Johnson, S. M. (2004). *The practice of emotionally focused couple therapy: Creating connection* (2nd ed.). New York, NY: Brunner-Routledge.

Johnson, S. M. (2008). Emotionally focused couple therapy. In A. S. Gurman (Ed.), *Clinical handbook of couple therapy* (4th ed., pp. 107–137). New York, NY: Guilford Press.

Johnson, S. M. (2009). Emotionally focused couple therapy. In H. T. Reis & S. K. Sprecher (Eds.), *Encyclopedia of human relationships* (Vol. 1, pp. 497–500). Thousand Oaks, CA: Sage.

Johnson, S. M., & Greenberg, L. S. (1995). The emotionally focused approach to problems in adult attachment. In N. S. Jacobson & A. S. Gurman (Eds.), *Clinical handbook of couple therapy* (pp. 121–141). New York, NY: Guilford Press.

Jones, D., & Hill, K. (1993). Criteria of facial attractiveness in five populations. *Human Nature, 4,* 271–296.

Jones, M. (1993). Influence of self-monitoring on dating motivations. *Journal of Research in Personality, 27,* 197–206.

Jones, M. (1998). Sociosexuality and motivations for romantic involvement. *Journal of Research in Personality, 32,* 173–182.

Jose, A., O'Leary, K. D., & Moyer, A. (2010). Does premarital cohabitation predict subsequent marital stability and marital quality? A meta-analysis. *Journal of Marriage and Family, 72,* 105–116.

Judkins, B., & Presser, L. (2008). Division of eco-friendly household labor and the marital relationship. *Journal of Social and Personal Relationships, 25,* 923–941.

Juhasz, A. M., Kaufman, B., & Meyer, H. (1986). Adolescent attitudes and beliefs about sexual behavior. *Child and Adolescent Social Work, 3,* 177–193.

Kalmijn, M., & Monden, C. W. S. (2011). The division of labor and depressive symptoms at the couple level: Effects of equity or specialization? *Journal of Social and Personal Relationships, 29,* 358–374.

Kamo, Y. (1993). Determinants of marital satisfaction: A comparison of the United States and Japan. *Journal of Social and Personal Relationships, 10,* 551–568.

Kanin, E. J. (1967). An examination of sexual aggression as a response to sexual frustration. *Journal of Marriage and the Family, 29,* 428–433.

Kanin, E. J. (1984). Date rape: Unofficial criminals and victims. *Victimology: An International Journal, 9,* 95–108.

Kanin, E. J. (1985). Date rapists: Differential sexual socialization and relative deprivation. *Archives of Sexual Behavior, 14,* 219–231.

Kaplan, H. S. (1979). *Disorders of sexual desire and other new concepts and techniques in sex therapy.* New York, NY: Simon & Schuster.

Karen, R. (1990, February). Becoming attached. *The Atlantic Monthly,* pp. 35–70.

Karlson, P., & Lüscher, M. (1959). "Pheromones": A new term for a class of biologically active substances. *Nature, 183,* 55–56.

Karney, B. R., & Bradbury, T. N. (1997). Neuroticism, marital interaction, and the trajectory of marital satisfaction. *Journal of Personality and Social Psychology, 72,* 1075–1092.

Karney, B. R., & Bradbury, T. N. (2000). Attributions in marriage: State or trait? A growth curve analysis. *Journal of Personality and Social Psychology, 78,* 295–309.

Karra, M. V., Stark, N. N., & Wolf, J. (1997). Male involvement in family planning: A case study spanning five generations of a South Indian family. *Studies in Family Planning, 28,* 24–34.

Karraker, A., DeLamater, J., & Schwartz, C. R. (2011). Sexual frequency decline from midlife to later life. *The Journals of Gerontology, Series B: Psychological Sciences and Social Sciences, 66,* 502–512.

Kato, T. (2014). A reconsideration of sex differences in response to sexual and emotional infidelity. *Archives of Sexual Behavior, 43,* 1281–1288.

Kayser, K. (1993). *When love dies: The process of marital disaffection.* New York, NY: Guilford Press.

Kayser, K. (1996). The Marital Disaffection Scale: An inventory for assessing emotional estrangement in marriage. *The American Journal of Family Therapy, 24,* 83–88.

Kayser, K., & Rao, S. S. (2006). Process of disaffection in relationship break-down. In M. A. Fine & J. H. Harvey (Eds.), *Handbook of divorce and dissolution* (pp. 201–221). Mahwah, NJ: Erlbaum.

Kellas, J. K., & Manusov, V. (2003). What's in a story? The relationship between narrative completeness and adjustment to relationship dissolution. *Journal of Social and Personal Relationships, 20,* 285–307.

Kelley, H. H., Berscheid, E., Christensen, A., Harvey, J. H., Levinger, G., McClintock, E., Peplau, L. A., & Peterson, D. R. (Eds.). (1983). *Close relationships.* New York, NY: Freeman.

Kelly, E. L., & Conley, J. J. (1987). Personality and compatibility: A prospective analysis of marital stability and marital satisfaction. *Journal of Personality and Social Psychology, 52,* 27–40.

Kelly, J. B., & Johnson, M. P. (2008). Differentiation among types of intimate partner violence: Research update and implications for interventions. *Family Court Review, 46,* 476–499.

Kenrick, D. T., Groth, G. E., Trost, M. R., & Sadalla, E. K. (1993). Integrating evolutionary and social exchange perspectives on relationships: Effects of gender, self-appraisal, and involvement level on mate selection criteria. *Journal of Personality and Social Psychology, 64,* 951–969.

Kenrick, D. T., Sadalla, E. K., Groth, G., & Trost, M. R. (1990). Evolution, traits, and the stages of human courtship: Qualifying the parental investment model. *Journal of Personality, 58,* 97–116.

Kephart, W. M. (1967). Some correlates of romantic love. *Journal of Marriage and the Family, 29,* 470–474.

Kerckhoff, A. C. (1974). The social context of interpersonal attraction. In T. L. Huston (Ed.), *Foundations of interpersonal attraction* (pp. 61–76). New York, NY: Academic Press.

Kerckhoff, A. C., & Davis, K. E. (1962). Value consensus and need complementarity in mate selection. *American Sociological Review, 27,* 295–303.

Khallad, Y. (2005). Mate selection in Jordan: Effects of sex, socio-economic status, and culture. *Journal of Social and Personal Relationships, 22,* 155–168.

Kiesler, S., Siegel, J., & McGuire, T. W. (1984). Social psychological aspects of computer-mediated communication. *American Psychologist, 39,* 1123–1134.

King, C. E., & Christensen, A. (1983). The Relationship Events Scale: A Guttman scaling of progress in courtship. *Journal of Marriage and the Family, 45,* 671–678.

Kinsey, A. C., Pomeroy, W. B., & Martin, C. E. (1948). *Sexual behavior in the human male.* Philadelphia, PA: W. B. Saunders.

Kinsey, A. C., Pomeroy, W. B., Martin, C. E., & Gebhard, P. H. (1953). *Sexual behavior in the human female.* Philadelphia, PA: W. B. Saunders.

Kisler, T. S., & Christopher, F. S. (2008). Sexual exchanges and relationship satisfaction: Testing the role of sexual satisfaction as a mediator and gender as a moderator. *Journal of Social and Personal Relationships, 25,* 587–602.

Kline, G. H., Stanley, S. M., Markman, H. J., Olmos-Gallo, P. A., St. Peters, M., Whitton, S. W., & Prado, L. M. (2004). Timing is everything: Pre-engagement cohabitation and increased risk for poor marital outcomes. *Journal of Family Psychology, 18,* 311–318.

Kline Rhoades, G., Stanley, S. M., & Markman, H. J. (2006). Pre-engagement cohabitation and gender asymmetry in marital commitment. *Journal of Family Psychology, 20,* 553–560.

Klohnen, E. C., & Luo, S. (2003). Interpersonal attraction and personality: What is attractive–self-similarity, ideal similarity, complementarity, or attachment security? *Journal of Personality and Social Psychology, 85,* 709–722.

Knee, C. R. (1998). Implicit theories of relationships: Assessment and prediction of romantic relationship initiation, coping, and longevity. *Journal of Personality and Social Psychology, 74,* 360–370.

Knee, C. R., & Bush, A. L. (2008). Relationship beliefs and their role in romantic relationship initiation. In S. Sprecher, A. Wenzel, & J. Harvey (Eds.), *Handbook of relationship initiation* (pp. 471–485). New York, NY: Psychology Press, Inc.

Knox, D., Vail-Smith, K., & Zusman, M. (2008). "Men are dogs": Is the stereotype justified? Data on the cheating college male. *College Student Journal, 42,* 1015–1022.

Koenig, B. L., Kirkpatrick, L. A., & Ketelaar, T. (2007). Misperception of sexual and romantic interests in opposite-sex friendships: Four hypotheses. *Personal Relationships, 14,* 411–429.

Koss, M. P., Gidycz, C. A., & Wisniewski, N. (1987). The scope of rape: Incidence and prevalence of sexual aggression and victimization in a national sample of higher education students. *Journal of Consulting and Clinical Psychology, 55,* 162–170.

Kowalski, R. M. (1993). Inferring sexual interest from behavioral cues: Effects of gender and sexually relevant attitudes. *Sex Roles, 29,* 13–36.

Krahé, B., Scheinberger-Olwig, R., & Kolpin, S. (2000). Ambiguous communication of sexual intentions as a risk marker for sexual aggression. *Sex Roles, 42,* 313–337.

Kumagai, F. (1995). Families in Japan: Beliefs and realities. *Journal of Comparative Family Studies, 26,* 135–163.

Kunkel, A. W., & Burleson, B. R. (1999). Assessing explanations for sex differences in emotional support: A test of the different cultures and skill specialization accounts. *Human Communication Research, 25,* 307–340.

Kurdek, L. A. (1991). Sexuality in homosexual and heterosexual couples. In K. McKinney & S. Sprecher (Eds.), *Sexuality in close relationships* (pp. 177–191). Hillsdale, NJ: Erlbaum.

Kurdek, L. A. (1993a). The allocation of household labor in gay, lesbian, and heterosexual married couples. *Journal of Social Issues, 49,* 127–139.

Kurdek, L. A. (1993b). Predicting marital dissolution: A 5-year prospective longitudinal study of newlywed couples. *Journal of Personality and Social Psychology, 64,* 221–242.

Kurdek, L. A. (1999). The nature and predictors of the trajectory of change in marital quality for husbands and wives over the first 10 years of marriage. *Developmental Psychology, 35,* 1283–1296.

Kurdek, L. A. (2000). Attractions and constraints as determinants of relationship commitment: Longitudinal evidence from gay, lesbian, and heterosexual couples. *Personal Relationships, 7,* 245–262.

Kurdek, L. A. (2002). Predicting the timing of separation and marital satisfaction: An eight-year prospective longitudinal study. *Journal of Marriage and Family, 64,* 163–179.

Kurdek, L. A. (2004). Are gay and lesbian cohabiting couples *really* different from heterosexual married couples? *Journal of Marriage and Family, 66,* 880–900.

Kurdek, L. A. (2005a). Gender and marital satisfaction early in marriage: A growth curve approach. *Journal of Marriage and Family, 67,* 68–84.

Kurdek, L. A. (2005b). What do we know about gay and lesbian couples? *Current Directions in Psychological Science, 14,* 251–254.

Kurdek, L. A. (2006). Differences between partners from heterosexual, gay, and lesbian cohabiting couples. *Journal of Marriage and Family, 68,* 509–528.

Kurup, R. K., & Kurup, P. A. (2003). Hypothalamic digoxin, hemispheric dominance, and neurobiology of love and affection. *International Journal of Neuroscience, 113,* 721–729.

Lacey, R. S., Reifman, A., Scott, J. P., Harris, S. M., & Fitzpatrick, J. (2004). Sexual–moral attitudes, love styles, and mate selection. *The Journal of Sex Research, 41,* 121–128.

Lambert, N. M., Gwinn, A. M., Baumeister, R. F., Strachman, A., Washburn, I. J., Gable, S. L., & Fincham, F. D. (2013). A boost of positive affect: The perks of sharing positive experiences. *Journal of Social and Personal Relationships, 30,* 24–43.

Lamm, H., & Wiesmann, U. (1997). Subjective attributes of attraction: How people characterize their liking, their love, and their being in love. *Personal Relationships, 4,* 271–284.

Laner, M. R., & Ventrone, N. A. (2000). Dating scripts revisited. *Journal of Family Issues, 21,* 488–500.

Langlois, J. H., Kalakanis, L., Rubenstein, A. J., Larson, A., Hallam, M., & Smoot, M. (2000). Maxims or myths of beauty? A meta-analytic and theoretical review. *Psychological Bulletin, 126,* 390–423.

Langlois, J. H., & Roggman, L. A. (1990). Attractive faces are only average. *Psychological Science, 1,* 115–121.

Lannutti, P. J. (2005). For better or worse: Exploring the meanings of same-sex marriage within the lesbian, gay, bisexual and transgendered community. *Journal of Social and Personal Relationships, 22,* 5–18.

Lannutti, P. J. (2011). Security, recognition, and misgivings: Exploring older same-sex couples' experiences of legally recognized same-sex marriage. *Journal of Social and Personal Relationships, 28,* 64–82.

Latty-Mann, H., & Davis, K. E. (1996). Attachment theory and partner choice: Preference and actuality. *Journal of Social and Personal Relationships, 13,* 5–23.

Lau, C. Q. (2012). The stability of same-sex cohabitation, different-sex cohabitation, and marriage. *Journal of Marriage and Family, 74,* 973–988.

Laumann, E. O., Paik, A., Glasser, D. B., Kang, J.-H., Wang, T., Levinson, B., Moreira, E. D., Nicolosi, A., & Gingell, C. (2006). A cross-national study of subjective well-being among older women and men: Findings from the Global Study of Sexual Attitudes and Behavior. *Archives of Sexual Behavior, 35*, 145–161.

Laurenceau, J.-P., Barrett, L. F., & Rovine, M. J. (2005). The interpersonal process model of intimacy in marriage: A daily-diary and multilevel modeling approach. *Journal of Family Psychology, 19*, 314–323.

Lavine, L. O., & Lombardo, J. P. (1984). Self-disclosure: Intimate and nonintimate disclosures to parents and best friends as a function of Bem sex-role category. *Sex Roles, 11*, 735–744.

Lavner, J. A., & Bradbury, T. N. (2010). Patterns of change in marital satisfaction over the newlywed years. *Journal of Marriage and Family, 72*, 1171–1187.

Lavner, J. A., Bradbury, T. N., & Karney, B. R. (2012). Incremental change or initial differences? Testing two models of marital deterioration. *Journal of Family Psychology, 26*, 606–616.

Lavner, J. A., Karney, B. R., & Bradbury, T. N. (2013). Newlyweds' optimistic forecasts of their marriage: For better or for worse? *Journal of Family Psychology, 27*, 531–540.

Lavrakas, P. J. (1975). Female preferences for male physiques. *Journal of Research in Personality, 9*, 324–334.

Lawrance, K., & Byers, E. S. (1995). Sexual satisfaction in long-term heterosexual relationships: The interpersonal exchange model of sexual satisfaction. *Personal Relationships, 2*, 267–285.

Lawson, H. M., & Leck, K. (2006). Dynamics of internet dating. *Social Science Computer Review, 24*, 189–208.

Lawson, J. F., James, C., Jannson, A. C., Koyama, N. F., & Hill, R. A. (2014). A comparison of heterosexual and homosexual mating preferences in personal advertisements. *Evolution & Human Behavior, 35*, 408–414.

Le, B., & Agnew, C. R. (2003). Commitment and its theorized determinants: A meta-analysis of the investment model. *Personal Relationships, 10*, 37–57.

Le, B., Korn, M. S., Crockett, E. E., & Loving, T. J. (2011). Missing you maintains us: Missing a romantic partner, commitment, relationship maintenance, and physical infidelity. *Journal of Social and Personal Relationships, 28*, 653–667.

Le, T. N. (2005). Narcissism and immature love as mediators of vertical individualism and ludic love style. *Journal of Social and Personal Relationships, 22*, 543–560.

Leavitt, G. C. (2003). Incest/inbreeding taboos. In J. J. Ponzetti, Jr. (Ed.), *International encyclopedia of marriage and family* (2nd ed., Vol. 2, pp. 869–876). New York, NY: Macmillan Reference USA.

Lebow, J. L., Chambers, A. L., Christensen, A., & Johnson, S. M. (2012). Research on the treatment of couple distress. *Journal of Marriage and Family Therapy, 38*, 145–168.

Leckman, J. F., & Herman, A. E. (2002). Maternal behavior and developmental psychopathology. *Biological Psychiatry, 51*, 27–43.

Leckman, J. F., Hrdy, S. B., Keverne, E. B., & Carter, C. S. (2006). A biobehavioral model of attachment and bonding. In R. J. Sternberg & K. Weis (Eds.), *The new psychology of love* (pp. 116–145). New Haven, CT: Yale University Press.

Lee, J. A. (1973). *Colours of love: An exploration of the ways of loving.* Toronto, Canada: New Press.

Lee, J. A. (1977). A typology of styles of loving. *Personality and Social Psychology Bulletin, 3,* 173–182.

Lee, J. A. (1988). Love-styles. In R. J. Sternberg & M. L. Barnes (Eds.), *The psychology of love* (pp. 38–67). New Haven, CT: Yale University Press.

Lee, Y.-S., & Waite, L. J. (2005). Husbands' and wives' time spent on housework: A comparison of measures. *Journal of Marriage and Family, 67,* 328–336.

Leeker, O., & Carlozzi, A. (2014). Effects of sex, sexual orientation, infidelity expectations, and love on distress related to emotional and sexual infidelity. *Journal of Marital and Family Therapy, 40,* 68–91.

LeFebvre, L., Blackburn, K., & Brody, N. (2015). Navigating romantic relationships on Facebook: Extending the relationship dissolution model to social networking environments. *Journal of Social and Personal Relationships, 32,* 78–98.

Le Gall, A., Mullet, E., & Shafighi, S. R. (2002). Age, religious beliefs, and sexual attitudes. *The Journal of Sex Research, 39,* 207–216.

Leiblum, S. R. (Ed.). (2010). *Treating sexual desire disorders: A clinical casebook.* New York, NY: Guilford Press.

Leitenberg, H., & Saltzman, H. (2000). A statewide survey of age at first intercourse for adolescent females and age of their male partners: Relation to other risk behaviors and statutory rape implications. *Archives of Sexual Behavior, 29,* 203–215.

Leites, E. (1982). The duty to desire: Love, friendship, and sexuality in some Puritan theories of marriage. *Journal of Social History, 15,* 383–408.

Leitz-Spitz, M. A. (2003). Stalking: Terrorism at our doors—how social workers can help victims fight back. *Social Work, 48,* 504–512.

Lemay, E. P., Jr., & Clark, M. S. (2008). How the head liberates the heart: Projection of communal responsiveness guides relationship promotion. *Journal of Personality and Social Psychology, 94,* 647–671.

Lennon, M. C., & Rosenfield, S. (1994). Relative fairness and the division of housework: The importance of options. *American Journal of Sociology, 100,* 506–531.

Lenton, A. P., & Francesconi, M. (2010). How humans cognitively manage an abundance of mate options. *Psychological Science, 21,* 528–533.

Leonard, R., Ling, L. C., Hankins, G. A., Maidon, C. H., Potorti, P. F., & Rogers, J. M. (1993). Sexual harassment at North Carolina State University. In G. L. Kreps (Ed.), *Sexual harassment: Communication implications* (pp. 170–194). Cresskill, NJ: Hampton.

Leone, C., & Hall, I. (2003). Self-monitoring, marital dissatisfaction, and relationship dissolution: Individual differences in orientations to marriage and divorce. *Self and Identity, 2,* 189–202.

Leone, C., & Hawkins, L. B. (2006). Self-monitoring and close relationships. *Journal of Personality, 74,* 739–778.

Lester, D. (1996). Trends in divorce and marriage around the world. *Journal of Divorce and Remarriage, 25,* 169–171.

Lester, D., Haig, C., & Monello, R. (1989). Spouses' personality and marital satisfaction. *Personality and Individual Differences, 10,* 253–254.

Lever, J. (1994, August 23). The 1994 *Advocate* survey of sexuality and relationships: The men. *The Advocate: The National Gay & Lesbian Newsmagazine,* pp. 17–24.

Lever, J. (1995, August 22). The 1995 *Advocate* survey of sexuality and relationships: The women. *The Advocate: The National Gay & Lesbian Newsmagazine,* pp. 22–30.

Levine, D. (2000). Virtual attraction: What rocks your boat. *CyberPsychology & Behavior, 3,* 565–573.

Levine, R., Sato, S., Hashimoto, T., & Verma, J. (1995). Love and marriage in eleven cultures. *Journal of Cross-Cultural Psychology, 26,* 554–571.

Levine, S. B. (1984). An essay on the nature of sexual desire. *Journal of Sex & Marital Therapy, 10,* 83–96.

Levinger, G. (1965). Marital cohesiveness and dissolution: An integrative view. *Journal of Marriage and the Family, 27,* 19–28.

Levinger, G. (1976). A social psychological perspective on marital dissolution. *Journal of Social Issues, 32,* 21–47.

Levinger, G. (1983). Development and change. In H. H. Kelley, E. Berscheid, A. Christensen, J. H. Harvey, T. L. Huston, G. Levinger, E. McClintock, L. A. Peplau, & D. R. Peterson (Eds.), *Close relationships* (pp. 315–359). New York, NY: Freeman.

Levinger, G., Senn, D. J., & Jorgensen, B. W. (1970). Progress toward permanence in courtship: A test of the Kerckhoff-Davis hypothesis. *Sociometry, 33,* 427–443.

Levinson, R. A., Sadigursky, C., & Erchak, G. M. (2004). The impact of cultural context on Brazilian adolescents' sexual practices. *Adolescence, 39,* 203–227.

Lewis, C. S. (1988). *The four loves.* New York, NY: Harcourt Brace. (Original work published 1960)

Li, N. P., Bailey, J. M., Kenrick, D. T., & Linsenmeier, J. A. W. (2002). The necessities and luxuries of mate preferences: Testing the trade-offs. *Journal of Personality and Social Psychology, 82,* 947–955.

Li, N. P., Valentine, K. A., & Patel, L. (2011). Mate preferences in the U.S. and Singapore: A cross-cultural test of the mate preference priority model. *Personality and Individual Differences, 50,* 291–294.

Lieberman, D., & Hatfield, E. (2006). Passionate love: Cross-cultural and evolutionary perspectives. In R. J. Sternberg & K. Weis (Eds.), *The new psychology of love* (pp. 274–297). New Haven, CT: Yale University Press.

Lin, L. W., & Huddleston-Casas, C. A. (2005). Agape love in couple relationships. *Marriage and Family Review, 37,* 29–48.

Lindahl, K., Clements, M., & Markman, H. (1998). The development of marriage: A 9-year perspective. In T. N. Bradbury (Ed.), *The developmental course of marital dysfunction* (pp. 205–236). Cambridge, England: Cambridge University Press.

Lippa, R. A. (2007). The preferred traits of mates in a cross-national study of heterosexual and homosexual men and women: An examination of biological and cultural influences. *Archives of Sexual Behavior, 36,* 193–208.

Litzinger, S., & Gordon, K. C. (2005). Exploring relationships among communication, sexual satisfaction, and marital satisfaction. *Journal of Sex & Marital Therapy, 31,* 409–424.

Lofquist, D., Lugaila, T., O'Connell, M., & Feliz, S. (2012). *Households and families: 2010. 2010 census briefs.* Retrieved from http://www.census.gov/prod/cen2010/briefs/c2010br-14.pdf

Logan, T. K., Leukefeld, C., & Walker, B. (2000). Stalking as a variant of intimate violence: Implications from a young adult sample. *Violence & Victims, 15,* 91–111.

Loh, C., Orchowski, L. M., Gidycz, C. A., & Elizaga, R. A. (2007). Socialization and sexual aggression in college men: The role of observational influence in detecting risk cues. *Psychology of Men & Masculinity, 8,* 129–144.

Luepnitz, D. A. (1988). *The family interpreted.* New York, NY: Basic Books.

Luo, S., & Zhang, G. (2009). What leads to romantic attraction: Similarity, reciprocity, security, or beauty? Evidence from a speed-dating study. *Journal of Personality, 77,* 933–963.

Lyndon, A., Bonds-Raacke, J., & Cratty, A. D. (2011). College students' Facebook stalking of ex-partners. *Cyberpsychology, Behavior, and Social Networking, 14,* 711–716.

Maccoby, E. E. (1990). Gender and relationships: A developmental account. *American Psychologist, 45,* 513–520.

MacGeorge, E. L., Graves, A. R., Feng, B., Gillihan, S. J., & Burleson, B. R. (2004). The myth of gender cultures: Similarities outweigh differences in men's and women's provision of and responses to supportive communication. *Sex Roles, 50,* 143–175.

MacNeil, S., & Byers, E. S. (2005). Dyadic assessment of sexual self-disclosure and sexual satisfaction in heterosexual dating couples. *Journal of Social and Personal Relationships, 22,* 169–181.

Madden, M., & Lenhart, A. (2006, March 5). *Online dating* (Report for the Pew Internet & American Life Project). Retrieved August 25, 2015 from http://www.pewinternet.org/2006/03/05/online-dating/

Maddox Shaw, A. M., Rhoades, G. K., Allen, E. S., Stanley, S. M., & Markman, H. J. (2013). Predictors of extradyadic sexual involvement in unmarried opposite-sex relationships. *Journal of Sex Research, 50,* 598–610.

Major, B. (1993). Gender, entitlement, and the distribution of family labor. *Journal of Social Issues, 49,* 141–159.

Malouff, J. M., Thorsteinsson, E. B., Schutte, N. S., Bhullar, N., & Rooke, S. E. (2010). The Five-Factor Model of personality and relationship satisfaction of intimate partners: A meta-analysis. *Journal of Research in Personality, 44,* 124–127.

Maran, D. A., Varetto, A., Zedda, M., & Munari, J. (2014). Stalking victimization among Italian university students. *Gender & Behaviour, 12,* 6070–6079.

Marazziti, D., Akiskal, H. S., Rossi, A., & Cassano, G. B. (1999). Alteration of the platelet serotonin transporter in romantic love. *Psychological Medicine, 239,* 741–745.

Mark, K. P., Herbenick, D., Fortenberry, J. D., Sanders, S., & Reece, M. (2014). A psychometric comparison of three scales and a single-item measure to assess sexual satisfaction. *Journal of Sex Research, 51,* 159–169.

Mark, K. P., & Jozkowski, K. N. (2013). The mediating role of sexual and non-sexual communication between relationship and sexual satisfaction in a sample of college-age heterosexual couples. *Journal of Sex & Marital Therapy, 39,* 410–427.

Mark, K. P., & Murray, S. H. (2012). Gender differences in desire discrepancy as a predictor of sexual and relationship satisfaction in a college sample of heterosexual romantic relationships. *Journal of Sex & Marital Therapy, 38,* 198–215.

Markey, P., & Markey, C. (2013). Sociosexuality and relationship commitment among lesbian couples. *Journal of Research in Personality, 47,* 282–285.

Markey, P. M., & Markey, C. N. (2007). Romantic ideals, romantic obtainment, and relationship experiences: The complementarity of interpersonal traits among romantic partners. *Journal of Social and Personal Relationships, 24,* 517–533.

Marshall, A. D., & Holtzworth-Munroe, A. (2002). Varying forms of husband sexual aggression: Predictors and subgroup differences. *Journal of Family Psychology, 16,* 286–296.

Martin, E. K., Taft, C. T., & Resick, P. A. (2007). A review of marital rape. *Aggression and Violent Behavior, 12,* 328–347.

Martin, P. D., Specter, G., Martin, D., & Martin, M. (2003). Expressed attitudes of adolescents toward marriage and family life. *Adolescence, 38,* 359–367.

Martin, P. V., & Hummer, R. A. (1989). Fraternities and rape on campus. *Gender & Society, 3,* 457–473.

Mashek, D., Aron, A., & Fisher, H. (2000). Identifying, evoking, and measuring intense feelings of romantic love. *Representative Research in Social Psychology, 24,* 48–55.

Masters, W. H., & Johnson, V. E. (1979). *Homosexuality in perspective.* Boston, MA: Little, Brown.

Matsick, J. L., Conley, T. D., Ziegler, A., Moors, A. C., & Rubin, J. D. (2014). Love and sex: Polyamorous relationships are perceived more favourably than swinging and open relationships. *Psychology & Sexuality, 5,* 339–348.

Mattingly, B. A., Clark, E. M., Weidler, D. J., Bullock, M., Hackathorn, J., & Blankmeyer, K. (2011). Sociosexual orientation, commitment, and infidelity: A mediation analysis. *The Journal of Social Psychology, 151,* 222–226.

Maurice, W. L. (2007). Sexual desire disorders in men. In S. R. Leiblum (Ed.), *Principles and practice of sex therapy* (4th ed., pp. 181–211). New York, NY: Guilford Press.

Maybach, K. L., & Gold, S. R. (1994). Hyperfemininity and attraction to macho and non-macho men. *The Journal of Sex Research, 31,* 91–98.

McAnulty, R. D. (Ed.). (2012). *Sex in college: The things they don't write home about.* Santa Barbara, CA: Praeger.

McCabe, M. P., & Collins, J. K. (1984). Measurement of depth of desired and experienced sexual involvement at different stages of dating. *Journal of Sex Research, 20,* 377–390.

McCarthy, B., & Farr, E. (2012). Strategies and techniques to maintain sexual desire. *Journal of Contemporary Psychotherapy, 42,* 227–233.

McCarthy, B. W., Ginsberg, R. L., & Fucito, L. M. (2006). Resilient sexual desire in heterosexual couples. *The Family Journal, 14,* 59–64.

McCormick, N. B. (1979). Come-ons and put-offs: Unmarried students' strategies for having and avoiding sexual intercourse. *Psychology of Women Quarterly, 4,* 194–211.

McCormick, N. B., & Jones, A. J. (1989). Gender differences in nonverbal flirtation. *Journal of Sex Education and Therapy, 15,* 271–282.

McCrae, R. R., & Costa, P. T., Jr. (1997). Personality trait structure as a human universal. *American Psychologist, 52,* 509–516.

McGinnis, R. (1958). Campus values in mate selection: A repeat study. *Social Forces, 36,* 368–373.

McGonagle, K. A., Kessler, R. C., & Schilling, E. A. (1992). The frequency and determinants of marital disagreements in a community sample. *Journal of Social and Personal Relationships, 9,* 507–524.

McKelvie, M., & Gold, S. R. (1994). Hyperfemininity: Further definition of the construct. *The Journal of Sex Research, 31,* 219–228.

McKenna, K. Y. A. (2008). MySpace or your place: Relationship initiation and development in the wired and wireless world. In S. Sprecher, A. Wenzel, & J. Harvey (Eds.), *Handbook of relationship initiation* (pp. 235–247). New York, NY: Psychology Press.

McKinney, K., & Sprecher, S. (Eds.). (1991). *Sexuality in close relationships.* Hillsdale, NJ: Erlbaum.

McNamara, J. R., & Grossman, K. (1991). Initiation of dates and anxiety among college men and women. *Psychological Reports, 69,* 252–254.

McNulty, J. K., & Hellmuth, J. C. (2008). Emotion regulation and intimate partner violence in newlyweds. *Journal of Family Psychology, 22,* 794–797.

McNulty, J. K., & Widman, L. (2013). The implications of sexual narcissism for sexual and marital satisfaction. *Archives of Sexual Behavior, 42,* 1021–1032.

Medora, N. P. (2003). Mate selection in contemporary India: Love marriages versus arranged marriages. In R. R. Hamon & B. B. Ingoldsby (Eds.), *Mate selection across cultures* (pp. 209–230). Thousand Oaks, CA: Sage.

Meeks, B. S., Hendrick, S. S., & Hendrick, C. (1998). Communication, love and relationship satisfaction. *Journal of Social and Personal Relationships, 15,* 755–773.

Meloy, J. R. (1989). Unrequited love and the wish to kill: Diagnosis and treatment of borderline erotomania. *Bulletin of the Menninger Clinic, 53,* 477–492.

Meloy, J. R. (2007). Stalking: The state of the science. *Criminal Behaviour and Mental Health, 17*, 1–7.

Ménard, K. S., & Pincus, A. L. (2012). Predicting overt and cyber stalking perpetration by male and female college students. *Journal of Interpersonal Violence, 27*, 2183–2207.

Metts, S. (2003). Sexual communication: Couple relationships. In J. J. Ponzetti, Jr. (Ed.), *International encyclopedia of marriage and family* (2nd ed., Vol. 3, pp. 1437–1443). New York, NY: Macmillan Reference USA.

Metts, S. (2004). First sexual involvement in romantic relationships: An empirical investigation of communicative framing, romantic beliefs, and attachment orientation in the passion turning point. In J. Harvey, A. Wenzel, & S. Sprecher (Eds.), *The handbook of sexuality in close relationships* (pp. 135–158). Mahwah, NJ: Erlbaum.

Metts, S., Sprecher, S., & Regan, P. C. (1998). Communication and sexual desire. In P. A. Andersen & L. K. Guerrero (Eds.), *Handbook of communication and emotion: Research, theory, applications, and contexts* (pp. 353–377). Orlando, FL: Academic Press.

Meyers, S., & Berscheid, E. (1996). The language of love: The difference a preposition makes. *Personality and Social Psychology Bulletin, 23*, 347–362.

Michael, R. T., Gagnon, J. H., Laumann, E. O., & Kolata, G. (1994). *Sex in America: A definitive survey*. Boston, MA: Little, Brown.

Michalski, J. H. (2005). Explaining intimate partner violence: The sociological limitations of victimization studies. *Sociological Forum, 20*, 613–640.

Mikula, G., Riederer, B., & Bodi, O. (2012). Perceived justice in the division of domestic labor: Actor and partner effects. *Personal Relationships, 19*, 680–695.

Mikulincer, M., & Shaver, P. R. (2009). An attachment and behavioral systems perspective on social support. *Journal of Social and Personal Relationships, 26*, 7–19.

Miller, A. C., & Karkazis, K. (2013). Health beliefs and practices in an isolated polygamist community of southern Utah. *Journal of Religion and Health, 52*, 597–609.

Miller, B. C., & Leavitt, S. C. (2003). Sexuality in adolescence. In J. J. Ponzetti, Jr. (Ed.), *International encyclopedia of marriage and family* (2nd ed., Vol. 3, pp. 1471–1476). New York, NY: Macmillan Reference USA.

Miller, L. (2012). Stalking: Patterns, motives, and intervention strategies. *Aggression and Violent Behavior, 17*, 495–506.

Mintz, E. E. (1980). Obsession with the rejecting beloved. *Psychoanalytic Review, 67*, 479–492.

Mischel, W. (1966). A social-learning view of sex differences in behavior. In E. E. Maccoby (Ed.), *The development of sex differences* (pp. 513–581). Stanford, CA: Stanford University Press.

Mongeau, P. A., Jacobsen, J., & Donnerstein, C. (2007). Defining dates and first date goals: Generalizing from undergraduates to single adults. *Communication Research, 34*, 526–547.

Mongeau, P. A., & Johnson, K. L. (1995). Predicting cross-sex first-date sexual expectations and involvement: Contextual and individual difference factors. *Personal Relationships, 2,* 301–312.

Mongeau, P. A., Morr Serewicz, M. C., & Therrien, L. F. (2004). Goals for cross-sex first dates: Identification, measurement, and the influence of contextual factors. *Communication Monographs, 71,* 121–147.

Monson, C. M., & Langhinrichsen-Rohling, J. (1998). Sexual and nonsexual marital aggression: Legal considerations, epidemiology, and an integrated typology of perpetrators. *Aggression and Violent Behavior, 3,* 369–389.

Montesi, J. L., Fauber, R. L., Gordon, E. A., & Heimberg, R. G. (2011). The specific importance of communicating about sex to couples' sexual and overall relationship satisfaction. *Journal of Social and Personal Relationships, 28,* 591–609.

Montoya, R. M., Horton, R. S., & Kirchner, J. (2008). Is actual similarity necessary for attraction? A meta-analysis of actual and perceived similarity. *Journal of Social and Personal Relationships, 25,* 889–922.

Moore, M. M. (1985). Nonverbal courtship patterns in women: Context and consequences. *Ethology and Sociobiology, 6,* 237–247.

Moore, M. M. (2010). Human nonverbal courtship behavior—A brief historical review. *Journal of Sex Research, 47,* 171–180.

Moreland, R. L., & Beach, S. R. (1992). Exposure effects in the classroom: The development of affinity among students. *Journal of Experimental Social Psychology, 28,* 255–276.

Morr Serewicz, M. C., & Gale, E. (2008). First-date scripts: Gender roles, context, and relationship. *Sex Roles, 58,* 149–164.

Morrison, E. R., Morris, P. H., & Bard, K. A. (2013). The stability of facial attractiveness: Is it what you've got or what you do with it? *Journal of Nonverbal Behavior, 37,* 59–67.

Morrow, G. D., Clark, E. M., & Brock, K. F. (1995). Individual and partner love styles: Implications for the quality of romantic involvements. *Journal of Social and Personal Relationships, 12,* 363–387.

Morse, B. J. (1995). Beyond the Conflict Tactics Scale: Assessing gender differences in partner violence. *Violence and Victims, 10,* 251–272.

Mosher, D. L., & Anderson, R. D. (1986). Macho personality, sexual aggression, and reactions to guided imagery of realistic rape. *Journal of Research in Personality, 18,* 150–163.

Mosher, D. L., & Sirkin, M. (1984). Measuring a macho personality constellation. *Journal of Research in Personality, 18,* 150–163.

Mouilso, E. R., & Calhoun, K. S. (2012). A mediation model of the role of sociosexuality in the associations between narcissism, psychopathology, and sexual aggression. *Psychology of Violence, 2,* 16–27.

Moustgaard, H., & Martikainen, P. (2009). Nonmarital cohabitation among older Finnish men and women: Socioeconomic characteristics and forms of union dissolution. *The Journals of Gerontology: Series B: Psychological Sciences and Social Sciences, 64B,* 507–516.

Muehlenhard, C. L. (1988). "Nice women" don't say yes and "real men" don't say no: How miscommunication and the double standard can cause sexual problems. *Women and Therapy, 7,* 95–108.

Muehlenhard, C. L., Goggins, M. F., Jones, J. M., & Satterfield, A. T. (1991). Sexual violence and coercion in close relationships. In K. McKinney & S. Sprecher (Eds.), *Sexuality in close relationships* (pp. 155–175). Hillsdale, NJ: Erlbaum.

Muehlenhard, C. L., & Hollabaugh, L. C. (1988). Do women sometimes say no when they mean yes? The prevalence and correlates of women's token resistance to sex. *Journal of Personality and Social Psychology, 54,* 872–879.

Muehlenhard, C. L., & Miller, E. N. (1988). Traditional and nontraditional men's responses to women's dating initiation. *Behavior Modification, 12,* 385–403.

Muehlenhard, C. L., & Rodgers, C. S. (1998). Token resistance to sex: New perspectives on an old stereotype. *Psychology of Women Quarterly, 22,* 443–463.

Muise, A., Giang, E., & Impett, E. A. (2014). Post sex affectionate exchanges promote sexual and relationship satisfaction. *Archives of Sexual Behavior, 43,* 1391–1402.

Muise, A., Impett, E. A., Kogan, A., & Desmarais, S. (2013). Keeping the spark alive: Being motivated to meet a partner's sexual needs sustains sexual desire in long-term romantic relationships. *Social Psychological and Personality Science, 4,* 267–273.

Mullen, P. E., & Pathé, M. (1994). Stalking and the pathologies of love. *Australian and New Zealand Journal of Psychiatry, 28,* 469–477.

Mumm, S. S., & Cupach, W. R. (2010). Turning points in the progression of obsessive relational intrusion and stalking. *Violence and Victims, 25,* 707–727.

Muram, D., Rosenthal, T. L., Tolley, E. A., Peeler, M. M., & Dorko, B. (1991). Race and personality traits affect high school senior girls' sexual reports. *Journal of Sex Education and Therapy, 17,* 231–243.

Murdock, G. P. (1967). Ethnographic atlas: A summary. *Ethnology, 6,* 109–236.

Murnen, S. K., & Byrne, D. (1991). Hyperfemininity: Measurement and initial validation of the construct. *The Journal of Sex Research, 28,* 479–489.

Murnen, S. K., Wright, C., & Kaluzny, G. (2002). If "boys will be boys," then girls will be victims? A meta-analytic review of the research that relates masculine ideology to sexual aggression. *Sex Roles, 46,* 359–375.

Murray, S. L., Holmes, J. G., & Griffin, D. W. (1996). The benefits of positive illusions: Idealization and the construction of satisfaction in close relationships. *Journal of Personality and Social Psychology, 70,* 79–98.

Murrow, C., & Shi, L. (2010). The influence of cohabitation purposes on relationship quality: An examination in dimensions. *The American Journal of Family Therapy, 38,* 397–412.

Murstein, B. I. (1970). Stimulus-value-role: A theory of marital choice. *Journal of Marriage and the Family, 32,* 465–481.

Murstein, B. I. (1976). *Who will marry whom? Theories and research in marital choice.* New York, NY: Springer.

Murstein, B. I. (1980). Mate selection in the 1970s. *Journal of Marriage and the Family, 42,* 777–792.

Murstein, B. I. (1987). A clarification and extension of the SVR theory of dyadic pairing. *Journal of Marriage and the Family, 49,* 929–947.

Murstein, B. I. (1988). A taxonomy of love. In R. J. Sternberg & M. L. Barnes (Eds.), *The psychology of love* (pp. 13–37). New Haven, CT: Yale University Press.

Murstein, B. I., Merighi, J. R., & Vyse, S. A. (1991). Love styles in the United States and France: A cross-cultural comparison. *Journal of Social and Clinical Psychology, 10,* 37–46.

Mwaba, K., & Naidoo, P. (2005). Sexual practices, attitudes toward premarital sex and condom use among a sample of South African university students. *Social Behavior and Personality, 33,* 651–656.

Naef, R., Ward, R., Mahrer-Imhof, R., & Grande, G. (2013). Characteristics of the bereavement experience of older persons after spousal loss: An integrative review. *International Journal of Nursing Studies, 50,* 1108–1121.

National Center for Health Statistics (2013). *Provisional number of divorces and annulments and rate: United States, 2000–2011.* Retrieved from http://www.cdc.gov/nchs/nvss/marriage_divorce_tables.htm

National Domestic Violence Hotline (2015). Is this abuse? Retrieved from http://www.thehotline.org/is-this-abuse/

Neff, L. A., & Karney, B. R. (2002). Judgments of a relationship partner: Specific accuracy but global enhancement. *Journal of Personality, 70,* 1079–1112.

Nemechek, S., & Olson, K. R. (1996). Personality and marital adjustment. *Psychological Reports, 78,* 26.

Neto, F., & Pinto, M. D. C. (2003). The role of loneliness, gender and love status in adolescents' love styles. *International Journal of Adolescence and Youth, 11,* 181–191.

Netting, N. S. (2010). Marital ideoscapes in 21st-century India: Creative combinations of love and responsibility. *Journal of Family Issues, 31,* 707–726.

Neyer, F. J., & Voigt, D. (2004). Personality and social network effects on romantic relationships: A dyadic approach. *European Journal of Personality, 18,* 279–299.

Nicholas, L. J. (2004). The association between religiosity, sexual fantasy, participation in sexual acts, sexual enjoyment, exposure, and reaction to sexual materials among black South Africans. *Journal of Sex & Marital Therapy, 30,* 37–42.

Noller, P., Feeney, J. A., Bonnell, D., & Callan, V. J. (1994). A longitudinal study of conflict in early marriage. *Journal of Social and Personal Relationships, 11,* 233–252.

Norris, S. L., & Zweigenhaft, R. L. (1999). Self-monitoring, trust, and commitment in romantic relationships. *Journal of Social Psychology, 139,* 215–220.

Nowatzki, J., & Morry, M. M. (2009). Women's intentions regarding, and acceptance of, self-sexualizing behavior. *Psychology of Women Quarterly, 33,* 95–107.

Odimegwu, C. O. (2005). Sexual behavior of Nigerian university students. *Journal of Child and Adolescent Mental Health, 17,* 35–38.

O'Leary, K. D., & Williams, M. C. (2006). Agreement about acts of violence in marriage. *Journal of Family Psychology, 20,* 656–662.

Oliver, M. B., & Hyde, J. S. (1993). Gender differences in sexuality: A meta-analysis. *Psychological Bulletin, 114,* 29–51.

Öner, B. (2002). Self-monitoring and future time orientation in romantic relationships. *The Journal of Psychology, 136,* 420–424.

O'Rourke, N., Claxton, A., Chou, P. H. B., Smith, J. Z., & Hadjistavropoulos, T. (2011). Personality trait levels within older couples and between-spouse trait differences as predictors of marital satisfaction. *Aging & Mental Health, 15,* 344–353.

Ortigue, S., Bianchi-Demicheli, F., Patel, N., Frum, C., & Lewis, J. W. (2010). Neuroimaging of love: fMRI meta-analysis evidence toward new perspectives in sexual medicine. *Journal of Sexual Medicine, 7,* 3541–3552.

Orvis, B. R., Kelley, H. H., & Butler, D. (1976). Attributional conflict in young couples. In J. H. Harvey, W. J. Ickes, & R. F. Kidd (Eds.), *New directions in attribution research* (Vol. 1, pp. 353–386). Hillsdale, NJ: Erlbaum.

O'Sullivan, L. F. (1995). Less is more: The effects of sexual experience on judgments of men's and women's personality characteristics and relationship desirability. *Sex Roles, 33,* 159–181.

O'Sullivan, L. F., & Byers, E. S. (1993). Eroding stereotypes: College women's attempts to influence reluctant male sexual partners. *Journal of Sex Research, 30,* 270–282.

O'Sullivan, L. F., & Gaines, M. E. (1998). Decision-making in college students' heterosexual dating relationships: Ambivalence about engaging in sexual activity. *Journal of Social and Personal Relationships, 15,* 347–363.

Othman, H., & Saadat, M. (2009). Prevalence of consanguineous marriages in Syria. *Journal of Biosocial Science, 41,* 685–692.

Oyamot, C. M., Fuglestad, P. T., & Snyder, M. (2010). Balance of power and influence in relationships: The role of self-monitoring. *Journal of Social and Personal Relationships, 27,* 23–46.

Pagelow, M. D. (1981). *Woman-battering: Victims and their experiences.* Beverly Hills, CA: Sage.

Painter, K., & Farrington, D. P. (1998). Marital violence in Great Britain and its relationship to marital and non-marital rape. *International Review of Victimology, 5,* 257–276.

Papp, L. M., Kouros, C. D., & Cummings, E. M. (2009). Demand-withdraw patterns in marital conflict in the home. *Personal Relationships, 16,* 285–300.

Parish, W. L., Luo, Y., Laumann, E. O., Kew, M., & Yu, Z. (2007). Unwanted sexual activity among married women in urban China. *The Journal of Sex Research, 44,* 158–171.

Parks, M. R. (2007). *Personal relationships and personal networks*. Mahwah, NJ: Erlbaum.

Parks, M. R., & Eggert, L. L. (1991). The role of social context in the dynamics of personal relationships. In W. H. Jones & D. Perlman (Eds.), *Advances in personal relationships: A research annual* (Vol. 2, pp. 1–34). Oxford, England: Jessica Kingsley Publishers.

Parrott, D. J., & Zeichner, A. (2003). Effects of hypermasculinity on physical aggression against women. *Psychology of Men & Masculinity, 4,* 70–78.

Pasch, L. A., Bradbury, T. N., & Davila, J. (1997). Gender, negative affectivity, and observed social support behavior in marital interaction. *Personal Relationships, 4,* 361–378.

Pathé, M. (2002). *Surviving stalking*. Cambridge, England: Cambridge University Press.

Pearce, A. R., Chuikova, T., Ramsey, A., & Galyautdinova, S. (2010). A positive psychology perspective on mate preferences in the United States and Russia. *Journal of Cross-Cultural Psychology, 41,* 742–757.

Pence, E., & Paymar, M. (1993). *Education groups for men who batter: The Duluth model*. New York, NY: Springer.

Penke, L., & Asendorpf, J. B. (2008). Beyond global sociosexual orientations: A more differentiated look at sociosexuality and its effects on courtship and romantic relationships. *Journal of Personality and Social Psychology, 95,* 1113–1135.

Penn, R. (2011). Arranged marriages in Western Europe: Media representations and social reality. *Journal of Comparative Family Studies, 42,* 637–650.

Pennebaker, J. W., Dyer, M. A., Caulkins, R. S., Litowitz, D. L., Ackreman, P. L., Anderson, D. B., & McGraw, K. M. (1979). Don't the girls get prettier at closing time: A country and western application to psychology. *Personality and Social Psychology Bulletin, 5,* 122–125. [Note: "Ackerman" is misspelled in the original article]

Peplau, L. A. (1983). Roles and gender. In H. H. Kelley, E. Berscheid, A. Christensen, J. H. Harvey, T. L. Huston, G. Levinger, E. McClintock, L. A. Peplau, & D. R. Peterson (Eds.), *Close relationships* (pp. 220–264). New York, NY: Freeman.

Peplau, L. A., Cochran, S. D., & Mays, V. M. (1997). A national survey of the intimate relationships of African American lesbians and gay men: A look at commitment, satisfaction, sexual behavior, and HIV disease. In B. Greene (Ed.), *Ethnic and cultural diversity among lesbians and gay men* (pp. 11–38). Thousand Oaks, CA: Sage.

Peplau, L. A., Cochran, S., Rook, K., & Padesky, C. (1978). Loving women: Attachment and autonomy in lesbian relationships. *Journal of Social Issues, 34,* 7–27.

Peplau, L. A., Fingerhut, A., & Beals, K. P. (2004). Sexuality in the relationships of lesbians and gay men. In J. H. Harvey, A. Wenzel, & S. Sprecher (Eds.), *The handbook of sexuality in close relationships* (pp. 349–369). Mahwah, NJ: Erlbaum.

Peplau, L. A., Rubin, Z., & Hill, C. T. (1977). Sexual intimacy in dating relationships. *Journal of Social Issues, 33,* 86–109.

Peplau, L. A., & Spalding, L. (2000). The close relationships of lesbians, gay men, and bisexuals. In C. Hendrick & S. S. Hendrick (Eds.), *Close relationships: A sourcebook* (pp. 111–123). Thousand Oaks, CA: Sage.

Perilloux, C., Fleischman, D. S., & Buss, D. M. (2011). Meet the parents: Parent-offspring convergence and divergence in mate preferences. *Personality and Individual Differences, 50,* 253–258.

Perlman, S. D., & Abramson, P. R. (1982). Sexual satisfaction among married and cohabiting individuals. *Journal of Consulting and Clinical Psychology, 50,* 458–460.

Perper, T., & Weis, D. L. (1987). Proceptive and rejective strategies of U.S. and Canadian college women. *Journal of Sex Research, 23,* 455–480.

Petersen, J. L., & Hyde, J. S. (2010). A meta-analytic review of research on gender differences in sexuality, 1993–2007. *Psychological Bulletin, 136,* 21–38.

Petersen, J. L., & Hyde, J. S. (2011). Gender differences in sexual attitudes and behaviors: A review of meta-analytic results and large datasets. *Journal of Sex Research, 48,* 149–165.

Peterson, C. D., Baucom, D. H., Elliott, M. J., & Farr, P. A. (1989). The relationship between sex role identity and marital adjustment. *Sex Roles, 21,* 775–787.

Peterson, D. R. (2002). Conflict. In H. H. Kelley, E. Berscheid, A. Christensen, J. H. Harvey, T. L. Huston, G. Levinger, E. McClintock, L. A. Peplau, & D. R. Peterson, *Close relationships* (pp. 360–396). Clinton Corners, NY: Percheron Press. (Original work published 1983)

Peterson, Z. D., & Muehlenhard, C. L. (2003). Rape. In J. J. Ponzetti, Jr. (Ed.), *International encyclopedia of marriage and family* (2nd ed., Vol. 3, pp. 1293–1297). New York, NY: Macmillan Reference USA.

Peterson, Z. D., Voller, E. K., Polusny, M.A., & Murdoch, M. (2011). Prevalence and consequences of adult sexual assault of men: Review of empirical findings and state of the literature. *Clinical Psychology Review,* 31, 1–24.

Pew Research Center (2014a). *Pew Research Center global attitudes project: Extramarital affairs.* Retrieved on October 17, 2014 from http://www.pewglobal.org/2014/04/15/global-morality/table/extramarital-affairs/

Pew Research Center (2014b). *Pew Research Center global attitudes project: Premarital sex.* Retrieved on October 17, 2014 from http://www.pewglobal.org/2014/04/15/global-morality/table/premarital-sex/

Pietropinto, A. (1986). Inhibited sexual desire. *Medical Aspects of Human Sexuality, 20,* 46–49.

Pinney, E. M., Gerrard, M., & Denney, N. W. (1987). The Pinney Sexual Satisfaction Inventory. *Journal of Sex Research, 23,* 233–251.

Planty, M., Langton, L., Krebs, C., Berzofsky, M., & Smiley-McDonald, H. (2013). *Special report: Female victims of sexual violence, 1994–2010.* U.S. Department of Justice/Bureau of Justice Statistics. Retrieved November 7, 2014 from http://www.bjs.gov/content/pub/pdf/fvsv9410.pdf

Prager, K. J. (2000). Intimacy in personal relationships. In C. Hendrick and S. S. Hendrick (Eds.), *Close relationships: A sourcebook* (pp. 228–242). Thousand Oaks, CA: Sage.

Prager, K. J., & Buhrmester, D. (1998). Intimacy and need fulfillment in couple relationships. *Journal of Social and Personal Relationships, 15,* 435–469.

Prager, K. J., & Roberts, L. J. (2004). Deep intimate connection: Self and intimacy in couple relationships. In D. J. Mashek & A. Aron (Eds.), *Handbook of closeness and intimacy* (pp. 43–60). Mahwah, NJ: Erlbaum.

Press, J. E., & Townsley, E. (1998). Wives' and husbands' housework reporting: Gender, class, and social desirability. *Gender & Society, 12,* 188–218.

Previti, D., & Amato, P. R. (2004). Is infidelity a cause or a consequence of poor marital quality? *Journal of Social and Personal Relationships, 21,* 217–230.

Pryor, J. B., & Merluzzi, T. V. (1985). The role of expertise in processing social interaction scripts. *Journal of Experimental Social Psychology, 21,* 362–379.

Qaqiesh, E., & Regan, P. C. (2004). Attitudes toward extrarelational sex as a function of participant's and third party's gender. *Psychological Reports, 95,* 965–968.

Quist, M. C., Watkins, C. D., Smith, F. G., Little, A. C., DeBruine, L. M., & Jones, B. C. (2012). Sociosexuality predicts women's preferences for symmetry in men's faces. *Archives of Sexual Behavior, 41,* 1415–1421.

Qureshi, K., Charsley, K., & Shaw, A. (2014). Marital instability among British Pakistanis: Transnationality, conjugalities and Islam. *Ethnic and Racial Studies, 37,* 261–279.

Rao, K. V., & DeMaris, A. (1995). Coital frequency among married and cohabiting couples in the United States. *Journal of Biosocial Science, 27,* 135–150.

Razeghi, N., Nikiju, M., Mujembari, A. K., & Masihi, A. Z. (2011). Relationship between big five personality factors and marital satisfaction. *Journal of Iranian Psychologists, 7,* 269–278.

Reece, M., Herbenick, D., Schick, V., Sanders, S. A., Dodge, B., & Fortenberry, J. D. (2010). Sexual behaviors, relationships, and perceived health among adult men in the United States: Results from a national probability sample. *Journal of Sexual Medicine, 7(suppl. 5),* 291–304.

Regan, P. C. (1996). Sexual outcasts: The perceived impact of body weight on sexuality. *Journal of Applied Social Psychology, 26,* 1803–1815.

Regan, P. C. (1998a). Minimum mate selection standards as a function of perceived mate value, relationship context, and gender. *Journal of Psychology and Human Sexuality, 10,* 53–73.

Regan, P. C. (1998b). Of lust and love: Beliefs about the role of sexual desire in romantic relationships. *Personal Relationships, 5,* 139–157.

Regan, P. (1998c). Romantic love and sexual desire. In V. C. de Munck (Ed.), *Romantic love and sexual behavior: Perspectives from the social sciences* (pp. 91–112). Westport, CT: Praeger.

Regan, P. C. (1998d). What if you can't get what you want? Willingness to compromise ideal mate selection standards as a function of sex, mate value, and relationship context. *Personality and Social Psychology Bulletin, 24,* 1288–1297.

Regan, P. C. (1999). Hormonal correlates and causes of sexual desire: A review. *The Canadian Journal of Human Sexuality, 8,* 1–16.

Regan, P. C. (2000a). Love relationships. In L. T. Szuchman & F. Muscarella (Eds.), *Psychological perspectives on human sexuality* (pp. 232–282). New York, NY: Wiley.

Regan, P. C. (2000b). The role of sexual desire and sexual activity in dating relationships. *Social Behavior and Personality, 28,* 51–60.

Regan, P. C. (2002). Functional features: An evolutionary perspective on inappropriate relationships. In R. Goodwin & D. Cramer (Eds.), *Inappropriate relationships: The unconventional, the disapproved, and the forbidden* (pp. 25–42). Mahwah, NJ: Erlbaum.

Regan, P. C. (2004). Sex and the attraction process: Lessons from science (and Shakespeare) on lust, love, chastity, and fidelity. In J. H. Harvey, A. Wenzel, & S. Sprecher (Eds.), *The handbook of sexuality in close relationships* (pp. 115–133). Mahwah, NJ: Erlbaum.

Regan, P. C. (2006). Love. In R. D. McAnulty & M. M. Burnette (Eds.), *Sex and sexuality. Vol. 2. Sexual function and dysfunction* (pp. 87–113). Westport, CT: Praeger.

Regan, P. C. (2015a). Attraction in close relationships. *Oxford bibliographies online: Psychology.* DOI: 10.1093/obo/9780199828340-0158

Regan, P. C. (2015b). Sexual desire: Conceptualization, correlates, and causes. In W. Hofmann & L. F. Nordgren (Eds.), *The psychology of desire* (pp. 347–368). New York, NY: Guilford.

Regan, P. C., & Anguiano, C. (2010). Romanticism as a function of age, sex, and ethnicity. *Psychological Reports, 107,* 972–976.

Regan, P. C., & Atkins, L. (2006). Sex differences and similarities in frequency and intensity of sexual desire. *Social Behavior and Personality, 34,* 95–102.

Regan, P. C., & Berscheid, E. (1995). Gender differences in beliefs about the causes of male and female sexual desire. *Personal Relationships, 2,* 345–358.

Regan, P. C., & Berscheid, E. (1997). Gender differences in characteristics desired in a potential sexual and marriage partner. *Journal of Psychology and Human Sexuality, 9,* 25–37.

Regan, P. C., & Berscheid, E. (1999). *Lust: What we know about human sexual desire.* Thousand Oaks, CA: Sage.

Regan, P. C., Durvasula, R., Howell, L., Ureño, O., & Rea, M. (2004). Gender, ethnicity, and the developmental timing of first sexual and romantic experiences. *Social Behavior and Personality, 32,* 667–676.

Regan, P. C., Kocan, E. R., & Whitlock, T. (1998). Ain't love grand! A prototype analysis of the concept of romantic love. *Journal of Social and Personal Relationships, 15,* 411–420.

Regan, P. C., Levin, L., Sprecher, S., Christopher, F. S., & Cate, R. (2000). Partner preferences: What characteristics do men and women desire in their short-term sexual and long-term romantic partners? *Journal of Psychology & Human Sexuality, 12,* 1–21.

Rehman, U. S., Rellini, A. H., & Fallis, E. (2011). The importance of sexual self-disclosure to sexual satisfaction and functioning in committed relationships. *Journal of Sexual Medicine, 8,* 3108–3115.

Reis, H. T., Clark, M. S., & Holmes, J. G. (2004). Perceived partner responsiveness as an organizing construct in the study of intimacy and closeness. In D. J. Mashek & A. Aron (Eds.), *Handbook of closeness and intimacy* (pp. 201–225). Mahwah, NJ: Erlbaum.

Reis, H. T., Maniaci, M. R., Caprariello, P. A., Eastwick, P. W., & Finkel, E. J. (2011). Familiarity does indeed promote attraction in live interaction. *Journal of Personality and Social Psychology, 3,* 557–570.

Reis, H. T., & Patrick, B. C. (1996). Attachment and intimacy: Component processes. In E. T. Higgins & A. Kruglanski (Eds.), *Social psychology: Handbook of basic principles* (pp. 523–563). New York, NY: Guilford Press.

Reis, H. T., & Shaver, P. (1988). Intimacy as an interpersonal process. In S. Duck (Ed.), *Handbook of personal relationships: Theory, research, and interventions* (pp. 367–389). Chichester, England: Wiley.

Reiss, I. L. (1960). Toward a sociology of the heterosexual love relationship. *Marriage and Family Living, 22,* 139–145.

Reiss, I. L. (1964). The scaling of premarital sexual permissiveness. *Journal of Marriage and the Family, 26,* 188–198.

Reiss, I. L. (1967). *The social context of premarital sexual permissiveness.* New York, NY: Holt, Rinehart & Winston.

Reiss, I. L. (1980). *Family systems in America* (3rd ed.). New York, NY: Holt, Rinehart & Winston.

Reiss, I. L. (1981). Some observations on ideology and sexuality in America. *Journal of Marriage and the Family, 43,* 271–283.

Reiss, I. L. (1986). *Journey into sexuality: An exploratory voyage.* Englewood Cliffs, NJ: Prentice Hall.

Renne, E. P. (1997). The meaning of contraceptive choice and constraint for Hausa women in a northern Nigerian town. *Anthropology & Medicine, 4,* 159–175.

Renninger, L. A., Wade, T. J., & Grammer, K. (2004). Getting that female glance: Patterns and consequences of male nonverbal behavior in courtship contexts. *Evolution and Human Behavior, 25,* 416–431.

Reyns, B. W., Henson, B., & Fisher, B. S. (2012). Stalking in the twilight zone: Extent of cyberstalking victimization and offending among college students. *Deviant Behavior, 33,* 1–25.

Rhoades, G. K., Stanley, S. M., & Markman, H. J. (2009a). Couples' reasons for cohabitation: Associations with individual well-being and relationship quality. *Journal of Family Issues, 30,* 233–258.

Rhoades, G. K., Stanley, S. M., & Markman, H. J. (2009b). The pre-engagement cohabitation effect: A replication and extension of previous findings. *Journal of Family Psychology, 23,* 107–111.

Richmond, L. D., Craig, S. S., & Ruzicka, M. F. (1991). Self-monitoring and marital adjustment. *Journal of Research in Personality, 25,* 177–188.

Richters, J., de Visser, R., Rissel, C., & Smith, A. (2006). Sexual practices at last heterosexual encounter and occurrence of orgasm in a national survey. *The Journal of Sex Research, 43,* 217–226.

Ridge, R. D., & Berscheid, E. (1989, May). *On loving and being in love: A necessary distinction.* Paper presented at the meeting of the Midwestern Psychological Association, Chicago, IL.

Robinson, I. E., Balkwell, J. W., & Ward, D. M. (1980). Meaning and behavior: An empirical study in sociolinguistics. *Social Psychology Quarterly, 43,* 253–258.

Robinson, J. P., Yerby, J., Fieweger, M., & Somerick, N. (1977). Sex-role differences in time use. *Sex Roles, 3,* 443–458.

Roche, J. P., & Ramsbey, T. W. (1993). Premarital sexuality: A five-year follow-up study of attitudes and behavior by dating stage. *Adolescence, 28,* 67–80.

Rodrigues, A. E., Hall, J. H., & Fincham, F. D. (2006). What predicts divorce and relationship dissolution? In M. A. Fine & J. H. Harvey (Eds.), *Handbook of divorce and dissolution* (pp. 85–112). Mahwah, NJ: Erlbaum.

Rollie, S. S., & Duck, S. (2006). Divorce and dissolution of romantic relationships: Stage models and their limitations. In M. A. Fine & J. H. Harvey (Eds.), *Handbook of divorce and dissolution* (pp. 223–240). Mahwah, NJ: Erlbaum.

Røsand, G-M. B., Slinning, K., Røysamb, E., & Tambs, K. (2014). Relationship dissatisfaction and other risk factors for future relationship dissolution: A population-based study of 18,523 couples. *Social Psychiatry and Psychiatric Epidemiology, 49,* 109–119.

Rosch, E. H. (1973). On the internal structure of perceptual and semantic categories. In T. E. Moore (Ed.), *Cognitive development and the acquisition of language* (pp. 111–144). New York, NY: Academic Press.

Rosch, E. (1975). Cognitive representations of semantic categories. *Journal of Experimental Psychology, 104,* 192–233.

Rosch, E. (1978). Principles of categorization. In E. Rosch & B. B. Lloyd (Eds.), *Cognition and categorization* (pp. 27–48). Hillsdale, NJ: Erlbaum.

Roscoe, B., Strouse, J. S., & Goodwin, M. P. (1994). Sexual harassment: Early adolescent self-reports of experiences and acceptance. *Adolescence, 29,* 515–523.

Rose, S., & Frieze, I. H. (1993). Young singles' contemporary dating scripts. *Sex Roles, 28,* 499–509.

Rosenfeld, L. B., & Bowen, G. L. (1991). Marital disclosure and marital satisfaction: Direct-effect versus interaction-effect models. *Western Journal of Speech Communication, 55,* 69–84.

Rotenberg, K. J., & Korol, S. (1995). The role of loneliness and gender in individuals' love styles. *Journal of Social Behavior and Personality, 10,* 537–546.

Rowatt, W. C., Cunningham, M. R., & Druen, P. B. (1998). Deception to get a date. *Personality and Social Psychology Bulletin, 24,* 1228–1242.

Rowatt, W. C., DeLue, S., Strickhouser, L., & Gonzalez, T. (2001). The limited influence of self-monitoring on romantic partner preferences. *Personality and Individual Differences, 31,* 943–954.

Rubenstein, A. J., Langlois, J. H., & Roggman, L. A. (2001). What makes a face attractive and why: The role of averageness in defining facial beauty. In G. Rhodes & L. A. Zebrowitz (Eds.), *Facial attractiveness: Evolutionary, cognitive, and social perspectives* (pp. 1–33). Westport, CT: Ablex Publishing.

Rubin, L. (1976). *Worlds of pain: Life in the working class family.* New York, NY: Basic Books.

Rubin, Z. (1970). Measurement of romantic love. *Journal of Personality and Social Psychology, 16,* 265–273.

Rubin, Z. (1973). *Liking and loving: An invitation to social psychology.* New York, NY: Holt, Rinehart & Winston.

Rubin, Z., Hill, C. T., Peplau, L. A., & Dunkel-Schetter, C. (1980). Self-disclosure in dating couples: Sex roles and the ethic of openness. *Journal of Marriage and the Family, 42,* 305–317.

Rusbult, C. E. (1983). A longitudinal test of the investment model: The development (and deterioration) of satisfaction and commitment in heterosexual involvements. *Journal of Personality and Social Psychology, 45,* 101–117.

Rusbult, C. E., Agnew, C. R., & Arriaga, X. B. (2012). The investment model of commitment processes. In P. A. M. Van Lange, A. W. Kruglanski, & E. T. Higgins (Eds.), *Handbook of theories of social psychology* (Vol. 2, pp. 218–231). Thousand Oaks, CA: Sage.

Rusbult, C. E., & Buunk, B. P. (1993). Commitment processes in close relationships: An interdependence analysis. *Journal of Social and Personal Relationships, 10,* 175–204.

Rusbult, C. E., Johnson, D. J., & Morrow, G. D. (1986). Predicting satisfaction and commitment in adult romantic involvements: An assessment of the generalizability of the investment model. *Social Psychology Quarterly, 49,* 81–89.

Rusbult, C. E., Martz, J. M., & Agnew, C. R. (1998). The Investment Model Scale: Measuring commitment level, satisfaction level, quality of alternatives, and investment size. *Personal Relationships, 5,* 357–391.

Rusbult, C. E., & Van Lange, P. A. M. (2003). Interdependence, interaction, and relationships. *Annual Review of Psychology, 54,* 351–375.

Rusbult, C. E., Zembrodt, I. M., & Gunn, L. K. (1982). Exit, voice, loyalty, and neglect: Responses to dissatisfaction in romantic relationships. *Journal of Personality and Social Psychology, 43,* 1230–1242.

Sabini, J., & Green, M. C. (2004). Emotional responses to sexual and emotional infidelity: Constants and differences across genders, samples, and methods. *Personality and Social Psychology Bulletin, 30,* 1375–1388.

Sagarin, B. J., Martin, A. L., Coutinho, S. A., Edlund, J. E., Patel, L., Skowronski, J. J., & Zengel, B. (2012). Sex differences in jealousy: A meta-analytic examination. *Evolution and Human Behavior, 33,* 595–614.

Sagrestano, L. M., Christensen, A., & Heavey, C. L. (1998). Social influence techniques during marital conflict. *Personal Relationships, 5,* 75–89.

Saify, K., & Saadat, M. (2012). Consanguineous marriages in Afghanistan. *Journal of Biosocial Science, 44,* 73–81.

Salusso-Deonier, C. J., Markee, N. L., & Pedersen, E. L. (1993). Gender differences in the evaluation of physical attractiveness ideals for male and female body builds. *Perceptual and Motor Skills, 76,* 1155–1167.

Samson, J. M., Levy, J. J., Dupras, A., & Tessier, D. (1991). Coitus frequency among married or cohabiting heterosexual adults: A survey in French-Canada. *Australian Journal of Marriage & Family, 12,* 103–109.

Sassler, S., & Miller, A. J. (2011). Class differences in cohabitation processes. *Family Relations, 60,* 163–177.

Saxbe, D. E., Repetti, R. L., & Graesch, A. P. (2011). Time spent in housework and leisure: Links with parents' physiological recovery from work. *Journal of Family Psychology, 25,* 271–281.

Scanzoni, J., Polonko, K., Teachman, J., & Thompson, L. (1989). *The sexual bond: Rethinking families and close relationships.* Newbury Park, CA: Sage.

Schatzel-Murphy, E. A., Harris, D. A., Knight, R. A., & Milburn, M. A. (2009). Sexual coercion in men and women: Similar behaviors, different predictors. *Archives of Sexual Behavior, 38,* 974–986.

Scheib, J. E. (2001). Context-specific mate choice criteria: Women's trade-offs in the contexts of long-term and extra-pair mateships. *Personal Relationships, 8,* 371–389.

Schewe, P. A., Adam, N. M., & Ryan, K. M. (2009). A qualitative analysis of the temptation to use force in sexual relationships. *Violence and Victims, 24,* 219–231.

Schwartz, P. (1994). *Peer marriage: How love between equals really works.* New York, NY: Free Press.

Schwartz, P., & Rutter, V. (1998). *The gender of sexuality.* Thousand Oaks, CA: Pine Forge.

Scott, S. B., Rhoades, G. K., Stanley, S. M., Allen, E. S., & Markman, H. J. (2013). Reasons for divorce and recollections of premarital intervention: Implications for improving relationship education. *Couple and Family Psychology: Research and Practice, 2,* 131–145.

Sedikides, C., Oliver, M. B., & Campbell, W. K. (1994). Perceived benefits and costs of romantic relationships for women and men: Implications for exchange theory. *Personal Relationships, 1,* 5–21.

Shadish, W. R., & Baldwin, S. A. (2005). Effects of behavioral marital therapy: A meta-analysis of randomized controlled trials. *Journal of Consulting and Clinical Psychology, 73,* 6–14.

Shaeer, O., & Shaeer, E. (2013). The Global Online Sexuality Survey: Public perception of female genital cutting among Internet users in the Middle East. *Journal of Sexual Medicine, 10,* 2904–2911.

Shaffer, D. R., & Bazzini, D. G. (1997). What do you look for in a prospective date? Reexamining the preferences of men and women who differ in self-monitoring propensities. *Personality and Social Psychology Bulletin, 23,* 605–616.

Shaver, P., Schwartz, J., Kirson, D., & O'Connor, C. (1987). Emotion knowledge: Further exploration of a prototype approach. *Journal of Personality and Social Psychology, 52,* 1061–1086.

Sheridan, L., Gillett, R., & Davies, G. (2002). Perceptions and prevalence of stalking in a male sample. *Psychology, Crime & Law, 8,* 289–310.

Sheridan, L., Gillett, R., Davies, G. M., Blaauw, E., & Patel, D. (2003). "There's no smoke without fire": Are male ex-partners perceived as more "entitled" to stalk than acquaintances or stranger stalkers? *British Journal of Psychology, 94,* 87–98.

Sherwin, R., & Corbett, S. (1985). Campus sexual norms and dating relationships: A trend analysis. *Journal of Sex Research, 21,* 258–274.

Shotland, R. L., & Hunter, B. A. (1995). Women's "token resistance" and compliant sexual behaviors are related to uncertain sexual intentions and rape. *Personality and Social Psychology Bulletin, 21,* 226–236.

Siegert, J. R., & Stamp, G. H. (1994). "Our first big fight" as a milestone in the development of close relationships. *Communication Monographs, 61,* 345–360.

Sillars, A., Roberts, L. J., Leonard, K. E., & Dun, T. (2000). Cognition during marital conflict: The relationship of thought and talk. *Journal of Social and Personal Relationships, 17,* 479–502.

Simon, W., & Gagnon, J. H. (1986). Sexual scripts: Permanence and change. *Archives of Sexual Behavior, 15,* 97–120.

Simpson, J. A., Campbell, B., & Berscheid, E. (1986). The association between romantic love and marriage: Kephart (1967) twice revisited. *Personality and Social Psychology Bulletin, 12,* 363–372.

Simpson, J. A., & Gangestad, S. W. (1991). Individual differences in sociosexuality: Evidence for convergent and discriminant validity. *Journal of Personality and Social Psychology, 60,* 870–883.

Simpson, J. A., & Gangestad, S. W. (1992). Sociosexuality and romantic partner choice. *Journal of Personality, 60,* 31–51.

Simpson, J. A., & Rholes, W. S. (2012). Adult attachment orientations, stress, and romantic relationships. In P. Devine & A. Plant (Eds.), *Advances in experimental social psychology* (Vol. 45, pp. 279–328). San Diego, CA: Academic Press.

Simpson, J. A., Wilson, C. L., & Winterheld, H. A. (2004). Sociosexuality and romantic relationships. In J. H. Harvey, A. Wenzel, & S. Sprecher (Eds.), *The handbook of sexuality in close relationships* (pp. 87–112). Mahwah, NJ: Erlbaum.

Simpson, L. E., Gattis, K. A., & Christensen, A. (2003). Therapy: Couple relationships. In J. J. Ponzetti, Jr. (Ed.), *International encyclopedia of marriage and family* (2nd ed., Vol. 4, pp. 1626–1634). New York, NY: Macmillan Reference USA.

Sims, K. E., & Meana, M. (2010). Why did passion wane? A qualitative study of married women's attributions for declines in sexual desire. *Journal of Sex & Marital Therapy, 36,* 360–380.

Sinclair, H. C., & Frieze, I. H. (2002). Initial courtship behavior and stalking: How should we draw the line? In K. E. Davis, I. H. Frieze, & R. D. Maiuro (Eds.), *Stalking: Perspectives on victims and perpetrators* (pp. 186–211). New York, NY: Springer.

Sinclair, H. C., & Frieze, I. H. (2005). When courtship persistence becomes intrusive pursuit: Comparing rejecter and pursuer perspectives of unrequited attraction. *Sex Roles, 52,* 839–852.

Singh, D. (1994). Body fat distribution and perception of desirable female body shape by young black men and women. *International Journal of Eating Disorders, 16,* 289–294.

Singh, D. (1995). Female judgment of male attractiveness and desirability for relationships: Role of waist-to-hip ratio and financial status. *Journal of Personality and Social Psychology, 69,* 1089–1101.

Singh, D., Dixson, B. J., Jessop, T. S., Morgan, B., & Dixson, A. F. (2010). Cross-cultural consensus for waist-hip ratio and women's attractiveness. *Evolution and Human Behavior, 31,* 176–181.

Singh, D., & Luis, S. (1995). Ethnic and gender consensus for the effect of waist-to-hip ratio on judgment of women's attractiveness. *Human Nature, 6,* 51–65.

Slep, A. M. S., Foran, H. M., Heyman, R. E., & United States Air Force Family Advocacy Research Program. (2014). An ecological model of intimate partner violence perpetration at different levels of severity. *Journal of Family Psychology, 28,* 470–482.

Smith, A., Lyons, A., Ferris, J., Richters, J., Pitts, M., Shelley, J., & Simpson, J. M. (2011). Sexual and relationship satisfaction among heterosexual men and women: The importance of desired frequency of sex. *Journal of Sex & Marital Therapy, 37,* 104–115.

Smith, C. A., Konik, J. A., & Tuve, M. V. (2011). In search of looks, status, or something else? Partner preferences among butch and femme lesbians and heterosexual men and women. *Sex Roles, 64,* 658–668.

Smith, T. W. (2006). Sexual behavior in the United States. In R. D. McAnulty & M. M. Burnette (Eds.), *Sex and sexuality. Vol. 1. Sexuality today: Trends and controversies* (pp. 103–132). Westport, CT: Praeger.

Snyder, M. (1974). The self-monitoring of expressive behavior. *Journal of Personality and Social Psychology, 30,* 526–537.

Snyder, M. (1987). *Public appearances/private realities: The psychology of self-monitoring.* New York, NY: Freeman.

Snyder, M., Berscheid, E., & Glick, P. (1985). Focusing on the exterior and the interior: Two investigations of the initiation of personal relationships. *Journal of Personality and Social Psychology, 48,* 1427–1439.

Snyder, M., & Simpson, J. A. (1984). Self-monitoring and dating relationships. *Journal of Personality and Social Psychology, 47,* 1281–1291.

Soames, M. (1979). *Clementine Churchill.* London, England: Cassell.

Sollie, D. L., & Fischer, J. L. (1985). Sex-role orientation, intimacy of topic, and target person differences in self-disclosure among women. *Sex Roles, 12,* 917–929.

Solomon, B. C., & Jackson, J. J. (2014). Why do personality traits predict divorce? Multiple pathways through satisfaction. *Journal of Personality and Social Psychology, 106,* 978–996.

Solomon, S. E., Rothblum, E. D., & Balsam, K. F. (2004). Pioneers in partnership: Lesbian and gay male couples in civil unions compared with those not in civil unions and married heterosexual couples. *Journal of Family Psychology, 18,* 275–286.

Solomon, S. E., Rothblum, E. D., & Balsam, K. F. (2005). Money, housework, sex, and conflict: Same-sex couples in civil unions, those not in civil unions, and heterosexual married siblings. *Sex Roles, 52,* 561–575.

Spanier, G. B., & Margolies, R. L. (1983). Marital separation and extramarital sexual behavior. *Journal of Sex Research, 19,* 23–48.

Spence, J. T., & Helmreich, R. L. (1978). *Masculinity and femininity: Their psychological dimensions, correlates, and antecedents.* Austin: University of Texas Press.

Spitzberg, B. H., & Cupach, W. R. (1996, July). *Obsessive relational intrusion: Victimization and coping.* Paper presented at the meeting of the International Society for the Study of Personal Relationships, Banff, Alberta, Canada.

Spitzberg, B. H., & Cupach, W. R. (Eds.). (1998). *The dark side of close relationships.* Mahwah, NJ: Erlbaum.

Spitzberg, B. H., & Cupach, W. R. (2001). Paradoxes of pursuit: Toward a relational model of stalking-related phenomena. In J. A. Davis (Ed.), *Stalking crimes and victim protection: Prevention, intervention, and threat assessment* (pp. 97–136). Boca Raton, FL: CRC Press.

Spitzberg, B. H., & Cupach, W. R. (2002). The inappropriateness of relational intrusion. In R. Goodwin & D. Cramer (Eds.), *Inappropriate relationships: The unconventional, the disapproved, and the forbidden* (pp. 191–219). Mahwah, NJ: Erlbaum.

Spitzberg, B. H., & Cupach, W. R. (2003). What mad pursuit? Obsessive relational intrusion and stalking-related phenomena. *Aggression and Violent Behavior, 8,* 345–375.

Spitzberg, B. H., & Cupach, W. R. (2007). The state of the art of stalking: Taking stock of an emerging literature. *Aggression and Violent Behavior, 12,* 64–86.

Spitzberg, B. H., Cupach, W. R., & Ciceraro, L. D. L. (2010). Sex differences in stalking and obsessive relational intrusion: Two meta-analyses. *Partner Abuse, 1,* 259–285.

Spitzberg, B. H., Nicastro, A. M., & Cousins, A. V. (1998). Exploring the interactional phenomenon of stalking and obsessive relational intrusion. *Communication Reports, 11,* 33–47.

Spreadbury, C. L. (1982). First date. *Journal of Early Adolescence, 2,* 83–89.

Sprecher, S. (1989). Importance to males and females of physical attractiveness, earning potential, and expressiveness in initial attraction. *Sex Roles, 21,* 591–607.

Sprecher, S. (1992). How men and women expect to feel and behave in response to inequity in close relationships. *Social Psychology Quarterly, 55,* 57–69.

Sprecher, S. (1998). Social exchange theories and sexuality. *Journal of Sex Research, 35,* 32–43.

Sprecher, S. (2002). Sexual satisfaction in premarital relationships: Associations with satisfaction, love, commitment, and stability. *The Journal of Sex Research, 39,* 190–196.

Sprecher, S. (2009). Relationship initiation and formation on the Internet. *Marriage & Family Review, 45,* 761–782.

Sprecher, S., Aron, A., Hatfield, E., Cortese, A., Potapova, E., & Levitskaya, A. (1994). Love: American style, Russian style, and Japanese style. *Personal Relationships, 1,* 349–369.

Sprecher, S., & Cate, R. M. (2004). Sexual satisfaction and sexual expression as predictors of relationship satisfaction and stability. In J. H. Harvey, A. Wenzel, & S. Sprecher (Eds.), *The handbook of sexuality in close relationships* (pp. 235–256). Mahwah, NJ: Erlbaum.

Sprecher, S., & Chandak, R. (1992). Attitudes about arranged marriages and dating among men and women from India. *Free Inquiry in Creative Sociology, 20,* 59–69.

Sprecher, S., Christopher, F. S., & Cate, R. (2006). Sexuality in close relationships. In A. Vangelisti & D. Perlman (Eds.), *The Cambridge handbook on personal relationships* (pp. 463–482). New York, NY: Cambridge University Press.

Sprecher, S., & Felmlee, D. (2008). Insider perspectives on attraction. In S. Sprecher, A. Wenzel, & J. Harvey (Eds.), *Handbook of relationship initiation* (pp. 297–313). New York, NY: Psychology Press.

Sprecher, S., Felmlee, D., Metts, S., & Cupach, W. (2014). Relationship initiation and development. In M. Mikulincer, P. R. Shaver, J. A. Simpson, & J. F. Dovidio (Eds.), *APA handbook of personality and social psychology, Volume 3: Interpersonal relations* (pp. 211–245). Washington, DC: American Psychological Association.

Sprecher, S., & Hatfield, E. (1995). Premarital sexual standards among U.S. college students: Comparison with Russian and Japanese students. *Archives of Sexual Behavior, 25,* 261–288.

Sprecher, S., Hatfield, E., Cortese, A., Potapova, E., & Levitskaya, A. (1994). Token resistance to sexual intercourse and consent to unwanted sexual intercourse: College students' dating experiences in three countries. *The Journal of Sex Research, 31,* 125–132.

Sprecher, S., & Hendrick, S. S. (2004). Self-disclosure in intimate relationships: Associations with individual and relationship characteristics over time. *Journal of Social and Clinical Psychology, 23,* 857–877.

Sprecher, S., McKinney, K., Walsh, R., & Anderson, C. (1988). A revision of the Reiss premarital sexual permissiveness scale. *Journal of Marriage and the Family, 50,* 821–828.

Sprecher, S., & Metts, S. (1989). Development of the "Romantic Beliefs Scale" and examination of the effects of gender and gender-role orientation. *Journal of Social and Personal Relationships, 6,* 387–411.

Sprecher, S., & Metts, S. (1999). Romantic beliefs: Their influence on relationships and patterns of change over time. *Journal of Social and Personal Relationships, 16,* 834–851.

Sprecher, S., Metts, S., Burleson, B., Hatfield, E., & Thompson, A. (1995). Domains of expressive interaction in intimate relationships: Associations with satisfaction and commitment. *Family Relations: Journal of Applied Family & Child Studies, 44,* 203–210.

Sprecher, S., & Regan, P. C. (1998). Passionate and companionate love in courting and young married couples. *Sociological Inquiry, 68,* 163–185.

Sprecher, S., & Regan, P. C. (2000). Sexuality in a relational context. In C. Hendrick & S. S. Hendrick (Eds.), *Close relationships: A sourcebook* (pp. 217–227). Thousand Oaks, CA: Sage.

Sprecher, S., & Regan, P. C. (2002). Liking some things (in some people) more than others: Partner preferences in romantic relationships and friendships. *Journal of Social and Personal Relationships, 19,* 463–481.

Sprecher, S., Regan, P. C., & McKinney, K. (1998). Beliefs about the outcomes of extramarital sexual relationships as a function of the gender of the "cheating spouse." *Sex Roles, 38,* 301–311.

Sprecher, S., Regan, P. C., McKinney, K., Maxwell, K., & Wazienski, R. (1997). Preferred level of sexual experience in a date or mate: The merger of two methodologies. *Journal of Sex Research, 34,* 327–337.

Sprecher, S., Schmeeckle, M., & Felmlee, D. (2006). The principle of least interest: Inequality in emotional investment in romantic relationships. *Journal of Family Issues, 27,* 1255–1280.

Sprecher, S., & Schwartz, P. (1994). Equity and balance in the exchange of contributions in close relationships. In M. J. Lerner & G. Mikula (Eds.), *Entitlement and the affectional bond: Justice in close relationships* (pp. 11–42). New York, NY: Plenum.

Sprecher, S., Sullivan, Q., & Hatfield, E. (1994). Mate selection preferences: Gender differences examined in a national sample. *Journal of Personality and Social Psychology, 66,* 1074–1080.

Sprecher, S., & Toro-Morn, M. (2002). A study of men and women from different sides of earth to determine if men are from Mars and women are from Venus in their beliefs about love and romantic relationships. *Sex Roles, 46,* 131–147.

Sprecher, S., Treger, S., Wondra, J. D., Hilaire, N., & Wallpe, K. (2013). Taking turns: Reciprocal self-disclosure promotes liking in initial interactions. *Journal of Experimental Social Psychology, 49,* 860–866.

Sprecher, S., Zimmerman, C., & Abrahams, E. M. (2010). Choosing compassionate strategies to end a relationship: Effects of compassionate love for partner and the reason for the breakup. *Social Psychology, 41,* 66–75.

Stanik, C. E., & Bryant, C. M. (2012). Marital quality of newlywed African American couples: Implications of egalitarian gender role dynamics. *Sex Roles, 66,* 256–267.

Stanik, C. E., & Ellsworth, P. C. (2010). Who cares about marrying a rich man? Intelligence and variation in women's mate preferences. *Human Nature, 21,* 203–217.

Stafford, L., Kline, S. L., & Rankin, C. T. (2004). Married individuals, cohabiters, and cohabiters who marry: A longitudinal study of relational and individual well-being. *Journal of Social and Personal Relationships, 21,* 231–248.

Steinfeldt, J. A., Gilchrist, G. A., Halterman, A. W., Gomory, A., & Steinfeldt, M. C. (2011). Drive for muscularity and conformity to masculine norms among college football players. *Psychology of Men & Masculinity, 12,* 324–338.

Sternberg, R. J. (1986). A triangular theory of love. *Psychological Review, 93,* 119–135.

Sternberg, R. J. (1988). Triangulating love. In R. J. Sternberg & M. L. Barnes (Eds.), *The psychology of love* (pp. 119–138). New Haven, CT: Yale University Press.

Sternberg, R. J. (1997). Construct validation of a triangular love scale. *European Journal of Social Psychology, 27,* 313–335.

Sternberg, R. J. (1998). *Cupid's arrow: The course of love through time.* Cambridge, England: Cambridge University Press.

Sternberg, R. J. (2006). A duplex theory of love. In R. J. Sternberg & K. Weis (Eds.), *The new psychology of love* (pp. 184–199). New Haven, CT: Yale University Press.

Sternberg, R. J., & Barnes, M. L. (Eds.). (1988). *The psychology of love.* New Haven, CT: Yale University Press.

Sternberg, R. J., & Weis, K. (Eds.). (2006). *The new psychology of love.* New Haven, CT: Yale University Press.

Straus, M. A. (2004). Prevalence of violence against dating partners by male and female university students worldwide. *Violence Against Women, 10,* 790–811.

Straus, M. A., Hamby, S. L., Boney-McCoy, S., & Sugarman, D. B. (1996). The revised Conflict Tactics Scales (CTS2): Development and preliminary psychometric data. *Journal of Family Issues, 17,* 283–316.

Straus, M. A., & Ramirez, I. L. (2007). Gender symmetry in prevalence, severity, and chronicity of physical aggression against dating partners by university students in Mexico and USA. *Aggressive Behavior, 33,* 281–290.

Stroebe, M. S., & Stroebe, W. (1987). *Bereavement and health: The psychological and physical consequences of partner loss.* London, England: Cambridge University Press.

Stuart, F. M., Hammond, D. C., & Pett, M. A. (1987). Inhibited sexual desire in women. *Archives of Sexual Behavior, 16,* 91–106.

Stuart, G. L., Moore, T. M., Gordon, K. C., Hellmuth, J. C., Ramsey, S. E., & Kahler, C. W. (2006). Reasons for intimate partner perpetration among arrested women. *Violence Against Women, 12,* 609–621.

Surra, C. A. (1985). Courtship types: Variations in interdependence between partners and social networks. *Journal of Personality and Social Psychology, 49,* 357–375.

Suter, E. A., Bergen, K. M., Daas, K. L., & Durham, W. T. (2006). Lesbian couples' management of public-private dialectical contradictions. *Journal of Social and Personal Relationships, 23,* 349–365.

Tabi, M. M., Doster, C., & Cheney, T. (2010). A qualitative study of women in polygynous marriages. *International Nursing Review, 57,* 121–127.

Tagler, M. J. (2010). Sex differences in jealousy: Comparing the influence of previous infidelity among college students and adults. *Social Psychological and Personality Science, 1,* 353–360.

Tagler, M. J., & Gentry, R. H. (2011). Gender, jealousy, and attachment: A (more) thorough examination across measures and samples. *Journal of Research in Personality, 45,* 697–701.

Tamplin, R. (1995). *Famous love letters: Messages of intimacy and passion.* New York, NY: Andromeda Oxford.

Tannen, D. (1990). *You just don't understand: Women and men in conversation.* New York, NY: William Morrow.

Tannen, D. (2001). *Talking from 9 to 5: Women and men at work.* New York, NY: William Morrow. [Reprint edition]

Tashiro, T., & Frazier, P. (2003). "I'll never be in a relationship like that again": Personal growth following romantic relationship breakups. *Personal Relationships, 10,* 113–128.

Tashiro, T., Frazier, P., & Berman, M. (2006). Stress-related growth following divorce and relationship dissolution. In M. A. Fine & J. H. Harvey (Eds.), *Handbook of divorce and dissolution* (pp. 361–384). Mahwah, NJ: Erlbaum.

Tassy, F., & Winstead, B. (2014). Relationship and individual characteristics as predictors of unwanted pursuit. *Journal of Family Violence, 29,* 187–195.

Taylor, S. E., Saphire-Bernstein, S., & Seeman, T. E. (2010). Are plasma oxytocin in women and plasma vasopressin in men biomarkers of distressed pair-bond relationships? *Psychological Science, 21,* 3–7.

Teachman, J., Tedrow, L., & Hall, M. (2006). The demographic future of divorce and dissolution. In M. A. Fine & J. H. Harvey (Eds.), *Handbook of divorce and dissolution* (pp. 59–82). Mahwah, NJ: Erlbaum.

Tellegen, A. (1985). Structures of mood and personality and their relevance to assessing anxiety, with an emphasis on self-report. In A. H. Tuma & J. D. Maser (Eds.), *Anxiety and the anxiety disorders* (pp. 681–706). Hillsdale, NJ: Erlbaum.

Tennov, D. (1979). *Love and limerence.* New York, NY: Stein & Day.

Theiss, J. A. (2011). Modeling dyadic effects in the associations between relational uncertainty, sexual communication, and sexual satisfaction for husbands and wives. *Communication Research, 38,* 565–584.

Theiss, J. A., & Estlein, R. (2014). Antecedents and consequences of the perceived threat of sexual communication: A test of the relational turbulence model. *Western Journal of Communication, 78,* 404–425.

Thibaut, J. W., & Kelley, H. H. (1959). *The social psychology of groups*. New York, NY: Wiley.

Thornton, A., & Young-DeMarco, L. (2001). Four decades of trends in attitudes toward family issues in the United States: The 1960s through the 1990s. *Journal of Marriage and Family, 63*, 1009–1037.

Tidwell, N. D., Eastwick, P. W., & Finkel, E. J. (2013). Perceived, not actual, similarity predicts initial attraction in a live romantic context: Evidence from the speed-dating paradigm. *Personal Relationships, 20*, 199–215.

Tjaden, P., & Thoennes, N. (2000). Prevalence and consequences of male-to-female and female-to-male intimate partner violence as measured by the National Violence Against Women Survey. *Violence Against Women, 6*, 142–161.

Tolhuizen, J. H. (1989). Communication strategies for intensifying dating relationships: Identification, use, and structure. *Journal of Social and Personal Relationships, 6*, 413–434.

Toma, C. L., Hancock, J. T., & Ellison, N. B. (2008). Separating fact from fiction: An examination of deceptive self-presentation on online dating profiles. *Personality and Social Psychology Bulletin, 34*, 1023–1036.

Tooby, J., & Cosmides, L. (1992). The psychological foundations of culture. In J. H. Barrow, L. Cosmides, & J. Tooby (Eds.), *The adapted mind: Evolutionary psychology and the generation of culture* (pp. 19–136). Oxford, England: Oxford University Press.

Tornstam, L. (1992). Loneliness in marriage. *Journal of Social and Personal Relationships, 9*, 197–217.

Toro-Morn, M., & Sprecher, S. (2003). A cross-cultural comparison of mate preferences among university students: The United States vs. the People's Republic of China (PRC). *Journal of Comparative Family Studies, 34*, 151–170.

Townsend, J. M., & Levy, G. D. (1990). Effects of potential partners' costume and physical attractiveness on sexuality and partner selection. *Journal of Psychology, 124*, 371–389.

Tracy, J. K., & Junginger, J. (2007). Correlates of lesbian sexual functioning. *Journal of Women's Health, 16*, 499–509.

Træen, B., & Thuen, F. (2013). Relationship problems and extradyadic romantic and sexual activity in a web-sample of Norwegian men and women. *Scandinavian Journal of Psychology, 54*, 137–145.

Treas, J. (2003). Infidelity. In J. J. Ponzetti, Jr. (Ed.), *International encyclopedia of marriage and family* (2nd ed., Vol. 2, pp. 895–901). New York, NY: Macmillan Reference USA.

Trudel, G. (1991). Review of psychological factors in low sexual desire. *Sexual and Marital Therapy, 6*, 261–272.

Tucker, J. S., Kressin, N. R., Spiro, A., III, & Ruscio, J. (1998). Intrapersonal characteristics and the timing of divorce: A prospective investigation. *Journal of Social and Personal Relationships, 15*, 210–225.

Tucker, P., & Aron, A. (1993). Passionate love and marital satisfaction at key transition points in the family life cycle. *Journal of Social and Clinical Psychology, 12*, 135–147.

Turmanis, S. A., & Brown, R. I. (2006). The Stalking and Harassment Behaviour Scale: Measuring the incidence, nature, and severity of stalking and relational harassment and their psychological effects. *Psychology and Psychotherapy: Theory, Research and Practice, 79,* 183–198.

Turner, R. H. (1970). *Family interaction.* New York, NY: Wiley.

Tyson, S. Y., Herting, J. R., & Randell, B. P. (2007). Beyond violence: Threat reappraisal in women recently separated from intimate-partner violent relationships. *Journal of Social and Personal Relationships, 24,* 693–706.

Uebelacker, L. A., Courtnage, E. S., & Whisman, M. A. (2003). Correlates of depression and marital satisfaction: Perceptions of marital communication style. *Journal of Social and Personal Relationships, 20,* 757–769.

Ullery, E. K., Millner, V. S., & Willingham, H. A. (2002). The emergent care and treatment of women with hypoactive sexual desire disorder. *The Family Journal: Counseling and Therapy for Couples and Families, 10,* 346–350.

United Nations Economic Commission for Europe. (2014). *UNECE statistical database. Regional divide in women's mean age at first marriage.* Retrieved December 13, 2014 from http://www.unece.org/statistics/news/news-women-first-marriage.html

U.S. Census Bureau. (1994). *Statistical abstracts of the United States.* Washington, DC: Government Printing Office.

U.S. Census Bureau. (1998). *Marital status and living arrangements: March 1998* (Current Population Reports, Series P20–514). Washington, DC: Government Printing Office.

U.S. Census Bureau. (2007a). Table 76: Live births, deaths, marriages, and divorces: 1950 to 2004. *Statistical abstract of the United States: 2007.* Retrieved from http://www.census.gov/compendia/statab/tables/07s0076.xls

U.S. Census Bureau. (2007b). Table 1312: Marriage and divorce rates, by country: 1980 to 2003. *Statistical abstract of the United States: 2007.* Retrieved from http://www.census.gov/compendia/statab/tables/07s1312.xls

U.S. Census Bureau. (2012a). *2012 American Community Survey. Table S1201. Marital status.* Retrieved from http://factfinder.census.gov

U.S. Census Bureau. (2012b). *Statistical abstract of the United States: 2012. Table 1336. Marriage and divorce rates by country: 1980 to 2008.* Retrieved from http://www.census.gov/compendia/statab/2012/tables/12s1336.pdf

U.S. Census Bureau (2013). *Current Population Survey. Table MS-2. Estimated median age at first marriage, by sex: 1890 to the present.* Retrieved December 13, 2014 from http://www.census.gov/hhes/families/data/marital.html

U.S. Department of Justice (2008). *Domestic violence awareness handbook.* Retrieved from http://www.da.usda.gov/shmd/aware.htm

U.S. Department of Justice (2012, January 6). Attorney General Eric Holder announces revisions to the Uniform Crime Report's definition of rape. Retrieved April 5, 2013 from http://www.fbi.gov/news/pressrel/press-releases/attorney-general-eric-holder-announces-revisions-to-the-uniform-crime-reports-definition-of-rape

U.S. Department of Justice (2014). *What is domestic violence?* Retrieved December 1, 2014, from http://www.justice.gov/ovw/domestic-violence#dv

Useche, B., Villegas, M., & Alzate, H. (1990). Sexual behavior of Colombian high school students. *Adolescence, 25,* 291–304.

Vail-Smith, K., Whetstone, L. M., & Knox, D. (2010). The illusion of safety in "monogamous" undergraduate relationships. *American Journal of Health Behavior, 34,* 12–20.

Valkenburg, P. M., & Peter, J. (2011). Online communication among adolescents: An integrated model of its attraction, opportunities, and risks. *Journal of Adolescent Health, 48,* 121–127.

van Anders, S. M., Goodson, J. L., & Kingsbury, M. A. (2013). Beyond "oxytocin = good": Neural complexities and the flipside of social bonds. *Archives of Sexual Behavior, 42,* 1115–1118.

van den Berghe, P. L. (1979). *Human family systems: An evolutionary view.* New York, NY: Elsevier.

van der Bruggen, M., & Grubb, A. (2014). A review of the literature relating to rape victim blaming: An analysis of the impact of observer and victim characteristics on attribution of blame in rape cases. *Aggression and Violent Behavior, 19,* 523–531.

Vangelisti, A. L., & Daly, J. A. (1997). Gender differences in standards for romantic relationships: Different cultures or different experiences? *Personal Relationships, 4,* 203–219.

Van Lange, P. A. M., & Rusbult, C. E. (1995). My relationship is better than—and not as bad as—yours is: The perception of superiority in close relationships. *Personality and Social Psychology Bulletin, 21,* 32–44.

Vannier, S. A., & O'Sullivan, L. F. (2010). Sex without desire: Characteristics of occasions of sexual compliance in young adults' committed relationships. *The Journal of Sex Research, 47,* 429–439.

Vannier, S. A., & O'Sullivan, L. F. (2011). Communicating interest in sex: Verbal and nonverbal initiation of sexual activity in young adults' romantic dating relationships. *Archives of Sexual Behavior, 40,* 961–969.

van Rooyen, L., & Hartell, C. (2010). The traditional custom of chastity and sexual restraint in the education of the young Swazi girl. *International Journal of Adolescence and Youth, 15,* 319–342.

van Steenbergen, H., Langeslag, S. J. E., Band, G. P. H., & Hommel, B. (2014). Reduced cognitive control in passionate lovers. *Motivation and Emotion, 38,* 444–450.

Villasmil Prieto, M. C. (1997). Social representation of feminine sexuality: An interpretation from a gender perspective. *Sociologica, 12,* 159–182.

von Krafft-Ebing, R. (1945). *Psychopathia sexualis* (12th ed.). New York, NY: Pioneer. (Original work published 1886)

Vorauer, J. D., Cameron, J. J., Holmes, J. G., & Pearce, D. G. (2003). Invisible overtures: Fears of rejection and the signal amplification bias. *Journal of Personality and Social Psychology, 84,* 793–812.

Vorauer, J. D., & Ratner, R. K. (1996). Who's going to make the first move? Pluralistic ignorance as an impediment to relationship formation. *Journal of Social and Personal Relationships, 13,* 483–506.

Wadsworth, P., & Records, K. (2013). A review of the health effects of sexual assault on African American women and adolescents. *Journal of Obstetric, Gynecologic, & Neonatal Nursing: Clinical Scholarship for the Care of Women, Childbearing Families, & Newborns, 42,* 249–273.

Wallace, H., & Silverman, J. (1996). Stalking and posttraumatic stress syndrome. *Police Journal, 69,* 203–206.

Wallace, P. (1977). Individual discrimination of humans by odor. *Physiology & Behavior, 19,* 577–579.

Walster, E., Aronson, V., Abrahams, D., & Rottmann, L. (1966). Importance of physical attractiveness in dating behavior. *Journal of Personality and Social Psychology, 4,* 508–516.

Walster, E., Walster, G. W., & Berscheid, E. (1978). *Equity: Theory and research.* Boston, MA: Allyn & Bacon.

Ward, C. C., & Tracey, T. J. G. (2004). Relation of shyness with aspects of online relationship involvement. *Journal of Social and Personal Relationships, 21,* 611–623.

Watson, D. (2002). Positive affectivity: The disposition to experience pleasurable emotional states. In C. R. Snyder & S. J. Lopez (Eds.), *Handbook of positive psychology* (pp. 106–119). New York, NY: Oxford University Press.

Watson, D., & Clark, L. A. (1984). Negative affectivity: The disposition to experience aversive emotional states. *Psychological Bulletin, 96,* 465–490.

Weaver, S. E., & Ganong, L. H. (2004). The factor structure of the Romantic Beliefs Scale for African Americans and European Americans. *Journal of Social and Personal Relationships, 21,* 171–185.

Weber, A. L. (1998). Losing, leaving, and letting go: Coping with nonmarital breakups. In B. H. Spitzberg & W. R. Cupach (Eds.), *The dark side of close relationships* (pp. 267–306). Mahwah, NJ: Erlbaum.

Wegner, H., Jr. (2005). Disconfirming communication and self-verification in marriage: Associations among the demand/withdraw interaction pattern, feeling understood, and marital satisfaction. *Journal of Social and Personal Relationships, 22,* 19–31.

Weigel, D. J., Bennett, K. K., & Ballard-Reisch, D. S. (2006). Influence strategies in marriage: Self and partner links between equity, strategy use, and marital satisfaction and commitment. *The Journal of Family Communication, 6,* 77–95.

Weinberg, M. S., Swensson, R. G., & Hammersmith, S. K. (1983). Sexual autonomy and the status of women: Models of female sexuality in U.S. sex manuals from 1950 to 1980. *Social Problems, 30,* 312–324.

Wells, B. E., & Twenge, J. M. (2005). Changes in young people's sexual behavior and attitudes, 1943–1999: A cross-temporal meta-analysis. *Review of General Psychology, 9,* 249–261.

Wesley, S., & Waring, E. M. (1996). A critical review of marital outcome research. *Canadian Journal of Psychiatry, 41,* 421–428.

Whisman, M. A., Gordon, K. C., & Chatav, Y. (2007). Predicting sexual infidelity in a population-based sample of married individuals. *Journal of Family Psychology, 21,* 320–324.

Whisman, M. A., & Snyder, D. K. (2007). Sexual infidelity in a national survey of American women: Differences in prevalence and correlates as a function of method of assessment. *Journal of Family Psychology, 21,* 147–154.

Whitaker, D. J., Haileyesus, T., Swahn, M., & Saltzman, L. S. (2007). Differences in frequency of violence and reported injury between relationships with reciprocal and nonreciprocal intimate partner violence. *American Journal of Public Health, 97,* 941–947.

White, E. M., Pearce, A. R., & Khramtsova, I. (2011). Character strengths are prominent as mate preferences of Turkish students. *Journal of International Students, 1,* 64–68.

White, G. L., & Mullen, P. E. (1989). *Jealousy: Theory, research, and clinical strategies.* New York, NY: Guilford Press.

Whitty, M. T. (2004). Cyber-flirting: An examination of men's and women's flirting behaviour both offline and on the Internet. *Behaviour Change, 21,* 115–126.

Whitty, M. T., & Carr, A. N. (2003). Cyberspace as potential space: Considering the web as a playground to cyber-flirt. *Human Relations, 56,* 869–891.

Whitty, M. T., & Carr, A. N. (2006). *Cyberspace romance: The psychology of online relationships.* New York, NY: Palgrave Macmillan.

Widmer, E. D., Treas, J., & Newcomb, R. (1998). Attitudes toward nonmarital sex in 24 countries. *The Journal of Sex Research, 35,* 349–358.

Wiederman, M. W. (1997). Extramarital sex: Prevalence and correlates in a national survey. *The Journal of Sex Research, 34,* 167–174.

Wiederman, M. W., & Allgeier, E. R. (1992). Gender differences in mate selection criteria: Sociobiological or socioeconomic explanation? *Ethology and Sociobiology, 13,* 115–124.

Wiederman, M. W., & Allgeier, E. R. (1996). Expectations and attributions regarding extramarital sex among young married individuals. *Journal of Psychology and Human Sexuality, 8,* 21–35.

Wiederman, M. W., & Kendall, E. (1999). Evolution, sex, and jealousy: Investigation with a sample from Sweden. *Evolution and Human Behavior, 20,* 121–128.

Wile, D. B. (1993). *After the fight: A night in the life of a couple.* New York, NY: Guilford Press.

Wilkie, J. R., Ferree, M. M., & Ratcliff, K. S. (1998). Gender and fairness: Marital satisfaction in two-earner couples. *Journal of Marriage and the Family, 60,* 577–594.

Willetts, M. C., Sprecher, S., & Beck, F. D. (2004). Overview of sexual practices and attitudes within relational contexts. In J. H. Harvey, A. Wenzel, & S. Sprecher (Eds.), *The handbook of sexuality in close relationships* (pp. 57–85). Mahwah, NJ: Erlbaum.

Williams, L., & Philipguest, M. (2005). Attitudes toward marriage among the urban middle-class in Vietnam, Thailand, and the Philippines. *Journal of Comparative Family Studies, 36,* 163–186.

Williams, S. L., & Frieze, I. H. (2005). Courtship behaviors, relationship violence, and breakup persistence in college men and women. *Psychology of Women Quarterly, 29,* 248–257.

Willoughby, B. J. (2010). Marital attitude trajectories across adolescence. *Journal of Youth and Adolescence, 39,* 1305–1317.

Willoughby, B. J., Carroll, J. S., & Busby, D. M. (2011). The different effects of "living together": Determining and comparing types of cohabiting couples. *Journal of Social and Personal Relationships, 29,* 397–419.

Willoughby, B. J., Carroll, J. S., & Busby, D. M. (2014). Differing relationship outcomes when sex happens before, on, or after first dates. *Journal of Sex Research, 51,* 52–61.

Willoughby, B. J., Farero, A. M., & Busby, D. M. (2014). Exploring the effects of sexual desire discrepancy among married couples. *Archives of Sexual Behavior, 43,* 551–562.

Wong, J., & Mellor, D. (2014). Intimate partner violence and women's health and well-being: Impacts, risk factors and responses. *Contemporary Nurse, 46,* 170–179.

Wood, J. T. (2000). Gender and personal relationships. In C. Hendrick & S. S. Hendrick (Eds.), *Close relationships: A sourcebook* (pp. 300–313). Thousand Oaks, CA: Sage.

Wood, J. T. (2007). *Gendered lives: Communication, gender, and culture* (7th ed.). Belmont, CA: Wadsworth Thomson Learning.

Wood, J. T. (2009). Communication, gender differences in. In H. T. Reis & S. K. Sprecher (Eds.), *Encyclopedia of human relationships* (Vol. 1, pp. 252–256). Thousand Oaks, CA: Sage.

Wood, J. T. (2013). Becoming gendered: Theories of gendering processes in early life. In M. A. Fine & F. D. Fincham (Eds.), *Handbook of family theories: A content-based approach* (pp. 301–315). New York, NY: Routledge/Taylor & Francis Group.

Wright, P. J., Tokunaga, R. S., & Bae, S. (2014). More than a dalliance? Pornography consumption and extramarital sex attitudes among married U.S. adults. *Psychology of Popular Media Culture, 3,* 97–109.

Xu, X., & Whyte, M. K. (1990). Love matches and arranged marriages: A Chinese replication. *Journal of Marriage and the Family, 52,* 709–722.

Yan, Y. K. (2006). Sexual responses and behaviors of university students in Hong Kong. *International Journal of Adolescence and Youth, 13,* 43–54.

Yeh, H.-C., Lorenz, F. O., Wickrama, K. A. S., Conger, R. D., & Elder, G. H., Jr. (2006). Relationships among sexual satisfaction, marital quality, and marital instability at midlife. *Journal of Family Psychology, 20,* 339–343.

Yoo, H., Bartle-Haring, S., Day, R. D., & Gangamma, R. (2014). Couple communication, emotional and sexual intimacy, and relationship satisfaction. *Journal of Sex & Marital Therapy, 40,* 275–293.

Yost, M. R., & Zurbriggen, E. L. (2006). Gender differences in the enactment of sociosexuality: An examination of implicit social motives, sexual fantasies, coercive sexual attitudes, and aggressive sexual behavior. *Journal of Sex Research, 43,* 163–173.

Young, B. J., & Furman, W. (2008). Interpersonal factors in the risk for sexual victimization and its recurrence during adolescence. *Journal of Youth and Adolescence, 37,* 297–309.

Young, B. J., & Furman, W. (2013). Predicting commitment in young adults' physically aggressive and sexually coercive dating relationships. *Journal of Interpersonal Violence, 28,* 3245–3264.

Young, M., Denny, G., Luquis, R., & Young, T. (1998). Correlates of sexual satisfaction in marriage. *Canadian Journal of Human Sexuality, 7,* 115–127.

Yucel, D., & Gassanov, M. A. (2010). Exploring actor and partner correlates of sexual satisfaction among married couples. *Social Science Research, 39,* 725–738.

Zajonc, R. B. (1968). Attitudinal effects of mere exposure. *Journal of Personality and Social Psychology, 9,* 1–27.

Zajonc, R. B. (2001). Mere exposure: A gateway to the subliminal. *Current Directions in Psychological Science, 10,* 224–228.

Zellman, G. L., & Goodchilds, J. D. (1983). Becoming sexual in adolescence. In E. A. Allgeier & N. B. McCormick (Eds.), *Changing boundaries: Gender roles and sexual behavior* (pp. 49–63). Palo Alto, CA: Mayfield.

Zhang, N., Parish, W. L., Huang, Y., & Pan, S. (2012). Sexual infidelity in China: Prevalence and gender-specific correlates. *Archives of Sexual Behavior, 41,* 861–873.

Zhao, J., Settles, B. H., & Sheng, X. (2011). Family-to-work conflict: Gender, equity and workplace policies. *Journal of Comparative Family Studies, 42,* 723–738.

Zuo, X., Lou, C., Gao, E., Cheng, Y., Niu, H., & Zabin, L. S. (2012). Gender differences in adolescent premarital sexual permissiveness in three Asian cities: Effects of gender-role attitudes. *Journal of Adolescent Health, 50,* S18–S25.

# Author Index

# Subject Index

Eye contact, as flirting behavior, 35–37
Eyebrow flash, as flirting behavior, 35

Facial features, as determinant of sex appeal, 235–236
Familiarity:
  and mere exposure effect, 27
  as determinant of attraction, 27–28
  as factor in sexual boredom, 270
Family interaction lab, 104
Fatal attractions, 62
Fatuous love, 155
Fidelity, evolutionary importance of, 8. *See also* Infidelity; Sexual exclusivity
Field of availables, and accessibility to partners, 31
Filter Theory, 54–55
First date, 41–46
  and "good night kiss," 45
  and sexual activity, 45
  beliefs about, 45–46
  events during, 44–45
  fear of rejection and, 42–43
  initiation of, 42
  pluralistic ignorance and, 43
  sexual script and, 42
  script of, 44–45
  signal amplification bias and, 43
Flirting, 34–39
  behaviors involved in, 34–36
  effectiveness of, 36–38
  in online (computer-mediated) environment, 38–39. *See also* Cyber-flirting
Free choice marriage, 84
Friendliness, misperceived as sexual interest, 46
Friendship:
  and companionate love, 154
  as feature of love, 164, 165, 188
  as type of love, 152, 158
  *See also* Liking

Friendship-based love. *See* Companionate Love; Storge

Game-playing love. *See* Ludus
Gender. *See* Psychological gender
Gender differences. *See* Sex differences
Gender roles:
  and domestic abuse, 214
  and relationship satisfaction, 299, 301
  and sexual assault, 275
  and sexual decision making, 229–231
  in marriage, 84–85
  *See also* Psychological gender; Sex role
Gender role orientation, 291–292, 301
Genetic fitness, preferences for and importance of, 7
Grief, 121–123. *See also* Relationship dissolution

Heterosexual sexual script. *See* Sexual script
Homogamy, 82
Homosexual couples. *See* Same-sex couples
Honeymoon effect, 253
Hyperfemininity, and sexual assault, 275
Hypergender, 275
Hypermasculinity, and sexual assault, 275
Hypothetical scenarios, problems with use of, 19–20, 283–285

Idealization, as feature of passionate love, 171–172
Implicit relationship theories, 321. *See also* Attachment style; Rejection sensitivity; Romanticism
In love, state of being. *See* Erotic love; Passionate love
Incest taboo, 82

Romantic beliefs. *See* Love at first
sight; Relationship beliefs;
Romanticism
Romanticism, 329–330
and age, 330
and relationship experiences, 330
definition of, 329
measurement of, 329–330
sex differences in levels of, 330
*See also* Relationship beliefs
Rubin's Love Scale, 190

Same-sex couples:
and cohabitation, 92–93
and division of household
labor, 95
and relationship dissolution, 110
and sexual infidelity, 278
attitudes toward "couplehood"
among, 90
marriage among, 90–92
relationship satisfaction among, 95
sexual assault among, 274
sexual frequency among, 251–252
sexual practices among, 255–256
sexual preferences among, 257–258
sexual satisfaction among,
258–259
sexuality and relationship
satisfaction among, 263
Same-sex marriage, 90–92
Secondary love styles, 158–159
Self-disclosure:
about sex, 260–262
and relational stalking, 200–201
and relationship development,
57–59
and relationship dissolution, 58
and relationship satisfaction, 58
as relationship initiation
strategy, 47
as relationship maintenance
strategy, 59
breadth of, 57
depth of, 57

intimacy and reciprocity of,
57–58
sex differences in, 292–293
*See also* Communication; Intimacy
Theory; Social Penetration
Theory
Self-monitoring, 312–316
and mate preference, 313–314
and relational outcomes, 314–316
definition of, 312
measurement of, 312–313
sex differences in, 313–314
Self-report methodologies:
for assessing mate preference,
9–10
for assessing relational
aggression, 209
for assessing sexual jealousy, 281
for measuring love, 156, 159, 160–
162, 180, 181–182, 190, 191
for measuring rejection
sensitivity, 327
for measuring romanticism, 330
for measuring self-monitoring,
312–313
for measuring sex role orientation,
298–299
for measuring sociosexual
orientation, 316
problems with, 19–20, 283–285
Self-revelation, role in relationship
development of, 55
Sex appeal:
as determinant of romantic
attraction, 234
and mate preference, 13
characteristics associated with,
234–237
sociosexual orientation and
preferences for, 316–317
Sex differences:
and demand-withdraw pattern,
108–109
and desired level of premarital
sexual involvement, 225–226

# About the Author

**Pamela C. Regan** is Professor of Psychology at California State University, Los Angeles. She received her PhD in psychology from the University of Minnesota and her undergraduate degree in English from Williams College. Her research interests are in the areas of close relationships and human sexuality, with an emphasis on passionate love, sexual desire, and mate preference. She has published more than 100 journal articles, book chapters, and reviews (and has given over 75 professional presentations) on the dynamics of sex, love, and human mating, and she is the author of *Close Relationships* (Routledge, 2011), the coauthor (with Ellen Berscheid) of *The Psychology of Interpersonal Relationships* (Pearson, 2005) and *Lust: What We Know About Human Sexual Desire* (Sage, 1999), and the coauthor (with Bruce King) of *Human Sexuality Today* (Pearson, 2014). In 2007, she was honored with the Outstanding Professor Award by her university for excellence in instruction and professional achievement.